T H E
SOUTHEAST ASIA COOKBOOK

THE
SOUTHEAST ASIA COOKBOOK

Ruth Law

Primus

DONALD I. FINE, INC.
NEW YORK

Library of Congress Cataloging-in-Publication Data

Law, Ruth.
    The Southeast Asia cookbook / by Ruth Law.
       p.   cm.
    ISBN 1-55611-469-9 (alk. paper)
    1. Cookery, Southeast Asian.   I. Title.
TX724.5.568L.39   1990
641.5959—dc20

Manufactured in the United States of America

10   9   8   7   6   5   4   3   2

DESIGNED BY STANLEY S. DRATE/FOLIO GRAPHICS COMPANY, INC.

To my patient and understanding mother, Gertrude Thompson, who presented me with my first wok, and my children, Sarah and Grant, who have been adventuresome, creative and supportive in all my endeavors.

CONTENTS

Acknowledgments

No book of this kind can be written without the help of hundreds of people. I have been extremely fortunate in getting to know many Asians both in Southeast Asia and in the United States and value tremendously their friendship and their warm hospitality. This book is a result of those experiences and the generosity of scores of talented chefs and home cooks who opened their professional and home kitchens to me and shared their knowledge.

For my children, Sarah and Grant, my sincere thanks for years of adventures with exotic aromas and tastes. They were my chief "guinea pigs" for many tasting sessions as I adapted authentic Southeast Asian recipes for preparation in the American home kitchen. In addition, Sarah, an accomplished art student, has contributed her creative talents by illustrating this book, and Grant introduced me to the wonders of computers while exhibiting tremendous patience toward his electronically inept mother.

Next, I want to thank some very special family friends, whom I'm sure did not know how deeply involved they would become when they first volunteered to help: Mary May, who organized testers and gave her own opinions on many of the foods I cooked. Lionel Go, who was offered food the very first minute he walked into my kitchen, and whom I found to have an excellent palate.

In my classroom and on my journeys to the Orient, my many students and tour participants—including the chefs of the American Culinary Federation—have been a great source of inspiration. Their joy in preparing a tantalizing dish, their tourist's delight with a fabulous entree, their complete fascination with ceremony and tradition have inspired me to write this book so that you all may share in my love for Southeast Asia.

Appreciation must also go to Susan Schwartz, my talented senior editor of my publisher, Donald I. Fine, Inc., Jane Dystel, my literary agent and Jay Harlow, a creative writer, who helped convey my thoughts into writing and for his supportive comments.

I am sincerely grateful to my faithful testers Lee Kellum, Jan Lord, Dave Parta, Karen Reed, Sally and Timothy Reis, and John Borscha plus Bob and Marsha Gordon, Richard Gordon, Tad and Jack Hillery, Joan and Norm Schuessler, Kathie and Rich Weber, Peter Rudiger, Julie and Philip Bonello, and Carel and Bill Seith. Their previous limited exposure to Southeast Asian cooking was actually a valuable asset since they approached each dish as would an American home cook. They tested all the recipes, asked all the important questions concerning shopping and preparation, and were always there with ideas to improve my writing skills to make the recipes more understandable. Their enthusiasm encouraged me immensely.

Thanks go, as well, to Klaus D. Doelling, vice president—food and beverage, Hyatt International Hotels, for his generosity and cooperation. His chefs contributed many of the recipes and photographs. They and the other chefs—plus the home cooks—who provided recipes are credited appropriately throughout the book.

Others who deserve recognition for their advice, counsel and other contributions are "Gourmet on the Go" Edward Robert Brooks, L. Edwin Brown, executive director, American Culinary Federation, Inc., Gerald Picolla, John Semone, Pacific Area Travel Association; my friends, Charlie Soo, head, Asian American Small Business Association, Lucy Lau, Regent International Hotels, Sandra Groben, Eddie Lopez, Bette Peters, Jean Spring, and Eddie Sunggoraneewan.

I hope you enjoy the wonderful cuisines of Southeast Asia as much as I have enjoyed compiling and writing this book.

My sincere gratitude to the following who read my manuscript and verified the information and spellings contained in each chapter.

INDONESIA: Hidayat, Consulate General of the Republic of Indonesia.

MALAYSIA: Noor Ahmad Hamid, Tourist Development Corporation.

THE PHILIPPINES: Imelda M. Alviso and Laura B. C. Coronel, Philippines Department of Tourism.

SINGAPORE: Min-Seng Chew, Singapore Tourist Promotion Board

THAILAND: Charal Plangtrakul, Royal Thai Consulate-General.

VIETNAM: Ngoan Le, Special Assistant on Asian Affairs for Governor James R. Thompson of Illinois.

CHINESE TRANSLATIONS: San O, Southeast Asian Center, Chicago.

I would also like to express my appreciation to the many others who assisted me in this immense undertaking, many of whom are recognized in the individual chapters, plus . . .

INDONESIA

Consul General Prawirosuhardjo Surahman, Consulate of the Republic of Indonesia; Makarim Wibisono, Embassy of Indonesia; Joop Ave, Udin Saifuddin, and Ir. George Oemint, Directorate General of Tourism; Atman Ferdy, Satriavi Tours & Travel; Djoko Judojono, Garuda Indonesia Airlines.

MALAYSIA

Abdullah Jonid, and Amarrudin Abu, Tourist Development Corporation of Malaysia; Rashid Khan, Malaysia Airlines.

THE PHILIPPINES

Deputy Consul General George P. Aducayen, Jr., Philippine Consulate General; Wally Reyes, Department of Tourism; Leslie Espino, Philippine Air Lines.

SINGAPORE

Evelyn Sen, Kay-Yew Koh, Adriaan Arends, and Hazunah Adnan, Singapore Tourist Promotion Board.

THAILAND

Consul General Prida Apirat, Royal Thai Consulate-General; Dharmnoon Prachuabmoh, Sumontha Nakornthab, and Pangsai Wangsai; Tourism Authority of Thailand; Robert O. Jotikasthira and Suchai Suriyayothin, Turismo Thai; and Rene L. Cortez, Thai Airways International Limited.

VIETNAM

Phuong Chung, and Dung Dinh Hguyen, Vietnamese Association of Illinois.

INTRODUCTION

When I close my eyes and think of Thailand, I can see ornate tile-roofed temples and saffron-robed Buddhist monks, smell the mingled aromas of spices and fresh basil in a chicken curry. The mention of Indonesia brings up memories of the elaborate religious rituals of Bali, the sounds, colors, and smells of an enormous open-air market in the Sumatran highlands, and the most intricately spiced sizzling satay I have ever tasted. My memories of Singapore include the New Year festivities, rich in food, customs and spirit; the whole city splashed in the luck-bringing color of red, symbolizing good fortune for the New Year; enticing adventures to an exotic island where a seafood restaurant high upon stilts over the water's surface serves the ultimate succulent, spicy chile crab and sparkling fresh fish plucked from the water moments earlier and delicately steamed to perfection.

Since my first trip to the Orient more than ten years ago, I have been in love with Southeast Asia: the friendly people, the warm tropical climate, the lush scenery, the varied and complex cultural and religious traditions—and above all, the food. I have returned many times, traveling to Thailand, Malaysia, Singapore, Indonesia, and the Philippines, each time gaining a greater appreciation for these countries and their heritage. This book is a result of these travel experiences; it is an attempt to share my enchantment with Southeast Asia and to acquaint you with the peoples, the cultures, and the delightful cuisines.

Whenever I visit a country, I like to wander through the streets, smell the marvelous aromas, taste the tantalizing foods from the local street vendors, visit the fascinating markets and kitchens and talk to the people. These first-hand meetings allow me to understand how the people really eat and live. I like to see what fruits and vegetables grow in a region, and even taste the local beer or rice wine to see how it blends with the foods.

1

This sense of discovery continues at the table. I enjoy tasting the luscious first fresh fruits of the season, breaking open divinely fresh lobsters, succulent crabs, and juicy jumbo prawns fresh from the water, preparing my own creative delights by dipping into the accompanying dips and sauces, the informality of eating with my fingers, the wonderful relaxed experience of sharing the foods together. All of this gives me an incredible sense of the Southeast Asian daily celebration of life.

I like to taste the creative combination of flavors and textures. The soft, the crunchy, and the slippery; the hot, sour, sweet, and salty are all present. The Southeast Asian cook pays great attention to the freshness and natural qualities of ingredients, and intuitively knows what textures and tastes will combine most successfully. Proportions and techniques are passed down from generation to generation. These are adventurous people and cooking is not done with a measuring spoon!

The book was written with two objectives in mind: to take you on a culinary journey to Southeast Asia and to introduce you to the exotic dishes of this fascinating part of the world. The chapter introductions and the traditional menus—Balinese Barbecue, Kadazan Tribal Fare from Borneo, Javanese *Slametan,* Tantalizing Thai Temptations, Chinese New Year's Eve Dinner, Tandoor Restaurant's Indian Feast, Philippine Fiesta Buffet, and Fabulous Vietnamese Fondue—should acquaint you with the traditions and cuisines. Whenever possible, I have included the cultural background behind the recipes. I feel that the more a person knows about the country, the more interesting it will be to both the cook and the diner. It is also my hope that you might share my passion for this part of the world.

The techniques and cooking processes in the book are the result of my travels and research into the kitchens of Southeast Asia. The recipes are authentic; most of them I have learned by standing beside master chefs, homecooks, and street vendors, watching them, and taking copious notes and photographs of every step. The recipes are adapted so that you may cook them in your American kitchen and serve exciting meals to your family and guests. Time-saving tips such as the use of the food processor, blender, and microwave oven are given when appropriate. Many of the recipes can be prepared in advance, especially the delicate soups, fragrant curries, and aromatic simmered and braised dishes as well as the refreshing salads. All a Southeast Asian meal takes is a little careful planning, which can be done by reading the advance preparation tips which accompany the recipes.

In my large collection of recipes, I may have many versions of the same recipe from several different countries. Some of the Malaysian recipes, for example, might just as well be in the Singapore or Indonesia chapter. I have chosen to put each dish in the chapter on the country where I obtained the particular recipe. In the case of *Soto Ayam,* a delightful chicken soup popular throughout Singapore, Malaysia, and Indonesia, I have included two distinctly different versions, one from Malaysia and one from Indonesia.

Since Southeast Asian entrees are usually served at the same time, classifying the recipes was also a problem. Should *Satay* (grilled meat on a skewer) be an appetizer, a snack, or a main course? It is served in all three ways. Should *Laksa Lemak,* a soupy dish of chicken, shrimp, and rice noodles in coconut sauce, be under soup or noodles? (It's under soup.) Throughout the book, you may find other instances that you might think are discrepancies. Perhaps that's why I am so fond of Southeast Asian food—it's a marvelous conglomeration of tantalizing flavors, textures, and tastes that blend together harmoniously, just like the people and cultures of this wonderful part of the world.

ABOUT SOUTHEAST ASIAN FOOD

Southeast Asian food is colorful, fragrant, flavorful, healthful, and thoroughly satisfying. From the simplest noodle soup to an elaborately spiced curry or a fiery chile sauce, this is food that delights all the senses. Not all of it is hot with chiles, by any means; hot flavors are just part of a whole flavor spectrum along with sweet, sour, salty, and bitter, which often come together in surprising but delicious combinations.

Geographically, Southeast Asia consists of all the mainland countries east of India and Bangladesh and south of China, plus the Philippine and Indonesian archipelagoes. This book focuses on cuisines and foods that I especially enjoy: Thailand, both the royal court cuisine of the south and the more rustic cuisine of the northern highlands; the spice-laden food of Muslim Malays and the hybrid Nonya or "Straits Chinese" cuisine; the varied Chinese, Malay, and Indian foods of charming Malaysia and the bustling Republic of Singapore; the enormously diverse cuisines of Indonesia's 13,000 islands; the exuberant Malay-Chinese-Spanish-American amalgam of the Philippines; and the subtle, refined, Chinese- and French-influenced foods of Vietnam.

Southeast Asia has for centuries been a crossroads of trade and cultural exchange between the Far East and India, the Middle East, and the West. The indigenous Malayo-Polynesian and Austro-Asiatic peoples of Southeast Asia have survived waves of conquest and immigration from India, China, Arabia, and Europe. Each group of conquerors or traders has added its unique overlay on the culture of the region, affecting the language, religion, and cuisine.

Certain foods are found throughout the region and recur in every cuisine. Rice, first domesticated in Asia at least 5,000 years ago, is the major staple carbohydrate of rich and poor alike, except in certain far-

4

flung islands of Indonesia. Noodles, whether made from rice flour, wheat flour, or bean starch, are another important staple.

Coconuts and coconut milk are nearly as essential as rice to authentic Southeast Asian cooking. Grating the meat of a mature coconut and squeezing out the liquid produces a milk that flavors everything from curries, soups, and sauces to desserts. Grated coconut is also a common ingredient in both sweet and savory dishes.

Much of the distinctive flavor of Southeast Asian food comes from the spices native to the region, including pepper, cloves, nutmeg, cinnamon, coriander, cardamom, and cumin. Although not native—they were introduced by the Portuguese—chile peppers of various types have become an essential part of the cuisine. In addition to the familiar spices, Southeast Asian cooking uses a great variety of fresh and dried herbs: several varieties of fresh mint and basil, plus fresh coriander (also known as Chinese parsley or cilantro), lemon grass, and even the leaves of citrus trees.

Several members of the onion family, including garlic, green onions, and shallots, are used throughout Southeast Asian cooking. And there are various aromatic roots of the ginger family, including ginger, galangal, and turmeric (which when dried and ground becomes the familiar yellow spice in curry powder and prepared mustard). Even the roots of the coriander plant are used in Thailand for their special flavor, which is slightly different from that of the leaves.

Since most of the population live near saltwater or in well-watered lowlands, fish and shellfish are the major sources of animal protein. Chickens, ducks, cows, and pigs are also important, as are goats among Muslims, who do not eat pork. The upper classes in the cities, as everywhere else in the world, eat more meat than village people. Soybeans, in the form of tofu and tempeh, are also important sources of protein for millions.

As a whole, the Southeast Asian diet is a sensible and healthful one. If eaten in authentic proportions (see Meal Patterns, following), the diet is based largely on complex carbohydrates (from rice, vegetables, and fruits), with modest proportions of protein and fat.

MEAL PATTERNS

In the villages and the countryside, people generally eat the same dishes, based on local ingredients, that their grandparents and remote ancestors ate. But residents of the large, multi-ethnic cities have a much wider choice. The restaurants and markets of Bangkok, Jakarta, Kuala Lumpur, Singapore, and Manila offer not only the local cuisine, but those of other Southeast Asian countries, China, Japan, and Europe. And everyone enjoys a wide range of street foods, which have been raised to the level of high art by the sidewalk and market-stall vendors of every major city. Ethnic Chinese in Bangkok may not cook Thai food at home, but they enjoy Thai curries when dining out, and the Thais gleefully devour Chinese-style noodles in the Chinese marketplace.

To those accustomed to Western meal patterns, Southeast Asian meals must seem odd at first. Everything usually arrives on the table at once, including soup, appetizers, salads, and main dishes. When you give up your preconceived notions, however, it's a very sensible way to eat: instead of eating one course at a time, you can nibble on a spicy dish, then some rice to put out the fire, take a bit of salad for a refreshing change of texture and flavor, and sip some soup whenever the mood strikes.

Another common Western mistake is to underestimate the role of rice in a meal. To the Asian mind, rice and food are practically synonymous; a bowl of rice is the center of the meal, and everything else plays a supporting role. If you think of a curry not as a stew or soup but as a sauce to flavor rice, it is easier to understand why many curries are so hot.

Dessert as we know it is not a part of most Asian meals. Sweet—sometimes intensely sweet—treats are popular, but are eaten mainly between meals. Restaurants catering to travelers often serve elaborate desserts, but home meals usually end with fresh seasonal fruit.

6

Meals without any beverages are not unusual. Soup often serves as a beverage. But this doesn't stop foreigners from enjoying local beers or even imported wines with their meals, and a cold beer is certainly a good way to quench the fires of really hot food. Tea or coffee may be served at the end of a meal. Fruit juices and soft drinks are extremely popular, but again, they are taken mostly away from the table. Strong spirits are occasionally served before, during, or after a celebration.

A standard place setting consists of a plate, a soup bowl, sometimes a separate rice bowl, and a spoon and fork (in the villages, the abundant banana leaves sometimes take the place of plates). Knives rarely appear at the table—the food is always cut into small pieces before cooking, both to conserve fuel and to enable the foods to increase the absorption of spices and sauce flavors during the cooking process.

A spoon and fork are really the ideal utensils for this kind of food. The spoon does most of the work, such as picking up some rice and a bit of an accompanying dish or *sambal* and transferring it to the mouth; the fork, usually held in the left hand, is mainly for pushing food into the spoon, not for spearing it Western style. Chopsticks are the everyday utensils among only ethnic Chinese and Vietnamese; others use them when eating Chinese food, and often with any kind of noodles.

But the most traditional "silverware" of all are the fingers. Some would argue that food never tastes quite so good as when you pick up a small handful of rice, roll it into a compact morsel with some sauce or other accompaniment, and pop it into your mouth. Many families that ordinarily use flatware return to the old method for special meals. In general, only the fingers of the right hand are used, especially among Muslims, who consider the left hand unclean and unfit for eating.

THE SOUTHEAST ASIAN KITCHEN

The basic cooking techniques of Southeast Asian cooking are quite simple, and they have evolved on the simplest of cooking equipment: an open fire of wood or charcoal. The stove may be as simple as three stones that create a stable base for a pot or grill, or a charcoal stove generally built from cement, with a large opening below for the charcoal. The stovetop has three prongs to support a wok or saucepan. A live fire is still the rule in all but the most modern city dwellings. For sautéing, stir-frying, or other quick cooking methods, the cook fans the fire to get a higher temperature. Otherwise, a small fire is fine for simmered and braised dishes. For grilling, a metal grate is simply laid over the fire.

Apart from pots for cooking rice, the most common form of cookware is a shallow metal pan with a rounded bottom. The exact shape and material varies, but this pan is immediately recognizable as a relative of the Chinese wok.

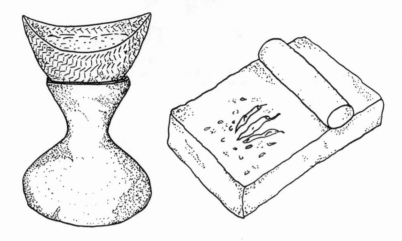

The next most important piece of equipment in the traditional kitchen is a mortar and pestle and possibly a grinding stone. These ageless tools are used daily for grinding spices and producing the pounded mixtures of ingredients so characteristic of Southeast Asian cooking—Thai curry pastes, Malay and Nonya *rempahs,* and the subtle liquid sauces of Vietnam, to name a few. A food processor, blender, and spice or coffee grinder can take its place in a Western kitchen and make short work of these rather laborious tasks.

Although the recipes in this book give measurements in cups, teaspoons, and tablespoons, these implements are rarely found in traditional kitchens. Most cooking is done without careful measurement, but by estimation and experience. A new bride does not take a cookbook into her new home, but rather what she has learned from her mother, grandmother, or aunts—how to tell by taste when a sauce is seasoned properly, how to tell if a pounded mixture is pounded enough by the feel of the ingredients in the mortar, how much water to use for new-crop rice or for older rice, and so on. I hope you will get into the true spirit of Southeast Asian cooking by adding a touch of this and a dab of that, using your own experience and ingenuity until your dish reaches your highest expectations.

The menus in each chapter are examples of traditional Southeast Asian meals. But don't feel you have to tackle a whole menu the first time out. Try a single main dish, along with some rice, and fill out the menu with familiar dishes. Or try a new appetizer in an otherwise Western meal. As you gain a little experience with these dishes, you will be ready to serve a complete meal of the delicious, healthful, exciting foods of Southeast Asia.

COOKING UTENSILS

Little equipment is absolutely essential to the Southeast Asian kitchen.

THE WOK

Of all the equipment in the Southeast Asian kitchen, the wok is the most versatile. Its design has many advantages, as it is shallow enough for pan-frying, yet deep enough for braising, parboiling, simmering, steaming, and deep-frying. Woks are made from carbon steel, cast iron, aluminum, stainless steel, or copper. Today, there are many woks on the market suitable for both kitchen and tabletop cooking.

Its bowl shape lends itself to the constant stirring and tossing of stir-frying. The metal heats quickly and distributes heat evenly. Because of its shape, less oil is used in cooking.

The 14-inch wok is best for home use and is the size most

commonly sold in sets, which usually include a wok ring, cover, a ladle and spatula, and often a Chinese-style wire strainer.

Carbon steel woks must be seasoned before using. First, wash it with a scouring pad and detergent to remove the protective oil coating. Rinse. Dry the wok well and place it on your stove to dry over a medium burner until all the moisture has evaporated. When the metal has dried completely, rub the inside of the wok with a paper towel dipped in approximately two tablespoons of cooking oil. Continue this procedure until all the oil is absorbed and the towel comes out clean. After each use, wash the wok with a soft sponge. After rinsing and drying, set the wok over medium heat until all the moisture has evaporated. Rub ¼ teaspoon of cooking oil in the wok to prevent rusting. If a carbon steel wok is not kept entirely dry between uses, it will rust.

MORTAR AND PESTLE, FOOD PROCESSOR, BLENDER, AND SPICE GRINDER

For most Southeast Asian cooks, the mortar and pestle is essential to the traditional kitchen. It is used for pulverizing spices into a powder and pounding aromatics into seasoning pastes. Its major advantage is that it can handle small quantities and that the ingredients are mashed into a smooth paste rather than chopped, producing a wonderfully fragrant blend that releases the flavors more effectively than does a machine.

Because our time is so limited, I have found processing the small amounts used in home cooking with a miniprocessor, small food processor, or in the small accessory jar of the blender to produce satisfying results. For grinding whole spices to a powder, a miniprocessor, electric spice mill, or coffee grinder is useful.

When preparing a paste in the small food processor, mince the harder ingredients first by hand. Add the remaining ingredients through the feed tube and process in pulses, stopping the machine often, to scrape down the sides of the work bowl.

In Southeast Asian cooking the spices and aromatics are often ground to a paste, then heated in oil in a wok or pan before adding other ingredients, to allow their full flavor to be enhanced. If you use a miniprocessor, small food processor, or blender, you may have to add some extra liquid to allow the mixture to blend properly. If you should have to do this, check with your recipe before proceeding. Is the spice mixture to be fried or simmered? If it is to be fried, add oil to aid in the mixing, and omit it when you add the paste to the heated pan on the stove; the oil you have used will produce the necessary frying action. If it is to be simmered, add water or coconut milk and proceed as directed in the recipe.

STEAMERS

METAL STEAMERS

There are two types of steamers: bamboo and metal. While limited steaming can be done in a wok, I prefer the utilitarianism of the 12-inch multi-tiered metal steamer, usually made of aluminum for heavy duty steaming, for fish and other foods that might impregnate my bamboo steamers with cooking odors. It is sturdier than the bamboo steamer and lets you steam several foods at the same time.

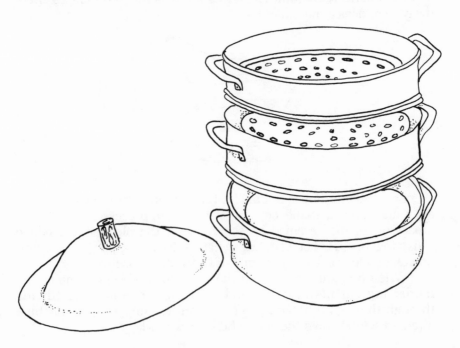

Bamboo Steamers

A bamboo steamer is more pleasing esthetically and is preferable for steaming buns or other doughy foods because the moisture does not drip from the top of the steamer onto the cooked foods. It makes a wonderful serving vessel. Place 2 to 3 cups of water in a wok and place the bamboo steamer trays into the wok.

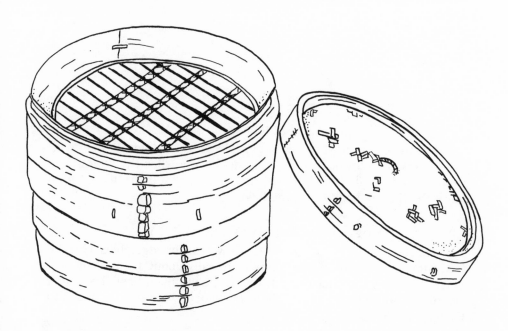

Cleavers and Knives

A Chinese cleaver, a large-bladed vegetable knife, and a small sharp knife will take care of practically any cutting task. Because so much depends upon the proper slicing and chopping, as with any knife, it should be kept razor sharp.

Electric Rice Cooker

An electric rice cooker makes the cooking of rice very easy and frees the burners for other cooking. I must say I could not live without one. However, I use it only for plain rice.

CUTTING TECHNIQUES

SLICING

Meat is easier to slice when partially frozen. Hold the food with the fingers curled under and the knuckles one slice-thickness back from the edge. Slice, using the knuckles to guide the blade, then move the fingers back along the food.

SHREDDING AND JULIENNE CUTTING

This technique is used for meat as well as for vegetables. Cut the food into slices of the desired length, usually about 1½ to 2 inches. Stack the slices and slice down through the bundle into sticks, which are square in cross section. Shreds are usually very fine, about ⅛ to 1/16 inch thick.

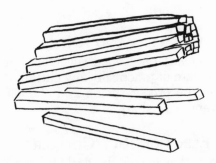

DICING, CHOPPING, AND CUBING

Cut the food into slices. Stack the slices on top of each other and cut them lengthwise into strips, as in shredding. Stack the strips and cut crosswise into evenly sized cubes or dice. (Often uniform cubes are unnecessary. When making curry or other pastes in the mortar or processor, the process will be made easier and faster by chopping the ingredients first.)

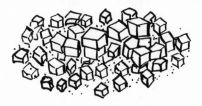

MINCING

To mince an ingredient is to cut it into very small pieces, about ¹⁄₁₆ inch. It is often used for ingredients that must retain their texture in ground or processed foods.

SMASHING AND BRUISING

Ginger, garlic, and green onions are often crushed to release their flavors. Cut to the desired size. Place the pieces on a board and hit firmly with the flat side of a cleaver or knife blade. This can also be done prior to mincing an ingredient, making the process much easier.

COOKING TECHNIQUES

STIR-FRYING

One of the most basic techniques in Southeast Asian cooking is stir-frying. Introduced by the Chinese, it has found its way into many non-Chinese kitchens. It is an ideal cooking method to produce tasty, nutritional, and colorful dishes in a short time.

A wok is ideal for stir-frying, but you may also use a large skillet. (A large skillet will use more oil than a wok.) Because stir-frying is extremely fast cooking, organization of the foods before cooking is of utmost importance. Have all of the ingredients, utensils, and equipment prepared completely before starting to cook.

Heat the wok. Add the oil in a thin stream around the sides of the wok. By the time the oil reaches the bottom, it should be hot. Add the first ingredient to be cooked to the wok and cook until the desired doneness. Meat and vegetables are often added separately, as they usually require different cooking times. Add the ingredients in the order listed in your recipe so that all will be finished at once. If a recipe has a "sauce mixture," add it when specified. If it is added too soon, the stir-fry will be braised and the ingredients will not be crisp.

If you are cooking on an electric stove, using a recipe that requires you to reduce the heat, it is best to preheat two burners. Have one burner on high and the other on low. Then you can move the wok from burner to burner.

STEAMING

Steaming is the least demanding and one of the most useful cooking techniques. It is a nutritious method of preparing food, since all the vitamins and minerals are preserved, rather than being boiled away in water. The texture and flavor of the finished dish is outstanding. There is no better way to cook a delicate fish than steaming, or to preserve the color and nutritional values of vegetables. It is also a wonderful way to reheat cooked dishes.

16

In steaming, the food is placed in a shallow heatproof container and suspended over boiling water in a metal or bamboo steamer to generate an intense flow of steam. It may also be done on a steaming rack in a wok. Wok steaming is hard on the seasoned surface and you will have to reseason it, both to avoid rust and to prepare it for stir-frying.

To steam successfully, the water in the steamer must be boiling before the food is placed in the container. The food should be suspended well above the boiling water, at least 2 inches, so that no water will touch the cooking food. There should be at least a 1½-inch space between the heatproof steaming dish and the steamer rim to allow the steam to circulate properly. Check the water level occasionally to be sure that it has not boiled away.

GRILLING

Grilling or barbecuing is one of the most popular of Southeast Asian cooking techniques. In a Southeast Asian kitchen, the same fire is often used to grill and to cook foods in pots. Bamboo skewers should be soaked in water for 1 hour before use so that they do not burn. If you prefer, most of the grilled foods in this book can be cooked under an oven broiler.

DEEP-FRYING

Deep frying produces interesting textures and seals in flavors and juices. Oil temperature is of extreme importance. It should be between 360° F and 380° F. At this temperature, the surface of the food is sealed immediately, preventing absorption of the oil. Too cool oil—below 350° F—will allow absorption of the oil into the food. If the oil is too hot, around 400° F, the oil will begin to burn the outside of the food before it is fully cooked inside.

To test the temperature of heated oil, drop a small piece of ginger, garlic, or green onion into the oil. If it rises to the surface quickly and begins to turn light brown without burning, the oil is the right temperature. If it drops to the bottom of the oil and sits there, the oil is not hot enough.

Another method of testing is by using chopsticks. Place a clean and dry chopstick vertically in the middle of the hot oil touching the bottom of the wok. If many bubbles appear immediately along the side of the chopstick, the oil is ready for deep-frying.

To keep the temperature constant during deep-frying, do not add too many pieces of food at a time. It is best to fry in batches to allow the oil to maintain the correct temperature.

Shallow-Frying or Pan-Frying

Similar to sautéing, this technique involves more oil than stir-frying but less than deep-frying. Food is fried first on one side and then on the other. Often, the excess oil is drained off and a sauce added to finish the entree. A frying pan is ideal for shallow-frying.

Blanching

Vegetables are frequently plunged into a large pan of boiling water and cooked rapidly to keep them crisp and their color bright. The vegetables should be cooked until almost tender, but still crunchy, drained immediately, then rinsed under cold running water to stop the cooking process.

BASICS

RICE

Central to almost every Southeast Asian meal is rice, which is served three times a day. Long-grain is preferred for meals by most Southeast Asians because it cooks into separate, fluffy grains. Most of the rice grown in the southern United States is long-grain and thus perfect for Southeast Asian food. Short-grain or glutinous rice is used mainly for desserts.

The failure of Westerners to understand the practice of eating almost everything mixed with rice has many people believing that Southeast Asian foods are too chile hot and spicy. One must remember that almost every dish was prepared to be consumed with a large quantity of rice. If you should find your mouth on fire from eating hot, spicy foods, just take a mouthful of rice. A drink of water will often only intensify the hot effect.

As many Southeast Asians will tell you, there are as many methods of cooking rice as there are areas and countries that eat it. This is a subject that should be definitely avoided at an Asian gathering!

Asian cooks wash their rice before cooking. Although directions for rice packaged in the United States says washing the rice is unnecessary and removes some of the nutrients, Southeast Asians believe that washing gives it a better texture and taste. You can experiment by trying it both ways and decide for yourself. If you purchase rice shipped from Asia, the rice should be washed before cooking to remove the excess dusting of starch that is used to prevent the rice from absorbing moisture in the humid climate.

An electric rice cooker produces perfect rice every time if the manufacturer's directions are followed. These are very common even in the most meager and remote Southeast Asian kitchens.

Steamed Rice

The amount of water used when cooking rice will vary upon the strain and age of the rice and the depth of the pan. Therefore, the measurements given are approximate.

½ to ¾ cup uncooked long-grain rice per person
2 cups water for the first measured cup of rice
1½ cups water for each additional cup of rice

Place the rice in a container and rub the grains together between the palms of your hands until the water becomes cloudy. Pour the rice into a colander to drain. Repeat the washing procedure 3 to 5 times until the water is clear. Drain thoroughly.

Select a pan with a tight-fitting lid. (Be sure to allow for room for expansion as rice triples in volume when cooked.) Place the drained rice in the pan. Bring the water to a boil over high heat. Reduce the heat. Cover the pan and simmer until all the water is absorbed, about 18 to 20 minutes. Do not lift the lid during this time. At the end of this period, open the cover long enough to check to see that all the water has been absorbed. Cover again. Turn off the heat and let stand 10 minutes. Fluff the rice with a fork. Serve warm.

ADVANCE PREPARATION: If the rice cools, it can be reheated in a non-metallic container in the microwave.

TIP: If you prefer to cook rice by Southeast Asian measurements, you may do the following after washing the rice. Add water to cover the rice by about 1 inch, remembering that there are no precise measurements. To double check the amount of water, put the tip of your index finger on top of the rice. The water should come to the point where your first joint begins.

Glutinous Rice

Glutinous rice is the short-grained pearly-white rice which is also known as sticky rice or sweet rice. It is sweet smelling, soft, and sticky.

⅓ cup uncooked glutinous rice per person
1½ cups water for first cup of rice
1 cup water for each additional cup of rice

Wash the rice until the water runs clear. Soak the rice in warm water to cover, at least 2 hours but preferably overnight. Drain.

Line a covered steamer basket with moistened cheesecloth. Spread the rice in the basket in an even layer. Steam over boiling water for 25 minutes or until soft. Serve hot, warm, or at room temperature.

Rice Mold

Cooked foods placed in the center of a rice mold make an attractive presentation.

Prepare cooked long-grain rice. Rinse a ring mold in cold water. Press the freshly cooked hot rice firmly into the mold. Invert mold over a platter. Unmold.

Ground Toasted Rice

Place uncooked long-grain rice in a dry skillet, and cook over moderate heat until the rice is a light golden brown, stirring frequently to prevent burning. Remove from the heat. Let the rice cool to room temperature. Grind to a fine powder in a processor, blender, or spice or coffee grinder. Ground toasted rice keeps indefinitely in an airtight container.

COCONUT MILK

Coconut milk is an essential ingredient in Southeast Asian cuisine. It is the liquid squeezed from the grated flesh of the mature coconut, *not* the liquid which is found inside the fresh coconut. That liquid is used in mixed tropical drinks and has none of the properties of coconut milk. You may want to chill the liquid and enjoy its refreshing taste.

Coconut milk is prepared by grinding coconut meat with water and pressing out the liquid. Thick coconut milk is produced from the first pressing from the ground coconut mixture, and thin coconut milk is produced from the second pressing. It can also be prepared from frozen or dried unsweetened coconut milk, which is available in Asian and health food stores. Many of the recipes call for either thick

or thin coconut milk. When creamed or dried unsweetened coconut flakes is called for, it is specified in the recipe. The recipes in this book were prepared using canned coconut milk, as I feel this is the milk most people will use when cooking, as fresh coconuts are not always readily available and preparation of fresh coconut milk is time consuming. Many of my Asian friends living in America use the canned Chaokoh brand coconut milk from Thailand. Creamed coconut, frozen grated coconut, and frozen coconut milk are also available.

Preparation of Fresh Coconut Milk

Choose a fresh coconut, free from cracks. Shake it well to make sure the nut is full of liquid.

To break open a coconut, hold it in one hand, with the three "eyes" upward. Hit the shell an inch or two away from the eyes with a hammer or the unsharpened side of a heavy cleaver. The shell will crack. After the first crack appears, drain the liquid into a bowl. Taste the liquid to make sure it is sweet, and not sour or rancid. If it is rancid, the coconut is not fresh and should be discarded. When a large crack appears, use a screwdriver, not a good kitchen knife, to pry the shell open. Remove the tough outer shell and cut the coconut meat into small pieces. It is not necessary to remove the thin brown skin unless the recipe calls for grated fresh coconut.

To prepare about 1½ cups coconut milk, add 2 cups grated coconut to a blender or food processor. Add 1¼ cups very hot water. Blend or process at high speed for 1 minute. Strain the mixture through a fine sieve, pressing hard with a wooden spoon to extract as much liquid as possible. For recipes calling for coconut milk, this is the liquid to use. If the milk is allowed to stand for a while, the thick milk will rise to the top. For recipes calling for thick coconut milk, spoon it from the top. The bottom will then be thin coconut milk.

A second extraction from the same coconut milk can be made by repeating the above steps. This will make a thinner coconut milk.

Fresh coconut milk should be refrigerated as soon as possible; it will keep for 1 to 2 days. For longer storage, it can be frozen in plastic containers. Once frozen, coconut milk does not have quite the smooth texture of the fresh or canned coconut milk.

Canned Coconut Milk

Canned coconut milk is very convenient and is quite delicious. The quality varies, and I prefer to use Chaokoh brand from Thailand. Sometimes the liquid may have a gray discoloration on top. If so, the coconut milk should be discarded. The thick coconut milk rises to the top of the can, as it does in fresh coconut milk. If a recipe calls for thick coconut milk, remove the top of the can and use the thick milk in your recipe. If a recipe specifies thin coconut milk, use the contents of the bottom of the can, just below the thick coconut milk. When "coconut milk" is called for, shake the can before opening to completely mix the milk. If it is too thick, you may dilute it with a little water.

Preparation of Coconut Milk from Dried Coconut Flakes

Empty an 8-ounce package of unsweetened dried coconut flakes into a food processor. Add 1⅞ cup of very hot, almost boiling, water. Process with quick on and off pulses for 20 seconds or until well mixed. Strain the mixture through a fine sieve, pressing hard with a wooden spoon to extract as much liquid as possible.

To make a thinner coconut milk, repeat the above steps.

Coconut Cream

This is available in block form and can be made into coconut milk by mixing equal amounts of creamed coconut and hot water. This very thick coconut milk should be put into dishes at the final stage of cooking.

Fried Shallot and Garlic Flakes

Fried shallot and garlic flakes are served throughout Southeast Asia as a garnish and to add flavor to many vegetable, meat, and rice dishes. Once cooked, the flakes will keep in an airtight container for one week, or they can be frozen.

The fried flakes are even easier to prepare when using purchased dehydrated onion or garlic flakes, which are usually much less expen-

sive in Asian markets. In many Asian markets, you can purchase the commercially fried shallot and garlic flakes. Just open the bag and use them!

Fried Shallot or Garlic Flakes

No amounts are given as they are so easy to cook when needed. If you prefer, you may prepare extra and store them in an airtight jar for several weeks.

Peanut or vegetable oil
Very thinly sliced shallots or garlic

Lightly oil a small skillet, preferably nonstick. Heat pan over medium-low flame, and add shallots or garlic. Cook for approximately 5 to 7 minutes, stirring or shaking the pan to allow them to brown slowly and evenly. When golden brown, remove from the oil and drain on paper toweling until cool. They will become crispy and turn darker brown as they stand.

ADVANCE PREPARATION: Cook ahead. Store in an airtight container for 1 to 2 weeks. The flakes may be frozen for 1 month.

TIP: Small, very thinly sliced onions may be substituted for the shallots. It is very important to have all the slices cut the same thickness to allow the flakes to cook evenly.

Fried Shallot or Garlic Flakes II

These flakes are so easily prepared that I have not given exact amounts. I usually cook the desired amount at the time needed.

Peanut or vegetable oil
Dehydrated onion or garlic flakes

Heat a small nonstick skillet over medium heat and lightly oil the pan. When the oil is hot, add the flakes, stirring until lightly browned. Remove. Drain on paper towels. Cool. Serve at room temperature.

ADVANCE PREPARATION: Store cooked flakes in an airtight container for 1 to 2 weeks.

TAMARIND

Tamarind produces the tart flavor in many dishes throughout Southeast Asia. It is the thick flesh inside the pods of the tamarind tree.

This recipe makes a medium-strength tamarind water. If the recipe needs another proportion, it will be specified in the individual recipe. The tamarind water will keep for several weeks if refrigerated in a tightly covered glass jar. Therefore, you might want to prepare a larger amount.

Prepared tamarind concentrate is available in Thai and Indian grocery stores and is very convenient. Use about 1 teaspoon tamarind concentrate to 3 tablespoons of water.

Tamarind Water

1 teaspoon tamarind pulp
2 teaspoons hot water

Place the tamarind pulp in a small container and add the hot water. Let the tamarind soak until it dissolves, squeezing the pulp with your fingers to break it apart and separate the seeds and strings. Strain the tamarind "water" through a fine wire strainer, reserving the liquid. Discard the pulp. Use immediately, or store tightly covered in a glass container in the refrigerator.

EGGS

EGG PANCAKE, EGG SHREDS, OR EGG STRIPS
Thin egg pancakes are often cut into shreds and used as a garnish.

1 egg, beaten thoroughly, strained
Pinch salt
Vegetable oil

Heat a well-seasoned or nonstick wok or skillet to moderate temperature. Lightly brush the pan with an oiled paper towel. Pour a thin layer of egg into the pan and slowly tilt the pan, forcing the egg to spread thinly over as wide an area as possible. Cook until slightly colored on the bottom. Turn over and cook briefly on the other side.

Let the pancake cool. To make strips for garnishing, roll up tightly and cut crosswise into the desired thickness. Unroll to make long, thin strips.

BANANA LEAVES

Banana leaves give a subtle aroma to cooked foods and are frequently used for steaming and grilling. Frozen banana leaves from the Philippines are available in Asian grocery stores. If unavailable, aluminum foil may be substituted; however, the pleasant fragrance of the banana leaf will be missing.

To wrap food in a banana leaf, start with a 12-inch-square leaf, and pour boiling water over the leaf to make it pliable. With the leaf fibers horizontal, place the food in the center of the leaf, allowing 4 inches of leaf on all sides. Fold the far and near edges over the food, making a neat parcel. Secure with a toothpick, metal skewer, staples, or string. Banana leaves are fragile and split easily, but you can patch the leaf with another leaf.

I have seen many chefs in Southeast Asia put aluminum foil outside the leaves if splitting occurs. The fragrance of the banana leaves will be imparted, and the aromatic seasonings will not be lost during cooking.

SPICE PASTES

The intrinsic flavor of a Thai, Malay, or Indonesian curry is the paste, a mixture of spices, herbs, and aromatic vegetables. Traditionally the pastes are pounded by hand in a mortar and pestle, but a miniprocessor, food processor, or blender can be used as well (see page 11).

The first step in cooking a curry paste is to fry the paste on moderate heat in oil or coconut cream, which allows the flavors and aromatics to be released. It is important to have the paste as dry as possible so that the mixture will fry rather than stew while cooking.

SPICE MIXTURES

Garam Masala I

This aromatic mixture of spices used in Indian cooking is best when freshly ground, as it is more flavorful.

1 tablespoon black cardamom pods
1-inch-stick cinnamon
1 teaspoon whole cloves
2 teaspoons black peppercorns

Break open the cardamom pods. Remove the seeds. Set aside. Crush the cinnamon with a rolling pin or mallet. Grind to a fine powder. Store in an airtight jar for 1 month.

Garam Masala II

This version is not as aromatic, but easier to prepare.

1 tablespoon ground cinnamon
¼ teaspoon ground cloves
1 teaspoon ground cardamom
1 teaspoon black pepper

Combine the spices. Keep in a tightly covered jar for about 1 month.

TIP: Prepared *garam masala* can be purchased in Indian grocery stores.

Szechuan Peppercorn Salt

4 tablespoons coarse salt
2 teaspoons Szechuan peppercorns
1 teaspoon freshly ground black pepper

Heat salt with Szechuan peppercorns in a dry pan on low heat for a few minutes, shaking the pan until the salt turns golden and you can smell the aroma from the peppercorns. Remove and cool. Crush the mixture with a rolling pin or in a food processor. Remove the husks of the peppercorns. Store in a tightly covered jar. The mixture will keep for months.

THAILAND

Sawasdee! Welcome!

Every time I visit Thailand, I feel a change come over me almost immediately. I know I am visiting a fascinating country with unique culinary, cultural, religious, archaeological, and physical attractions. But beyond its immediately obvious qualities, Thailand is for me a state of mind. Within a matter of hours after arriving in this magical, mystical kingdom, I begin to feel completely at peace.

Perhaps it is the calming influence of Buddhism, reinforced by the country's approximately 30,000 temples. Or maybe it is just the tranquil nature of the Thai people. The Thais are always smiling, justly giving their country the name "The Land of Smiles."

The Thai word *sanuk* means "fun," and the Thais' love of *sanuk* and joy of living is deep-rooted and irrepressible: it pervades almost every aspect of their daily existence. Going to a festival, having a simple bowl of noodles at a good restaurant, making a trip to the movies or to the countryside is *sanuk*. It reveals an ingrained sense of joy without which life would be dull and purposeless. The Thais seem to be at peace with themselves and to enjoy making people happy.

Bangkok, the capital of Thailand, is a bewildering conglomeration of old and new, East and West, exotic and ordinary, tranquility and chaos, all thrown together following no perceptible recipe. You might be lulled by the rhythmic sounds of chanting priests in a hushed temple and at the next moment risk your life crossing a street that has some of the most lethal traffic in all of Asia. (The traffic is bad, but the first time I was caught in it, I thought the automobiles had no horns. During this mad rush there was a distinct silence;

29

nobody honks the horn, and nobody shouts. The Thais are content to sit and wait.)

When I arrive in Bangkok, I visit Wat Po, one of the city's oldest and largest *wats* (temple-monastery), to get into the typically Thai spirit. The four large pointed pagodas, or *chedis*, memorials to the first four Bangkok kings, seem to hold up the sky ever so gently. The 160-foot-long Reclining Buddha, the largest in Thailand, splendidly shows Buddha in the position in which he entered nirvana. The gigantic figure is entirely covered with gold leaf, and the soles of the feet marvelously inlaid with mother-of-pearl designs depicting the 108 auspicious signs of the Buddha.

A short walk from Wat Po is the extravagantly glorious Grand Palace and the sacred Temple of the Emerald Buddha. The square-mile compound is a vast display of glittering gilded spires, colorful mosaics, jewel-encrusted shrines, and beautifully landscaped gardens. The mysterious blend of the temporal and spiritual essence so typical of Thailand is strikingly visible here. The Temple of the Emerald Buddha, the centerpiece of the Palace complex, is the king's personal chapel and perhaps the most beautiful temple in Asia. The two-foot-tall Emerald Buddha is the country's most sacred object; King Bhumibol Adulyadej, Rama IX, personally changes its robes three times a year, dressing it in blue for the rainy season, gold for the cool season, and in diamond-studded finery for the hot season. The Emerald Buddha plays a vital role in the lives of the Thais, many of whom prostrate themselves before it in prayer or meditation.

I am entranced by the monks with their flowing saffron robes and shaved heads. Emulating the Buddha, they have cast aside all worldly possessions, and all over Thailand they can be found in the early morning with their heads bowed, holding their alms bowls, which will be filled with offerings of food. To feed a monk is an honor and it is believed to bring you luck.

The exotic architecture of the wats is mirrored in the "spirit houses," miniature structures looking like a cross between a doll's house and an elaborate birdhouse, standing on posts in beautiful gardens in front of Thai homes. They are homes for *Pra Poom,* the spirit of the land on which the house, shop, or office is built. The spirit houses are usually elaborately decorated and are kept well supplied with offerings of fresh flowers, food, and fragrant incense to prevent the land spirits from becoming jealous.

Traveling by long-tailed boat along Bangkok's canals, called *klongs*, takes me instantly out of the modern world and into a waterborne Thailand that has hardly changed in centuries. Although the busy streets are just a short distance away, the atmosphere on the klongs is one of quiet calm. I admire the beautiful flowers and enjoy their fragrance while observing the peaceful lifestyle along the waterways. I will never forget the sight of a group of young monks, their saffron robes hanging neatly from tree branches along the banks, splashing merrily in a *klong*.

Of course, there are more than spiritual reasons for visiting Thailand. They are evident everywhere in the city, from the street vendors to the markets to the local restaurants. The visitor is bombarded with the sights and smells of food. In food stands on nearly ever street corner, vendors offer countless varieties of fast food—noodles, noodles, and more noodles, barbecued chicken, roasted ears of corn, fried bananas, and small savories and sweets. The many markets display tumbling avalanches of silvery fish, cascades of glistening clams, exotic fruits and vegetables, all arranged artistically in true Thai fashion. The smells are magnificent.

In the floating markets—particularly Damnern Saduak, about an hour's drive outside Bangkok I can glimpse the still-active waterborne life of Thailand. Hundreds of long-tailed boats loaded with freshly picked fruits and vegetables, dried fish, rice, and other products are paddled by attractive women wearing broad-brimmed lampshade-style hats. In other boats, vendors stir-fry tasty noodle dishes, prepare delicious fried bananas, and sell thirst-quenching fresh coconut milk and tasty sweets. The scenes and smells are colorful and exotic.

Although many Westerners think of Thai food as simply hot, there is much more to it than that. Thai food is colorful, aromatic, and altogether delicious. Many authentic dishes are quite hot, but chiles are just part of a complex melding of flavors, all conspiring to bring pleasure: a little garlic, ginger, galangal, coriander, shallots, mint; perhaps a blend of spices—peppercorns, cloves, nutmeg, cardamom, cinnamon, cumin; and the inevitable fish sauce, *nam pla,* to tie it all together. No matter how fiery the initial bite, I find myself unable to resist another bite! Like the country itself, the food leaves an enjoyable sensation that lingers long after the meal is over.

Thai soups, often a meal in themselves, are eaten whenever they are ready, rather than as an introduction to a meal. Two all-time favorites are *Tom Yum Koong,* a spicy and sour soup with prawns and mushrooms, and *Kai Tom Kha,* an herbed chicken and coconut soup.

There are aromatic, fiery curries, the freshest of fish and seafood cooked in numerous ways, fried noodles, and sparkling salads that combine grilled meat or poultry with a tantalizing combination of seasonings and herbs. Desserts tend to be less intensely sweet than those of other Southeast Asian countries: mangoes with sticky rice, coconut ice cream topped with corn and peanuts, and delicious, aromatic fresh fruits, as often as not carved into elaborate leaf and flower patterns.

During a stay at the gracious and luxurious Regent of Bangkok, I learned about the intricacies of Thai cuisine from Head Chef Pajongchit Pitaksakorn of the hotel's delightful Spice Market Restaurant. Here I enjoyed traditional Thai foods: crispy *Tord Man Khao Phod,* corn fritters with sweet and sour sauce; *Som Tam,* a vividly delicious papaya salad; sweet *Mee Krob,* crispy rice noodles with pork and shrimp; *Kung Sarm Rod,* gigantic pan-fried river prawns, and *Kaeng Kiew Warn Kai,* a wonderful blending of spices in green curry with chicken.

On other visits, I have enjoyed the hospitality of Danny Mc-Cafferty, general manager of the Dusit Thani Hotel, and many meals in the royal Thai style in the hotel's famous Dusit-Bussaracum Restaurant. In the tradition of the kings of Siam and their courts, many of the dishes are intricately decorated. *Krathong Thong* are tiny flower-shaped, coconut-flavored pastries filled with chicken, shrimp, and pork. Another appetizer, *Cho Muang,* encases a tasty chicken and shallot stuffing in an indigo-colored rice-flour dough fashioned into a beautiful flower. *Saengwa,* a grilled prawn salad seasoned with chile, onion, and lemon grass, is served in an intricately carved squash and garnished with delicate shreds of fried catfish, a marvelous juxtaposition of textures and flavors. All of the dishes were beautifully adorned with elegant fruit and vegetable carvings. One of the desserts was *Look Choob,* Marzipan-like "fruits", a mixture of green mung beans, sugar, coconut milk, jasmine, and agar-agar perfectly shaped into miniature cherries, apples, green and purple grapes, and bananas. Many of the recipes in this chapter are from Boonchoo Pholwatana, head chef of the Dusit Bussaracum Restaurant and Culinary Academy and one of the "grand dames" of Royal Thai cuisine, having taught and been a chef for over forty years.

Looking out the window of my room at the Dusit Thani one morning, I spotted a gathering of people who seemed to be exercising in Lumpini Park, one of the few grassed areas in Bangkok. It was six A.M., and I decided to explore. I was surprised to see a gathering of middle-aged people twisting away to disco music from a boom-box. They had incredibly serious faces, and it was quite apparent that they were here for health reasons and not for pleasure. In another corner, elderly men and women were stretching and bending in unison, practicing the ancient Chinese Tai Chi exercises. Young students in sweats were practicing for Bangkok's upcoming marathon. Outside the park, an array of breakfast stalls sold the health devotees vegetarian dishes and other healthy foods such as rice porridge, to be garnished with ginger, preserved radish, and chiles.

The Thai Cooking School at The Oriental offers still another taste of Thailand. A quick ferry ride across the Chao Phraya River from the hotel's private dock takes students to an airy room in a former riverside mansion converted into a teaching kitchen. School director

Chalie Amatyakul offers a week-long immersion in Thai culture while teaching marvelously flavorful cooking. Students learn the dishes from the very beginning, opening and grating coconuts, pounding curry pastes by hand in a mortar—to the end—how to wrap noodles around meatballs to be fried into *Moo Sarong,* how to achieve the proper crisp and crumbly texture in the fried noodle dish, *Mee Krob.* Carving specialists from the hotel's kitchen staff demonstrate the intricate carved fruit and vegetable garnishes that are so much a part of this elegant cuisine.

Some 350 miles to the north of Bangkok lies Chiang Mai, often called the "Rose of the North." The relaxed atmosphere and cool climate is a refreshing contrast to the hot lowlands. I start my visit by climbing the 306 steps to the Wat Phra That, the magnificent Buddhist temple on Doi Suthep mountain. From this high spot, I have a panoramic view of the town, its fertile valley and lush forests, as well as the surrounding mountains that form the lower ranges of the Himalayas.

Back in town, I enjoy the smells of the open-air markets selling *Kao Soi,* a Thai-Burmese dish that is a cross between a simple noodle dish and a curry. It is served with pork, meat, or chicken with some crispy noodles sprinkled on top and optional accompaniments of pickled vegetables, garlic, lime, and chile sauce. Tasty barbecued honey chicken and heavily spiced pork sausages prepared by Thailand's best sausage makers are other local specialties.

The best introduction to northern Thai food is to savor a *Khantoke* dinner. This is the favorite form of celebration meal in the north, served for the ordination of monks, weddings, and housewarmings.

Khan literally means "bowl," and *toke* is a small, low table, usually made of rattan, lacquerware, or brass, around which diners sit cross-legged on the floor and share a succession of dishes such as *Kaeng Hang Le,* pork curry with garlic, ginger, and spices; *Nam Prik Ong,* minced pork cooked with tomato, cucumber, onion, and chiles; *Kaeng Kai,* chicken and vegetable curry; and *Larb Nua,* minced beef with chiles. Other dishes might include marinated grilled chicken and green papaya salad. Sticky rice is rolled into a ball and used to lift the food from the bowl. *Nam Prik Num,* a spicy chile sauce prepared from chiles and baby eggplant, accompanies the meal.

The ceremony is usually held outside. Mats are placed on the grass and five or six people sit around each low table. If it is a formal ceremony, special dances such as *Fawn-Tien* (candle dancing) and *Fawn-Dab* (sword dancing) are performed after dinner.

Chiang Mai was also the starting point for a trip through the beautiful highlands to the north. The scenery is breathtaking yet serene, with magnificent panoramas of rugged mountain ranges and valleys stretching northward toward Burma. An unforgettable part of the trip was an elephant trek through dense jungles and green open valleys. Hugging the slopes amid the hilly terrain, a cluster of thatched huts comprised the village of the Yao hill tribe. I was told that this village was probably much the same as it had been hundreds of years ago. There were many women, all wearing colorfully embroidered outfits. The children were busily playing *look khang,* a game of spinning a wooden top. Cows, horses, pigs, dogs, and chickens roamed freely.

The Yao are among a half-dozen major tribes (the others are the Karen, Meo, Lahu, Akha, and Lisu) inhabiting the pine- and teak-forested mountains of northern Thailand. Numbering more than 500,000 in Thailand, these tribes speak languages more closely related to those of Burma, Tibet, and southwest China than that of the Siamese Thai. Each tribe has its own distinct culture and traditional dress, but all share a love of richly embroidered costumes, massive headdresses, and silver ornaments.

The Yao's staple food is rice grown on the mountain slopes. Their eating table is of circular-shaped woven bamboo, and they eat with chopsticks, like the Chinese. Besides rice, their diet includes pork, pumpkin, potatoes and other root vegetables, plus chiles and salt. Chicken is served when there is an occasion to pay respect to the spirits, a practice similar to the Chinese. A very potent alcoholic beverage prepared from locally grown maize, millet, or wheat is often drunk before meals.

The hill people are basically shy and superstitious. They believe that their lives, health, and luck are influenced by invisible spirits present in their houses, the hills, forests, and waterways. They protect their homes and villages with altars, fertility symbols, and other objects to ward off evil spirits. They can also be open and friendly and are just as curious about us as we are about them. Although they speak different languages than the Thai and Lao people of the lowlands, there has always been commerce in goods and foodstuffs between them. Many of the popular dishes of northern Thai cookery, such as *Larb Nua, Kai Pad Bai Ka Pho,* and *Ma Hor* are thought to have originated among the hill people.

The sights, the sounds, the sensations, the magnificent cuisine, and the gentle, fun-loving Thai people keep me returning to Thailand. And each trip I discover more.

Kin Hai Aroy! Enjoy your dinner!

THAI MENUS

TANTALIZING THAI TEMPTATIONS
AN EXOTIC THAI BUFFET

16 people

Grilled Beef, Chicken or Pork on Skewers, *Satays*
◆
Spicy Peanut Sauce, *Naam Jim Satay**
◆
Sweet and Sour Cucumbers, *Kwa Brio Wan†*
◆
Spicy Beef in Lettuce Packages, *Larb Nua†*
◆
Stuffed Green Peppers, *Kai Kred Kaew**
◆
Fried Rice Noodles with Pork, Chicken, and Shrimp, *Mee Krob*
◆
Red Chicken Curry, *Kaeng Pet Kai**
◆
Herbed Fruit Salad, *Yum Polamai†*
◆
Spiced Seafood Salad, *Yum Pla Talay†*
◆
Pineapple Fried Rice, *Kao Pad Saparod†*
◆
Rice
◆
Chile Sauce, *Naam Prik**
◆
Siamese Gems, *Tab Tim Krob**
◆
Bangkok Delight, *Bangkok Sook***
◆

*double recipe   †triple recipe   **quadruple recipe

Fresh Pineapple or Fruit Juice

•

Singha Beer

•

Coffee or Tea

Here is a colorful and sparkling menu for an exotic buffet. Your friends will enjoy the relaxed, friendly atmosphere and will have great fun experimenting with the many taste sensations this menu provides.

Have plenty of fragrant fresh flowers and exotic fruits on your table to create a sensational Thai ambience. The festivities will be off to a roaring start when you serve ambrosial Bangkok Delights. One word of caution—this is a deceptively potent beverage, so one or two per guest will be ample. I suggest you have a delectable fresh fruit juice such as Fresh Pineappleade (page 168) to serve as well.

So your guests may dine in typical Thai manner, set each place with a fork and soup spoon; the fork is used to push the food onto the spoon, which delivers the food to your mouth.

Thai food is usually served at room temperature, making this an easy buffet. The peanut sauce, chicken curry, and chile sauce may be prepared several days ahead. The day before your big event, prepare the Sweet and Sour Cucumbers, cook the beef for the Spicy Beef in Lettuce Packages, prepare the stuffing for the green peppers, the fruit and seafood for the salads, the Siamese Gems, Bangkok Delight, and fruit juice.

The morning of the dinner, hollow out oranges and pineapples to be used as serving dishes for the Herbed Fruit Salad and Pineapple Fried Rice. Prepare the Pineapple Fried Rice and *Mee Krob* as specified in the Advance Preparation tips for each recipe.

Before serving, bring the peanut sauce, cucumbers, and chile sauce to room temperature. Arrange the Spicy Beef on a lettuce-lined platter, and combine the seafood salad and the fruit salad with their dressings. Place the fruit salad in the hollowed-out oranges and the Pineapple Fried Rice in the hollowed-out pineapple. Bake the Pineapple Fried Rice as specified in the directions. Assemble the green peppers and steam. Grill the satays, and reheat the *Mee Krob* and Red Chicken Curry as specified in the recipe directions.

Relax and enjoy the culinary delights of Thailand!

AN ENCHANTING EVENING AT THE SPICE MARKET

6 people

Corn Fritters, *Tord Man Khao Phod*

◆

Sweet and Sour Cucumbers, *Kwa Brio Wan*

◆

Galloping Horses, *Ma Hor*

◆

Hot and Spicy Shrimp Soup, *Tom Yum Koong*

◆

Spicy Chicken Salad, *Yum Kai*

◆

Mussaman Beef Curry, *Kaeng Mussaman Nua*

◆

Rice

◆

Chile Sauce, *Naam Prik*

◆

Fresh Fruits

◆

Coffee or Tea

◆

Singha Beer

Entering the cozy, enchanting Spice Market Restaurant in Bangkok's Regent Hotel, one is greeted by a dramatic array of Thai spices, whose wonderful aromas permeate this tastefully decorated room. Sacks of dried chiles, tubs of rice, dried beans, and lentils, braids of garlic, and cubbies of coriander, lemon grass, citrus leaves, and coconuts stimulate your taste sensations. A beautiful Thai girl named Varin delicately carves papayas, watermelons, apples, carrots, and many other fragrant fruits and vegetables to become various shapes of enchantingly delicate flowers that are intricate in detail, yet beautiful in their simplicity.

Short of hopping on the next plane for Bangkok, the best way to enjoy the specialties of this delightful restaurant is with this menu given to me by Head Chef Pajongchit Pitaksakorn. You can create your own "Spice Market" ambience by making an arrangement of fresh lemon grass, red and green chiles, coriander, and coconuts. Surround this with small baskets of dried spices such as cumin, coriander powder, cloves, and cardamom, or even some exotic fruits.

The Corn Fritters, Sweet and Sour Cucumbers, Mussaman Beef Curry, Chile Sauce, and fruit may be prepared a day ahead. The Hot and Spicy Shrimp Soup may be prepared ahead, but add the shrimp a few minutes before serving so they won't be overcooked. Galloping Horses and Spicy Chicken Salad are served at room temperature and may be prepared ahead and assembled several hours before your dinner. At serving time, prepare the rice, and reheat the Corn Fritters and Mussaman Beef Curry as specified in the recipe directions.

Enjoy an enchanting evening in Bangkok!

STARTERS

Son-in-Law Eggs, *Khai Look Kaey*
Corn Fritters, *Tord Man Khao Phod*
Stuffed Cucumbers, *Tang Khua Yad Sai*
Fat Horses, *Ma Uon*
Grilled Beef, Chicken or Pork on Skewers, *Satays*
Pork in Golden Threads, *Moo Sarong*
Galloping Horses, Ma Hor
Pork and Shrimp Dip, *Kao Tang Na Tang*
Fish Cakes, *Tord Man*
Coconut Shrimp, *Koong Tord*
Shrimp Rolls, *Prataad Lom*

SOUPS

Corn and Crab Soup, *Kaeng Poo Kab Kao Phod*
Stuffed Cucumber Soup, *Kaeng Chud Tang Khua Yad Sai*
Herbed Chicken and Coconut Soup, *Kai Tom Kha*
Hot and Spicy Shrimp Soup, *Tom Yum Koong*

MEAT

Chile Beef, *Nua Pad Prik*
Beef with Oyster Sauce, *Nua Pad Nam Man Hoy*
Spicy Beef in Lettuce Packages, *Larb Nua*

POULTRY

Chicken with Fresh Basil, *Kai Pad Bai Ka Phao*
Ginger Chicken, *Kai Pad Khing*
Sweet and Sour Chicken, Pork, and Shrimp, *Pad Preeowahn Sarm Kasat*
Barbecued Chicken, Thai Style, *Kai Yang*

FISH AND SEAFOOD

Fish with Spicy Tamarind Sauce, *Kaeng Som Pla*
Aromatic Steamed Fish, *Pla Nueng*
Baked Coconut Shrimp, *Koong Som*

CURRIES

Red Curry Paste, *Nam Prik Krung Kaeng Ped*
Green Curry Paste, *Nam Prik Kaeng Kiew Warn*
Mussaman Curry Paste, *Nam Prik Kaeng Mussaman*
Green Curry with Chicken, *Kaeng Kiew Warn Kai*
Red Chicken Curry, *Kaeng Pet Kai*
Mussaman Chicken Curry, *Kaeng Mussaman Kai*
Mussaman Beef Curry, *Kaeng Mussaman Nua*
Thick Curry with Beef, *Panaeng Nua*
Green Curry with Shrimp, *Kaeng Kiew Warn Koong*

SALADS AND VEGETABLES

Green Mango Salad, *Yum Ma Muang*
Green Apples with Spicy Sauce, *Yum Apples Kiew*
Sweet and Sour Cucumbers, *Kwa Brio Wan*
Spicy Beef Salad, *Yum Nua*
Spicy Chicken Salad, *Yum Kai*
Herbed Fruit Salad, *Yum Polamai*
Spiced Seafood Salad, *Yum Pla Talay*
Stuffed Green Peppers, *Kai Kred Kaew*

RICE AND NOODLES

Classic Thai Fried Rice, *Kao Pad*
Pineapple Fried Rice, *Kao Pad Saparod*
Thai Fried Noodles, *Pad Thai*
Fried Rice Noodles with Pork, Chicken, and Shrimp, *Mee Krob*

SAUCES AND ACCOMPANIMENTS

Thai Cucumber Sauce, *Arjard*
Chile Sauce, *Naam Prik*
Chile Jam, *Naam Prik Pad*
Spicy Peanut Sauce, *Naam Jim Satay*
Barbecue Chicken Sauce, *Naam Jim Kai-Nua*

DESSERTS AND BEVERAGES

Siamese Gems, *Tap Tim Krob*
Mangoes and Sticky Rice, *Khao Niew Mam Uang*
Banana Fritters, *Kluay Tord*
Bangkok Delight, *Bangkok Sook*
Thai Iced Tea, *Cha Yen*
Thai Iced Coffee, *Kar Fae Yen*
Lemon Grass Tea, *Cha Takai*

STARTERS

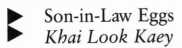 Son-in-Law Eggs
Khai Look Kaey

There are many stories regarding this dish. One of them is that a prospective bridegroom wanted to impress his future mother-in-law with his culinary skills. He prepared this dish, and she was delighted.

> 3 cups oil
> 6 hard-boiled eggs, shelled, cut in half crosswise
> 3 tablespoons light brown sugar
> 3 tablespoons fish sauce (*nam pla*)
> 2 tablespoons tamarind water (page 25)

GARNISH:

> 1 to 2 fresh red chiles, seeded, thinly shredded into 1 inch
>   lengths
> 1 to 2 tablespoons oil
> 3 tablespoons fried onion flakes (optional, page 24)
> Coriander leaves

Heat oil in wok. Add eggs and deep-fry the eggs, flat side down, until the outsides are golden and blistered, about 3 to 4 minutes. Remove. Drain on paper towels. Remove all but 2 tablespoons of oil from wok. Add the sugar, fish sauce, and tamarind water. Stir until sugar is dissolved. Reduce the heat. Let simmer gently for approximately 5 minutes until the mixture is thickened and well blended. Add the eggs and stir very gently over the heat for 1 to 2 minutes. Transfer with a slotted spoon to a serving plate. Serve yolk-side up. Garnish with chiles, onion flakes, and coriander leaves.

YIELD: 3 to 4 servings.

ADVANCE PREPARATION: Prepare eggs and sauce ahead. Add eggs to sauce mixture and heat together at serving time.

 ## Corn Fritters
Tord Man Khao Phod

A favorite Thai snack from the Regent of Bangkok's Spice Market Restaurant. Serve these tasty fritters as an appetizer or as part of your meal.

½ cup rice flour
½ cup flour
½ teaspoon salt (optional)
2 teaspoons baking powder
½ teaspoon pepper
½ to 1 teaspoon chili powder
2 teaspoons sugar
1 tablespoon minced fresh coriander leaves
2 teaspoons minced garlic
3 tablespoons minced shallots
½ cup water
1½ cups corn, blanched until tender-crisp
½ cup oil for frying
Plum Sauce
Thai Cucumber Sauce (page 94)

Sift flours, salt, and baking powder together. Combine all ingredients except the corn and beat until smooth. Add the corn. Mix well. Pour the oil into a frying pan and heat over medium-high heat to 350° F. When oil is hot, drop batter by spoonfuls into hot oil, pressing down with fork to flatten. The fritters should be about 3 inches in diameter and ¼ inch thick. Fry about 2½ minutes on each side or until golden brown. Remove and drain on paper towels. Do not fry more than 6 fritters at a time or they will not cook properly. Serve with plum sauce and/or Thai Cucumber Sauce.

YIELD: 6 to 8 servings.

ADVANCE PREPARATION: The fritters may be fried ahead and reheated in the oven.

Inspired by a recipe from Head Chef Pajongchit Pitaksakorn, The Spice Market Restaurant, The Regent of Bangkok.

Stuffed Cucumbers

Tang Khua Yad Sai

Stuffed cucumbers are a delightful, mild appetizer.

2 cucumbers, peeled, trim ends, cut crosswise into ¾-inch pieces
4 ounces pork, minced
4 ounces shrimp, shelled, deveined, minced
½ teaspoon freshly ground black pepper
1 tablespoon minced fresh coriander leaves
1 tablespoon minced garlic
1 teaspoon sugar
1 to 3 tablespoons fish sauce *(nam pla)*
2 tablespoons cornstarch
Soy sauce
Chile Sauce (page 94)

GARNISH:

Fresh coriander leaves
12 very small cooked shrimp (optional)

Scoop out seeds from one side of each cucumber section to make a well, being careful not to cut completely through the section. Mix pork and shrimp together in a bowl. Add black pepper, coriander, garlic, sugar, and 1½ tablespoons fish sauce. Mix well. Dust the hollowed-out section of the cucumbers lightly with cornstarch to prevent the filling from falling out. Fill the cucumbers with the mixture, mounding the filling and smoothing it with a wet spoon or knife. Place an a heatproof platter. Place a coriander leaf on the stuffing. Steam the stuffed cucumbers over boiling water for about 8 minutes or until the cucumber and the pork are cooked and firm. Remove from heat. When serving, place a cooked shrimp on each cucumber section. Serve at room temperature with soy sauce and Chile Sauce if desired.

YIELD: 10 to 12 stuffed cucumbers.

TIP: Zucchini may be used as a substitute for cucumbers.

ADVANCE PREPARATION: Prepare cucumbers and refrigerate, covered with plastic wrap. Steam and garnish at serving time.

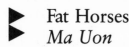 Fat Horses
Ma Uon

A lightly seasoned classic Thai snack, these also make an attractive appetizer on a buffet table. Head Chef Boonchoo Pholwatana of the Dusit-Bussaracum Restaurant serves these in the traditional banana-leaf cups. I have substituted lightly oiled heatproof cups.

1 tablespoon minced fresh coriander root
4 cloves garlic, minced
½ teaspoon freshly ground black pepper
1 chicken breast, boned, skinned, minced
4 ounces crabmeat, shredded
4 ounces ground pork
1 tablespoon fish sauce (*nam pla*)
1 tablespoon light brown sugar
2 tablespoons thick coconut milk
2 eggs, lightly beaten
1 tablespoon oil
Small heatproof containers or heatproof paper cups

GARNISH:

2 to 3 tablespoons thick coconut milk
12 to 14 coriander leaves
1 fresh red chili, shredded into 1-inch lengths

Pound or process coriander root, garlic, and black pepper in a mortar or processor. To aid in processing, you may add a little chicken breast to the coriander mixture. Add chicken breast, crabmeat, and pork. Puree until smooth. Add fish sauce, sugar, coconut milk, and eggs, reserving 1 tablespoon of egg. Process to completely blend ingredients, being careful not to overprocess mixture.

Divide the mixture. Put in lightly oiled small heatproof cups or heatproof paper cups. Brush tops lightly with reserved egg. Place on a steaming rack over boiling water. Steam until mixture is set and firm, about 5 to 8 minutes. Cool until comfortable to hold. Invert cups onto a large heat-proof platter and tap gently to remove the molds. Garnish with 1 teaspoon thick coconut milk, a coriander leaf, and 2 to 3 chile shreds. Steam for 1 minute. Remove from heat. Serve warm or at room temperature on a lettuce lined platter.

YIELD: 4 to 6 servings.

ADVANCE PREPARATION: Prepare ahead completely and refrigerate. Bring to room temperature before serving.

VARIATION: If coriander roots are unavailable, use 1½ tablespoons coriander stems.

 ### Grilled Beef, Chicken or Pork on Skewers
Satays

A favorite Thai snack or appetizer, this satay, when accompanied by the robust, aromatic, Thai Spicy Peanut Sauce and Thai Cucumber Sauce is a favorite of all my students. Serve it as an appetizer, a snack, or part of a meal with rice.

> 1½ cups thin coconut milk
> 1½ teaspoons turmeric powder
> ¾ teaspoon Oriental curry powder
> 1 pound beef, chicken, or pork, or an assortment of all, cut across
>   the grain into thin slices ¼ inch wide by 3 to 4 inches long
> 12″ bamboo skewers, soaked in water for 1 hour to prevent
>   burning
> Spicy Peanut Sauce (page 96)
> Thai Cucumber Sauce (page 94)

Combine 1½ cups thin coconut milk, turmeric, and curry powder. Thread the meat strips on the skewers, 3 or 4 to each stick. Marinate the skewered meat in the mixture for about 1 hour. Grill the satay over charcoal or broil in the oven, basting occasionally. Serve with Spicy Peanut Sauce and Thai Cucumber Sauce. If the satay is a main course, serve with rice.

YIELD: 6 to 8 servings as an appetizer.

ADVANCE PREPARATION: The satay may be marinated and then frozen. Layer skewers in a container, placing plastic wrap between layers of satay. Grill when frozen. The satay sauce may be prepared ahead and refrigerated.

Inspired by a recipe from Chalie Amatyakul, director, The Thai Cooking School, The Oriental, Bangkok.

 ## Pork in Golden Threads
Moo Sarong

Wrapped with golden egg noodles, these tasty morsels make a delicious and attractive presentation. They are delightfully pleasing to the eye as well as to the palate. At The Oriental, they are served as an appetizer with Thai Cucumber Salad, Plum Sauce, and Sriracha Chile Sauce.

> 4 ounces dried, long flat egg noodles (⅛ to ¼ inches wide),
>   soaked in hot water until softened, about 10 to 20 minutes
> 1 tablespoon finely minced coriander stems
> 1 tablespoon finely minced garlic
> ¾ teaspoon freshly ground black pepper
> ½ pound ground pork
> ¼ cup finely minced water chestnuts
> 4 Chinese dried black mushrooms, soaked in water until
>   softened, about 20 minutes, stems discarded, finely minced
> ¼ cup minced bamboo shoots
> 1 egg yolk, lightly beaten
> 1 tablespoon cornstarch
> 3 cups oil for frying
> Chile Sauce (page 94), soy sauce, Plum Sauce and/or Thai
>   Cucumber Salad (page 94)

Drain the soaked noodles and set aside, tossing occasionally to prevent sticking.

Pound or process the coriander, garlic, and pepper to a smooth paste in a mortar or small processor. (If using a processor, you may add a small amount of pork and grind with the coriander and garlic.) In a small bowl, combine the ground pork with the paste. Add the water chestnuts, black mushrooms, bamboo shoots, egg yolk, and cornstarch.

Shape the mixture into small balls, using about 1 tablespoon of the mixture for each. Wrap each ball with 2 or 3 noodles. Press the noodles onto the surface of each ball and continue wrapping until each ball is covered.

Heat oil in a wok to 350° F. Fry in batches, turning, until the noodles are golden brown and the meat is cooked through, about 4 minutes. Drain on paper towels. Serve hot, warm, or at room temperature with Chile Sauce, soy sauce, Plum Sauce, and/or Thai Cucumber Salad.

YIELD: approximately 30 balls.

TIPS: If noodles are soaked too long, they will break when wrapping. Plum Sauce and Sriracha Chile Sauce may be purchased at Asian markets.

VARIATION: Ground chicken, beef, shrimp, or a combination of these may be substituted.

Inspired by a recipe from Chalie Amatyakul, director, The Thai Cooking School, The Oriental, Bangkok.

Galloping Horses
Ma Hor

There is no better way to be taught cooking than amid the lush greens and exotic flowers surrounding the pool at The Regent of Bangkok! This easily prepared attractive appetizer is a favorite among Thais and is a specialty of The Spice Market Restaurant.

> 2 tablespoons oil
> 1 tablespoon minced garlic
> 12 ounces ground pork
> 2 tablespoons fish sauce (*nam pla*)
> 4 tablespoons light brown sugar
> ⅛ teaspoon freshly ground black pepper
> ½ cup coarsely chopped roasted peanuts
> 1 head lettuce, separated into leaves
> 4 tangerines, peeled, pith and white fibers removed, cut
>   horizontally into ⅓-inch slices

GARNISH:

> Mint or coriander leaves
> 2 fresh red chiles, seeded, cut into thin shreds

Heat wok. Add oil and heat. Add garlic and fry until fragrant. Add pork, fish sauce, brown sugar, and black pepper. Stir-fry until pork is cooked throughout. Stir in peanuts and mix thoroughly. Remove from heat and let cool.

Place the lettuce leaves on a serving platter. Arrange the tangerine slices on the lettuce. Put a heaping teaspoon of the cooked pork mixture on each tangerine slice. Garnish with mint or coriander leaves and chile shreds. Chill until ready to serve.

YIELD: 8 to 10 servings.

TIP: Pineapple wedges may be substituted for the tangerines.

ADVANCE PREPARATION: Prepare the pork mixture 1 day ahead. Refrigerate. Assemble 1 to 2 hours prior to serving. Cover with plastic wrap. Refrigerate.

Inspired by a recipe from Head Chef Pajongchit Pitaksakorn, The Spice Market Restaurant, The Regent of Bangkok.

Pork and Shrimp Dip
Kao Tang Na Tang

A mild and slightly sweet dish traditionally served over fried, crisp rice. Head Chef Boonchoo Pholwatana prepares this dish as a dip with crunchy shrimp chips. It is delightful when served at room temperature as an appetizer or as part of a meal.

2½ tablespoons chopped fresh coriander stems
3 cloves garlic, chopped
1 teaspoon white pepper
¾ cup thin coconut milk
8 ounces lean ground pork
8 ounces shrimp, shelled, deveined, and chopped
⅓ cup chopped shallots
2 tablespoons tamarind water
4 tablespoons fish sauce (*nam pla*)
½ cup light brown sugar
½ cup finely chopped unsalted peanuts
⅓ cup thick coconut milk
1 to 2 tablespoons paprika for color

GARNISH:

Fresh coriander leaves
1 to 2 fresh red chiles, cut into thin shreds (optional)
Fried shrimp chips (page 267)

Combine the coriander, garlic, and white pepper. Pound or process to a smooth paste. To aid in processing, you may add a little of the coconut milk to the coriander mixture. Heat ¾ cup thin coconut milk in a saucepan over medium heat until it is just simmering. Stir in coriander paste, pork, shrimp, and shallots. Bring to a boil and reduce heat to simmer. Cook, stirring, uncovered for approximately 5 minutes or until pork is cooked throughout. Stir in tamarind water, fish sauce, brown sugar, and peanuts. Cook until sugar dissolves. Remove from heat. Add thick coconut milk and paprika to desired color. Stir. Garnish with coriander leaves and chile shreds. Serve with shrimp chips or fried crispy rice.

YIELD: 4 to 6 servings as a dip.

ADVANCE PREPARATION: Prepare 1 day in advance. Serve at room temperature. The flavors and texture improve and the sauce will thicken upon standing. If dip is too thick, add more coconut milk.

VARIATION: Serve with broccoli, green beans, and zucchini cut into bite-size pieces.

Inspired by a recipe from Head Chef Boonchoo Pholwatana, Dusit Bussaracum Cooking School and Restaurant, Bangkok.

 ## Fish Cakes
Tord Man

Spicy, chewy, and crisp, this is a traditional Thai favorite. The fish cakes are usually very spicy, but you may reduce the amount of red curry paste if you desire less heat. Serve with Thai Cucumber Sauce.

¾ pounds catfish or any white-fleshed fish fillet
1½ tablespoons fish sauce *(nam pla)*
1 to 2 tablespoons Red Curry Paste (page 69)
1 tablespoon minced galangal
1 egg, lightly beaten
8 Kaffir lime leaves, stems removed, finely shredded (optional)
½ cup oil
Thai Cucumber Sauce (page 94)

Remove white part of the fish with a spoon, being careful not to use the oily parts of the fish. Place fish, fish sauce, curry paste, galangal, and egg in a food processor or blender. Process until blended into a smooth paste, being careful not to overprocess. Remove. Add Kaffir lime leaves and mix well. Moisten hand with water. Pick up fish mixture and shape into small cakes, about 3 inches in diameter by ¼ inch thick. Heat oil to 350° F. Fry a few cakes at a time, pressing down with a spatula, until both sides are light brown. Drain on paper towels. Serve with Thai Cucumber Sauce.

YIELD: 4 servings.

ADVANCE PREPARATION: The fish cakes may be made ahead, frozen, and fried at serving time. They may also be fried ahead and reheated in the oven.

Inspired by a recipe from Head Chef Pajongchit Pitaksakorn, The Spice Market Restaurant, The Regent of Bangkok.

Coconut Shrimp
Koong Tord

Vorachoon Yuchinda, the soft-spoken owner of Lemongrass Restaurant, Bangkok, served me this cool, refreshing dish. For a beverage, he suggested his wonderful Lemon Grass Tea (page 101), which had a delicate flavoring of lemon grass and was sweetened with sugar cane. It was a perfect foil for this delightful, easily prepared appetizer.

> ½ pound medium shrimp, peeled, deveined, tails intact
> ¼ cup fresh lime juice
> ½ cup medium coconut milk
> Salt to taste

GARNISH:

> 1 shallot, thinly sliced
> 1 or 2 fresh red or green chiles, seeds removed, thinly sliced

Place shrimp in a small glass bowl. Add lime juice and toss well. Marinate for 30 minutes, stirring occasionally. The shrimp should be almost opaque throughout and firm. Drain. Pour coconut milk over the shrimp. Stir. Season with salt to taste. Garnish with shallots and chiles. Chill, covered with plastic wrap, for 4 hours.

YIELD: 3 to 4 servings.

TIP: A very brief cooking in the lime juice is authentic. You may marinate the shrimp up to 8 hours for a more complete cooking.

ADVANCE PREPARATION: Prepare completely in advance. Refrigerate.

► Shrimp Rolls ◄
► *Prataad Lom* ◄

Bean curd sheets (tofu sheets)
24 large shrimp, shelled, deveined, tails left intact
1 teaspoon minced coriander root
1 teaspoon minced garlic
1 teaspoon white pepper
1 tablespoon fish sauce *(nam pla)*
2 egg yolks, beaten
3 cups oil for deep frying
Soy sauce, Plum Sauce, Sriracha Chile Sauce, or Chile Sauce
    (page 94)

Sprinkle or brush bean curd sheets with water to allow to soften. Make small slits in the inner curve of the shrimp to allow them to lie flat.

Process the coriander root, garlic, and pepper to a smooth paste. Add the fish sauce and mix. Marinate the prawns in the mixture for 10 minutes, turning once.

Cut the softened bean curd sheet into 3-inch squares. Place one shrimp on each square near the top, allowing the tail to extend over the edge. Fold the top of the square over the shrimp. Roll up tightly, leaving tail extended. Brush the lower edge of the bean curd sheet with egg yolk to seal the package. Place rolls on a rack until ready to fry, making sure they do not touch one another.

Heat oil in wok to 350° F. Deep-fry shrimp, a few at a time, until golden brown. Drain on paper towels. Serve immediately with soy sauce, Plum Sauce, Sriracha Chile Sauce, or Chile Sauce.

YIELD: 24 shrimp rolls.

TIPS: Bean curd sheets are available fresh, frozen, or dried in Asian grocery stores. To prevent cracking, they should be moistened with water before using. When purchasing dried bean curd sheets, check them to make sure they are not broken, as they might be too broken up to be useful.

Bottled Plum Sauce and Sriracha Chile Sauce may be purchased in Asian markets.

ADVANCE PREPARATION: The rolls may be assembled 1 hour

ahead. Cover with plastic wrap to keep the wrappers moist; if they become too dry, they will break. Fry just before serving.

Inspired by a recipe from Chalie Amatyakul, director, The Thai Cooking School, The Oriental, Bangkok.

SOUPS

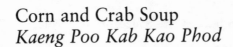

Corn and Crab Soup
Kaeng Poo Kab Kao Phod

This is the Thai version of an easily prepared, subtly seasoned soup of Chinese origin.

> 2 tablespoons oil
> 2 garlic cloves, minced
> 2 shallots, minced
> 3 cups chicken stock
> 1½ tablespoons fish sauce (*nam pla*)
> ½ pound crabmeat
> 16-ounce can cream-style corn
> 1 large egg, beaten with ¼ teaspoon salt
> Dash white pepper
> 2 tablespoons chopped fresh coriander leaves

Heat a large saucepan over high heat. Add oil and heat. Add garlic and shallots. Fry until fragrant. Add chicken stock, fish sauce, crabmeat, and creamed corn. Stir until soup comes to a boil. Reduce heat to low and simmer 1 minute. Pour in beaten egg in a wide circle over the surface. Stir gently a few times with chopsticks to form ribbons. Adjust seasonings by adding more salt and fish sauce if desired. Pour into a soup tureen. Sprinkle with white pepper. Garnish with coriander.

YIELDS 4 to 6 servings.

TIP: Shrimp may be substituted for crabmeat.

ADVANCE PREPARATION: Soup may be prepared ahead. Add the beaten egg at serving time.

Inspired by a recipe from Head Chef Pajongchit Pitaksakorn, The Spice Market Restaurant, The Regent of Bangkok.

 ## Stuffed Cucumber Soup

Kaeng Chud Tang Khua Yad Sai

Mildly spiced, this soup is a nice palate refresher during a Thai meal. It reflects the Chinese influence on Thai cuisine.

> 2 small cucumbers, peeled, trim ends, cut crosswise into ¾-inch
>   pieces
> 4 ounces pork, minced
> 4 ounces shrimp, minced
> ½ teaspoon freshly ground black pepper
> 1 tablespoon minced fresh coriander leaves
> 1 tablespoon minced garlic
> 1 teaspoon sugar
> 1 to 3 tablespoons fish sauce (*nam pla*)
> 2 tablespoons cornstarch
> 6 cups chicken stock

GARNISH:

> Fresh coriander leaves

Scoop out seeds from one end of each cucumber section to make a well, being careful not to cut completely through the section. Mix pork and shrimp together in a bowl. Add black pepper, coriander, garlic, sugar, and 1½ tablespoons fish sauce. Mix well. Dust the hollowed-out sections of the cucumbers lightly with cornstarch. Fill the cucumbers with the mixture, mounding the filling and smoothing it with a wet spoon or knife. Place on a heatproof platter. Steam the stuffed cucumbers for 10 to 15 minutes, or until the cucumber and the pork are cooked and firm. Remove from heat. Bring the chicken stock to a boil. Add the stuffed cucumbers. Remove from the heat. Season with remaining fish sauce to taste. Garnish with coriander leaves. Serve immediately.

YIELD: 4 to 6 servings.

ADVANCE PREPARATION: Steam cucumbers one day ahead. Cover with plastic wrap and refrigerate. Reheat chicken stock at serving time and add cucumbers, cooking until cucumbers are heated through. Season with fish sauce. Serve hot.

Inspired by a recipe from Head Chef Pajongchit Pitaksakorn, The Spice Market Restaurant, The Regent of Bangkok.

 ### Herbed Chicken and Coconut Soup
Kai Tom Kha

This is a creamy, slightly sweet, fragrant classic Thai soup with a hint of fire.

> 6 garlic cloves, chopped
> 7 fresh coriander roots, chopped, or 2 tablespoons chopped fresh
>   coriander stems
> 2 stalks lemon grass, bottom 6 inches only, finely sliced
> 3 shallots, sliced
> 4 tablespoons chopped, peeled galangal
> ½ teaspoon white pepper
> 2 cups thick coconut milk
> 2 cups thin coconut milk
> ¾ pound skinless, boneless chicken breasts, cut into strips 2 by
>   ¼ by ¼ inches
> 4 to 5 tablespoons fish sauce *(nam pla)*, or to taste
> 4 to 5 tablespoons lime juice, or to taste
> 4 to 6 fresh red chiles, seeded, chopped
> 7 Kaffir lime leaves, finely shredded
> 2 tablespoons chopped fresh coriander leaves

Pound or process the garlic, coriander, lemon grass, shallots, galangal, and pepper to a smooth paste. In a wok, bring 1 cup thick coconut milk to a boil. Add the spice-paste mixture and stir-fry for 4 to 5 minutes. Add the chicken and stir-fry over moderately high heat until it is no longer pink. Add the remaining coconut milk. Bring the mixture to a boil, stirring. Reduce the heat to simmer and cook for 1 minute or until the chicken is cooked and is tender. At serving time, check seasonings, adding more fish sauce and lime juice if desired. Garnish with chiles, Kaffir lime leaves, and coriander. Serve hot or at room temperature.

YIELD: 6 servings, with other dishes.

TIP: One-half teaspoon lime zest, chopped, may be substituted for the Kaffir lime leaves.

ADVANCE PREPARATION: Prepare ahead. Reheat and garnish at serving time.

Inspired by a recipe from Chalie Amatyakul, director, The Thai Cooking School, The Oriental, Bangkok.

 ## Hot and Spicy Shrimp Soup
Tom Yum Koong

This piquant soup is probably the best known and loved of all Thai soups. It is rich with the flavors of shrimp, lemon grass, coriander, and chiles, and can be one of the spiciest dishes in Thai cuisine. Tender shrimp and straw mushrooms give an added texture.

You may want to increase or decrease the amount of lime juice and chile to suite your taste. Head Chef Pajongchit says there should be an even balance between the sour and hot flavors.

1 pound medium shrimp with shells
1 tablespoon oil
5 cups chicken stock
2 stalks lemon grass
1½ tablespoons minced coriander stems
2 cloves garlic, peeled, minced
2 to 4 fresh chiles, seeds removed, minced
4 Kaffir lime leaves, chopped
½ teaspoon lime zest, slivered
½ teaspoon white pepper
15-ounce can straw mushrooms, drained
Fish sauce to taste, about 1 tablespoon
Juice of 1 lime, about 3 to 4 tablespoons, or to taste
2 fresh red chile, seeds removed, shredded into 1½-inch lengths
2 tablespoon coarsely chopped coriander leaves

Peel, wash, and devein shrimp, reserving shells. Cut shrimp in half lengthwise. Heat oil in saucepan and fry shells until they turn pink. Add chicken stock. Cut off tops of lemon grass stalks. Bruise with the side of a cleaver or knife. Add to stock. Slice remaining bottom 5 inches of lemon grass into paper-thin slices. In a blender or small processor, combine sliced lemon grass, coriander, garlic, chiles, Kaffir lime, lime zest, and white pepper. Pound or process to a paste in a mortar or small processor or blender. Add paste to stock. Stir to combine. Bring to a boil. Cover. Reduce heat and simmer for 20 minutes. Strain the mixture through a sieve. Return stock to pan and bring to a boil. Add the shrimp and mushrooms to the stock and cook 2 to 3 minutes, or until the shrimp are pink and opaque. Reduce heat to a simmer. Season to taste with fish sauce and lime juice. Stir. Remove from heat. Pour into a tureen. Garnish with red chile and coriander leaves. Serve hot.

YIELD: 4 to 6 servings.

TIP: If Kaffir lime is unavailable, double the amount of lime zest used. If straw mushrooms are large, cut into quarters or halves.

Inspired by a recipe from Head Chef Pajongchit Pitaksakorn, The Spice Market Restaurant, The Regent of Bangkok.

MEAT

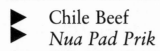 Chile Beef
Nua Pad Prik

A spicy, hot, and colorful Thai stir-fry.

½ pound flank steak, cut into paper-thin slices 1 inch wide by 2
    inches long
1 tablespoon light brown sugar
2 tablespoons soy sauce
4 tablespoons oil
15-ounce can miniature corn, drained
2 green peppers, cored, seeded, cut into ½-inch squares
1 medium onion, thinly sliced
6 Chinese dried black mushrooms, soaked in warm water for 20
    minutes or until spongy, stems removed, shredded
4 fresh red chiles, seeds removed, shredded into 1½" lengths
1 tablespoon minced ginger
2 tablespoons minced garlic

SAUCE: Combine in a bowl and set aside

1 tablespoon fish sauce *(nam pla)*
1 tablespoon soy sauce
2 tablespoons oyster sauce

In a bowl, combine beef, sugar, and soy sauce. Let marinate 20 to 30
minutes. Heat 2 tablespoons oil in a wok. Add corn, green peppers,
onion, mushrooms, and chiles. Stir-fry for 1 to 2 minutes, or until
green peppers and onions are done. Remove and set aside. Add 2
tablespoons oil to wok. Heat. Add ginger and garlic and stir until
fragrant. Add beef. Stir-fry 3 to 4 minutes or until cooked. Add the
cooked vegetables to the wok. Stir-fry until the vegetables are heated
throughout. Add the sauce mixture and cook until it begins to bubble.
Serve with cooked rice or in a rice mold (page 21).

YIELD: 2 to 3 servings.

ADVANCE PREPARATION: The vegetables and meat may be cut up
and refrigerated in plastic wrap one day ahead. Cook the vegetables
and meat separately several hours in advance. Combine all ingredients when serving.

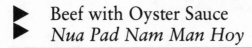 **Beef with Oyster Sauce**
Nua Pad Nam Man Hoy

The Thai influence is shown in the use of hot chiles in this Chinese stir-fry. For a less spicy dish, omit the chile peppers.

1 pound flank steak, cut into thin 1-inch by 2-inch slices
1 tablespoon dry sherry
1 tablespoon cornstarch
Dash pepper
3 tablespoons oil
3 garlic cloves, minced
2 teaspoons minced fresh ginger

SAUCE: Combine and set aside

3 tablespoons oyster sauce
1½ tablespoons soy sauce
1 tablespoon honey
1 tablespoon lemon juice

4 fresh red chiles, seeds removed, shredded
3 green onions, shredded into 1½-inch lengths
6 to 8 lettuce leaves

Place beef in a bowl. Add sherry, cornstarch, and pepper. Allow beef to marinate 15 to 20 minutes. Heat wok over high heat. Add 2 tablespoons oil. Heat. Add garlic and ginger. Stir until fragrant. Add beef. Stir-fry until beef is cooked through. Add sauce mixture and stir-fry until sauce is slightly thickened and translucent. Add chiles and green onions. Stir until thoroughly mixed. Arrange lettuce leaves on platter. Place beef on top of lettuce. Serve with rice.

YIELD: 4 servings.

Spicy Beef in Lettuce Packages
Larb Nua

A northeastern Thai delight, this tangy hot and sour dish is served with assorted raw vegetables at The Regent of Bangkok's Spice Market Restaurant. When wrapped with lettuce, it makes a wonderful appetizer.

1 pound ground beef
1 tablespoon toasted long-grain rice (page 21)
2 tablespoons minced garlic
2 tablespoons minced shallots
2 green onions, coarsely chopped
1 stalk lemon grass, bottom 6 inches only, minced
2 to 3 teaspoons minced fresh red chiles (seeds removed)
⅓ cup tightly packed fresh mint leaves, minced
⅛ cup tightly packed fresh coriander leaves, minced
3 tablespoons fresh lime juice
1 teaspoon sugar
2 to 3 tablespoons fish sauce *(nam pla)*

Assorted raw vegetables cut into serving-size pieces: carrots, green beans, zucchini, broccoli

OR

Boston or romaine lettuce, cored, leaves detached, washed, dried

GARNISHES:

Mint leaves
Lime wedges

Shape beef into 1-inch balls. Fill a large saucepan with water. Bring to a boil. Add the beef balls and cook approximately 2 to 3 minutes, until no longer pink in the center, stirring occasionally. Drain beef balls immediately. Put in a bowl and crumble into small pieces. In a coffee grinder, miniprocessor, or mortar, grind or pound toasted rice to a powder.

Thoroughly mix into the crumbled meat the garlic, shallots, green onions, lemon grass, chiles, rice powder, mint, coriander, lime juice, and sugar. Add fish sauce to taste. Serve with the raw vegetables or make lettuce packages. Garnish with mint leaves and lime wedges.

To serve with the vegetables, arrange the vegetables attractively on one side of a platter and place the beef mixture on the other. Scoop up the beef with the vegetables.

To serve with lettuce, place lettuce on a serving platter and arrange the salad in the center. Spoon the meat mixture on a lettuce leaf. Wrap the lettuce leaf around the meat and eat with your fingers.

YIELD: 4 servings.

ADVANCE PREPARATION: Prepare the meat one day ahead. Combine the salad several hours before serving. Serve at room temperature.

Inspired by a recipe from Head Chef Pajongchit Pitaksakorn, The Spice Market Restaurant, The Regent of Bangkok.

POULTRY

 Chicken with Fresh Basil
Kai Pad Bai Ka Phao

The Riverside Restaurant in beautiful Chiang Mai serves this popular Thai dish. Their baby corn, native to northern Thailand, was the sweetest I have ever tasted. Most Thais prefer hot basil, which has a much stronger taste than our milder sweet basil.

1 teaspoon shrimp paste *(kapee),* (optional)
6 dried chiles, seeds removed, soaked in hot water for 30 minutes
2 tablespoons chopped garlic
2 tablespoons chopped shallots
4 tablespoons oil
2 chicken breasts, boned, skinned, cut into 1½- by 1-inch strips
½ cup straw mushrooms
½ cup baby corn
3 tablespoons fish sauce *(nam pla)*
2 teaspoons sugar
¾ cup fresh basil leaves

GARNISH:

2 fresh red chiles, seeds removed, shredded into 1½-inch lengths
    (optional)
Boston or romaine lettuce leaves

Wrap shrimp paste in foil and toast in a dry frying pan for 1 to 2 minutes on each side. Remove. Pound or process chiles, garlic, shallots, and toasted shrimp paste in a mortar, blender, or small food processor until a smooth paste is formed. Heat 2 tablespoons oil. Add the paste and fry on moderate heat, stirring until fragrant, about 2 to 3 minutes, being careful not to burn. Add 2 tablespoons oil. Turn heat to high. Add the chicken and stir-fry until well mixed and cooked throughout. Add the mushrooms and baby corn. Mix well. Add the fish sauce, sugar, and basil leaves. Stir until the sugar has dissolved and the basil leaves have wilted. Garnish with chiles. Serve on lettuce leaves.

YIELD: 3 to 4 servings.

TIP: Canned baby corn and straw mushrooms are available in Asian markets.

VARIATION: If fresh basil is unavailable, substitute fresh mint. Do not use dried basil.

 ### Ginger Chicken
Kai Pad Khing

A marvelous stir-fry combining chicken and ginger—a Thai favorite!

2 tablespoons light soy sauce
2 tablespoons fish sauce (*nam pla*)
2 tablespoons rice vinegar
1 to 2 teaspoons sugar
3 tablespoons oil
1 small onion, thinly sliced
3 cloves garlic, minced
2 tablespoons fresh ginger, peeled, shredded
2 large chicken breasts, skinned, boned, cut into bite-size pieces
6 Chinese dried black mushrooms, soaked in hot water, about 20
    minutes or until soft, stems removed, sliced
5 green onions, thinly sliced
2 fresh red chiles, seeds removed, thinly shredded into 1½-inch
    lengths
2 tablespoons chopped fresh coriander leaves

Combine soy sauce, fish sauce, rice vinegar, and sugar. Set aside. Heat oil in wok. Add onion. Stir-fry until soft and translucent. Add garlic and ginger, and stir-fry about 10 seconds. Add chicken. Stir-fry until chicken changes color, about 2 minutes. Add mushrooms, green onions, and chiles. Stir. Continue cooking until chicken is cooked throughout. Add soy sauce mixture to wok. Stir until well mixed. Add coriander leaves. Stir. Serve hot with rice.

YIELD: 2 to 3 servings.

  Sweet and Sour Chicken, Pork and Shrimp
Pad Preeowahn Sarm Kasat

This colorful, spicy stir-fry is a favorite of my students.

   2 small cucumbers
   4 tablespoons oil
   1 tablespoon minced garlic
   4 ounces pork, sliced thinly into 1½-inch pieces
   4 ounces chicken breast, skinned, boned, cubed
   4 ounces shrimp, shelled, deveined
   1 large onion, cut into small wedges
   ¾ cup drained baby corn
   3 to 5 red or green chiles, seeds removed, sliced diagonally
   2 tomatoes, cut into small cubes
   3 green onions, cut into 1-inch lengths

SAUCE: Combine and set aside.

   ⅓ cup tomato ketchup
   4 tablespoons fish sauce (*nam pla*)
   4 tablespoons rice vinegar
   4 tablespoons sugar
   1 tablespoon cornstarch dissolved in 2 tablespoons water

GARNISH:

   Fresh coriander leaves

Peel cucumbers. Trim off ends, cut in half, remove seeds. Cut each half lengthwise into 4 to 5 strips. Cut each strip into 2-inch lengths. In a wok, heat 2 tablespoons oil. Add garlic and fry about 10 seconds.

Add pork. Stir-fry 1 minute or until half-done. Add chicken and shrimp. Stir until cooked. Remove and set aside. Add 2 tablespoons oil. Heat. Add cucumbers, onion, baby corn, and chiles. Stir-fry for 1 to 2 minutes, or until cucumbers are slightly translucent. Add tomatoes and cook until heated throughout. Add cooked pork, chicken, and shrimp. Stir. Add green onions and sauce mixture. Stir until slightly thickened and translucent. Remove and serve. Garnish with coriander.

YIELD: 4 servings.

Inspired by a recipe from Head Chef Boonchoo Pholwatana, Dusit-Bussaracum Restaurant and Culinary Academy, Bangkok.

 ## Barbecued Chicken, Thai Style
Kai Yang

Barbecued chicken is a Thai favorite and is available in the many street stands in Thailand. A Thai friend of mine calls herself a "plastic bag cook." She purchases barbecued chicken in a plastic bag from a street vender and serves it to her family for dinner.

1 whole chicken (2½ to 3 pounds)
2 stalks fresh lemon grass, bottom 6 inches only, chopped
1 tablespoon chopped fresh ginger
1 tablespoon chopped garlic
2 tablespoons chopped fresh coriander root
1 teaspoon ground turmeric
1 tablespoon light brown sugar
1 to 2 tablespoons fish sauce (*nam pla*)
2 tablespoons oil

Rinse chicken and pat dry. Split the chicken in half down the breast or cut into serving-size pieces. Place in a large bowl.

Pound or process lemon grass, ginger, garlic, and coriander root in a mortar, blender, or small processor until a smooth paste is formed, adding a little of the oil if necessary. Add turmeric, brown sugar, fish sauce, and oil. Blend until smooth. Pour mixture over the chicken, cover, and marinate in refrigerator for 2 hours or overnight. Turn the pieces periodically to allow them to marinate evenly.

Prepare hot coals for barbecuing or preheat the broiler. Grill the chicken until juices from the thickest part run clear, about 20 to 30 minutes. Serve with Barbecued Chicken Sauce (page 97).

YIELD: 3 to 4 servings.

TIP: Substitute 3 tablespoons chopped coriander stems for coriander root.

FISH AND SEAFOOD

 ## Fish with Spicy Tamarind Sauce
Kaeng Som Pla

Spicy red Thai curry paste combined with ginger and tart tamarind produce a marvelous combination of flavors. A favorite of my students, I am sure you will find it the highlight of your dinner. Red snapper is my preference.

¼ cup tamarind water (1½ tablespoons tamarind pulp dissolved
   in ½ cup hot water)
6 tablespoons fish sauce (*nam pla*)
¼ cup light brown sugar
¼ cup light soy sauce
3 to 6 cups oil for frying
3 tablespoons minced garlic
1 to 2 tablespoons Red Curry Paste (page 69)
3 tablespoons minced ginger
3 green onions, minced
1 whole 1½- to 2-pound firm-fleshed white fish (red snapper, sea
   bass), cleaned, scaled, head and tail intact
¼ cup all-purpose flour
¼ cup cornstarch
½ teaspoon salt
¼ teaspoon freshly ground black pepper

GARNISH:

2 green onions, shredded into 2-inch lengths
3 tablespoons coriander leaves
3 fresh red chiles, shredded into 2-inch lengths
Fried shallot flakes (page 23)

Place tamarind in warm water and mix with your fingers. Let stand for 20 minutes. Strain tamarind water, pressing to extract liquid. Discard pulp.

In a small bowl, combine ¼ cup tamarind water, fish sauce, sugar, and soy sauce. In a wok or skillet, heat 2 tablespoons oil over high heat. Add garlic and stir-fry until lightly browned, about 10 seconds. Add curry paste and fry 1 to 2 minutes. Add tamarind mixture and cook until sugar dissolves and the sauce thickens slightly, approximately 1 minute. Add ginger and minced green onions and stir-fry for 30 seconds. Reduce heat to a simmer and cook for 2 minutes. Set aside.

Wash the fish and pat dry. Make 3 diagonal slashes 1 inch apart on each side of the fish. Combine the flour, cornstarch, and salt. Coat the fish completely, shaking off any excess mixture.

In the meantime, over high heat, heat a wok or shallow roasting pan large enough to hold fish. Add the oil and heat to 375° F. Gently lower the fish into the oil head first and immerse it in the oil. Ladle the hot oil over the fish. Deep fry on each side, turning carefully, about 4 to 8 minutes, depending upon the size of the fish, or just long enough for the fish to be firm and delicately browned. Baste with oil and shift the fish occasionally while frying. Remove gently with 2 spatulas, tilting it over the wok to drain. Place on a large, heated serving platter. Reheat the sauce and pour over the fish. Garnish with green onions, coriander, and chiles. Serve immediately with Fried Shallot Flakes (page 23), Thai Cucumber Salad (page 94), and rice.

YIELD: 2 to 3 servings as a main course.

ADVANCE PREPARATION: Prepare sauce ahead. Fry fish ahead. Heat oil, fry a second time to reheat. Reheat sauce and pour over fish.

Inspired by a recipe from Chalie Amatyakul, director, The Thai Cooking School, The Oriental, Bangkok.

Aromatic Steamed Fish
Pla Nueng

A fragrant, pleasantly spiced freshly steamed fish is always a highlight. Easily prepared, low in cholesterol and calories and a delight to the eye, this dish is destined to be a winner. If you prefer to lower your calories even further, you may omit the unsmoked bacon and the last finishing touch of the hot glistening oil. In Thailand, a freshly caught pomfret is always a prized fish for steaming. Pomfret can be purchased frozen in some Asian grocery stores.

1 whole 1½- to 2-pound fish (pomfret, pompano, red snapper, or
    sea bass) cleaned, scaled, with head and tail intact
2 garlic cloves, chopped
3 tablespoons peeled, shredded fresh ginger
2 Chinese pickled plums, pitted, chopped
½ teaspoon freshly ground black pepper
2 ounces lean unsmoked bacon, cut into thin strips (optional)
2 tablespoons light soy sauce
1 tablespoon cornstarch
4 to 6 Chinese dried black mushrooms, soaked in hot water until
    spongy, about 20 minutes, stems discarded, shredded
3 fresh red chiles, seeded, shredded
2 sprigs fresh coriander
3 green onions, cut on the diagonal into 2-inch lengths
2 tablespoons celery leaves (optional)
2 tablespoons peanut oil
1 tablespoon Chinese sesame oil

Score the fish, making 3 or 4 equal diagonal cuts across the body on each side of the fish. Place the fish on a heatproof plate for steaming. Pound or process the garlic, half the ginger, the pickled plums, and pepper to a paste. Add the unsmoked bacon. Combine the soy sauce and cornstarch and combine with the mixture. Place the paste mixture inside the fish, in the slits, and over and around the fish. Place half of the mushrooms and half of the chiles, and the remaining ginger shreds inside the slits in a decorative manner. Scatter the remaining mushrooms around the fish.

Bring water to a boil in a Chinese steamer. Place the fish dish in the top of the steamer. Cover and steam the fish about 10 minutes per pound over medium-high heat, or until the fish is no longer translucent. Remove the plate from the steamer. Remove the steamed vegetables scattered around the fish, leaving only those in the slits on the fish. Garnish with coriander, green onions, celery leaves, and the remaining chile shreds. Heat the peanut and sesame oils to smoking point and pour the oil over the fish to produce a sheen and add richness and flavor. Serve.

YIELD: 2 to 3 servings with other dishes.

TIP: Smoked ham may be substituted for the unsmoked bacon.

ADVANCE PREPARATION: Assemble the fish and ingredients on a heatproof platter several hours before cooking. Cover with plastic wrap. Refrigerate. Steam just before serving.

Inspired by a recipe from Chalie Amatyakul, director, The Thai Cooking School, The Oriental, Bangkok.

Baked Coconut Shrimp
Koong Som

Vorachoon Yuchinda, owner of the charming Lemongrass Restaurant in Bangkok, served this to me on one of my visits to Thailand. The dish was made all the more interesting as our dining table was a mah jongg table with little drawers for the players' chips. Vorachoon's collection of handpainted batik and reproductions of royal barges graced the walls, lending a most delightful atmosphere.

½ pound medium shrimp, peeled, deveined, tails intact
¼ cup lime juice
2 tablespoons thick coconut cream
1 shallot, thinly sliced
1 or 2 small fresh red or green chiles, seeds removed, thinly
    sliced
Salt to taste

Place shrimp in an ovenproof dish. Add lime juice and toss well. Marinate for 30 minutes, stirring occasionally. Shrimp should be almost opaque and firm. Drain. Pour coconut cream over the shrimp. Stir. Bake in a 350° F oven until heated through and coconut milk and lime juice have blended. Garnish with shallot slices and chiles.

YIELD: 3 to 4 servings with other dishes.

CURRIES

Nam Prik Kaeng

The heart of Thai cooking is the curry paste. The family recipe is passed down from generation to generation, and a Thai housewife is taught to take the "correct" amount of each spice and pound them together in a mortar and pestle.

Although every Thai curry is slightly different, there are a few general styles of curry pastes, the most common of which are red, green, and Mussaman. Red curry paste, *Nam Prik Kaeng Ped,* based on dried red chiles, is fairly hot, with a strong flavor of lemon grass and galangal. Green curry paste, *Nam Prik Kaeng Kiew Warn,* based on the fiery fresh green chiles plus coriander root and other green herbs, is typically the hottest of all. Mussaman curry, *Nam Prik Kaeng Mussaman,* derives its name from the Thai pronunciation of "Muslim," and reflects the complex blends of dry spices typical of North Indian Muslim cookery.

Today many Thai women living in this country use canned curry pastes, "freshening" them with a little coriander, lime zest, and garlic. Curry pastes are also packaged dry in envelopes. But to taste really authentic Thai curries, do try making your own. Though time-consuming, they are more aromatic and show the full spectrum of flavors. Curry pastes may be stored in a tightly covered glass container in the refrigerator for several weeks or frozen for 2 months.

A coffee grinder is excellent for grinding dried spices, although the small size of the grinder may require that you grind the spices in batches. For the wet spices, use a mini-processor, small food processor, or blender. If necessary, add a little oil to the paste to aid in the blending of the spices.

A Thai curry usually has a thin sauce, which will thicken upon standing. If the curry becomes too thick, thin with coconut milk or water to the desired consistency. Most of the curries can be made ahead and refrigerated; the flavors will improve upon standing. If the curry seems too mild, garnish with fresh chile peppers.

To hasten the cooking of a curry, heat 2 tablespoons oil over low heat. Add coconut milk and curry paste. Simmer for about 5 minutes, or until curry paste has completely changed consistency and has an oily surface. Proceed with next cooking steps.

Curries are always served with lots of steaming hot rice. Some of the condiments that may be served with curries are salted peanuts, crisply fried shallots or garlic, (page 24) chopped green onions, chopped chile peppers, coriander leaves, pineapple chunks, grated coconut, and Thai Cucumber Salad (page 94).

Red Curry Paste
 Nam Prik Kaeng Ped

A hot, rich, and fragrant curry paste that originated in northern Thailand, this is one of the most versatile of the curry pastes, as it not only makes an exotic curry, but is an important ingredient in Peanut Sauce for Satay and Fish with Spicy Tamarind Sauce as well as many other dishes. Head Chef Boonchoo Pholwatana of the Dusit-Bussaracum Cooking School says soaking the red chiles allows the flavors to mellow.

14 dried red chiles, seeds removed, soaked in water
2 teaspoons galangal, chopped
1 lemon grass stalk, bottom 6 inches only, sliced
1 teaspoon shredded lime zest
10 coriander roots, chopped
4 garlic cloves, chopped
1 shallot, chopped
1 teaspoon shrimp paste *(kapee)*
10 black peppercorns
2 tablespoons oil

Pound or process all of the ingredients in a mortar, blender, or processor to a smooth even paste. (If necessary, add a little more oil when processing.)

YIELD: 3 tablespoons.

TIP: Red curry paste may be purchased in jars or cans in some Oriental grocery stores. This paste is a time saver but lacks the intricate flavorings of homemade red curry paste.
    You may substitute 16 coriander stems for coriander roots.

ADVANCE PREPARATION: The curry paste will keep tightly covered in a glass container in the refrigerator for 2 weeks or may be frozen for 2 months.

Inspired by a recipe from Head Chef Boonchoo Pholwatana, Dusit-Bussaracum Restaurant and Culinary Academy, Bangkok.

► Green Curry Paste
► Nam Prik Kaeng Kiew Warn

Green curry is usually the hottest of Thai curries, as it is prepared with tiny green Thai chiles that are fiery hot. In this recipe, I have used green Serrano chiles, making the paste a milder variation. You may adjust the amount of chiles used for the paste, and the amount of green curry paste for each dish, to suit your taste.

8 fresh green Serrano chiles, seeds removed, chopped
2 stalks lemon grass, bottom 6 inches only, chopped
2 teaspoons chopped coriander roots
1½ tablespoons chopped shallots
1 tablespoon chopped garlic
2 teaspoons chopped galangal
3 Kaffir lime leaves, chopped
2 teaspoons minced lime zest
½ teaspoon shrimp paste *(kapee)*

DRIED SPICES:

3 cardamom seeds
½ teaspoon coriander seeds
8 black peppercorns
¼ teaspoon nutmeg
¼ teaspoon mace

1 to 2 tablespoons oil (optional)

Pound or process the green chiles, lemon grass, coriander, shallots, garlic, galangal, Kaffir lime leaves, lime zest, and shrimp paste in a mortar, blender, or small processor to a smooth paste, adding 1 tablespoon oil, if necessary, to aid in mixing the paste.

Place the dried spices in a mortar or electric spice or coffee grinder, and pound or grind to a smooth powder. (If using a spice or coffee grinder, this may require several separate grindings.) If using powdered spices, add after grinding the whole spices. Add the spice powders to the paste mixture. Pound or process until smooth. Refrigerate in a glass container.

YIELD: approximately 8 tablespoons.

TIP: Green curry paste may be purchased in jars or cans in Asian markets. This paste is a time saver but lacks the intricate flavorings of homemade green curry paste.

ADVANCE PREPARATION: The curry paste will keep tightly covered in a glass container in the refrigerator for two weeks, or may be frozen for 2 months.

Inspired by a recipe from Head Chef Boonchoo Pholwatana, Dusit-Bussaracum Culinary Academy, Bangkok

 ## Mussaman Curry Paste
Nam Pril Kaeng Mussaman

A rich, flavorful curry paste that contains cinnamon and nutmeg not usually used in Thai curries, making it reminiscent of many Indian curries. It is usually used in meat and chicken dishes that contain potatoes.

10 dried red chiles, seeded, soaked in hot water 30 minutes, drained
7 shallots, chopped
7 cloves garlic, chopped
1 teaspoon galangal, chopped
2 stalks lemon grass, bottom 6 inches only, chopped
8 tablespoons chopped coriander roots or stems
1 teaspoon shredded lime zest
4 cardamom pods, outside shells removed
½-inch piece of cinnamon
5 bay leaves
10 cloves
½ teaspoon shrimp paste (*kapee*)

GROUND SPICES:

½ teaspoon ground nutmeg
½ teaspoon freshly ground black pepper

Over moderate heat in a dry wok or small frying pan, toast the chiles, shallots, garlic, galangal, shrimp paste, lemon grass, coriander, lime zest, cardamom, cinnamon, bay leaves, and cloves for approximately 3 to 5 minutes. Be very careful not to burn the ingredients.

In a mortar, blender, or processor, combine the toasted ingredients with the nutmeg and black pepper, and pound or process to a juicy, pungent paste.

YIELD: 6 tablespoons.

TIP: Mussaman curry paste can be purchased in jars or cans in some Asian grocery stores. It will lack the special aromas and flavorings of homemade paste but is a time saver.

ADVANCE PREPARATION: Prepare completely ahead. Store in a tightly covered glass jar in the refrigerator for 2 weeks, or freeze for 2 months.

Inspired by a recipe from Head Chef Boonchoo Pholwatana of the Dusit-Bussaracum Restaurant and Culinary Academy, Bangkok.

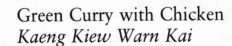

► Green Curry with Chicken
► *Kaeng Kiew Warn Kai*

A popular Thai curry combining the heat of chiles, smoothness of coconut milk, and tang of lime. Head Chef Pajongchit prepares this dish, using small Thai pea eggplants, but you may substitute green peas. Adjust the amount of curry paste to your desired degree of hotness.

> 1¼ cups thick coconut milk
> 2 to 4 tablespoons Green Curry Paste (page 70)
> 2 whole chicken breasts, boned, skinned, cut into 1-inch pieces
> 1½ cups thin coconut milk
> 2 to 3 small Thai pea eggplants, quartered
> 4 to 6 fresh green chiles, seeds removed, chopped
> 2 tablespoons fish sauce *(nam pla)*
> 1 teaspoon light brown sugar
> 4 Kaffir lime leaves, shredded
> ½ cup sweet basil leaves

GARNISH:

> 1 or 2 fresh red chiles, seeded, finely shredded into 1-inch
>   lengths

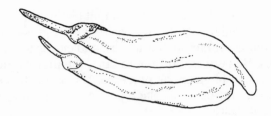

In a 10- or 12-inch frying pan, bring 1 cup thick coconut milk to a boil on moderate heat. Continue boiling, stirring, until the coconut milk thickens and has an oily surface. Add the curry paste. Continue cooking and stirring until the appearance has changed considerably and the oil has separated from the curry, about 3 to 5 minutes. Be careful not to burn the curry. Add the chicken and stir-fry until the chicken is whitish in color. Add the thin coconut milk gradually, stirring. Return to a gentle boil. Reduce the heat, add the Thai eggplant, chiles, fish sauce, sugar, Kaffir lime leaves, and half of the basil leaves, and simmer 5 to 10 minutes until chicken and eggplant are tender. Add ¼ cup thick coconut milk and heat, but do not boil. Garnish with remaining sweet basil leaves and red chiles. Serve with rice and a Thai salad.

YIELD: 3 to 4 servings.

ADVANCE PREPARATION: Prepare ahead completely, but do not add final ¼ cup of thick coconut milk. Refrigerate or freeze. Reheat at moderate heat in microwave or on top of stove, adding more thin coconut milk if necessary. Be careful not to allow the curry to come to a boil. Add final ¼ cup of thick coconut milk just before serving. This curry tastes better when prepared ahead and the flavors have a chance to mellow.

VARIATION: Substitute ¼ cup green peas for Thai eggplant. If using frozen green peas, add at end of cooking and cook until done.

Inspired by a recipe from Head Chef Pajongchit Pitaksakorn, The Spice Market Restaurant, The Regent of Bangkok.

Red Chicken Curry

Kaeng Pet Kai

Chef "Jack" Witthaya Ramwatthanakul, of Siam Square Restaurant, Evanston, Illinois, taught me this aromatic red Thai curry. His use of pumpkin or acorn squash gives it an interesting flavor and texture.

2 cups plus 3 tablespoons thick coconut milk
2 to 3 tablespoons Red Curry Paste (page 69)
2 to 3 tablespoons Madras curry powder
2 whole chicken breasts, boned, skinned, cut into small chunks
2 tablespoons fish sauce *(nam pla)*
2 cups thin coconut milk
2 cups pumpkin or acorn squash, peeled, diced
2 tablespoons light brown sugar
2 tablespoons chopped fresh basil or 1 teaspoon dried sweet basil
2 fresh green chiles, seeded, shredded into 1-inch lengths
1 tablespoon chopped coriander leaves

In a 10- or 12-inch frying pan, simmer 2 cups thick coconut milk over moderate heat, stirring until it thickens and oil appears around the edge. At this point increase the heat. Add the curry paste and cook for approximately 5 minutes, or until the appearance changes considerably and the oil has separated from the paste. Add the curry powder and cook, stirring, until thoroughly dissolved. Add the chicken and stir-fry until done. Reduce the heat. Add the fish sauce and stir-fry for 2 minutes.

With a slotted spoon, remove the chicken and set aside. Add the thin coconut milk, sliced pumpkin, and sugar. Bring to a boil. Reduce the heat to simmer. Cook for 10 to 15 minutes until the pumpkin is soft. Add the cooked chicken, basil, and chiles, and simmer for 5 minutes. Adjust seasonings, adding more fish sauce if desired. Place in a serving bowl. Heat 3 tablespoons thick coconut milk and place in the center of the bowl of curry. Sprinkle with coriander leaves. Serve with rice and a Thai salad.

YIELD: 6 servings.

TIP: Beef may be substituted for chicken.

ADVANCE PREPARATION: Prepare 1 day ahead. Refrigerate. Reheat when serving.

Mussaman Chicken Curry
Kaeng Mussaman Kai

This dish has a smooth, rich, mildly hot and spicy flavor and demon-strates the Indian influence on Thai cuisine. It should be served with substantial amounts of rice. Chef Boonchoo Pholwatana says it is very important to add the thick coconut milk in small amounts to allow the curry to thicken properly and to allow the flavors to develop gradually.

4 to 6 tablespoons oil
2 to 3 pounds frying chicken, boned, skinned, cut into bite-size
    pieces
2 medium potatoes, peeled, cut into bite-size pieces
10 small white onions, halved
¼ cup whole roasted, unsalted peanuts
3 cups thin coconut milk
2 cups thick coconut milk
3 tablespoons Mussaman Curry Paste (page 71)
3 tablespoons fish sauce (*nam pla*)
⅓ cup palm or light brown sugar
¼ cup tamarind water

GARNISH:

1 or 2 fresh red chiles, seeded, shredded
2 tablespoons chopped roasted, unsalted peanuts
6 fresh basil leaves

Heat oil, fry the chicken pieces, potatoes, onions and peanuts sepa-rately until very lightly browned and place in a saucepan with the thin coconut milk. Bring to a boil. Reduce the heat and cook for 10 to 20 minutes, or until the chicken, potatoes, and onions are tender.

Put ½ cup thick coconut milk in a small frying pan. Add the curry paste, and cook over moderate heat, stirring, until the sauce becomes pale and tan. Be careful not to allow mixture to burn. Add the remaining thick coconut milk, ¼ cup at a time, and cook until the sauce becomes slightly thick after each addition. Add to the cooked chicken mixture and bring it to a boil. Remove from heat. Stir in the fish sauce, sugar, and tamarind water. Continue stirring until sugar is dissolved. Garnish with red chiles, peanuts, and basil leaves. Serve with rice and a Thai salad.

YIELD: 4 to 6 servings.

TIP: Chicken breasts may be substituted for the whole chicken if desired.

ADVANCE PREPARATION: The flavors of the curry improve if made a day ahead and refrigerated. It may also be frozen if desired, but some of the aromatics will be lost. Reheat in the microwave on medium power or on top of the stove, being careful not to allow the curry to boil.

Inspired by a recipe from Head Chef Boonchoo Pholwatana, Dusit-Bussaracum Culinary Academy and Restaurant, Bangkok.

 ## Mussaman Beef Curry
Kaeng Mussaman Nua

This northern Thai curry is mildly hot, with a sweet and spicy flavor, and is a favorite of Westerners. Head Chef Pajongchit often uses potato in her preparation. It is served as part of a traditional Kantoke dinner in the area of Chiang Mai.

> 4 tablespoons oil
> 1 pound sirloin or top round, trimmed, cut into ½-inch cubes
> 1 large potato, peeled, cut into bite-size pieces
> 2 cups thin coconut milk
> 2 cups thick coconut milk
> 3 tablespoons Mussaman Curry Paste (page 71)
> 12 cardamom seeds
> 3 tablespoons fish sauce (*nam pla*)
> ½ cup light brown sugar
> 2 tablespoons tamarind water

GARNISH:

> 1 or 2 fresh red chiles, seeded, shredded
> 4 tablespoons chopped roasted, unsalted peanuts

Heat oil in a pan. Fry beef and potato separately over medium-high heat until very lightly browned. Place cooked meat, potato, thin coconut milk, and 1 cup thick coconut milk in a saucepan. Bring to a boil. Reduce heat and simmer 20 to 30 minutes, or until meat is tender.

Heat a wok or frying pan. Add ½ cup of thick coconut milk and the curry paste. Stir the mixture over moderate heat for 3 to 5 minutes, until the oil has separated from the coconut milk and the appearance has changed considerably. Be careful not to burn. Add cardamom seeds. Add the remaining thick coconut milk ¼ cup at a time, stirring over high heat until the sauce becomes slightly thick after each addition. Add the thick coconut milk mixture to the cooked beef and potato mixture. Bring to a boil. Add the fish sauce, sugar, and tamarind water. (The gravy should remain thick, but still liquid.) Garnish with red chiles and peanuts. Serve with rice and a Thai salad.

YIELD: 4 to 6 servings.

TIP: It is important to add the thick coconut milk in small amounts to allow the flavors to develop gradually.

ADVANCE PREPARATION: When prepared in advance, flavors will improve. Store covered in refrigerator or freezer. To serve, heat on moderate heat in the microwave on medium power, or on top of the stove without letting the curry boil. If necessary, add more coconut milk to desired thickness.

Inspired by a recipe from Head Chef Pajongchit Pitaksakorn, The Spice Market Restaurant, The Regent of Bangkok.

Thick Curry with Beef
Panaeng Nua

A moderately hot, slightly sweet, rich curry that originated in Penang, Malaysia. According to Chalie Amatyakul, this curry first appeared in Thailand around 1930. He says that fresh basil must be used as it will add to both the flavor and color of this thick and creamy curry. If you prefer a milder curry, reduce the chiles.

    2 cups thin coconut milk
    1 pound sirloin or top round steak, sliced into thin 1½- by ½-inch
        strips
    Pinch of salt
    1 cup plus 3 tablespoons thick coconut milk
    3 tablespoons Red Curry Paste (page 69)
    2 to 3 tablespoons fish sauce (*nam pla*)
    2 tablespoons light brown sugar
    1 cup roasted, unsalted crushed peanuts
    5 Kaffir lime leaves, shredded
    1 cup sweet basil leaves
    2 or 3 fresh red chiles, seeded, shredded

Bring 2 cups thin coconut milk to a boil. Add beef and salt. Reduce heat and simmer until beef is tender. In a wok or saucepan, heat 1 cup thick coconut milk over moderate heat. Continue cooking until it thickens and oil appears around the edges. Add the curry paste and fry for 3 to 5 minutes, or until the oil has separated from the coconut milk. You will notice a distinct change in appearance. Be careful not to allow the mixture to burn. Add the fish sauce and sugar, and stir until the sugar has dissolved. Add the cooked beef and coconut milk. Stir. Add three quarters of the peanuts, lime leaves, basil leaves, and chiles. Stir. Pour into a serving dish. Heat the remaining 3 table-spoons thick coconut milk and place in the center of the curry. Garnish with remaining basil, lime leaves, chiles, and peanuts. Serve with rice and a Thai salad.

YIELD: 4 servings.

TIP: If Kaffir lime leaf is unavailable, use 2 tablespoons finely shred-ded lime zest.

ADVANCE PREPARATION: Prepare in advance, and refrigerate or freeze. Reheat, but do not boil. When serving, heat 3 tablespoons thick coconut milk and place in center of curry. Garnish as above.

Inspired by a recipe from Chalie Amatyakul, director, The Thai Cooking School, The Oriental, Bangkok.

► ► **Green Curry with Shrimp**
Kaeng Kiew Warn Koong ◄ ◄

A favorite of the Thais, this curry is usually very spicy. You may adjust the amount of curry paste to your taste. Chalie Amatyakul says you may prepare this curry ahead, up to the addition of the shrimp. He serves this with a Thai salad such as his Herbed Fruit Salad (page 85).

½ cup fresh basil leaves
½ cup plus 3 tablespoons thick coconut milk
2 to 3 tablespoons Green Curry Paste (page 70)
1½ cups thin coconut milk
6 Kaffir lime leaves, shredded
2 tablespoons fish sauce (*nam pla*)
2 teaspoons light brown sugar
White pepper to taste
8 ounces shrimp, washed, shelled, deveined

GARNISH:

1 or 2 fresh red or green chiles, seeded, finely shredded
(optional)

Shred half of the basil leaves. Add ½ cup thick coconut milk to a 10- or 12- inch frying pan. Bring to a boil. Stir until the oil rises to the surface. Add the curry paste. Continue to stir until the oil has separated from the coconut milk and the appearance has changed considerably, about 3 to 5 minutes. Be careful not to allow the mixture to burn. Gradually add the thin coconut milk, stirring. Bring to a boil. Add one-half of the shredded basil, Kaffir lime leaves, fish sauce, sugar, and pepper. Add the shrimp. Stir. Cover and cook over moderate heat until the shrimp is pink and cooked. Add more fish sauce and sugar if desired. Heat remaining 3 tablespoons thick coconut milk and place in the center of the curry. Transfer to a serving dish. Garnish with remaining basil leaves and chile shreds. Serve with rice and a Thai salad.

YIELD: 3 to 4 servings.

TIPS: Roast duck may be used in place of shrimp. Grapes, plums, jackfruit, or any sweet fruit may be added to this dish.

ADVANCE PREPARATION: The curry may be prepared ahead, up to the addition of the shrimp. Add shrimp and finish the cooking at serving time.

Inspired by a recipe from Chalie Amatyakul, director, The Thai Cooking School, The Oriental, Bangkok.

SALADS AND VEGETABLES

 ### Green Mango Salad
Yum Ma Muang

The unusual combination of green mangoes, pork, and chiles produces a salad full of surprises. Frozen green mangoes can be found in Asian grocery stores. You may substitute tart green apples such as Granny Smith. It may be prepared completely in advance.

> 2 large green mangoes or 3 large green cooking apples, peeled
>   and finely sliced
> 1 teaspoon salt mixed with 1 cup water
> 1½ tablespoons oil
> 3 cloves garlic, minced
> 4 green onions, thinly sliced
> 4 ounces pork, shredded

SAUCE MIXTURE: Combine and set aside

> 2 teaspoons dried shrimp powder
> 1½ tablespoons fish sauce (*nam pla*)
> 1½ tablespoons light brown sugar
> 2 tablespoons roasted, unsalted crushed peanuts
> Freshly ground pepper to taste
> Finely chopped red chiles or dried red chili flakes

Place sliced mangoes in a large bowl and pour salt water over them. Soak for 30 minutes to remove sourness. Rinse in cold water and pat dry.

Heat oil and stir-fry garlic and green onions until lightly browned. Remove and set aside. Add pork and stir-fry until cooked throughout. Add the sauce mixture and stir to mix. Remove from heat.

Combine the mangoes with the pork mixture, cooked garlic, and green onions. Add pepper to taste. Sprinkle chopped red chiles over the top. Serve chilled.

YIELD: 4 servings.

TIP: Pineapple may be substituted for the mangoes or apples.

  ## Green Apples with Spicy Sauce
  ## *Yum Apples Kiew*

In Thailand, this dish is made with green mangoes, which are crisp and sour and are wonderful with this sweet, spicy sauce. I have substituted Granny Smith apples for this unusual appetizer.

4 crisp, green Granny Smith apples, cored and sliced
1 teaspoon lemon juice
⅓ cup light brown sugar
¼ cup fish sauce (*nam pla*)
¼ to ½ teaspoon dried chili flakes
1 tablespoon minced red onion

Place apples in ice-cold water to cover. Add lemon juice and stir. Soak for 15 minutes. In a small pan, combine sugar and fish sauce. Cook over low heat until sugar has dissolved. Remove and set aside to cool for 10 minutes. Add chili flakes and onion. Stir. Drain the apples and arrange on a plate. Place the sauce in the center of the plate. Dip the apple slices into the sauce.

YIELD: 6 to 8 servings.

ADVANCE PREPARATION: Prepare the sauce one day ahead. Refrigerate.

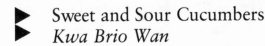

Sweet and Sour Cucumbers
Kwa Brio Wan

A cool, refreshing hot and sour salad, which accompanies many Thai meals.

> 2 cucumbers, peeled, cut in half, seeds removed
> 1 teaspoon salt
> ¼ cup minced red onion
> 2 tablespoons rice vinegar
> 2 teaspoons sugar
> 2 teaspoons minced fresh coriander
> 2 tablespoons finely chopped peanuts
> 2 fresh red chiles, seeded, shredded (optional)

Slice the cucumber into thin rounds. Place in a strainer and sprinkle with salt. Toss to coat the cucumbers well. Let stand for 15 minutes to 1 hour. Press out excess moisture. Place cucumbers in a serving bowl and toss with onion, rice vinegar, sugar, and coriander. Garnish with chopped peanuts and chiles.

YIELD: 4 to 6 servings.

TIP: Chili flakes may be substituted for fresh red chile peppers.

ADVANCE PREPARATION: The cucumbers may be prepared 1 day ahead and refrigerated. For optimum results serve within 2 to 3 hours.

Spicy Beef Salad
Yum Nua

In this tantalizing yum, *beef is vividly combined with chiles, garlic, coriander, lime, and mint. This is quite often served as a snack food in the late afternoon with Singha beer or Mekong whiskey. It is wonderful with Thai curries.*

> ¼ cup minced fresh coriander root
> 2 tablespoons minced garlic
> ¼ teaspoon ground black pepper
> ½ teaspoon salt
> 1 pound beef tenderloin or flank steak, trimmed of excess fat

3 to 5 fresh red chiles, seeded, minced
2 tablespoons fish sauce (*nam pla*)
6 tablespoons fresh lime juice
2 teaspoons sugar

GARNISH:

1 head lettuce, cored, separated into leaves
2 tomatoes, thinly sliced
½ cucumber, peeled, thinly sliced on the diagonal
1 small red onion, thinly sliced
1 stalk lemon grass, bottom 6 inches only, minced
½ cup torn mint leaves
½ cup coriander leaves
2 tablespoons dried red chili flakes, crushed
1 lime, cut into thin wedges

Pound or process the coriander root, 1 tablespoon garlic, the pepper, and salt to a coarse paste. (If using a blender, add a little oil to aid in blending.) Remove and cover beef thoroughly with paste. Let marinate for several hours or overnight in the refrigerator. Grill or broil the beef until rare. Let cool. Refrigerate for 2 hours to allow easier slicing. Slice across the grain in thin strips, 2 by ½ by ¼ inches. Set aside.

Prepare the dressing. Pound the remaining garlic and chiles in a mortar, or process in a processor or blender. Add the fish sauce, lime juice, and sugar. Continue processing until well mixed. Pour over the beef and toss to coat.

Arrange the lettuce leaves to cover a serving dish. Arrange the tomatoes around the outside edge, overlapping the slices. Place the cucumber slices inside the tomatoes. Remove the beef from the dressing and mound it in the center of the dish. Pour any remaining dressing over the meat. Sprinkle red onion, lemon grass, mint, coriander, and chili flakes over the salad. Garnish with lime wedges. Serve chilled.

YIELD: 4 to 6 servings.

ADVANCE PREPARATION: All ingredients may be prepared ahead and wrapped separately in plastic wrap and refrigerated. Arrange the salad 1 to 2 hours before serving time, cover with plastic wrap, and refrigerate.

Inspired by a recipe from Head Chef Pajongchit Pitaksakorn, The Spice Market Restaurant, The Regent of Bangkok.

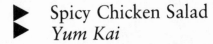

Spicy Chicken Salad
Yum Kai

A tantalizing salad combining chicken, mint, coriander, and citrus flavors with the bite of chile. Serve it with cocktails before dinner or during the meal.

4 garlic cloves, chopped
¼ cup chopped fresh coriander
2 teaspoons whole black peppercorns
¼ cup soy sauce
⅓ cup fish sauce (*nam pla*)
2 whole chicken breasts
6 tablespoons lime juice
2 tablespoons sugar
1 to 2 teaspoons ground red chili powder
2 stalks lemon grass, bottom 6 inches only, finely minced
¼ red onion, thinly sliced
1 head lettuce, washed and separated into leaves
1 lime, thinly sliced
10 to 20 fresh mint leaves (optional)
1 fresh red chile, seeded, finely shredded

Pound or process, in a blender or food processor, the garlic, 2 tablespoons of coriander and peppercorns, and blend to a paste. Add soy sauce and 2 tablespoons fish sauce. Blend to mix. Pour into a shallow pan. Add chicken and let marinate for 45 minutes. Remove chicken from the marinade and let drain. Grill or broil chicken, basting with the marinade until done, being careful not to overcook. Let cool. Tear the cooled cooked chicken into shreds. Place in a mixing bowl. Add remaining fish sauce, lime juice, sugar, and chili powder. Mix. Add remaining chopped coriander, lemon grass, and red onion. Toss lightly. Refrigerate.

Alternate batches of lettuce leaves and lime slices around the edge of a chilled platter. Place the chicken salad in the center. Garnish with mint leaves and chile shreds.

YIELD: 4 servings.

TIP: For a spicier salad, shrimp chili paste may be added.

Inspired by a recipe from Head Chef Pajongchit Pitaksakorn, The Spice Market Restaurant, The Regent of Bangkok.

Herbed Fruit Salad

Yum Polamai

Chalie Amatyakul serves this unusual salad in a crispy noodle basket or in an orange or grapefruit half. Local fruits such as mangosteen, roseapple, and pomelo are used. You may improvise with any exotic fruits in season. It is quite often served as an afternoon snack or as a vivid contrast during a meal.

½ cup fresh lime juice
1 small green apple, peeled, cored, diced
2 tablespoons oil
2 cloves garlic, thinly sliced
1 shallot, thinly sliced
1 to 2 teaspoons sugar (or to taste)
1 teaspoon kosher salt
½ cup red and green grapes, halved, seeded
1 small tangerine, peeled, sectioned
½ cup peeled grapefruit or pomelo sections
½ cup sliced strawberries
½ cup sliced water chestnuts
4 ounces cooked shrimp
4 ounces cooked chicken, cut into bite-size pieces (optional)
Bird's Nest Potato Basket (page 160, optional)

GARNISH:

2 tablespoons chopped, toasted, unsalted peanuts
1 or 2 fresh red chiles, seeds removed, shredded
Orange or grapefruit halves hollowed out for serving containers
(optional)

Pour a little of the lime juice on the diced apple to prevent discoloration. In 2 tablespoons oil, fry garlic and shallot over low heat, stirring until brown and crisp but not burned. Remove. Drain on paper towels.

Combine sugar, salt, and remaining lime juice in pan. Cook until sugar has dissolved. Set aside and let cool. Combine fruits, water chestnuts, cooked shrimp, and chicken, and half the garlic and shallot mixture. Add the lime dressing, and toss lightly to coat. Taste to adjust seasoning if necessary.

Garnish with remaining garlic, shallots, peanuts, and chiles. If desired, serve in a Bird's Nest Noodle Basket, or fill orange or grapefruit halves with the mixture. Serve chilled or at room temperature.

YIELD: 4 to 6 servings with other dishes.

ADVANCE PREPARATION: Prepare completely in advance and assemble ½ hour before serving.

Inspired by a recipe from Chalie Amatyakul, director, The Thai Cooking School, The Oriental, Bangkok.

 ## Spiced Seafood Salad
Yum Pla Talay

A refreshing, tangy salad for lovers of chiles! This salad is quite often served as a pre-meal starter with cocktails.

3 tablespoons lime juice
2 tablespoons fish sauce (*nam pla*)
2 to 4 fresh red chiles, crushed
2 teaspoons minced garlic
1 stalk lemon grass, bottom 6 inches only, finely sliced (optional)
2 tablespoons finely sliced shallots
1 tablespoon finely sliced galangal
½ cup peeled boiled shrimp, cut into ½-inch pieces
½ cup boiled scallops, cut into ½-inch cubes
½ cup boiled and diced firm fish
½ cup boiled and sliced baby squid
½ cup shelled boiled clams

GARNISH:

Lettuce leaves
Coriander sprigs
2-3 fresh red chiles, shredded

Combine lime juice and fish sauce. Add chiles, garlic, lemon grass, shallots, and galangal. Mix well. Add cooked shrimp, scallops, fish, squid, and clams. Toss to mix seasonings. Serve on a bed of lettuce. Garnish with coriander and chiles.

YIELD: 4 to 6 servings with other dishes.

ADVANCE PREPARATION: Cook seafood ahead and refrigerate. Prepare sauce ahead. Combine and garnish at serving time.

VARIATION: Any mixture totaling 2½ cups cooked seafood may be used.

Inspired by a recipe from Chalie Amatyakul, director, The Thai Cooking School, The Oriental, Bangkok.

 Stuffed Green Peppers
Kai Kred Kaew

A delicious, attractive appetizer, which can also be a light luncheon dish when served with rice. This is a delicate dish with subtle flavors.

> 2 to 4 dried red chiles, soaked in water to soften, seeds removed, chopped
> 2 shallots, chopped
> ½ teaspoon chopped galangal (optional)
> 2 cloves garlic, chopped
> 1 stalk lemon grass, bottom 6 inches only, sliced
> ¼ teaspoon shrimp paste *(kapee)*, (optional)
> 2 tablespoons fish sauce *(nam pla)*
> ½ cup thin coconut milk
> 1 ounce fine bean threads, soaked in water 20 minutes to soften, drained
> ½ pound shredded chicken breasts
> 4 small green peppers, cut in half lengthwise, seeds removed
> ½ cup thick coconut milk
> 24 fresh coriander leaves
> 1 fresh red chile, seeded, finely shredded

Combine the chiles, shallots, galangal, garlic, lemon grass, and shrimp paste. Pound or process the mixture to a paste in a mortar, blender, or processor.

Combine the paste mixture, fish sauce, and thin coconut milk in a bowl. Cut the soaked bean threads into 1-inch pieces. Add the bean threads and chicken to the bowl. Mix thoroughly. Fill the green pepper halves with the mixture. Spoon the thick coconut milk on top. Place the stuffed green peppers on a steaming rack. Steam over boiling water for 5 minutes. Garnish with coriander leaves and red chile shreds.

YIELD: 8 servings.

TIP: The green peppers may be cooked in the microwave on medium heat.

ADVANCE PREPARATION: Stuff the peppers several hours ahead. Refrigerate, covered with plastic wrap. Steam at serving time.

Inspired by a recipe from Head Chef Boonchoo Pholwatana, Dusit-Bussaracum Culinary Academy and Restaurant, Bangkok.

RICE AND NOODLES

 Classic Thai Fried Rice
Kao Pad

A delightfully spiced rice!

To make successful fried rice, you must start with cold, cooked, flaked rice. You may improvise by adding other vegetables and seafood or poultry and make this a one-dish meal. If Fried Rice is served during a Thai meal, plain rice should also be offered.

3 tablespoons oil
2 cloves garlic, minced
1 to 2 tablespoons Red Curry Paste (page 69)
1 to 2 fresh red chiles, seeded, minced
5 ounces pork, shredded
3½ cups cooked, cold rice (approximately 1 cup uncooked)
3 eggs, lightly beaten
2 tablespoons chopped dried shrimp (optional)
½ cup thawed frozen peas
3 tablespoons fish sauce (*nam pla*)
1 tablespoon chopped coriander leaves

GARNISH:

1 green onion, chopped
2 tablespoons chopped coriander leaves (optional)
2 to 3 fresh red chiles, seeded, thinly shredded

Heat wok or skillet. Add 2 tablespoons oil. Heat. Add garlic and stir until fragrant. Add curry paste and chiles, and stir over moderate heat for approximately 2 to 3 minutes, being careful not to burn. Add the pork. Stir-fry 2 to 3 minutes or until the pork is cooked throughout. Add the rice. Stir until the rice is colored with the paste and thoroughly heated. Make a well in the center of the rice. Add 1 tablespoon oil. Add the eggs and dried shrimp. Let set slightly. Start incorporating the egg mixture with the rice, stirring in a circular fashion with chopsticks. Add the peas, fish sauce, and chopped coriander. Stir to mix, and cook until peas are tender and heated throughout. Transfer to a serving dish. Garnish with green onion, coriander, and red chiles.

YIELD: 3 to 4 servings.

TIP: Red chili flakes may be substituted for the curry paste.

ADVANCE PREPARATION: Prepare ahead. Reheat in a 350° F oven at serving time.

 ## Pineapple Fried Rice
Kao Pad Saparod

Delightful to the eye as well as the palate, this dish is especially attractive when the pineapple is used as the serving container.

4 tablespoons oil
2 tablespoons dried shrimp (optional)
2 tablespoons chopped onion
6 ounces shrimp, cooked
4 Chinese dried black mushrooms, soaked in hot water until
    spongy, about 20 minutes, stems removed, shredded
2 to 3 tablespoons fish sauce *(nam pla)*
3 cups cold, cooked long-grain rice (1 cup uncooked)
2 eggs, lightly beaten
¾ cup bite-size pieces fresh pineapple
1 to 2 fresh red chile peppers, finely shredded into 1½-inch
    pieces
Coriander leaves (optional)

Heat wok. Add 2 tablespoons oil. Heat. Add the dried shrimp. Stir until lightly browned. Remove and set aside. Add the onion and stir-fry until translucent. Add the shrimp and Chinese black mushrooms. Stir. Add the fish sauce. Stir. Remove and set aside. Add 1 tablespoon oil. Heat. Add the rice, stirring rapidly, and cook until thoroughly heated without browning. Make a well in the center of the rice. Add 1 tablespoon oil. Add the eggs and let them set slightly. When they have a soft-scrambled consistency, start incorporating the rice, stirring in a circular fashion with chopsticks. When rice and eggs are blended, add the cooked onion, shrimp, mushrooms, and fish sauce combination. Add the pineapple. Stir until thoroughly combined and heated throughout. Place on a serving platter. Garnish with red chiles and cooked dried shrimp. Sprinkle coriander leaves over the fried rice.

YIELD: 3 to 4 servings.

VARIATION: Place cooked fried rice in a large pineapple which has been hollowed out. Bake in a preheated 375° F oven until heated throughout. Garnish with red pepper, dried shrimp, and coriander.

 Thai Fried Noodles
Pad Thai

A traditional Thai favorite, this shrimp and rice-noodle dish is usually served for luncheon, midday snack, or as a late supper. It is a meal-in-one and needs no accompaniment.

> ½ pound fresh rice noodles, cut into ½-inch slices, or flat dried
>   rice noodles
> 1 cup fresh bean sprouts
> ⅓ cup oil
> 1 tablespoon minced garlic
> 4 tablespoons minced shallots
> 2 teaspoons shrimp paste *(kapee)*
> 1 tablespoon chopped dried shrimp (optional)
> 10 medium shrimp, shelled, deveined
> 3 tablespoons fish sauce *(nam pla)*
> 1 tablespoon rice vinegar
> 2 tablespoons light brown sugar
> 2 tablespoons tomato ketchup
> ½ to 1 teaspoon chili powder (optional)
> 2 eggs, lightly beaten

GARNISHES:

> ⅓ cup coarsely ground unsalted peanuts
> ½ teaspoon dried red chili flakes (optional)
> 2 green onions, finely sliced
> 2 tablespoons chopped coriander leaves
> 2 limes, cut into wedges
> 1 small cucumber, sliced

If using dried rice noodles, soak in hot water for 20 minutes before cooking. Drain. In 4 quarts boiling water, cook fresh rice noodles 2 to 3 minutes or until just tender to the bite, *al dente*. Drain. Rinse. Drain for 30 minutes or until dry. In boiling water, blanch the bean sprouts for 30 seconds. Refresh under cold water. Drain.

Heat oil. Fry garlic and shallots until golden. Add the shrimp paste and dried shrimp. Stir. Add the shrimp and stir-fry until done. Add the fish sauce, vinegar, sugar, ketchup, and chili powder. Stir until sugar dissolves. Add the beaten eggs and let them set slightly. Then stir to scramble. Add the noodles and toss for about 2 minutes. Place the Pad Thai on a platter. Sprinkle the noodles with peanuts, chili flakes, green onions, and coriander. Arrange lime wedges around the edge of the platter. Serve with a side dish of fresh bean sprouts and cucumbers.

YIELD: 3 to 4 servings.

TIP: Shredded pork may be substituted for the shrimp, or you may use a combination of both ingredients.

ADVANCE PREPARATION: Prepare sauce and cook shrimp. Combine with noodles at serving time.

Inspired by a recipe from Head Chef Boonchoo Pholwatana, Dusit-Bussaracum Culinary Academy and Restaurant, Bangkok.

 ## Fried Rice Noodles with Pork, Chicken, and Shrimp
Mee Krob

Mee Krob is sometimes referred to as the Thai national dish. Fried rice noodles are served with a lightly sweetened, carmelized sauce, providing a marvelous counterpoint of textures and flavors. Quite often Mee Krob is served at the beginning of a meal as an appetizer.

Chalie Amatyakul said the texture in Mee Krob is crucial and the noodles should be crisp, loose, and crumbly, not crunchy. To achieve this, he moistened the dried rice noodles with water to seal their pores. He then toweled and air-dried them. Next, he dipped them in beaten egg, then towel and air-dried them again. The resulting tender crisp noodles keep their consistency after they are combined with the cooked sauce.

He says that while the noodles do not puff up as dramatically as the rice noodles straight from the package, they stay crunchy after saucing. The preparation of the noodles is time consuming, but well worth the effort. This is what makes this Mee Krob better than that served in most Thai restaurants in the United States.

> 8 ounces *sen mee* (Thai thin dried rice-stick noodles) or Chinese
>   thin rice-stick noodles
> 8 eggs
> 3 cups plus 3 tablespoons oil
> 6 ounces firm bean curd (tofu), cut into ½-inch cubes
> ¼ pound pork loin, minced
> ¼ pound skinless, boneless chicken breast, minced
> ¼ pound medium shrimp, shelled, deveined, cut into ½-inch
>   pieces
> ½ cup Fried Shallot Flakes (page 23)
> ½ cup Fried Garlic Flakes (page 23)
> ½ cup drained, preserved yellow bean sauce (*tao jaiw*), (optional)
> ¼ cup fish sauce (*nam pla*)
> 2 tablespoons rice vinegar
> 2 tablespoons tamarind water (page 25)
> 1 tablespoon fresh lime juice
> ¼ cup granulated sugar
> 1 tablespoon firmly packed light brown sugar
> ¼ teaspoon red pepper powder or to taste
> 1 tablespoon finely grated lime zest

GARNISH:

> 2 limes, cut into slices
> 2 fresh red chiles, seeded, thinly shredded
> Fresh coriander sprigs and leaves
> 1½ cups fresh bean sprouts, blanched in boiling water for 30
>   seconds, refreshed in cold water, drained

Tear the noodles apart in a large paper bag to prevent the noodles from scattering over your counter. Place them in a large mixing bowl. Cover with cold water and let soak to soften and seal in moisture, about 10 minutes. Remove. Drain, tossing occasionally to separate. Pat dry to remove any excess moisture. In another large bowl, beat 3 of the eggs until blended. Add the drained noodles to the eggs and stir gently to coat. Drain the noodles in a colander and spread them between paper toweling to remove any excess egg. Transfer the noodles to toweling or waxed paper and let them stand at room temperature for 20 minutes to set the egg coating.

Heat 3 cups oil in a wok to 375° F. Add the bean curd and fry in batches, stirring, until golden brown, about 1 to 2 minutes. Remove with a skimmer and drain on paper towels. Reheat the oil to 375° F. Add the egg-coated noodles in small batches and fry, stirring, until crisp and golden, about 45 seconds to 1 minute per handful. Remove with a skimmer. Drain on paper towels. Continue frying until all noodles are cooked. (In order for the noodles to cook properly the oil temperature must be maintained at 375° F while frying or the noodles will not become crisp. You may have to wait for the oil to heat up between batches.)

Discard the oil and wipe the wok clean. Heat the remaining 3 tablespoons oil. Add the pork, chicken, and shrimp. Stir until the pork is no longer pink. Add the fried shallot and garlic flakes, fried bean curd, and yellow soy bean sauce. Stir-fry for 10 seconds to mix. Add the remaining 5 eggs, one at a time, stir-frying between each addition, adding more oil to the pan if necessary. Stir in the fish sauce, vinegar, tamarind water, lime juice, the sugars, and red pepper powder. Stir-fry until all ingredients are blended and all liquid has evaporated, about 3 minutes. Add the lime zest and stir-fry until blended. Reduce the heat to moderate. Add the fried noodles and cook the mixture, stirring gently, until it is well blended and heated throughout. Transfer the Mee Krob to a large, round platter. Garnish with lime slices, chile slices, and the coriander. Surround the Mee Krob with bean sprouts. Serve immediately.

YIELD: 8 to 10 servings, with other dishes.

TIP: You can omit the soaking and egg procedures for the rice noodles if desired. Although they will not hold up as well as Chalie's method, they will probably taste like the Mee Krob you have had in a Thai restaurant in America. Deep-fry the rice noodles in batches in hot oil until puffed. Cook the remainder of the recipe as directed.

ADVANCE PREPARATION: Rice noodles may be fried several hours ahead and kept in an airtight container. Sauce may be prepared 1 to 2 hours ahead. At serving time, reheat the sauce. Add the cooked noodles and toss with the sauce mixture until thoroughly combined and heated throughout.

Inspired by a recipe from Chalie Amatyakul, director, The Thai Cooking School, The Oriental, Bangkok.

SAUCES AND ACCOMPANIMENTS

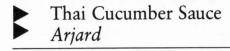 Thai Cucumber Sauce
Arjard

Sweet and sour, Thai Cucumber Sauce is usually served with satays, fish cakes, or any deep-fried appetizer.

> 1 cucumber, seeds removed, thinly sliced
> 5 tablespoons sugar
> 1 cup boiling water
> ½ cup distilled white vinegar
> 1 teaspoon salt
> ⅛ cup minced red onion
> 3 to 5 fresh red chiles, seeded, finely shredded

Arrange cucumbers in a bowl. Dissolve sugar in boiling water. Add vinegar and salt. Stir. Let cool. Pour over cucumbers. Add red onion and chiles. Chill.

YIELD: 1½ cups.

Chile Sauce
Naam Prik

Every Thai has his own version of this popular spice sauce served with many Thai dishes.

> ½ pound fresh red chiles, seeded, washed, and dried
> ½ cup garlic cloves, peeled
> 3 tablespoons sake
> 1 cup rice vinegar
> ¼ cup sugar
> ⅛ cup salt

Combine all ingredients and process until a coarse paste is formed. Store in tightly covered glass jar in the refrigerator for one week. The flavor improves upon standing.

YIELD: 8 to 10 servings.

TIPS: Dried chiles may be substituted for fresh red chiles. Soak the dried chiles in the vinegar for ½ hour before using. Rice vinegar may be substituted for sake.

Inspired by a recipe from Head Chef Boonchu Pholwatana, Dusit-Bussaracum Culinary Academy and Restaurant.

 ## Chili Jam
Naam Prik Pad

The Thais love Naam Prik Pad so much that Chalie Amatyakul calls this spirited sauce "Chili Jam." It can also be diluted with lime juice, fish sauce (nam pla), *and water.*

> 1 teaspoon dried shrimp paste *(kapee)*
> ⅔ cup dried shrimp, soaked in hot water to soften, about 10 minutes
> 10 garlic cloves, chopped
> 10 shallots, chopped
> ¼ cup oil
> 5 fresh red chiles, chopped
> 1 tablespoon fish sauce *(nam pla)*
> 2 tablespoons brown sugar
> 2 tablespoons tamarind water (page 25)

Wrap shrimp paste in foil and toast on moderate heat in a dry pan for 1 to 2 minutes on each side. Drain the soaked shrimp and chop coarsely. Preheat the oven to 350° F. Place the garlic and shallots on a baking sheet. Toss with 1 tablespoon oil. Bake for 30 minutes, stirring occasionally, until brown and crisp. Remove from oven. Let cool. In a mortar or processor, pound or process the toasted garlic, shallots, shrimp paste, and chiles to a coarse paste.

Heat 3 tablespoons oil in a wok. Add the paste and stir-fry over moderate heat, until fragrant, about 1 minute. Add the fish sauce, sugar, and tamarind water, and stir-fry until most of the liquid has evaporated, about 3 minutes. Let cool. Store in a tightly covered glass container in the refrigerator. Chili Jam will keep refrigerated for up to one month.

YIELD: 1½ cups, approximately.

TIP: If fresh chiles are unavailable, use 10 dried red chiles. Toast the chiles in a dry skillet over moderate heat until lightly browned. Chop.

Inspired by a recipe from Chalie Amatyakul, director, The Thai Cooking School, The Oriental, Bangkok.

 ## Spicy Peanut Sauce for Satay
Naam Jim Satay

This rich peanut sauce made with red curry paste transforms grilled satay into a savory delight and is one of the favorites of many of my students in both Bangkok and the United States. Head Chef Boonchoo Pholwatana says the sauce should have a more sweet than sour flavor. Be careful not to add too much tamarind water.

> 1 cup thick coconut milk
> 2 to 3 tablespoons Red Curry Paste (page 69)
> ¾ cup thin coconut milk
> 1 tablespoon fish sauce (*nam pla*)
> 2 tablespoons light brown sugar
> 1½ tablespoons tamarind water (page 25)
> ¼ cup ground unsalted dry roasted peanuts or 3 tablespoons
>   creamy peanut butter

In a pan, heat the thick coconut milk over low heat and cook until it thickens and becomes oily around the edges. Increase the heat. Add the curry paste and cook for 3 to 5 minutes, being careful not to burn. There will be a noticeable color and odor change as the mixture becomes properly cooked. Add the thin coconut milk gradually. Stir. Season with fish sauce, sugar, and tamarind water. Add the ground peanuts. Stir. Serve as a dipping sauce for Satay with Thai Cucumber Sauce (page 94).

YIELD: 6 to 8 servings as an appetizer.

ADVANCE PREPARATION: The satay sauce may be prepared several days in advance. Refrigerate and serve at room temperature. If sauce is too thick when serving, dilute with thin coconut milk or water. The sauce will become spicier and thicker as it stands.

Inspired by a recipe from Head Chef Boonchoo Pholwatana, Dusit-Bussaracum Restaurant and Culinary Academy, Bangkok.

Barbecued Chicken Sauce
Naam Jim Kai-Nua

1 teaspoon ground chile paste
2 teaspoons finely minced garlic
½ cup sugar
½ cup rice vinegar
½ cup water
Salt to taste

Combine chile paste, garlic, sugar, and rice vinegar, and mix well. Put in a small saucepan. Add water. Bring to a boil. Reduce heat and boil slowly until the mixture is reduced by one-half. The sauce will become thicker as it cools. Sauce will keep for 1 to 2 weeks in refrigerator.

YIELD: 3 to 4 servings.

DESSERTS AND BEVERAGES

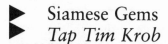 Siamese Gems
Tap Tim Krob

A colorful Thai dessert combining jewel-like water chestnuts with coconut milk.

1½ cups water chestnuts, diced into ¼-inch cubes
Food coloring: red, green, yellow, and blue, approximately 5 drops
    of each color
½ cup tapioca flour
⅓ cup sugar
½ teaspoon jasmine extract (optional)
2 cups coconut milk

Divide the water chestnuts into 5 groups. In separate dishes, mix each food coloring with ½ cup water. Dye 4 of the groups until they are pastel in color. Remove and drain well on paper towels. Toss all the water chestnuts in tapioca flour to coat. Place in a sieve and shake to remove excess tapioca flour.

Bring 5 cups water to a boil. Add water chestnuts and bring to a second boil. Cook 1 to 2 minutes until the water chestnuts start rising to the top and are almost translucent. Drain immediately. Chill in cold water. Combine the sugar and ½ cup water in a pan. Cook over moderate heat, stirring, until dissolved and slightly thickened. Remove from the heat. Add jasmine extract and coconut milk. Let chill. Add chilled water chestnuts to the coconut milk. Stir well. Serve in individual bowls.

YIELD: 6 to 8 servings.

TIP: Substitute rose water or any flowery extract for the jasmine extract.

ADVANCE PREPARATION: Prepare 1 day in advance. Refrigerate. Combine 1 hour before serving.

Inspired by a recipe from Head Chef Boonchoo Pholwatana, Dusit-Bussaracum Culinary Academy, Bangkok.

 ### Mangoes and Sticky Rice
Khao Niew Mam Uang

When mangoes are ripe in Thailand, everyone rushes to the street vendors to enjoy this tropical delight. Luscious, juicy mangoes served with creamy sticky rice make a fabulous ending to a Thai meal. Be sure to use ripe, sweet mangoes.

> 2 cups glutinous rice (sticky or sweet rice), washed, soaked
>   overnight (8 hours), and drained
> ½ cup sugar
> 1 teaspoon salt
> 1 cup thick coconut milk

TOPPING:

> 1 cup coconut milk
> ½ teaspoon salt
> ¼ cup sugar

> 5 ripe mangoes, peeled, halved, stone removed, each half cut into
>   4 transverse slices

Place the rice on cheesecloth and steam over water for 20 to 25 minutes, or until the rice is soft. Dissolve the sugar and salt in 1 cup thick coconut milk over medium heat. Bring slowly to a boil. Remove from the heat immediately. Add the cooked sticky rice to the hot coconut milk. Stir until well mixed. Cover and let stand 30 minutes.

Prepare the topping by bringing 1 cup coconut milk slowly to boil. Add salt and sugar. Stir to dissolve the sugar.

Reassemble the mango halves on a plate. Spoon the sticky rice in a mound beside it. Spoon the coconut topping over the sticky rice. Serve immediately or refrigerate.

YIELD: 4 to 5 servings.

Inspired by a recipe from Sompunee Srirath, as told to Wade Garretson, district sales manager, Thai Airways International Ltd.

 ## Banana Fritters
Kluay Tord

While in Bangkok, I often stop by a street vendor to enjoy these tasty treats. They are a sweet ending to a Thai dinner.

4 tablespoons butter
6 firm, fresh bananas, peeled and quartered lengthwise
6 tablespoons palm sugar or light brown sugar
Juice of two limes

Heat the butter in a pan until it bubbles. Add the quartered bananas. Fry on all sides until golden and soft. Sprinkle sugar into the pan. Stir until the sugar is dissolved and becomes syrupy. Mix to coat the bananas. Sprinkle with lime juice. Serve immediately.

YIELD: 6 servings.

TIP: If you prefer a less tart fritter, reduce the lime juice.

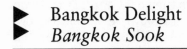

Bangkok Delight
Bangkok Sook

Each time I serve Bangkok Delight, it brings back the fondest of memories. Upon my arrival at the famous Oriental Hotel in Bangkok I was ushered to the charming veranda, abundant with exotic flowers and gleaming white wicker furniture. A few tables away Peter Ustinov enjoyed himself. At a different table was yet another famous personality. As the sun set over the beautiful Chao Phraya River, we relaxed and enjoyed our Bangkok Delight.

    ⅓ cup light rum
    ⅓ cup gin
    ⅓ cup cream of coconut
    ¼ cup pineapple juice
    ¼ cup orange juice
    ¼ cup lime juice
    Ice cubes
    Mint leaves for garnish

Combine all ingredients and 3 to 4 ice cubes in a blender or cocktail shaker. Shake thoroughly. Pour into a chilled glass. Garnish with mint leaves.

YIELD: 4 drinks.

TIP: A delightful dessert can be made by putting the ingredients in your ice cream maker and serving it frozen.

Thai Iced Tea
Cha Yen

Thai iced tea is made from a tea grown in northern Thailand. It is powdery in consistency, flavored with vanilla and roasted corn, and has a reddish earth color and is sold in Thai grocery stores. The tea is traditionally served in tall glasses. Boonchoo Pholwatana says this must be brewed in a muslin bag, but I have found it to be successfully made by brewing it through a coffee filter. Traditional tea may not be substituted.

½ cup Thai tea
3 cups water
14-ounce can sweetened condensed milk
Milk or half and half to taste, approximately 1½ cups

Place the tea in a coffee filter in a drip cone. Bring the water to a boil and pour it over the tea. Allow the tea to drip through. Repeat this procedure 5 or 6 times until it is a deep reddish orange color and is very strong.

Add the sweetened condensed milk to the hot tea and allow it to cool to room temperature. To serve, fill tall glasses with ice and add the tea/condensed milk mixture to fill the glass ½ to ¾ full. Add milk or half and half to fill the glass. Stir.

YIELD: 4 to 6 servings.

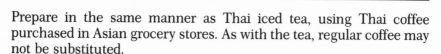

Thai Iced Coffee
Kar Fae Yen

Prepare in the same manner as Thai iced tea, using Thai coffee purchased in Asian grocery stores. As with the tea, regular coffee may not be substituted.

Lemon Grass Tea
Cha Takai

Vorachoon Yuchinda of the exotic Lemongrass Restaurant, Bangkok, served me this wonderful, refreshing beverage. He says you must use only the freshest of lemon grass. To make it even more fragrant, he added jasmine to the tea.

Lemon grass is sprinkled liberally into salads and curries to stimulate the appetite. It is customarily boiled with water and is then used by Thai women for a newborn baby's refreshing, cleansing, and fragrant bath.

8 stalks lemon grass, bottom 6 inches only
4 cups water
1 to 2 tablespoons sugar
3 to 4 drops jasmine extract (optional)

Wash lemon grass, smash with the side of a cleaver to crush and allow flavor to release. Boil for 20 minutes. Add sugar to taste and stir to dissolve. Refrigerate until ready to use. Strain. Add jasmine extract to taste. Serve with ice in a tall glass.

YIELD: 4 cups.

SINGAPORE

Huan Yin Kwan Lin! Welcome!

Singaporeans are absolutely passionate about their food. It is such a national obsession the locals greet each other not with the familiar "How are you?" but by asking "Have you eaten?" Once you have sampled some of the range of Singaporean cuisine, you may share this obsession.

Both the island and the nation of Singapore take their name from the capital city, the Sanskrit name of which means "lion city." But Singapore is hardly lion-sized: its 224 square miles make it about as big as the city of Chicago and only one-fifth as big as Rhode Island.

A former British colony located at the tip of the Malay Peninsula, Singapore was part of the Federation of Malaysia from 1963 to 1965, when it became an independent republic. Like southern Malaysia, Singapore's culinary heritage is the result of a cultural melting pot of Chinese, Malay, and Indian. The harmonious exchange of cooking techniques and ingredients among these and other ethnic groups has produced a cuisine with enormous diversity, and one that offers the widest variety of international food in all of Asia.

My exploration of Singapore's food secrets started with a trishaw ride to the Little India district, where we wandered through the enormous covered "wet market" (so-called because of the wet floors). Going from stall to stall, I saw cages full of live chickens, soon to be sold, weighed, then cleaned while the buyer waited. Everyday fare at the butcher's stall included crusty sides of streaky pork, a type of bacon baked in a barrel, long ruddy sausages hanging from hooks,

103

and an entire side of beef. In another stall, a Chinese medicine man claimed he could cure everything and anything with his concoction of animal bones, snake soup, and lizard skins, and he seemed to have many takers.

Around the corner was an overwhelming array of both exotic and familiar vegetables and fruits—fresh-picked Chinese greens, glossy aubergines (eggplants), huge mounds of fiery chiles, aromatic stalks of reefer-thin lemon grass, lustrous mangosteens (a tiny purple fruit with a succulent white interior), fuzzy red rambutans (a chestnut-sized fruit with juicy white flesh and a delicate, scented flavor), and most memorable of all, the yellowish-green durian.

Durian is a fruit the size of a coconut, with a thick rind covered with sharp, half-inch-long prickles. Southeast Asians love it, but acknowledge its dual character with the description "smells like hell, but tastes like heaven." A mature durian possesses a very strong odor so similar to robust overripe Roquefort cheese that most hotels forbid their guests to bring them into their rooms. The taste of the creamy-white pulp surrounding the seeds is sublime, although certainly an acquired taste.

Other shops displayed gray-pink shrimp as large as bananas, glittering on a bed of ice, heavy-clawed crabs hunched truculently in rows, and baked ducks, brown-glazed with soy sauce.

Fascinating and colorful to watch was the Indian spice merchant with his fragrant offerings—freshly ground turmeric, mustard seed, cardamom, cinnamon, clove, cumin, coriander, bay leaf, ginger, and chiles, all traditionally ground by hand with a mortar and pestle and combined according to the dictates of a particular recipe. The spice merchant is an artist who blends spices in the proper proportions by incorporating his knowledge of flavors with his instinct for what tastes good.

The delicious smells of the marketplace make you hungry, and hawkers' stalls turn out a huge array of tasty local dishes in various styles. One stall sells Hainanese chicken rice, flavored with chicken stock and served with steamed or soy-simmered chicken and a side dish of chile sauce and cucumber or tomatoes. Another offers fried Hokkien Mee, a popular dish of thick egg noodles and thin rice vermicelli fried with shrimp, pork, squid, bean sprouts and green vegetables in a small amount of rich pork stock, served with a squeeze of lime and a dish of chile sauce. Others sell tasty spring rolls or plump shrimp dumplings. All kinds of fresh fruit juices are made to order. You may choose a particular fruit juice or a combination of many. One of my favorites is a combination of star fruit, carrot, and orange, a refreshingly sweet concoction. Freshly squeezed sugar cane juice and sweet, creamy soy milk freshly pressed from soybeans are other treats.

After leaving the market, I stopped at Muthu's Curry Restaurant, a "banana leaf restaurant" with a stark tile and Formica decor. It is a haven for curry-hungry hordes of Singaporeans who are fond of the spicy southern Indian curries, sometimes known to make grown men cry. First I sampled their legendary specialty, a fiery Fish Head Curry. A fish head it is indeed, the cheeks and eyes being the delicacies. The window displayed other equally hot curries: jumbo shrimp, mutton, fried chicken, and a complete range of vegetables. All are served not on plates but on a piece of banana leaf (hence the genre "banana leaf restaurant"), with a huge mound of rice soaked in a tear-jerker of a hot curry sauce. I ate in native style, using the fingers of my right hand instead of utensils, which had a wonderful tactile quality once I got used to it. Thirst-quenching fresh lime juice from the sweet local limes put out the fire.

That night I had dinner in the beautiful Compass Rose Restaurant on the 73rd floor of the Westin Stamford Hotel—the tallest hotel in the world, according to the Guinness Book of World Records. The spectacular panoramic view of Singapore by night provided some major competition for a magnificent Continental dinner of fresh seafood in an "ice house" sculpture, seafood consommé with lobster mousse in wonton skin, delicately steamed garoupa seasoned with soy-flavored oil, fresh papaya sorbet, roast duck breast seasoned with Chinese rice wine, and sesame seed wild rice wrapped in a bamboo leaf. The Pineapple Compass Rose dessert with chocolate sauce and fresh raspberries was exquisite.

Sous Chef Joe Yap, a natural teacher and Singapore culinary team captain gold medalist, took me on a tour of the ultramodern, sparkling-clean stainless steel and white kitchens of the Westin Hotel. Reportedly one of the largest hotel kitchens in Asia, they are so vast that even Chef Yap called for a guide!

First stop was a well-chilled room where I watched Chef Artist Choo Heng Boy create an intricate vegetable carving of a bird of paradise. He chose a pumpkin for the body and graceful neck, large reddish carrots and cucumbers to imitate the long feathery tail, and broccoli flowerets to crown the exotic head. In another large kitchen lined with fish tanks, I watched Sous Chef Garde-manger William Tan prepare an elaborate shrimp paté with delicate patterns woven of seaweed, carrots, and cucumbers throughout. His lightning-quick execution made his magnificent presentation look effortless. Before leaving the kitchen for the dining room, each serving tray was garnished with breathtaking carvings—an elaborate lion, a golden phoenix, a serpentine dragon, a Chinese Buddha, and plenty of fanciful renditions from Chinese legends. I left the Westin in complete awe of the vastness of the kitchens and with a real appreciation for the wizardry of the artist chefs.

Sensing my passion and enthusiasm for the local food and customs, Joe Yap invited me to join him for a true Singaporean *Teochew* breakfast. And as many travelers and tourists know, nothing is more delightful or appreciated when you're away from home than to be led to a local haunt by a native. As we departed from the hotel at five-thirty A.M., I was filled with a great sense of adventure. I was about to see the market, the heart and soul of Singapore, come alive.

Joe drove to the Ellenborough Market on Tew Chew Street, where a row of old Chinese-style buildings overlooked the river. (The name of the street is probably yet another spelling of Teochew, named after a region of southeastern China that was home to a great number of the Chinese traders in Southeast Asia. Their cuisine, known in Hong Kong as *Chiu Chow,* is one of the more common styles of Chinese cooking in Singapore.) After climbing a narrow flight of stairs, we came upon many small open-air food vendors' stalls, each one with its own specialty. Picking his favorite from each stall, Chef Yap produced a Singaporean "breakfast of champions": fiery stir-fried crayfish with chiles, braised duck feet with sea cucumber, delicately steamed fish, and luscious stir-fried fresh bamboo shoots. The only condiment was a large bowl of chiles! The grand finale, though none was needed, was a steamed yam pudding laden with ginko nuts. The meal was as heady as it sounds, as were the beverages—cognac and beer. It was an unforgettable breakfast and a precious learning experience, mostly because of the kinship I shared with my host and guide, and through him, the people of Singapore.

I have also had the good fortune to be the guest of Alan Palmer, head of food and beverage of the Singapore Hotel Association Training and Educational Centre and Honorary Secretary of the Singapore Chef's Association, as well as a number of Singapore's award-winning chefs. It has always amazed me that this tiny island state has produced so many world-class chefs, plus a chefs' training school of equally remarkable excellence. Local teams do extremely well in international culinary competitions, and I have watched a victorious team of chefs returning to the school from overseas to a hero's reception, complete with cheerleaders. When they have competed in the United States, I have taken them grocery shopping and watched them create their native dishes using American foods and equipment. Our friendship and mutual exchange of guidance and inspiration has helped me tremendously in adapting Southeast Asian cooking techniques and ingredients to American methods.

One of the most interesting and distinctive of Singapore's cuisines is Nonya. This cooking style dates back four centuries to the exodus of Chinese men to the Straits settlements of Singapore, Penang, and Malacca. Since Chinese women were not allowed to emigrate with their men, the men married Malay women. Their descendants are known either as Peranaken or Straits Chinese; the ladies are traditionally called Nonyas and the men Babas. Nonya cooking, then, is the food served in a Nonya woman's home. Hotter and spicier than Chinese cooking, Nonya food draws on both Chinese and Malay traditions in both ingredients and techniques.

The Nonya kitchen is filled with pungent roots such as turmeric, ginger, galangal, shallots, and chives, plus candlenuts, shrimp paste, garlic, lemon grass, and of course, lots of chiles. For the tartness essential to Nonya food, lemons, limes, tamarinds, and green mangoes are used. Citrus leaves, coriander, and coconut milk are used, along with a vast variety of dried foods—mushrooms, lily buds, fermented black beans—found in Chinese kitchens.

What really sets Nonya cooking apart from Chinese is the use of a *rempah,* a mixture of ingredients pounded together in a mortar. Where a Chinese cook would slice or mince each ingredient separately, only combining them in the pan, many Nonya dishes begin with a *rempah* of up to a dozen ingredients that are thoroughly combined in the mortar. The whole mixture is then cooked in oil to release its flavor before the main ingredients are added.

According to the late Mrs. Lee Chin Koon, the grande dame of Nonya cooking (and the mother of Prime Minister Lee Kuan Yew), pounding the *rempah* is one of the essential skills of the Nonya cook. In traditional Nonya households, visitors "could tell by the sound of the mortar and pestle if there were good cooks in the house. There should be a rhythm to the pounding. From the sound of the pounding, we can tell which ingredient is being pounded and also whether the person who is pounding is an experienced cook." She added that because of their cooking prowess, "we were much sought after as prospective brides for the sons of other Straits-born Chinese."

Its unique blend of spicy Malay food and the original Chinese food has produced dishes like Curry Fish in Banana Leaves, Nonya Style, and *Satay Babi Goreng,* a Nonya pork satay.

In Nonya meals, all of the main courses are served at once. The traditional manner of eating is to mix and eat the spicy food with the fingers. (Noodles and some Chinese dishes are an exception; these are usually eaten with chopsticks. Sauced foods may also be eaten with a spoon and fork.) Fruit is seldom served with meals; the preferred dessert is the very sweet cake made from glutinous rice and coconut milk which is the trademark of the Nonyas. Malay coffee is preferred to Chinese tea.

Like all traditional cooks, Nonyas learn from their mothers how to pound *rempah* to just the right texture, how to fry garlic until golden brown, light, and crispy, and to combine spices and other ingredients by *agak,* estimation, rather than by strict measurement. Everything has to be learned by watching and practice.

I was fortunate to have as my teacher Nonya Violet Oon, well-known cooking and television personality and publisher of Singapore's monthly newspaper *The Food Paper*. In her spacious home kitchen, she taught me many Nonya dishes and demonstrated the use of traditional utensils including the *kuali* (wok), a Chinese cleaver, the *batu lesong* (mortar and pestle), and *batu giling* (a grinding stone for pulverizing herbs and spices). She also showed me how to use an electric blender, coffee grinder, or small food processor to replace the mortar and pestle and grinding stone. (See cooking techniques, page 11.)

In the recipes in this chapter, I have concentrated on Nonya dishes, but have included Chinese and northern Indian foods to give you an idea of the broad range of Singaporean cuisine. (Malay food, abundant in Singapore, is covered in the chapter on Malaysia.) Many of the recipes are my adaptations of dishes of the renowned chefs of Singapore.

The greatest feast in the East can be found in Singapore, where people view food with tremendous passion and pride.

Ching Sui Pien Che! Please eat!

SINGAPORE MENUS

SINGAPORE NONYA BUFFET

8 to 10 people

Nonya Five-Spice Rolls, *Ngoh Hiang*

♦

Beef Rendang, Nonya Style, *Rendang Daging*

♦

Curry Fish in Banana Leaves, Nonya Style, *Chiu Yip Kar Li Yu*

♦

Coconut-Flavored Rice, *Nasi Lemak*

♦

Vegetable Pickles, *Acar*

♦

Rice

♦

Accompaniments
(Peanuts, Hard Boiled Eggs, Cucumber and Tomato Slices,
Chopped Chiles)

♦

Fruit Compote, *Chup Kum Quo*

♦

Coffee

Perfect for year-round entertaining, this menu illustrates the way Nonya cooking has drawn threads from Chinese and Malay traditions into a distinctive local cuisine. Nonya Five-Spice Rolls are a delicate adaptation of the familiar Chinese egg roll, but bound in bean-curd skin. Beef Rendang, Nonya Style, is a rich, creamy curry native to Pandang in West Sumatra and popular throughout Southeast Asia. A large piece of banana leaf encloses a whole fish and its seasonings, adding its own pleasant fragrance to the complex mixture. Vegetable Pickles add flavor and texture, and smooth, gentle Coconut-Flavored

Rice provides a mild background for the myriad flavors. (Nonya cooks would also serve plain white rice, but this is optional.)

In Nonya meals, all of the main courses are served at once. The traditional manner of eating is to mix and eat the spicy food with the fingers. If you prefer, you can use spoons and forks, but you will miss out on some of the sensual pleasure of this style of food.

This buffet is easily prepared and stands well. Prepare the *Acar* one week in advance. Five-Spice Rolls and Beef Rendang can be prepared ahead and reheated at serving time. Combine the fruit several hours in advance and store in the refrigerator. Wrap the Curry Fish in the banana leaves several hours before your guests arrive, and cook just before serving. Prepare the accompaniments hours ahead.

SINGAPORE SEAFOOD SUPPER

6 to 8 people

Steamed Fish with Black Beans, *Dau Shi Ching Yu*

◆

Stir-Fried Shrimp in Tomato Sauce, Cantonese Style, *Har Loke*

◆

Spicy Seafood Salad, *Hoi Shin Lang Pun*

◆

Rice

◆

Fresh Fruit

◆

Tiger Beer

Being surrounded by water, Singapore has a marvelous variety of fresh seafood available. Fishing boats and fish farms produce a rainbow assortment of fish, plus crabs, shrimp, squid, and other shellfish.

Up and down Singapore's East Coast Parkway there are wonderful seafood restaurants serving freshly caught fish and seafood. The atmosphere is relaxed and casual, allowing the focus to be where it should be—on the seafood.

During one visit to Singapore, Alan Palmer took me to visit one of the few remaining fish farms. A short distance from the harbor the fishermen had set up a *kelong*, a wooden house built on stilts in the water. Many nets were suspended from poles near the house, then raised and lowered to catch the assorted fish, which have been caught in the sea and transported to these enclosures until ready to harvest. There were shrimp, ranging in size from huge whiskered specimens the size of a small lobster down to sweet little nothings the length of a thumbnail, tentacled squid, weighty red snapper, silver-white pomfret, and silver-gray mackerel being raised to the perfect size for serving to a fortunate diner. Several large guard dogs watched over the precious seafood.

Fish farming has become so expensive that most of the fishing industry has moved to the industrial suburb of Jurong in the western corner of Singapore. Fishing vessels from the coastal waters around Singapore and the southern part of Peninsular Malaysia jockey for position at the wharf. There, at the Central Fish Market, over 200 tons of seafood a day are auctioned to wholesalers during the dim hours before dawn.

After our visit to the fish farm, our fishing boat took us to the Ubin Seafood Restaurant, a small wooden building on stilts over the water, for a soul-satisfying seafood meal. A freshly caught red snapper was steamed to order, followed by large shrimp in tomato sauce and a refreshing seafood salad. We washed it all down with large glasses of Singapore's Tiger Beer.

The same meal is easy to make and serve at home. Prepare the seafood salad ingredients one day ahead and combine them just before serving. Stir-fry the shrimp while the fish steams and the rice cooks.

TANDOOR RESTAURANT'S INDIAN FEAST

6 people

Shrimp in Spiced Sauce, *Jhinga Samurkundh*

•

Potatoes, Cauliflower, and Peas, *Aloo Gobi Matar*

•

Tandoori Chicken, *Tandoori Murghi*

•

Indian Spiced Fruit Salad, *Chat*

•

Sweet Saffron Pilaf, *Zarda*

•

Cucumber Salad, *Raita*

•

Fresh Fruit

•

Tiger Beer

At Singapore's Tandoor Restaurant, Chef Kalam Kumar Channa prepares dishes in the northern Indian Moghul style. It's a highly refined form of court cooking which relies on subtle use of spices rather than the chile hotness associated with southern Indian cuisine. Tandoori dishes, named for the clay tandoor ovens in which they are cooked, are his specialty. In this type of cooking, the meat is marinated first to give it a delicate flavor before being roasted in the clay ovens.

You don't need a tandoor oven to prepare a delicious Tandoori Chicken dinner; a conventional oven or charcoal grill will do. Spiced Fruit Salad and Cucumber Salad are made ahead and served as palate refreshers during the meal. Shrimp in Spiced Sauce, and Potatoes, Cauliflower, and Peas are easily prepared ahead and reheated at the last moment. Tandoori Chicken and Sweet Saffron Pilaf can be cooking, demanding little attention, while you are entertaining.

STARTERS
Nonya Five-Spice Rolls, *Ngoh Hiang*
Fresh Spring Rolls, Nonya Style, *Poh Pia*
Money Bags, *Chien Dai*
Pork and Shrimp Dumplings, *Shao Mai*
Shrimp Puffs, *Tchar Har Kow*
Shrimp and Pork Wontons, *Har Yuk Wonton*

SOUPS
Chilled Orange Carrot Soup, *Hong Lo Bak Tchang Lang Tong*
Chicken and Cucumber Soup, *Huang Quar Gai Tong*

MEAT
Beef Rendang, Nonya Style, *Rendang Daging*
Nonya Pork Satay, *Satay Babi Goreng*
Grilled Lamb Kebabs, *Khana Kebabs*

POULTRY
Hainanese Chicken, *Hainanese Gai Fayn*
Cantonese Oyster Sauce Chicken, *Hauyou Gai*
Tandoori Chicken, *Tandoori Murghi*
Braised Coriander Chicken, *Yuan Sai Man Gai*
Stir-Fried Squab with Asparagus, *Butt Shuan Chao Bak Kab*

FISH AND SEAFOOD
Curry Fish in Banana Leaves, Nonya Style, *Chiu Yip Kar Li Yu*
Baked Curry Fish in Banana Leaves, *Chiu Yip Kar Li Yu*
Steamed Fish with Black Beans, *Dau Shi Ching Yu*
Fried Fish with Ginger Sauce, *Kaing Chup Yu*

Stir-Fried Shrimp in Tomato Sauce, Cantonese Style, *Har Loke*
Tamarind Shrimp, *Udang Goreng Asam*
Shrimp Curry with Pineapple, *Bor Lor Kar Li Har*
Shrimp in Spiced Sauce, *Jhinga Samurkundh*
Steamed Shrimp with Green Onions, *Chun Yau Ching Har*

SALADS AND VEGETABLES

Asparagus Sesame Salad, *Mar Yau Butt Shuan Lang Pun*
Vegetable Salad with Tangy Peanut Sauce, *Gado-Gado Singapore
Style*
Indian Spiced Fruit Salad, *Chat*
Spicy Chicken Shred, Vegetable and Noodle Salad, *Shau Shi Gai*
Spicy Seafood Salad, *Hoi Shin Lang Pun*
Potatoes, Cauliflower, and Peas, *Aloo Gobi Matar*
Grilled Eggplant, *Kaw Kar Chee*
Mixed Vegetable Medley, *Chup Kum Choy*

RICE, NOODLES, AND WRAPPERS

Yangchow Fried Rice, *Yangchow Chao Fayn*
Hainanese Chicken Rice, *Nasi Ayam Goreng Hainanese*
Coconut-Flavored Rice, *Nasi Lemak*
Sweet Saffron Pilaf, *Zardo*
Stir-Fried Rice Noodles with Chicken and Broccoli, *Kai Lan Gai
Chao Fun*
Bird's Nest, *Cheut Chaw*
Fresh Spring Roll Wrappers, *Poh Pia Wrappers*

ACCOMPANIMENTS AND SAUCES

Cucumber Pickles, *Acar Timun*
Vegetable Pickles, *Acar*
Cucumber Salad, *Raita*
Violet Oon's Chile Dipping Sauce, *Lak Chong*
Violet Oon's Chile Sauce for Hainanese Chicken, *Hainanese Gai Lak
Chong*
Ginger Sauce, *Kaing Yau*
Soy Vinegar Dipping Sauce, *Chong Yau Chit Cho Tiu Mee Chong*

DESSERTS AND BEVERAGES

Fruit Compote, *Chup Kum Quo*
Almond Float, *Hung Yum Cha*
The Original Singapore Sling
Fresh Pineappleade, *Bor Lor Chup*

STARTERS

 Nonya Five-Spice Rolls
Ngoh Hiang

A delightful combination of texture and taste, this is a favorite appetizer among the Nonyas. Violet Oon, who taught me these savories, dips the bite-size pieces of the rolls into tapioca flour before deep-frying to give an added dimension.

Bean curd skins, fresh, frozen, or dried
½ pound ground pork
¼ pound shrimp, shelled, deveined, coarsely chopped
1 small onion, chopped
1 egg, lightly beaten

SEASONING MIXTURE:

2 teaspoons soy sauce
¾ teaspoon Chinese five-spice powder
½ teaspoon Chinese sesame oil
1 teaspoon sugar
¼ teaspoon salt
¼ teaspoon pepper
2 teaspoons cornstarch
2 teaspoons oil

3 ounces cooked crabmeat, flaked
4 water chestnuts, minced
2 teaspoons flour mixed in 4 teaspoons water
½ cup tapioca flour

Run hot water over the bean curd skin to soften. Cut it into squares 5 inches by 5 inches.

In a large bowl, combine the pork, shrimp, onion, eggs, and seasoning mixture. Mix well. Add the crab and water chestnuts, and stir until well combined. Place approximately 2 tablespoons of the mixture on a wrapper. Cover the remaining bean curd skins with a damp towel. Moisten the flap of the envelope with warm water and flour and roll it into a cylinder, sealing it firmly. Set aside and repeat until all the filling has been used.

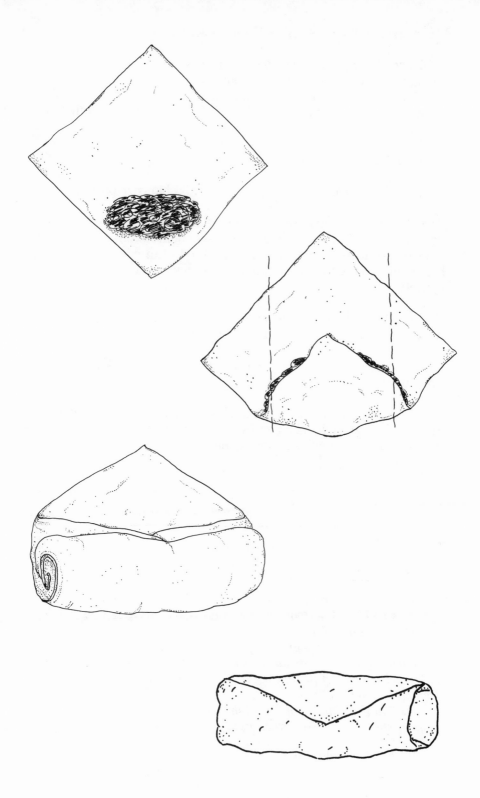

Place the rolls on an oiled bamboo steamer tray. Steam over boiling water for 10 minutes. Let cool.

Cut the rolls into bite-size pieces on the diagonal and roll in tapioca flour. Heat the oil in a wok to 375° F. Deep-fry rolls in batches until golden.

Serve with Violet Oon's Chile Sauce (page 164), Chinese plum sauce, and cucumber slices.

YIELD: 8 Five Spice Rolls or approximately 32 bite-size pieces.

TIPS: Bean curd skins are available fresh, frozen, or dried in Asian grocery stores. To prevent cracking, they should be moistened with water before using. When purchasing dried bean curd skins, check them to make sure they are not broken as they can be too broken up to be useful.

VARIATIONS: The rolls may be fried without using the tapioca flour. Cut into bite-sized pieces when serving.

If bean curd wrappers are unavailable, spring roll skins may be substituted.

ADVANCE PREPARATION: Make ahead and freeze after steaming. The rolls can be fried ahead and warmed at serving time in a 350° F oven. However, you will sacrifice some of the crispness of the rolls.

 ## Fresh Spring Rolls, Nonya Style
Poh Pia

Poh Pia are the Nonya version of a fresh Chinese spring roll and a popular snack in Singapore and Malaysia. They are refreshing, low calorie, and wonderful for entertaining.

They are an excellent party or do-it-yourself meal as everyone assembles his or her own, adding the desired ingredients to produce a tasty combination of flavors. Everything can be prepared ahead and assembled at serving time.

The Poh Pia *consists of the fresh wrappers, the cooked filling, and the garnishes, which are served in separate dishes.*

20 *Poh Pia* Wrappers (page 161)

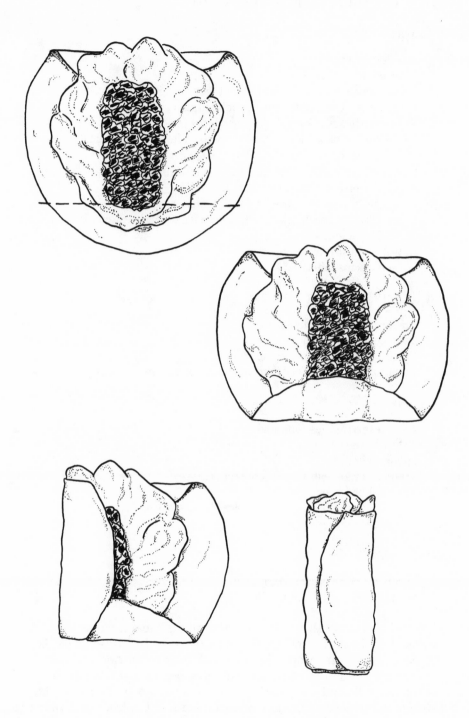

FILLING:

4 tablespoons oil
1 clove garlic, minced
2 teaspoons peeled, minced fresh ginger
8 ounces pork, shredded into 1-inch lengths
8 ounces shrimp, cleaned, deveined, chopped
6 Chinese dried black mushrooms, soaked in hot water for 20
    minutes or until spongy, stems removed, shredded
1 cup bamboo shoots, shredded into 1-inch lengths
½ cup carrots, shredded into 1-inch lengths
1 cup celery cabbage, shredded into 1-inch lengths
¾ cup Chinese turnip (lo bok, Japanese daikon), shredded into
    1-inch lengths
12 water chestnuts, chopped
6 green onions, chopped

SAUCE MIXTURE FOR FILLING: Combine and set aside.

2 tablespoons light soy sauce
2 teaspoons oyster sauce
1 tablespoon Chinese sesame oil
1 tablespoon cornstarch dissolved in 2 tablespoons water

GARNISHES:

2 Chinese sausages (optional)
2 cups bean sprouts
½ cucumber
8 ounces crabmeat, flaked (optional)
2–3 hard boiled eggs, chopped
20 to 24 Boston, romaine, or red leaf lettuce leaves, torn in half if
    large

CONDIMENTS:

¾ cup sweet soy sauce, kecap manis
½ cup chile sauce, Sambal Ulek page 321.

Prepare Poh Pia wrappers. Prepare the filling. Heat 2 tablespoons oil
in wok. Add the garlic and ginger and stir-fry for 5 to 10 seconds. Add
the pork and stir-fry until the shreds change color. Add the shrimp
and stir-fry until they turn pinkish. Remove and set aside. Add 2
tablespoons oil. Add the mushrooms, bamboo shoots, carrots, celery
cabbage, Chinese turnip, and water chestnuts. Cook for 2 minutes.
Add the cooked pork and shrimp mixture, and green onions, and stir

to mix. Add the sauce mixture and cook until the sauce begins to thicken and is transparent. Transfer the mixture to a plate to cool.

Steam Chinese sausage for 10 minutes. Cut on the diagonal into thin slices. Blanch bean sprouts in boiling water for 30 seconds. Drain. Refresh with cold water. Peel and seed cucumber. Cut into 2-inch shreds.

To serve: Arrange the ingredients in separate piles on a large serving platter or in individual bowls. If cold, reheat the pancakes in the foil package in a preheated 400° F oven for 3 to 5 minutes or until warm. Let each guest assemble his *Poh Pia*. Place a lettuce leaf on top of the pancake. Spread the lettuce with a small amount of chile sauce and a little sweet soy sauce. Put a spoonful of the cooked filling on the lettuce and a selection of ingredients from the garnishes. Roll up the wrapper, turning in the sides so the filling is completely enclosed. The *Poh Pia* should be eaten immediately or the pancakes will get soggy.

YIELD: 20 Poh Pia.

ADVANCE PREPARATION: All parts of the *Poh Pia* may be prepared ahead and refrigerated.

TIP: Prepared frozen spring-roll or lumpia wrappers may be purchased in Oriental grocery stores. They are a time-saver, but not as tasty as freshly made wrappers. Steam over boiling water to heat.

If desired, the filling may be served in lettuce leaves without the wrapper.

Inspired by Gottfried Schuetzenberger, southeast area executive pastry chef, Hyatt International.

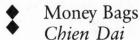

Money Bags
Chien Dai

Violet Oon suggests you prepare these tasty Money Bags for your guests for Chinese New Year. They will love you all the way to the bank when you serve these small golden pouches that look like real money bags.

2 tablespoons oil
½ pound shrimp, shelled, deveined, minced
½ pound fish fillet (sole or flounder), chopped, minced
6 water chestnuts, minced
1 green onion, chopped
1 tablespoon soy sauce
1 tablespoon dry sherry
½ teaspoon sugar
Dash white pepper
1 tablespoon cornstarch dissolved in 2 tablespoons water
20 to 30 wonton wrappers
15 green onions, cut in half lengthwise, or 30 watercress stems
½ teaspoon salt
3 cups oil

Heat wok or frying pan. Add 2 tablespoons of the oil and heat. Add the shrimp and fish. Stir-fry until the shrimp turns pink, about 30 seconds. Add the water chestnuts, green onion, soy sauce, sherry, sugar, and white pepper. Stir to mingle the flavors. Add cornstarch and water. Cook until translucent. Remove from the wok. Let filling cool before filling the Money Bags.

Cut the wonton wrappers into 3-inch circles with scissors. Spoon 1 tablespoon of the filling onto the center of each wonton wrapper. Form a bundle around the filling. Soak the green onions or watercress stems in salted water until pliable. Tie the parcel in place with green onion strips or watercress stems.

In a wok, heat the oil to 350° F. Deep-fry in batches of 6 until golden and the meat is cooked throughout. Drain on paper towels. Serve with Soy Vinegar Dipping Sauce (page 166).

YIELD: 36 Money Bags.

TIP: If the Money Bags are too large, the meat will not cook thoroughly.

ADVANCE PREPARATION: The Money Bags may be assembled several hours in advance or frozen for 2 months. Deep-fry ahead of time and reheat in a 350° F oven.

 ## Pork and Shrimp Dumplings
Shao Mai

Steamed dumplings are traditional snack foods served in the hawkers' stands. These tasty appetizers can be made ahead and frozen.

36 wonton wrappers

FILLING MIXTURE:

½ pound ground pork
½ pound shrimp, cleaned, shelled, deveined, diced into ¼-inch
    pieces
6 water chestnuts, minced
3 Chinese dried black mushrooms, soaked in hot water until
    spongy, about 20 minutes, stems removed, minced
3 green onions, minced
1½ tablespoons peeled, minced fresh ginger
1½ tablespoons soy sauce
2 teaspoons Chinese sesame oil
1 teaspoon dry sherry
1 teaspoon sugar
⅛ teaspoon white pepper
36 frozen peas (optional)

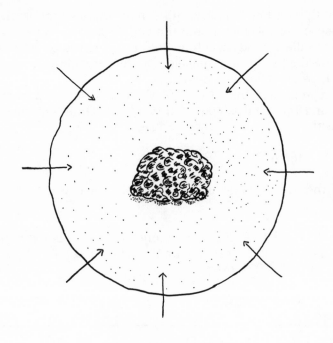

Combine the pork, shrimp, water chestnuts, mushrooms, green onions, ginger, soy sauce, sesame oil, dry sherry, sugar, and white pepper. Mix well with hands, but do not overmix.

Cut wontons into 3-inch circles. Place 1 tablespoon of the pork-shrimp mixture in the center of each circle. Gather the edges around the filling to form pleats. Lightly squeeze the center of the dumpling. With a spoon, smooth the meat surface. Place a pea in the center of the meat. Set the dumpling on a table and tap it on the table to make the bottom flat. Repeat procedure until all the dumplings are formed.

Oil the bottom of a bamboo steamer or heatproof platter. Place the dumplings on it, leaving a ½-inch space between the dumplings.

Cover and steam over medium-high heat for 20 minutes. Serve hot with Soy Vinegar Dipping Sauce (page 165).

YIELD: 36 dumplings.

TIP: Fresh mushrooms may be substituted for the Chinese dried black mushrooms. Commercially prepared Gyoza wrappers may be substituted for the wonton wrappers.

ADVANCE PREPARATION: The *Shao Mai* may be frozen for 2 months or may be cooked 1 day ahead, refrigerated, and reheated by steaming for 5 to 10 minutes. Some flavor will be lost if frozen.

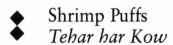 Shrimp Puffs
Tehar har Kow

Glistening white rice noodles impart a festive flair to these delicate shrimp puffs.

½ pound shrimp, shelled, deveined, minced
2 tablespoons finely minced pork or bacon fat
3 water chestnuts, minced finely
¼ teaspoon salt
¼ teaspoon sugar
1 ounce dried rice noodles
3 to 4 cups oil

Mix shrimp, pork fat, water chestnuts, salt, and sugar in a bowl until firm and well combined. Place rice noodles in a food processor or blender and turn on processor for a few seconds to break up rice noodles in small pieces. Form shrimp mixture into small balls. Roll in rice noodles. Heat oil in a wok to 350° F. Cook shrimp puffs in batches. Rice noodles should puff up immediately. Reduce heat to medium, and cook until shrimp puffs are cooked throughout.

Serve with Soy Vinegar Dipping Sauce (page 166) and a chile sauce such as *Sambal Ulek,* available in Asian grocery stores.

YIELD: 6 servings.

TIP: Rice noodles may be crumbled in a paper bag, using a rolling pin or other hard object.

Inspired by a recipe from Violet Oon, editor, *The Food Paper.*

Shrimp and Pork Wontons
Har Yuk Wonton

Delicious wontons are an interesting appetizer. The filled, uncooked wontons can be frozen successfully.

1 package wonton wrappers, about 30 skins

FILLING:

½ pound pork
½ pound shrimp, shelled, deveined, chopped
1 teaspoon minced fresh ginger
1 green onion, minced
8 water chestnuts, minced
5 Chinese dried black mushrooms, soaked in water until spongy, chopped
1 egg, lightly beaten
1 tablespoon dark soy sauce
½ teaspoon salt
¼ teaspoon Chinese sesame oil
1 teaspoon dry sherry

1 tablespoon cornstarch dissolved in 2 tablespoons water
1 egg, lightly beaten
3 to 4 cups oil for deep frying

Combine the filling ingredients in a bowl and mix well. Heat a wok over high heat. Add 2 tablespoons oil and heat. Add the pork and shrimp mixture. Stir-fry for 1 minute, or until the pork turns grayish. Stir the cornstarch mixture and add to the wok. Stir until the mixture is smooth and slightly thickened. Turn onto a plate and let cool before wrapping.

Place ¾ teaspoon of the cooked mixture in the center of each wrapper. Moisten the wrapper edges with the egg. Bring 1 corner up over the filling to the opposite corner, folding the wrapper at an angle so that 2 overlapping triangles are formed, with their points side by side about ½ inch apart. Press the edges together. Pull the two bottom corners of the folded triangle forward and below the folded edge so that they meet one another and slightly overlap, creating a frame around the mound of filling. Moisten with egg and pinch the ends together. Place the finished wontons on a plate, and cover with a towel until ready to cook.

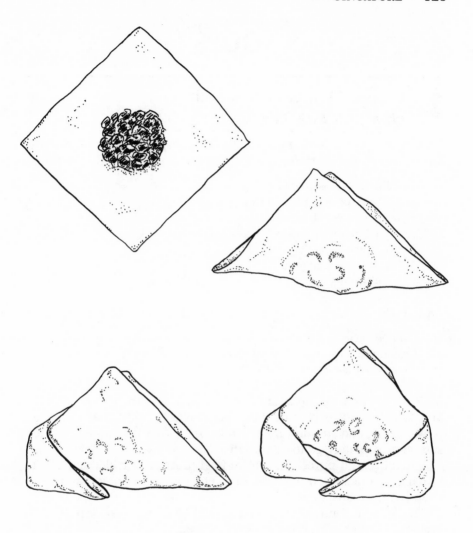

Heat 3 cups oil in a wok to 350° F. Fry the wontons, a few at a time, until crisp and golden. Remove and drain. Serve with Soy Vinegar Dipping Sauce (page 166).

ADVANCE PREPARATION: Uncooked wontons can be refrigerated for 1 day or frozen for 2 months. Fry the morning of serving and reheat on a rack in a 350° F oven. For optimum results, fry just before serving.

YIELD: 30 wontons.

SOUPS

◆ **Chilled Orange Carrot Soup**
◆ *Hong Lo Bak Tchang Lang Tong*

Serve chilled in a stemmed glass. This easily prepared, colorful, healthy, low calorie soup is perfect for a hot summer day.

2 tablespoons unsalted butter or oil
¾ teaspoon peeled, minced fresh ginger
1 pound carrots, chopped
½ cup sliced leeks, washed, white part only
3 cups chicken broth
1½ cups fresh orange juice
Salt and white pepper to taste

GARNISH:

Orange slices
Grated raw carrot
Fresh mint leaves

Melt the butter over moderate heat in a pan. Add the ginger, carrots, and leeks. Sauté until soft, but not browned. Add 2 cups chicken broth, cover, and simmer until carrots are cooked throughout and are soft, approximately 20 to 30 minutes.

Remove and puree mixture in food processor or blender. Stir in remaining chicken broth and enough orange juice to produce a slightly thick consistency. Season to taste with salt and white pepper. Chill. Place an orange slice and grated raw carrot on top of each serving. Garnish with mint leaves if desired.

YIELD: 6 servings.

ADVANCE PREPARATION: Prepare 1 to 2 days ahead. Chill.

♦
♦
Chicken and Cucumber Soup
Huang Quar Gai Tong

An easily prepared, light, tasty soup.

> 1 boned, skinless chicken breast, cut into 1- by 1- by ⅛-inch
>   pieces
> ½ egg white (beat egg white lightly, divide in half)
> 6 cups chicken stock
> ¼ teaspoon sugar
> 1 teaspoon light soy sauce
> 1 medium cucumber, peeled, cut in half lengthwise, seeded, and
>   sliced crosswise into ⅛-inch slices
> ½ teaspoon Chinese sesame oil
> ½ teaspoon salt (optional)
> ⅛ teaspoon white pepper

Combine chicken and egg white. Set aside. Combine chicken stock, sugar, and soy sauce. Heat to boiling. Stir in cucumber and chicken mixture. Cook, stirring with chopsticks, until soup boils again. As soon as it reaches the boiling point, remove from the heat. Stir in sesame oil, salt, and pepper. Serve immediately.

MEAT

♦
♦
Beef Rendang, Nonya Style
Rendang Daging

This rich, full-flavored curry, typical of the Nonya kitchens of Singapore and Malaysia, was taught to me by sous chef Joe Yap, team captain of the Singapore International Culinary Team. It is native to Padang, West Sumatra, where it is served very, very hot and has no sauce (page 271). He says that the addition of the tamarind not only adds flavor but helps in tenderizing the meat during cooking.

Prepare a large quantity because it keeps well, developing more flavor each day. It is ideal for entertaining. With rice, it can be a one-dish meal.

SPICE MIXTURE *(Rempah)*:

> 1 tablespoon chopped fresh ginger root
> 2 cloves chopped garlic
> 4 to 6 dried chiles, soaked in warm water to soften,
>   about 5 minutes
> 2 teaspoons coriander powder
> 2 teaspoons cumin powder
> 2 tablespoons paprika
>
> 4 tablespoons oil
> 3 cups thinly sliced onions
> 1 pound sirloin or top round steak, trimmed and cut into 1-inch
>   cubes
> 2 stalks bruised lemon grass, bottom 6 inches only
> 2½ cups coconut milk
> 2 tablespoons tamarind water (page 25)
> 1 tablespoon sugar
> ½ teaspoon salt

In a mortar or processor, pound or process the ginger, garlic, and chiles, and pound or blend to a paste. Add coriander, cumin, and paprika. Mix well.

In a wok or heavy pan, heat oil over medium-high heat. Add the ground spice paste and cook for 2 to 3 minutes, stirring. Add sliced onions. Cook until softened. Add meat and bruised lemon grass, and fry until meat is browned. Add the coconut milk gradually, stirring. Add the tamarind water, sugar, and salt. Bring to a boil. Reduce heat and simmer, uncovered, until meat is tender, about 1 hour, stirring occasionally. Serve with rice or *Nasi Lemak* (page 157).

YIELD: 4 servings.

ADVANCE PREPARATION: Prepare completely ahead. Refrigerate or freeze. Reheat on moderate heat in microwave or on top of the stove, adding about ½ cup of thin coconut milk or plain milk to obtain desired consistency.

Nonya Pork Satay
Satay Babi Goreng

An easily prepared entree with an aromatic blending of spices.

½ pound shallots or 1 medium onion, chopped
8 candlenuts or macadamia nuts
2 fresh red chiles, seeded, chopped
5 to 8 dried red chiles, soaked in warm water to soften, about 5
    minutes, chopped
½ teaspoon dried shrimp paste *(belacan)*
4 tablespoons oil
1 stalk lemon grass, bottom 6 inches only, crushed with the side
    of a cleaver
3 Kaffir lime leaves (optional)
1 tablespoon coriander powder
1 pound pork tenderloin, sliced ¼ inch thick
1¼ cups thick coconut milk
½ teaspoon salt
2 teaspoons sugar

Pound or process shallots, macadamias, fresh and dried chiles, and shrimp paste. Heat oil in a wok or 3-quart saucepan over medium-high heat. Add the paste mixture and fry for 2 to 3 minutes, stirring to prevent burning. Add the lemon grass, lime leaves, and coriander. Fry an additional 1 minute, stirring. Add the pork and stir-fry for 5 minutes or until it is no longer pink. Stir in the coconut milk and bring slowly to a boil. Reduce the heat to simmer, and cook 30 minutes, or until the pork is tender, stirring occasionally. Add sugar and salt. Stir until the sugar dissolves. Remove the lemon grass and Kaffir lime leaves. Serve with rice. *Satay Babi Goreng* should be dry but with a gravy that is thick and fragrant.

YIELD: 4 servings with other dishes.

TIP: Violet Oon prefers to use "streaky pork," a type of unsmoked bacon that contains a high amount of fat. To reduce the fat content, I have substituted pork tenderloin.

ADVANCE PREPARATION: Prepare 1 day ahead. Reheat at serving time.

Inspired by a recipe from Violet Oon, editor, *The Food Paper.*

Grilled Lamb Kebabs
Khana Kabab

Low in calories and easily prepared, this favorite northern Indian kebab has a symphony of exciting flavors.

> 1 pound lean boneless lamb shoulder or leg, cut into 1-inch
>   cubes
> Juice of 1 lemon
> 1 small onion, peeled, quartered
> 2 cloves garlic, peeled, chopped
> ½ teaspoon chili powder
> ½ teaspoon turmeric powder
> 1 tablespoon vinegar
> ½ teaspoon salt
> 1 teaspoon black pepper
> ½ cup unflavored yogurt
> Lemon wedges for garnish
> 12″ Bamboo skewers, soaked in water for 1 hour to prevent
>   burning.

Place lamb in a bowl. Add lemon juice. Mix. Put the onion, garlic, chili powder, turmeric, vinegar, salt, and pepper into a blender or small food processor, and process into a coarse mixture. Add the yogurt and mix. Pour on the lamb and mix well. Cover and marinate overnight in the refrigerator.

Put the meat on skewers. Barbecue over hot coals or broil the kebabs, turning and basting once or twice until tender and cooked, approximately 10 minutes.

Serve hot with wedges of lemon.

YIELD: 4 servings.

TIP: Beef may be substituted for the lamb.

Inspired by a recipe from sous chef Kalam Kumar Channa, Tandoor Restaurant.

POULTRY

◆ Hainanese Chicken
◆ *Hainanese Gai Fayn*

One of the favorites in the Singapore hawkers' stalls is Hainanese Chicken. Simplicity in itself, this dish is a classic. Hungry Singaporeans savor the chicken and rice as a snack food. With the addition of colorful vegetables, this national favorite becomes a festive buffet or colorful picnic presentation. It can be prepared ahead completely and is served at room temperature.

1 chicken, about 2½ to 3 pounds, or 1½ pounds chicken breasts
1 teaspoon salt
4 pieces fresh ginger, the size of a quarter, peeled, crushed
2 cloves garlic, peeled, crushed
4 green onions, crushed
12 cups water, approximately
2 tablespoons Chinese sesame oil
3 tablespoons soy sauce
½ cup chicken stock
1 clove garlic, chopped
1 teaspoon cornstarch dissolved in 2 teaspoons water

½ recipe Violet Oon's Chile Sauce (page 164)
Ginger Sauce (page 165)

Optional Accompaniments:
1 to 2 cucumbers, halved lengthwise, sliced
½ pineapple, cored, halved, cut into ¼-inch slices
4 tomatoes, sliced
Coriander sprigs

Clean the chicken, removing any fatty deposits. Rub the inside of the chicken cavity with salt. Place the ginger, garlic, and green onions in the chicken cavity. Bring the water to a boil in a deep, heavy pan into which the chicken fits snugly. Heat to boiling. Reduce heat to simmer. Cover and let the chicken simmer gently for 25 minutes, turning once during cooking. To check if the chicken is done, prick the underside of the thighs to see if the juices run clear and are no longer pinkish in color. Remove the chicken carefully from the cooking water. Plunge the chicken into a large bowl of ice water. Let the chicken remain in the ice water for five minutes, turning to chill the chicken completely. (This forces the juices to retract into the chicken, making it juicy.) Drain and pat dry. Cut into bite-size pieces. Heat the sesame oil in a pot. Add soy sauce and stock, and stir until the mixture comes to a boil. Stir the cornstarch mixture into sauce. Stir until thickened and translucent. Pour over the chicken. Serve with Hainanese Chicken Rice (page 156), Violet Oon's Chile Sauce (page 164), and Ginger Sauce.

TIP: For a festive presentation place the chicken in the center of a round platter. Arrange the cucumbers, pineapple, and tomatoes around the chicken. Pour the soy sauce mixture, Ginger Sauce, and some Chile Sauce on top of the chicken. Garnish with coriander sprigs.

Inspired by a recipe from Violet Oon, editor, *The Food Paper.*

 ## Cantonese Oyster Sauce Chicken
Hauyov Gai

An attractive presentation for this colorful, tasty cold appetizer, luncheon, or buffet dish. Violet uses a whole chicken, as she says it is more flavorful. If you wish, you may substitute 2 whole chicken breasts.

1 cooked chicken, prepared in the manner of Hainanese Chicken
(page 131)
2 tablespoons oyster sauce
¾ tablespoon light soy sauce
½ tablespoon dark soy sauce
2 tablespoons peanut oil
5 tablespoons chicken stock
½ teaspoon sugar
¼ teaspoon freshly ground black pepper

1 teaspoon cornstarch dissolved in 2 tablespoons cold water
½ teaspoon Chinese sesame oil
10 ounces broccoli flowerets, peeled, blanched, drained
1 green onion, sliced (optional)

In a small pan, combine the oyster sauce, soy sauces, peanut oil, chicken stock, sugar, and pepper and bring to a boil. Stir the cornstarch and water and add to the mixture. Cook, stirring, until the sauce is thickened and translucent. Remove from the heat. Add the sesame oil. Stir. Let cool.

Remove the bones from the chicken and cut it into bite-size pieces. Arrange the chicken in the center of a round platter. Place the cooked broccoli flowerets around the chicken, making a border on the outer edge of the platter. Pour the sauce over the chicken. Garnish with green onions. Serve at room temperature.

ADVANCE PREPARATION: Prepare ahead completely, 1 to 2 days in advance. Bring to room temperature and assemble one hour before serving.

Inspired by a recipe from Violet Oon, editor, *The Food Paper.*

◆ Tandoori Chicken ◆
Tandoori Murghi

A famous northern Indian dish, Tandoori Chicken has a distinctive flavor and is bright reddish orange in color. It is cooked with fragrant Indian spices in a tandoor oven, a large clay pit that has very hot, glowing coals in the bottom. The juices of the chicken, which is cooked on a long skewer in the center of the clay oven, drip down onto the coals, giving it a unique sweet aroma.

Sous Chef Channa says that one of the secrets of Tandoor Chicken is in the long marinating in fragrant spices, which flavor and tenderize the chicken.

I have designed this recipe for cooking in a conventional oven or charcoal grill, using Chef Channa's spices.

2 chickens, or 8 chicken legs or breasts
3 tablespoons lemon juice
1 teaspoon salt

MARINADE:

> 1 tablespoon peeled, minced fresh ginger
> 3 cloves garlic, minced
> 1½ teaspoons ground cumin
> 1 teaspoon chili powder
> 2 tablespoons paprika
> 1 teaspoon coriander powder
> ½ teaspoon cardamom powder
> ¾ cup unflavored yogurt
> Oil or ghee for basting
> Lemon slices for garnish

Remove the wings and neck of chicken. Cut into quarters and remove the skin. Dry with absorbent towels. With a sharp knife, make short slashes in the chicken about ½ inch deep and 1 inch apart. Rub the chicken with lemon juice and salt.

Add the ginger and garlic to a blender or processor and process to make a paste, adding 1 tablespoon of water if necessary. Add the cumin, chili powder, paprika, coriander, cardamom, and blend. Add the yogurt and blend quickly to a smooth paste. Do not overprocess. Rub the marinade thoroughly into the chicken and let stand in a covered bowl for 4 hours or overnight in the refrigerator.

Remove the chicken from the refrigerator 1 hour before cooking. Preheat the oven to 500° F. Brush the chicken with oil or ghee, and place on a wire rack in a large, shallow roasting pan. Place in the middle of the oven and cook for 20 to 30 minutes or until cooked throughout.

OUTDOOR BARBECUING METHOD:

Prepare coals for the barbecue 1 hour in advance. Coals are ready when a white ash forms. Rub the grill generously with oil and place 5 inches from the coals.

Place the chicken, slashed side up, on the grill and brush with oil. Cook for 10 minutes. Turn, baste the other side, and cook 10 minutes longer. Continue to cook, turning every 10 minutes, until the chicken is done.

Sweet Saffron Pilaf (page 158) and Potatoes, Cauliflower, and Peas (page 153) are nice accompaniments to this dish. See Northern Indian Dinner (page 111).

YIELD: 6 servings.

TIP: Marinating of the chicken is a tenderizing process. The cooking time will take less than that of the usual roasted or barbecued chicken.

Inspired by a recipe from sous chef Kalam Kumar Channa, Tandoor Restaurant.

 ## Braised Coriander Chicken
Yuan Sai Man Gai

This tender, juicy chicken in a savory sauce is ideal for a family meal as well as a Western buffet. It can be made a day ahead and can easily be doubled or tripled. Serve it with plenty of rice and a vegetable.

3 tablespoons dark soy sauce
3 tablespoons coriander powder
2 tablespoons sugar
1 teaspoon freshly ground black pepper
One 2- to 3-pound chicken, cut into 8 pieces
2 tablespoons oil
2 large onions, finely sliced
1 clove garlic, crushed
1 piece fresh ginger, the size of a quarter, smashed
3 cups water
1 tablespoon cornstarch dissolved in 2 tablespoons water
Salt and pepper to taste

Combine the soy sauce, coriander powder, sugar, and pepper. Add the chicken to the mixture and marinate for 20 to 30 minutes. Heat the oil in a wok. Add the onions, garlic, and ginger, and stir-fry over moderate heat until the onions are soft and translucent. Add the chicken and marinade and stir-fry until the chicken is lightly browned. Add the water and bring to a boil. Reduce the heat to simmer, and simmer for 20 to 30 minutes or until the chicken is tender. Add dissolved cornstarch to the wok. Cook, stirring, until the sauce has thickened and is translucent. Season to taste with salt and pepper. Serve with rice.

ADVANCE PREPARATION: Prepare 1 to 2 days in advance and refrigerate. Freeze for 1 to 2 months. Reheat at serving time.

◆ Stir-Fried Squab with Asparagus
◆ *Butt Shuan Chao Bak Kab*

Colors, textures, tastes, and contrasts abound in this simple but refreshing dish. For a superb presentation, offer your succulent dish in a Bird's Nest potato basket.

1 pound squab fillets

MARINADE:

1 egg white, lightly beaten
2 teaspoons soy sauce
2 teaspoons sherry
1 tablespoon cornstarch

½ pound fresh asparagus
4 tablespoons oil
1 clove garlic, minced
2 teaspoons peeled, minced fresh ginger
1 carrot, shredded into 1½-inch lengths
1 green onion, shredded into 1½-inch lengths

SAUCE MIXTURE: Combine and set aside.

1 tablespoon plus 2 teaspoons soy sauce
1 tablespoon plus 2 teaspoons oyster-flavored sauce
1 teaspoon Chinese sesame oil

Shredded lettuce for garnish
Bird's Nest (page 160) (optional)

Cut squab fillets into ½-inch slices. Combine marinade and add to the squab. Let marinate for 20 minutes.

Trim and discard the woody bottom ends of the asparagus spears. Peel the lower third of the spears. Cut them on the diagonal into 1½-inch-long pieces. Heat 2 tablespoons oil in a wok. Add the garlic and ginger. Stir until fragrant, about 10 seconds. Add squab and stir-fry until tender, about 2 minutes, or until the squab is cooked. Remove and set aside. Add 2 more tablespoons oil. Add the asparagus. Stir-fry for 1 minute. Add the carrot. Stir-fry for 2 minutes or until crispy tender. Add cooked squab and green onions. Stir. Stir the sauce mixture and add to the wok. Arrange lettuce on a plate. Place the cooked dish in Bird's Nests, if desired. Serve.

YIELD: 2 to 3 servings.

TIP: If squab is unavailable, substitute chicken breast.

Inspired by a recipe from Heinz Von Holzen, chef des cuisines, Hyatt Regency Singapore.

FISH AND SEAFOOD

 ### Curry Fish in Banana Leaves, Nonya Style
Chiu Yip Kar Li Yu

Violet Oon prepares this dish with white or silver pomfret, a highly prized fish regarded as a great delicacy. You may purchase frozen pomfret in Asian markets.

1 pomfret, red snapper, or pike, cleaned and scaled, head and tail
    intact, approximately 1½ to 2 pounds
6 shallots, chopped
2 cloves garlic, chopped
2 tablespoons chopped fresh ginger
2 to 3 fresh red chiles, seeded, minced
1½ tablespoons Oriental curry powder
1 tablespoon paprika
2 tablespoons tomato ketchup
6 tablespoons water
1 tablespoon oil
2 teaspoons brown sugar
½ teaspoon salt (optional)
Banana leaves (page 26)
1 fresh red chile, seeds removed, sliced
1 lemon, sliced
Parsley sprigs (optional)

Wash the fish and pat dry. Make 3 diagonal cuts almost to the bone on each side. In a mortar, blender, or mini-processor combine the shallots, garlic, ginger, and chiles. Pound or process to a paste. Add the curry powder, paprika, ketchup, water, oil, sugar, and salt and process into a coarse paste. Rub some of the mixture into the fish cavity. Spread the remaining mixture over the fish. Marinate for 30 minutes.

    Pour boiling water over the banana leaf to make it pliable and to prevent splitting. Place the fish in the middle of a large square of a

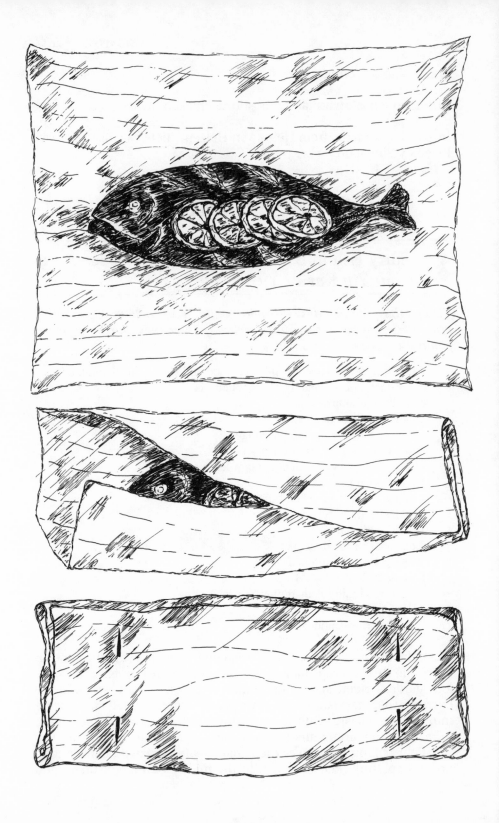

banana leaf. Place the chile, lemon slices and parlsey sprigs on top of the fish. Fold into a neat parcel, keeping the seam side on top. Secure with a metal skewer or a toothpick. Grill fish over glowing coals, allowing 10 minutes per inch of thickness of the fish. Serve fish in the banana leaves with rice, vegetables, and a sambal.

YIELD: 2 to 3 servings.

TIPS: Violet Oon prepares the fish by dry-frying the fish in a frying pan on medium heat on top of the stove. Cook one side, pressing down on the banana leaf, then turn over and cook the other side.

VARIATIONS: Fish fillets may be substituted. Overlap fillets and wrap in one or two packages.

Aluminum foil may be substituted for banana leaves, but the fish will not have the pleasant fragrance of the banana leaf. To prevent juices from leaking, wrap aluminum foil around banana leaf before grilling.

ADVANCE PREPARATION: Wrap fish several hours ahead. Refrigerate. Cook at serving time.

 ## Baked Curry Fish in Banana Leaves
Chui Yip Kar Li Yu

Prepare fish as for Curry Fish in Banana Leaves (page 137).
Preheat oven to 450° F. Bake package, allowing 10 to 12 minutes per inch of thickness of fish.

Steamed Fish with Black Beans
Dau Shi Ching Yu

Few seasonings complement the delicate flavor of fresh fish as well as fermented black beans. Topped with green onions and ginger, this dish is equally pleasing to the eye as to the palate.

    1 whole fish (red snapper, sea bass, pike), about 1½ to 2 pounds,
        cleaned, scaled, with head and tail intact
    2 tablespoons fermented (salted) black beans
    2 cloves garlic
    2 tablespoons light soy sauce
    2 tablespoons dry sherry
    ½ teaspoon sugar
    3 slices ginger, each the size of a quarter, shredded
    4 green onions, shredded into 2-inch lengths
    ½ red bell pepper, shredded into 2-inch lengths (optional)
    2 tablespoons peanut oil
    1 tablespoon Chinese sesame oil

Score the fish crosswise, cutting diagonally into the flesh, making 3 or 4 equal diagonal cuts deep to the backbone but not through.

Rinse the black beans with water. Drain. Coarsely chop the black beans and garlic together. (Do not make a paste or the beans will become bitter.) Combine the soy sauce, sherry, and sugar. Place the fish on a heatproof plate in an upright position. Pour the soy sauce mixture over the fish and rub into the fish. Scatter the black beans, garlic, shredded ginger, green onions, and red bell pepper over the fish.

Place the fish in a steamer large enough to hold the fish upright. If a large enough steamer is not available, cut the fish in half and reconstruct when serving. Steam the fish about 10 minutes per pound over high heat until the fish is no longer translucent.

When the fish is done, remove the plate from the steamer. Heat the oil and sesame oil in a small saucepan almost to the smoking point and pour the mixture over the fish to produce a sheen and add richness and flavor.

To serve, fillet the fish at the table. Start just below the head and make a horizontal cut down the backbone to the tail using the back of two spoons. Lift off the pieces of the fish from one side, then the other side. Serve with the pan juices.

YIELDS 2 to 3 servings.

Fried Fish with Ginger Sauce
Kaing Chup Yu

The tantalizing ginger sauce has interesting textures and a distinctive flavor. My preference for this dish is red snapper. This is a must for ginger lovers!

> 6 Chinese dried black mushrooms, soaked in hot water for 20 minutes or until spongy, stems removed, shredded
> ½ cup rice vinegar
> ⅔ cup light brown sugar
> 1½ cups water
> ⅓ cup dark soy sauce
> 4 green onions, thinly sliced
> ⅓ cup fresh peeled and minced ginger
> Juice of 2 limes
> 1 tablespoon cornstarch dissolved in 3 tablespoons cold water
> ⅓ cup cornstarch
> ½ teaspoon salt
> ¼ teaspoon freshly ground black pepper
> 1 whole white-fleshed fish, 2 to 2½ pounds (red snapper, sea bass, pike), scaled, cleaned, dried
> 4 to 6 cups oil

GARNISH:

> 4 tablespoons coriander leaves
> 2 to 3 fresh red chiles, cut into fine shreds

In a medium pan, combine mushrooms, vinegar, sugar, water, and soy sauce. Bring to boil over medium heat and continue boiling, stirring occasionally for 2 to 3 minutes. Add the green onions and ginger. Stir and continue cooking until the green onions are soft. Add the lime juice. Stir. Add dissolved cornstarch mixture to pan, stirring until the sauce is smooth and has a glaze. Remove from heat. Set aside.

Combine the cornstarch, salt, and pepper. Mix. Make deep scores on each side of the fish, almost to the center bone, forming diamond shapes on the fish. Dip the fish into the seasoned cornstarch to coat completely. Dust off the excess cornstarch.

Heat oil in a wok to 375° F. Slowly immerse the fish into the oil, head first. Ladle the hot oil over the fish to brown lightly on each side. Fry until crisp golden on the first side, approximately 3 to 6 minutes.

Using two spatulas, turn the fish carefully and fry on the other side until it is golden. Gently remove the fish with two spatulas. Drain on paper towels. Place on a large heated serving platter. Reheat the sauce and pour over the fish. Garnish with coriander leaves and red chiles. Serve immediately.

YIELD: 2 to 3 servings.

ADVANCE PREPARATION: Prepare sauce and fry fish several hours ahead. At serving time, reheat oil. Fry the fish again to crisp and reheat throughout. Drain on paper towels. Place on a heated serving platter. Reheat the sauce and pour over the top, covering the fish completely.

Inspired by a recipe from Violet Oon, editor, *The Food Paper.*

 ### Stir Fried Shrimp in Tomato Sauce, Cantonese Style
Har Loke

Violet Oon, editor of The Food Paper, *showed me the preparation of this popular tangy Chinese stir-fry. Seasoned with garlic, ginger, black beans, ketchup, and oyster sauce, this dish is full of flavor and aroma.*

- 1 pound large shrimp, shelled and deveined
- 2 cloves garlic, chopped
- 1½ teaspoons chopped fresh ginger
- 4 teaspoons dry sherry
- 1 tablespoon fermented (salted) black beans
- 6 tablespoons ketchup
- 4 teaspoons oyster sauce
- 2 tablespoons sugar
- ½ teaspoon salt
- 2 tablespoons oil
- 2 green onions, shredded, for garnish

Combine the shrimp, garlic, ginger, and sherry and let marinate for 20 minutes. Rinse the black beans with water. Drain. Chop finely and mix with ketchup, oyster sauce, sugar, and salt. Heat wok. Add oil. Add the shrimp and stir-fry over high heat until they turn pink. Add the bean mixture, and stir until combined and the shrimp are coated, about 30 seconds. Add the green onions and stir. Remove from wok and serve.

YIELD: 3 to 4 servings.

◆◆ Tamarind Shrimp
Udang Goreng Asam
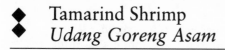

A popular dish, served both in Singapore and Malaysia. Singapore's famous Violet Oon, editor of The Food Paper, *served this as part of a buffet. It is equally good hot or at room temperature.*

3 tablespoons tamarind paste
½ cup boiling water
½ teaspoon chili powder
½ teaspoon salt
½ teaspoon sugar
1½ pounds jumbo shrimp, shells intact
⅔ cup vegetable oil
1 cucumber, cut in half, seeds removed, cut into thin slices

In a small bowl combine the tamarind paste with ½ cup boiling water. Let stand for 30 minutes. Strain, pressing hard, to obtain a thick paste. Add the chili powder, salt, and sugar, and stir to mix. Add the shrimp and stir, covering each shrimp well. Marinate, stirring occasionally, for at least 30 minutes.

Remove shrimp and drain well. In a large skillet or wok, heat oil until hot but not smoking. Add shrimp and fry, stirring, for 3 to 4 minutes until they are firm, crisp, and brown. Drain on paper towels. Place on a platter and serve garnished with cucumber.

YIELD: 4 servings.

TIP: Shrimp may be shelled and deveined before cooking if preferred. The taste will not be quite as succulent.

◆ Shrimp Curry with Pineapple
◆ Bor Lor Kar Li Har

This delicious Nonya curry is made even more interesting and colorful by the addition of pineapple.

1 stalk lemon grass, bottom 6 inches only, thinly sliced
5 dried red chiles, soaked in warm water for 5 minutes or until
    softened
2 to 4 fresh red chiles, chopped
5 green onions, chopped
3 cloves garlic, minced
3 tablespoons coriander powder
1 teaspoon turmeric powder
¾ teaspoon shrimp paste (*belacan*)
2 tablespoons oil
2 cups thin coconut milk
¾ pound medium-size shrimp, shelled, cleaned, deveined
1 small pineapple, skinned, cored, cut into bite-size triangular
    wedges
⅓ cup thick coconut milk
Salt to taste

In a mortar or processor, pound or process lemon grass, chiles, green onions, garlic, coriander, turmeric, and shrimp paste to a smooth paste. Heat frying pan. Add oil and heat. Add paste mixture. Stir the mixture over moderate heat for 3 to 5 minutes. If necessary, add 2 to 3 tablespoons thin coconut milk to keep the mixture in the pan moist and prevent burning. Add shrimp and stir for 1 minute. Add remaining thin coconut milk and pineapple. Cook until pineapple is soft. Add thick coconut milk and continue cooking for 1 minute, or until heated throughout. Add salt to taste. Serve with rice.

YIELD: 2 to 3 servings.

ADVANCE PREPARATION: Prepare ahead completely. Reheat at serving time.

Shrimp in Spiced Sauce
Jhinga Samurkundh

An easily prepared spicy Northern Indian shrimp dish.

- 8 tablespoons oil
- 1 small onion, peeled, chopped
- 1 tablespoon peeled, finely minced fresh ginger
- 1 tablespoon finely minced garlic

SEASONINGS: Combine and set aside in a small dish

- 1 teaspoon red chili powder
- 1 tablespoon *garam masala* (page 27)
- 1 teaspoon coriander powder (optional)
- 1 teaspoon turmeric powder
- ½ teaspoon salt

- 1 pound shrimp, shelled, deveined
- 2 tablespoons tomato paste
- 2 tablespoons fresh coriander leaves
- 1 cup cream

Heat oil in frying pan over moderate flame. Add chopped onion, ginger, and garlic. Stir until softened. Add the seasonings to the pan and stir to mix. Cook over moderate heat for 1 to 2 minutes to blend spices. Add the shrimp and tomato paste. Cook for 2 minutes or until shrimp are cooked. Add the coriander leaves and cream and cook until heated throughout. Serve.

YIELD: 4 servings.

Inspired by a recipe from Sous Chef Kalam Kumar Channa, Tandoor Restaurant.

◆ Steamed Shrimp with Green Onions ◆
◆ *Chun Yau Ching Har* ◆

I first experienced this easily prepared, attractive, delicately flavored shrimp dish during a Chinese New Year celebration at the Garden Seafood Restaurant with Violet Oon, editor of The Food Paper. *The beautiful large shrimp available in Southeast Asia made this a very impressive and inviting dish.*

> 1 pound jumbo shrimp, shelled, deveined
> 1 tablespoon oil
>
> SAUCE MIXTURE: Combine and set aside
>
> 1 tablespoon Chinese rice wine or pale dry sherry
> ½ teaspoon five-spice powder
> ½ teaspoon salt
> ¼ teaspoon white pepper
> 2 teaspoons Chinese sesame oil
>
> 2 teaspoons finely shredded peeled fresh ginger
> 2 tablespoons chopped green onions
> 2 egg whites, lightly beaten

Fill a steamer with 2 to 3 inches of water or put a rack into a wok or large deep pan and fill it with water almost to the rack. Bring the water to a boil.

Pat the shrimp dry. Cut shrimp in half lengthwise. Arrange the shrimp in a pinwheel pattern on a lightly oiled heatproof serving plate. Pour the sauce mixture over the shrimp. Sprinkle the ginger and green onions over the shrimp. Pour the egg whites over the shrimp, covering the entire plate.

Gently lower the plate into the steamer. Cover the pan tightly and lower the heat. Steam for approximately 5 to 10 minutes, or until the shrimp are pink, springy in texture, and cooked throughout. Check the water level of the steamer occasionally and replenish with water if necessary.

YIELD: 4 to 6 servings with other dishes.

ADVANCE PREPARATION: Assemble the shrimp dish several hours before steaming. Cover with plastic wrap and refrigerate.

VARIATION: Sprinkle 1 to 2 teaspoons hot chili oil over the cooked shrimp, for a more spirited dish.

YIELD: 3 to 4 servings.

SALADS AND VEGETABLES

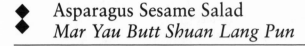

Asparagus Sesame Salad
Mar Yau Butt Shuan Lang Pun

A cool, refreshing, easily prepared do-ahead salad.

> 1 pound asparagus, stems peeled, tough ends removed, cut on
> diagonal into 1½-inch pieces

SALAD DRESSING: Combine and set aside.

> 2 tablespoons lemon juice
> 2 tablespoons oil
> Salt to taste
> Dash white pepper
>
> Lettuce (optional)
> 1 green onion, shredded into 1½-inch lengths
> ¼ cup toasted white sesame seeds

In a steamer over boiling water, steam the asparagus for 2 to 4 minutes. Remove. Rinse with cold water. Cool. (The asparagus should be crisp.) Pour the dressing over salad. Refrigerate until chilled. Serve on a bed of lettuce. Garnish with green onion shreds and sesame seeds.

YIELD: 4 servings.

TIP: To toast sesame seeds, heat a small pan over medium-high heat. Add the sesame seeds and toast, stirring occasionally, until lightly browned.

◆ Vegetable Salad with Tangy Peanut Sauce
◆ Gado-Gado, *Singapore Style*

A bouquet of color will greet your guests when you serve this cool and refreshing do-ahead Nonya salad. This presentation is perfect for a summer dinner, a picnic, or a formal buffet. The zesty peanut sauce is even better when prepared a day ahead and the flavors have a chance to mellow.

½ teaspoon dried shrimp paste *(belacan)*
2 to 4 fresh red chile peppers, seeds removed, minced
3 tablespoons dark soy sauce
¼ cup fresh lime juice
2 tablespoons brown sugar
2 teaspoons granulated sugar
¾ cup peanut butter
½ cup water
½ teaspoon salt (optional)
8 ounces firm bean curd (tofu), cut in half horizontally
1 cup oil
2 cups tightly packed watercress, washed, drained, lower stems
    removed
12 green beans, tips removed, cut into 2-inch lengths
3 carrots, peeled, cut into slices
2 zucchini, cut into ¼-inch-thick slices
6 ounces Chinese cabbage, finely shredded
2 medium potatoes
4 hard-boiled eggs, quartered lengthwise

Wrap shrimp paste in foil. Toast in a dry frying pan on moderate heat for 1 minute on each side. Remove from heat.

In a blender or processor, process the toasted shrimp paste, chiles, soy sauce, lime juice, and sugars to a smooth paste. Add peanut butter and water. Add salt if desired. Process to a smooth sauce. Set aside.

Put the bean curd halves on a plate and set another plate on top of the bean curd. Place a 4- to 5-pound weight on the plate. Press the bean curd for 30 minutes. Drain. Pat dry. Cut into 1-inch by 1-inch pieces. Add oil to a heated pan. Heat to 375° F and fry the bean curd until the exterior of the cubes forms a crisp, golden brown skin. Drain and set aside on paper towels.

In a saucepan, bring 3 quarts water to a boil. Add watercress and blanch for 15 to 20 seconds. Remove with a strainer. Drain. Refresh with cold water. Blanch the green beans, carrots, and zucchini separately for 2 minutes each. Remove with a strainer. Drain. Refresh with cold water. Add the cabbage and blanch for 30 seconds. Drain. Refresh with cold water. Cook potatoes in water until done. Let cool. Peel and cut into ¼-inch slices. Arrange the ingredients in separate mounds in a decorative fashion on a large platter. Pour the sauce over the vegetables. Garnish with hard-boiled eggs. Serve.

YIELD: 6 to 8 servings with other dishes.

TIP: Choose your own selection of vegetables, making sure they are cut and cooked according to their density.

ADVANCE PREPARATION: Prepare completely in advance. Assemble hours before serving. Cover with plastic wrap and refrigerate. Pour peanut sauce over the salad when serving. Serve warm, room temperature, or cold.

 ## Indian Spiced Fruit Salad
Chat

In central and northern India, this flavorful combination of spiced fruits is served as an accompaniment to the main course to refresh the palate and sooth the senses. Sous Chef Channa uses fresh fruits in season when preparing his Chat.

It is great for a Western meal as an appetizer, a dinner accompaniment, or a spiced dessert.

2 small oranges, peeled, sectioned, outer white membrane
     removed
2 bananas, peeled, sliced
2 apples, peeled, sliced into ¼-inch bite-size slices
2 pears, peeled, sliced into ¼-inch bite-size slices
1 large fresh mango, peeled, sliced thinly into bite-size pieces
20 seedless grapes
Juice of 1 to 2 limes
1 tablespoon peeled fresh ginger, shredded
2 to 4 hot red or green chiles, seeds removed, finely shredded
2 teaspoons *garam masala* (page 27)
1 tablespoon sugar
Salt to taste
Fresh mint leaves for garnish (optional)

Put the fruit in a bowl. Add the lime juice and mix well to keep the fruit from discoloring. In a small bowl, combine the ginger, chiles, *garam masala,* sugar, and salt. Mix. Add the mixture to the fruit. Toss until the fruit is coated. Chill in refrigerator for 2 hours. Garnish with mint leaves.

YIELD: 6 servings.

TIP: If oranges are large, cut sections into halves. Mandarin oranges may be substituted for the oranges.

ADVANCE PREPARATION: Prepare completely in advance. Store in refrigerator for several hours covered with plastic wrap.

Inspired by a recipe from Chef Kalam Kumar Channa, Tandoor Restaurant.

 ## Spicy Chicken Shred, Vegetable, and Noodle Salad
Shau Shi Gai

A delightful cold noodle salad combining fresh egg noodles, chicken and vegetables. Serve as a meal-in-one or as an impressive and attractive buffet or dinner dish with other entrees. If you wish, you may make this a vegetarian salad by adding more vegetables of your choice and omitting the chicken.

This is a salad which I serve often. It can be prepared in advance, doubled or tripled.

8 ounces fresh thin Chinese egg noodles
3 tablespoons Chinese sesame oil
2 cups bean sprouts
1 chicken breast, skinned, boned
½ cup soy sauce
¼ cup Chinese black vinegar
2½ tablespoons creamy peanut butter
2 tablespoons sugar
2 tablespoons oil
2 to 6 dried red peppers
1 tablespoon peeled, minced ginger
2 teaspoons minced garlic
2 cups Chinese cabbage or leafy lettuce, shredded

    1 cup green onions, shredded into 1½-inch pieces
    2 cups cucumbers halved, seeded, shredded
    1 red bell pepper, shredded into 1½-inch lengths
    ⅓ cup chopped roasted peanuts

Cook the noodles in 4 quarts water until *al dente*. Rinse with cold water. Chill. Drain well. Toss with 1 tablespoon sesame oil. Place in a plastic bag. Chill. Blanch the bean sprouts in water to cover for 45 seconds. Remove. Refresh with cold water. Drain.

    Steam chicken breasts in a heatproof bowl over boiling water for 20 minutes or until tender. Let the chicken cool in the cooking liquid. Remove. Drain. Shred into ½-inch strips. Chill.

    Combine soy sauce, vinegar, peanut butter, and sugar. Mix well with a whisk. Heat wok. Add remaining sesame oil and oil. Heat. Add the dried peppers and press against the side of the wok until peppers have darkened. Add ginger and garlic and stir until fragrant, about 10 seconds. Stir in the soy sauce mixture. Cook, stirring, for about 10 seconds or until blended. Remove from the heat. Let cool to room temperature.

    Place the chilled noodles on a serving platter. Sprinkle the cabbage, bean sprouts, and half the green onions on the noodles. Arrange the chicken shreds neatly on the cabbage mixture. Place the shredded cucumber around the edge of the platter. Pour the sauce over the chicken just before serving. Sprinkle the remaining green onions, red bell pepper, and peanuts over the top in a decorative fashion. Serve at room temperature. Toss the salad just before eating.

TIP: Substitute cooked shrimp or pork for chicken. Omit chicken and use vegetables of your choice.

If substituting thin dry vermicelli, use 6 ounces. Cook *al dente*.

ADVANCE PREPARATION: Prepare all ingredients and salad dressing ahead. Assemble the salad several hours before serving. Cover with plastic wrap. Refrigerate. Bring to room temperature when serving. Combine with sauce when ready to serve.

◆ Spicy Seafood Salad
◆ *Hoi Shin Lang Pun*

A colorful, easily prepared salad with interesting textures and refreshing flavors. It is perfect for a buffet or a light summer supper.

½ pound shrimp, shelled, cleaned, deveined
½ pound scallops
1 cup oil
½ cup slivered blanched almonds
4 egg roll wrappers, cut into ¼-inch strips
1 small head romaine lettuce, rinsed, dried, shredded into ¼-inch shreds
½ pound snow peas

SALAD DRESSING: Combine and set aside

1 clove garlic, peeled, minced
1 tablespoon peeled, minced fresh ginger
2 tablespoons light soy sauce
1 tablespoon red wine vinegar
1 tablespoon Chinese sesame oil
1 to 2 teaspoons hot chile oil
2 teaspoons sugar
Salt to taste

Cook the shrimp in boiling water until just pink. Drain. Rinse under cold running water. Drain. Cut into ¼-inch slices. Set aside. Cook the scallops in boiling water until firm and translucent. Drain. Rinse with cold water. Drain. Pat dry with paper towels. Cut crosswise into ¼-inch slices. Set aside. In wok, heat 1 cup oil to 350° F. Cook almonds in oil until golden, about 15 seconds. Remove and drain. Fry the egg roll strips, a few at a time, until golden. Remove and drain on paper towels. Set aside. Place the lettuce on a serving dish. Add shrimp, scallops, and snow peas. Pour the dressing over the salad. Garnish with egg roll strips and slivered almonds.

YIELD: 3 to 4 servings.

ADVANCE PREPARATION: Salad dressing may be prepared several days ahead. Prepare remaining ingredients 1 day in advance. Combine ingredients one-half hour before serving.

◆ Potatoes, Cauliflower, and Peas
Aloo Gobi Matar

A very attractive, colorful Northern Indian entree traditionally served during banquets and weddings. Chef Kalam Kumar Channa highlights this with a touch of Kashmiri influenced spices.

You may vary his combination of vegetables by substituting green beans, zucchini, green peppers, and/or mushrooms.

1 cup cauliflowerets
2 medium potatoes, peeled, cut into bite-size cubes
1½ cups fresh green peas, or 10 ounces frozen green peas
½ teaspoon turmeric powder
1 teaspoon cumin powder
¾ teaspoon chili powder
1 teaspoon coriander powder
4 tablespoons oil or ghee
1½ cups pureed or finely chopped fresh ripe tomatoes
Salt to taste
2 tablespoons chopped coriander leaves

Parboil separately the cauliflower, potatoes, and fresh peas until almost tender. Drain. Set aside to dry on paper towels.

Combine the turmeric, cumin, chili, and coriander powders. Heat ghee in frying pan over moderate flame. Add the seasonings to the pan. Stir a few seconds to release flavors. Add the cauliflower, potatoes, and peas, and stir-fry until they are very lightly browned. Add the tomatoes and continue cooking over low heat for 1 to 2 minutes, crushing the tomatoes with back of a spoon. Add about ¼ cup water. Reduce heat to simmer. Cover and cook, stirring occasionally, for about 5–10 minutes, or until vegetables are tender. Add salt to taste. Garnish with coriander leaves. Serve.

YIELD: 4 servings.

TIP: If using frozen peas, add during last 5 minutes of cooking time and cook until tender.

ADVANCE PREPARATION: Prepare ahead and reheat.

Inspired by a recipe from Sous Chef Kalam Kumar Channa, Tandoor Restaurant.

Grilled Eggplant
Kaw Kar Chee

Simply prepared, Grilled Eggplant is an interesting vegetable preparation.

4 Chinese eggplants
1 teaspoon pepper
1 tablespoon dark soy sauce
2 tablespoons oil

Cut the eggplants in half. Score the inside of the eggplants in a criss-cross manner. Marinate the eggplants with the pepper, soy sauce, and oil for 15 minutes. Grill or broil for 4 to 6 minutes on each side. Serve with Chile Sauce (page 321).

YIELD: 4 servings.

TIP: If Chinese eggplants are unavailable, substitute small eggplants. Cut into 1-inch slices and treat as above.

Mixed Vegetable Medley
Chup Kum Choy

A bouquet of colors and flavors graces this easily prepared stir-fry.

2 tablespoons oil
2 teaspoons minced fresh ginger
1 teaspoon minced garlic
2 cups bok choy hearts, cut into bite-size pieces
12 snow peas, strings removed
One 8-ounce can baby corn, drained
One 8-ounce can straw mushrooms, drained
½ cup sliced bamboo shoots
¼ cup sliced water chestnuts
12 cherry tomatoes, halved

SAUCE MIXTURE: Combine and set aside.

2 tablespoons light soy sauce
1 tablespoon dry sherry
1 to 2 teaspoons hot chile oil (optional)
1 teaspoon sugar

Heat wok. Add 2 tablespoons oil. Heat. Add the ginger and garlic. Stir until fragrant. Add the bok choy and snow peas. Stir-fry until the snow peas turn jade green in color. Add the baby corn, straw mushrooms, bamboo shoots, and water chestnuts. Stir-fry until heated throughout, about 1 minute. Add the sauce mixture. Stir. Add the tomatoes and cook until heated throughout. Serve.

VARIATION: Chicken or shrimp may be cooked and added to the above dish.

RICE, NOODLES AND WRAPPERS

 ### Yangchow Fried Rice
Yangchow Chao Fayn

Fried rice is always a favorite. It can be prepared in many ways, but the highest form of preparation is in the style of Yangchow, considered the best in China. Traditionally the frying is done in lard. I have substituted oil. Yangchow Fried Rice is often served at the end of a festive Chinese banquet.

For good fried rice, the rice should be cold and firm so that it may be separated to prevent lumping during the fast stir-frying process.

4 ounces shrimp, shelled, deveined, cut into ¼-inch pieces
½ teaspoon cornstarch
½ teaspoon dry sherry
½ teaspoon salt
4 to 5 tablespoons oil
3 eggs, lightly beaten with a pinch of salt and white pepper
3 cups cold, cooked, long-grain rice (1 cup uncooked rice)
½ cup frozen peas, defrosted
4 ounces Chinese barbecued pork, *char siew,* cut into ¼-inch cubes
1 tablespoon light soy sauce
¼ teaspoon sugar
½ cup minced green onions
Salt to taste

Pat the shrimp dry. Marinate the shrimp in cornstarch and sherry for 15 minutes. Add 2 tablespoons oil to the wok. Heat. Add the shrimp. Stir-fry until the shrimp turn pink, about 30 seconds. Remove and set aside. Add 2 tablespoons oil to wok. Heat. Add the rice, stirring rapidly, and cook until thoroughly heated, without browning. Quickly make a well in the center of the rice. Add 1 tablespoon oil, if necessary. Add the egg mixture, stirring constantly. When it has a soft-scrambled consistency, start incorporating the rice, stirring it in a circular fashion with chopsticks. When the rice and eggs are blended, add the peas and stir to mix. Stir in the cooked shrimp, barbecued pork, soy sauce, and sugar, and continue stir-frying for about 2 minutes or until well combined and heated throughout. Add the green onions and salt. Combine. Remove from heat and serve.

YIELD: 4 servings with other dishes.

TIP: If you do not care to make barbecued pork, purchase it in your local Chinese restaurant. Diced roast pork or ham may be substituted for barbecued pork.

ADVANCE PREPARATION: The cooked rice can be kept warm, covered in a serving bowl in a 250 ° F oven for 30 minutes. Add the green onions when serving.

Inspired by a recipe from Violet Oon, editor, *The Food Paper.*

 ## Hainanese Chicken Rice
Nasi Ayam Goreng Hainanese

A taste treat that is usually served with Hainanese Chicken.

    2 cups long-grain rice
    2½ tablespoons peanut oil
    2 cloves garlic, peeled, finely minced
    5 shallots, peeled, finely minced
    3½ cups chicken stock (from Hainanese chicken)
    ½ teaspoon salt

Wash rice well and drain in colander. Set aside for one-half hour to dry.

Heat wok. Add oil. Heat. Add garlic and shallots. Stir-fry over high heat until soft. Add the rice and stir for a few minutes, making sure the rice does not stick to the wok. Transfer to a deep pot and add the Hainanese chicken stock and salt. Bring to a boil over high heat. When water evaporates to the level of the rice, turn the heat to simmer. Cover and cook for 40 minutes. Serve with Hainanese Chicken.

YIELD: 4 to 6 servings.

Inspired by a recipe from Violet Oon, editor, *The Food Paper.*

 ## Coconut-Flavored Rice
Nasi Lemak

An easily prepared classic Nonya rice dish.

Nasi Lemak *is like the proof of the pudding as far as Nonya tradition goes. Legend has it that if the groom's mother presented* Nasi Lemak *to the bride's mother twelve days after the wedding, the bride was indeed a virgin.*

> 1½ cups long-grain rice
> 2½ cups coconut milk
> 1 pandan or bay leaf
> Salt to taste

Wash rice in several changes of water. Drain. Place rice and coconut milk in a heavy pan. Add pandan leaf. Bring to boil, stirring once or twice, then lower the heat and simmer, uncovered, until all the milk has been absorbed into the rice. Stir once, then lower the heat. Cover the pan with a tight-fitting cover. Cook on very low heat for 10 minutes. Serve hot. Typical accompaniments are sliced hard-boiled eggs, sliced cucumber, and fried peanuts.

YIELD: 4 servings.

TIP: In Singapore, pandan leaves would be used for this rice. Powdered daun pandan (screwpine leaf) is available in Oriental grocery stores. Use ½ teaspoon of the powdered daun pandan.

Inspired by a recipe from sous chef Joe Yap, Westin Hotel, and Singapore Culinary Team Captain.

Sweet Saffron Pilaf
Zarda

Yellow, glistening, sweet saffron rice is a favorite of the Muslims. They enjoy this flavorful golden yellow rice with hot, spicy foods or alone as a snack. Sous Chef Channa says that to enjoy this festive rice to its fullest, it is best to use high-quality saffron. Because saffron is expensive, you may substitute or add yellow food coloring to obtain the bright, traditional color. However, the wonderful aromatics of the saffron will be lacking.

This elegant pilaf goes with all Northern Indian and Moghul dishes such as Tandoori Chicken. It is also good with seafood and other Singaporean and Malaysian curries.

1 cup basmati or other long-grain white rice, washed (page 21)
½ teaspoon saffron threads
1¾ to 2 cups water
4 tablespoons oil or ghee
2 tablespoons unsalted, shelled pistachios
5 whole cardamom pods
1½-inch stick of cinnamon
5 whole cloves
⅓ teaspoon salt
5 to 7 tablespoons sugar, depending upon sweetness desired
2 tablespoons golden raisins

Place washed rice in a bowl. Add 4 cups cold water and let soak for 30 minutes. Drain thoroughly. Crumble saffron in a small bowl. Add 2½ tablespoons boiling water. Stir. Soaĸ for 15 minutes. Heat the oil over medium heat in a heavy-bottom pan. When hot, add the pistachios. Stir-fry for 5 seconds or until very lightly browned. Remove. Chop. Set aside. Add cardamom, cinnamon, and cloves, and fry until they are lightly browned and puffed (about 1 minute). Add drained rice, and fry until the rice is thoroughly coated with the oil and begins to brown (about 3 minutes), stirring to prevent burning. Add 1⅓ cups water, saffron and saffron soaking water, salt, sugar, and raisins. Stir well to keep rice from settling. Bring to a boil. Reduce heat and simmer partially covered, for approximately 10 minutes or until most of the water is absorbed and the surface of the rice has steamy holes. Cover the pan with a tight-fitting lid and very gently simmer for 10 minutes. Remove from heat and let rice rest, covered, for 5 minutes to allow the fragile grains to firm up. Do not stir the rice during the final 15 minutes of steaming and resting. Uncover and fluff the rice with a fork. Remove the cardamom, cinnamon, and cloves. Place rice in a serving bowl. Sprinkle with chopped pistachios.

YIELD: 4 servings.

TIP: The rice will remain warm for 20 minutes after resting.

Inspired by a recipe from Sous Chef Kalam Kumar Channa, Tandoor Restaurant.

 ## Stir-Fried Rice Noodles with Chicken and Broccoli
Kai Lan Gai Chao Fun

Delicately seasoned vegetables and chicken top charred rice noodles in this delectable one-dish meal.

> 8 ounces fresh flat rice noodles, cut into ½-inch slices, or 6
>   ounces flat dried ½-inch rice noodles
> ½ pound broccoli
> ¼ cup oil
> 3 cloves garlic, minced
> 6 Chinese dried black mushrooms, soaked in hot water for 20
>   minutes or until spongy, stems removed, shredded
> 1 pound chicken breast, shredded into 1½ inch matchstrick strips

SAUCE MIXTURE: Combine in a bowl and set aside.

> 1 tablespoon oyster sauce
> 1 tablespoon plus 2 teaspoons soy sauce
> 1 tablespoon fish sauce *(nam pla)*
> ½ teaspoon sugar
> ½ cup chicken stock
> 1 tablespoon cornstarch dissolved in 2 tablespoons water

Blanch the fresh rice noodles in boiling water for 15 to 20 seconds. Rinse. Drain. Set aside. (If using dried rice noodles, soak in hot water for 20 minutes or until soft and pliable.)

Separate the broccoli into flowerets, and peel and cut the stems on the diagonal in ¼-inch slices. Heat 3 tablespoons oil in wok. Add garlic and cook until fragrant. Add rice noodles. Stir-fry for 3 minutes or until lightly browned, being careful not to break the noodles. Remove and place on a serving platter. Add 2 tablespoons oil. Add the broccoli and black mushrooms. Stir-fry for 3 minutes or until the broccoli is tender. Remove and set aside. Add 2 tablespoons oil to wok. Add the chicken. Stir-fry for 3 minutes or until done. Add the cooked vegetables to the wok and stir until heated throughout. Add the sauce mixture and cook until translucent. Serve immediately on top of the warm noodles. Serve with *Sambal Ulek* (page 321).

YIELD: 3 to 4 servings.

TIP: Beef or pork may be substituted for chicken.

 ## Bird's Nest
Cheut Chaw

Dress up your stir-frys and salads by serving them in this attractive "potato basket."

¾ pound baking potatoes, peeled, shredded
2 to 3 tablespoons cornstarch
½ teaspoon salt
Oil for frying
Shredded lettuce

Place the potato shreds in a colander. Rinse with cold water to remove the starch. Drain completely. (If not frying the nests immediately, store in cold water to prevent darkening.) Place the shreds in a clean towel. Wring the potato shreds in the towel to squeeze out any excess moisture. Blot dry.

Place the dry potatoes in a bowl. Add cornstarch and salt. Toss the mixture with the potatoes to coat them evenly. Meanwhile, heat oil for frying in a wok to 375° F. Dip a 5-inch slotted strainer with a long handle into the hot oil and remove. Spread the potato shreds out evenly in the strainer. Dip another 5-inch strainer into the hot oil and place on top of the potato shreds. Deep-fry the potato shreds for 5 minutes on high heat. Be sure the potato nest stays completely immersed during the cooking. Remove carefully and drain on absorbent toweling. Continue to make nests using remaining potato shreds. Serve on a bed of lettuce.

YIELD: 4 potato nests.

TIPS: Sweet potatoes or taro root may be substituted for the potato.

You may use any size strainer for the nests. Be sure to use two that are the same size to make an even nest.

ADVANCE PREPARATION: Cooked potato nests will keep in the refrigerator for 3 to 4 days. They can be frozen for 1 month. Be sure to pack them carefully to avoid breakage. Reheat in a 350° F oven.

◆ **Fresh Spring Roll Wrappers**
◆ *Poh Pia Wrappers*

4½ tablespoons cornstarch
2 cups all-purpose flour
Pinch salt
6 eggs, lightly beaten
1 tablespoon oil
2 cups cold water (approximately)

Sift the flour, cornstarch, and salt together in a bowl. Add the eggs and oil and beat in about 2 cups cold water to make a smooth batter. Allow to rest for 30 minutes.

Food processor method: Process the flour, cornstarch, and salt with two 5-second pulses. Add eggs and oil. With the machine running, pour cold water through the food chute within 8 seconds. Process 5 seconds. Scrape down the sides of the container. Process 10 seconds. Stop motor and scrape down the sides of the container. Process a few seconds longer. Allow to rest for 30 minutes. (If there is froth on top of the batter when ready to cook wrappers, remove before cooking.)

Heat an 8" non-stick skillet or crepe pan. Lightly oil the pan with a piece of paper towel dipped in oil. Using a ladle, pour in just enough batter to cover the bottom (about 2 tablespoons). Swirl the pan quickly to make a thin coating and pour off any excess batter. Cook over medium heat for approximately 30 seconds to 1 minute, or until wrapper is set and light bubbles form. Turn over and cook the other side for a few seconds. The wrappers should not brown. Transfer to a plate and repeat with the remaining batter, adding more oil if necessary. Place a sheet of waxed paper in between the pancakes and wrap loosely in foil. Refrigerate until ready to use.

YIELD: 20 to 24 wrappers.

TIPS: Frozen spring roll or lumpia wrappers may be purchased in

Oriental grocery stores. These are a time-saver, but not as tasty as the freshly made wrappers.

ADVANCE PREPARATION: The wrappers may be prepared 1 day in advance and refrigerated or frozen for 1 month. Reheat by steaming.

ACCOMPANIMENTS AND SAUCES

 ## Cucumber Pickles
Acar Timun

A delightful accompaniment for curries.

3 cucumbers
2 teaspoons salt
4 tablespoons sugar
3 tablespoons malt vinegar

Wash and dry cucumbers. Cut lengthwise into quarters. Remove seeds. Cut on the diagonal into 1½-inch pieces. Sprinkle with 2 teaspoons salt and let stand for 1 hour. Pour off the excess liquid and drain thoroughly. Squeeze out the excess moisture with towel. Combine the cucumbers with sugar and vinegar. Let marinate at least ½ hour before serving.

YIELD: 8 servings with other dishes.

ADVANCE PREPARATION: The cucumber pickles may be made ahead and stored in a glass container overnight. The flavor improves upon standing.

 ## Vegetable Pickles
Acar

Serve this crispy, spirited, colorful vegetable condiment cold with other dishes. The Acar *can be prepared in large quantities and stored in airtight containers in the refrigerator for up to one month.*

1¼ cups white vinegar
1 cucumber, halved, seeded, cut into 1½-inch matchstick strips

3 carrots, peeled, cut into 1½-inch matchstick strips

10 long Chinese green beans, cut in half, cut into 1½-inch lengths

½ pound cabbage, cored, cut into 1½-inch shreds

½ pound cauliflower, cut into small flowerets

1 to 2 fresh red chiles, halved lengthwise, seeded, chopped

1 to 2 fresh green chiles, halved lengthwise, seeded, chopped

7 dried red chiles, soaked in hot water until softened, about 5 minutes

6 shallots, chopped

4 garlic cloves, chopped

5 macadamia nuts, chopped

1½ teaspoons turmeric powder

1 teaspoon laos powder (galangal)

5 tablespoons oil

¾ cup sugar

1 teaspoon salt

¾ cup coarsely ground dry-roasted unsalted peanuts

In a saucepan, combine ¾ cup of the vinegar with 1½ cups water. Bring to a boil. Blanch the vegetables one variety at a time until each is cooked to the crunchy stage. Remove each of the vegetables with a slotted spoon, draining as much moisture as possible into the pan. Drain the vegetables in a colander. When all the vegetables have been cooked and well drained, place them in a large bowl.

Pound or process all the chiles, shallots, garlic, and macadamias to a paste. Add the turmeric and laos, and mix. Heat the oil in a wok on medium heat. Add the chile paste mixture and fry until fragrant, about 2 to 3 minutes. Add the remaining ½ cup vinegar, sugar, and salt. Stir in the peanuts and toss thoroughly. Remove from the heat. Let the mixture cool. Add the cooled mixture to the blanched vegetables. Toss well. Place in a tightly covered glass container and refrigerate overnight to allow the flavors to blend. Serve as an accompaniment with other dishes.

YIELD: 6 to 8 servings.

TIP: If Chinese long green beans are unavailable, substitute regular green beans.

ADVANCE PREPARATION: Prepare completely at least one day in advance. The Acar will keep several weeks, refrigerated.

Inspired by a recipe from sous chef Saw Siew Sim, Golden Sands Hotel.

◆◆ Cucumber Salad ◆◆
Raita

An Indian meal is never considered complete without Raita, a cool refreshing yogurt salad. Sous Chef Channa used Indian yogurt, which is thick, creamy, and sweet, and prepared from buffalo milk.

In this recipe, homemade yogurt is preferred. However, you may use a commercially prepared yogurt as a substitute. If the commercial yogurt tastes a little tangy, add a small amount of sour cream to enrich the flavor.

Raita is a wonderful addition to a Western barbecue or grilled meal.

1 small cucumber, peeled, seeds removed, finely shredded into
½-inch lengths
1 small onion, peeled, finely chopped
2½ cups unflavored yogurt
1 teaspoon Kosher salt
1 tablespoon chopped mint or coriander leaves
1 fresh red chile, seeded, finely sliced (optional)

Place cucumber, onion, yogurt, and salt in a bowl. Stir to mix. Chill in refrigerator. When serving, garnish with mint and chile.

YIELD: 4 to 6 servings.

TIP: Chopped tomatoes or pineapple may also be added to the Raita.

Inspired by a recipe from Sous Chef Kamal Kumar Channa, Tandoor Restaurant.

◆◆ Violet Oon's Chile Dipping Sauce ◆◆
Lak Chong

A great dipping sauce for Spring Rolls and other fried foods.

1 tablespoon dry mustard
1 tablespoon sugar
1 tablespoon lime juice
1 cup Worcestershire sauce
¼ cup water
6 to 9 fresh red chiles, seeded, chopped

Combine and mix well. Serve at room temperature or refrigerate for 1 week in a tightly closed glass container.

YIELD: approximately 1⅓ cups.

◆ Violet Oon's Chile Sauce for Hainanese Chicken ◆
Hainanese Gai Lak Chong

½ pound fresh red chiles, seeds removed (24 chiles, approximately)
3 tablespoons peeled, chopped shallots
3 tablespoons peeled, chopped garlic
3 tablespoons peeled, chopped young ginger
½ cup chicken stock
3 teaspoons lime juice
½ teaspoon rice vinegar
1½ teaspoons sugar
½ teaspoon salt

Place chiles, shallots, garlic, and ginger in blender or small processor. Process until a smooth paste forms. Put puree into a bowl. Pour ½ cup boiling chicken stock over the mixture. Add the remaining ingredients. Cool before serving.

ADVANCE PREPARATION: The sauce will keep refrigerated for 1 to 2 weeks in a tightly covered glass container. The flavor improves upon standing.

◆ Ginger Sauce ◆
Kaing Yau

Serve this tasty sauce with Hainanese Chicken.

½ cup grated ginger
½ teaspoon salt
1 tablespoon oil

Process ginger until a puree has formed. Add salt and oil. Mix together. Refrigerate.

YIELD: ½ cup.

Inspired by a recipe from Violet Oon, editor, *The Food Paper.*

◆ Soy Vinegar Dipping Sauce
◆ Chong Yau Chit Cho Tiu Mee Chong

A tasty dipping sauce for Shao Mai, Wontons, Money Bags, Spring Rolls, and other appetizers.

> 2 teaspoons peeled, finely minced fresh ginger
> 2 teaspoons peeled, finely minced garlic
> ½ cup soy sauce
> 2 tablespoons rice vinegar
> 1 to 2 teaspoons hot chile oil (optional)
> 2 tablespoons sugar

Combine all ingredients. Mix well.

ADVANCE PREPARATION: The sauce will keep refrigerated in a tightly closed glass container for 1 week.

DESSERTS AND BEVERAGES

◆ Fruit Compote
◆ Chup Kum Quo

A delicious, refreshing ending to a Southeast Asian feast! You may choose any fresh fruits in season or, if you prefer, omit the rum, canned lychees and kumquats, and candied ginger to have a fresh fruit compote.

> 1 ripe pineapple
> 1 pint strawberries, hulled
> 2 apples, peeled, cored, sliced into thin wedges
> 2 oranges, peeled, sliced into segments
> 1 small cantaloupe, cut into 1-inch cubes
> 2 bananas, sliced diagonally
> One 11-ounce can lychee nuts, drained
> ½ cup preserved whole kumquats, drained, syrup reserved
> ¾ cup white rum (optional)
> 2 tablespoons chopped candied ginger (optional)

Cut off the top of the pineapple and trim the bottom so that it will stand upright. Using a sharp knife, cut away the skin, trimming any eyes. Cut away the core. Slice in ½-inch wedges.

Combine all ingredients in a large bowl. Let chill for at least 2 hours.

◆
◆ **Almond Float**
 Hung Yum Cha

A meltingly smooth, not too sweet ending to a delicious dinner. In the original version of this classic Chinese dessert, agar-agar, a type of seaweed, was used instead of gelatin, and ground almonds were used instead of almond extract. Today, it can be found in ready-to-make powdered form in packets in Asian grocery stores. However, I much prefer this version to the pre-packaged dessert.

The almond "jelly" can be topped with canned lychees, loquats, mandarin oranges, or any fresh fruits in sugar syrup. It is also wonderful when made with orange sections and fresh orange juice.

    2 envelopes unflavored gelatin
    3½ cups water
    ½ cup evaporated milk
    3 tablespoons plus 2 teaspoons sugar
    2 teaspoons almond extract
    Two 11-ounce cans mandarin oranges, chilled

Put the gelatin into a small bowl. Add ½ cup water to soften the gelatin. Heat, but do not boil, the evaporated milk and remaining water. Add the sugar and stir to dissolve. Slowly add the softened gelatin and cook, stirring over low heat to dissolve completely. Let cool slightly. Stir in the almond extract. Pour the liquid into a shallow dish and refrigerate 4 hours or until firm. To serve, cut into squares or diamond shapes and put into serving bowl. Add the chilled mandarin oranges and the canned liquid, and serve.

YIELD: 6 servings.

TIP: Amaretto may be substituted for the almond extract. Decrease the sugar to 2 tablespoons or to taste.

ADVANCE PREPARATION: The "almond jelly" may be prepared 1 to 2 days in advance. Refrigerate, covered with plastic wrap. Cut up several hours before serving. Cover with plastic wrap. Refrigerate. Pour mandarin oranges over the jelly at serving time.

The Original Singapore Sling

In 1915 Ngian Tong Boon created this world-famous drink at the famous Raffles Hotel. It is said that Raffles Hotel is the largest consumer of gin in the world: 20,160 bottles are required per year.

In 1985, 131 Singapore Slings were drunk by five gentlemen in two hours, which makes 26.2 per head and is one Sling every 4.6 minutes. On good days around 2,000 Singapore Slings are sold at Raffles and an estimated 12,000 in Singapore.

2½ ounces gin
¾ ounce fresh lime juice
4½ ounces pineapple juice
1 drop Angostura Bitters
1 dash Benedictine liqueur
1 dash Cointreau
¾ ounce Cherry Heering or cherry brandy

Combine all ingredients and 3 or 4 ice cubes in a cocktail shaker. Shake thoroughly. Strain into a tall cocktail glass. Add ice cubes, if desired. For garnish, insert a wooden pick through a pineapple wedge and cherry.

YIELD: 2 drinks.

Courtesy of Raffles Hotel.

Fresh Pineappleade
Bor Lor Chup

A favorite of the Singapore hawkers' stands, this refreshing, easily prepared treat is wonderful on a hot summer day.

2 cups sugar
8 cups water
1 medium pineapple, cored, outer covering removed, cut into
    chunks
½ cup lime juice

Heat 2 cups water with the sugar and stir until sugar dissolves.

Place pineapple chunks and lime in a blender or food processor and blend to a puree. Add the sugar water to the pineapple puree and blend well. Add remaining water and stir to mix well. Chill. Serve in tumblers with ice.

YIELD: 2 quarts.

TIP: 1½ to 2 ounces rum may be added to each serving.

ADVANCE PREPARATION: Make ahead and refrigerate.

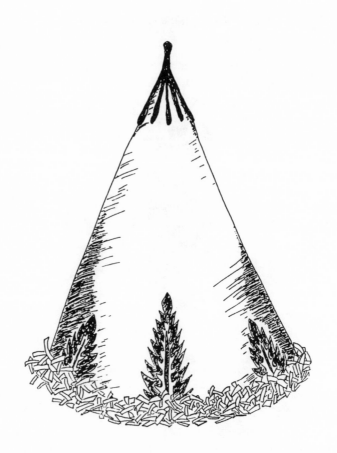

MALAYSIA

Selamat Datang! Welcome!

The peoples and cuisines of Malaysia—the modern republic that includes most of the mainland Malay Peninsula and a portion of the island of Borneo—are as varied as the landscape, which ranges from hilly temperate regions to tropical lowlands, often within a few miles of each other.

Unlike in Indonesia, where many of the individual islands or regions are ethnically uniform, in Malaysia people of several different cultures—primarily Malay, Chinese, and Indian—live side by side. Each racial and ethnic group has much to contribute to the quality of life, and each does so while respecting the religious and cultural traditions of others.

Malaysia has always been a trading center. The sea lanes that connect China and Japan with India, Arabia, and the West pass around the tip of the Malay Peninsula, and centuries of traders left their influence on the native Malay cuisine. (Note that Malay refers to the indigenous ethnic group, while Malaysian refers to the country as a whole.) In fact, many of the spices and ingredients that characterize all Malaysian cooking were introduced by Chinese, Indian, Indonesian, and Arab traders and settlers.

Malay food is generally rich and spicy. Although each state has its distinctive tastes and style of preparation, most of them have a common set of ingredients. The curries of Malay cooks have a distinct flavor, quite different from those of their Indian neighbors. They rely heavily on fresh ingredients such as lemon grass, galangal, chile, and fragrant citrus, coriander, and curry leaves. Coconut is the basis of the curries as well as many other dishes. Southern Malaysian cooking

171

is also influenced by that of the nearby Indonesian island of Sumatra.

Family-style Malay meals generally consist of one meat or fish dish, one or two vegetables, and possibly a soup, and are generally served at room temperature. The mainstay of the meal is rice. Because Malays are mostly Muslim, pork is not used, as it is forbidden in the Islam religion. It is traditional to eat with the fingers of the right hand, which is used to knead rice and seasonings together before tucking the food into the mouth. Today, forks and spoons are common, but many feel that manual eating brings out the true flavors in the food.

The Chinese community is Malaysia's largest immigrant group. Chinese merchants established themselves in Malacca as long ago as 1500, and a large number of Chinese immigrants came in the early 19th century to make their fortunes in the tin fields. The descendants of these Chinese men and their Malay wives enjoy the distinctive Nonya cuisine, which carefully blends the best of Chinese and Malay cuisines (See Singapore chapter, page 103).

Indians constitute the second largest minority in Malaysia. There is a great diversity of Indian people in Malaysia, both Hindu and Muslim, and a corresponding diversity in Indian cooking. Spices, imaginatively used, are the most important feature of Indian cooking. They do not use the all-purpose "curry powder" we use in this country; true Indian curry powders are varied combinations of spices, usually blended by the Indian spice merchant for a specific dish. They may be hot or mild, pungent or bland. Fresh herbs and roots are added to the dish while cooking, giving a wonderful spicy, aromatic result.

Kuala Lumpur, with its arabesque arches and minarets, is the capital of modern Malaysia, and it shows all these influences. It is a Muslim city with Chinese influence and a flourish of Hindu flavor and color. With the diversity of culture, there are many celebrations and festivals of Malay, Chinese, Indian, and Arab origin. Everyone joins in on most celebrations, even though it may not be his holiday.

While in Kuala Lumpur, I enjoyed a grandiose brunch in the Regent's luxurious Suasa Brasserie. Magnificent ice carvings were surrounded by the freshest of fruits and perfumed flowers. Indian chefs flung thin *murtaba* dough in the air to get the finest sheet possible, then stretched it over a large, flat round metal surface to cook. They filled it with a tasty curry filling and folded it into a square pancake. Absolutely wonderful! Other chefs served spicy Beef Rendang, a luxurious lamb curry called *Kari Kambing,* tasty vegetable curry dishes, and the spicy *sambals* that accompany every meal. Before our eyes, they prepared wonderful fresh fruit juices from our choice of rambutans, mangoes, papayas, guavas, pineapples, and bananas.

Penang, often called "the pearl of the Orient," is a beautiful island off the west coast of peninsular Malaysia. The outer rim of the island has miles upon miles of white, sandy beaches lined with beautiful palms. Here, all of the hustle and bustle of Georgetown, the capital, is left behind for a peaceful and unhurried life.

Georgetown, in the center of the island, is a charming town, from its crowded streets to the thriving port from which Malaysia's exports find their way to the world's markets. It is also the home of northern Nonya cooking, which is heavily influenced by Thai cuisine (Thailand lies just a hundred miles to the north). Penang Nonya cooking is hot, spicy, and rich, and makes liberal use of pungent roots (galangal, lemon grass, turmeric, ginger), aromatic leaves, shrimp paste (*belacan*), chiles, lime, tamarind, and coconut milk.

It was in Georgetown that I dined with Mr. Khor Cheang Kee, the soft-spoken, refined owner of the famous Dragon King Nonya Restaurant, a restaurant with old-world charm. Mr. Khor is dedicated to preserving the Penang Nonya cultural heritage. In his words, "Singapore Nonyas have gone astray, as they have developed too fast and have forgotten the true Nonya foods of the past. Penang Nonya cooking uses much more tamarind (a sour ingredient) than that in Singapore and Malacca, and it is much more refined in the pounding and mixing of the ingredients, which is a time-consuming and exacting task."

We had *Kueh Pie Tee* (top hat), a crisp appetizer consisting of tiny hat-shaped pastry shells filled with shredded vegetables, topped with crab, fried green onions, garlic, and red chiles; Penang Spring Rolls seasoned with cinnamon and soy sauce; *Lo Bak*, a delicately flavored homemade Chinese sausage; *Kerabu*, a salad that includes chopped shrimp, chicken, onions, ginger flowers, and spices in a sour dressing; *Kari Kapitan*, a wonderful chicken curry; and *Lam Mee*. He explained that *Lam Mee* is an almost forgotten dish that is served at a typical Nonya wedding, birthday, or anniversary, and symbolizes longevity. Blanched bean sprouts and cooked homemade egg noodles are placed on a heatproof platter, then topped with shrimp, crab, green onions, and a sprinkling of red chiles. A light sauce is prepared from shrimp and chicken stock to which many seasonings have been added, providing a tangy, sweet, spicy flavor to the dish. The beautiful presentation is served on a silver chafing dish. Dessert was many *Nonya Kueh*, sweet Nonya cakes. The tastes were like none I had been served before, as they were extremely delicate but at the same time intricate.

From Penang, I crossed the peninsula and the South China Sea to mysterious Borneo, where the tribesmen were immortalized as the headhunters of old.

The state of Sabah is situated in the northern portion of Borneo, and about 70 percent of the state is under jungle cover. The terrain is irregular, from level land to rolling hills and mountainous areas, with many swift rivers running down the numerous valleys. Kota Kinabalu, the state capital, is the gateway to Sabah's attractions of rain forests, bird and animal life, and traditional villages. It is a gentle, unimposing town with an elevated water village on one side and Chinese shop houses crowded together on the other. It is possibly the narrowest city in Asia; turn any corner and in less than five minutes you are climbing a hill or wading in water.

While in Kota Kinabalu, executive chef Roslan of the Tanjung Aru Beach Hotel, located in a breathtaking setting of white sandy beaches, lush tropical flowers, palms, and brilliant, clear blue-green water, treated me to a delicious feast of tribal Kadazan food, which is featured in a special menu at the end of this chapter (page 198).

The state of Sarawak, the largest in Malaysia, lies on the north-west coast of Borneo. Three-quarters of the land is covered by rich rain forests criss-crossed by many rivers.

Sarawak is the world's largest exporter of pepper (India produces more, but much of it stays at home). On a visit to a pepper plantation, I saw neat rows of pepper vines curling around hard wooden posts to form gigantic cone-shaped plants six to eight feet tall. (Imagine a tropical Christmas tree farm and you get the picture.) The berries, which ripen over a three-month period during the dry season, are usually harvested by hand. Most of the picking is done by women, who load up large wicker baskets with the pepper berries.

When the berries are picked and how they are processed determines the final color (black, white, or green), with each form having a distinctive flavor. Black peppercorns are produced by picking berries while they are green and drying them in the sun for about ten days. They turn gradually from green to brown and finally to black before they are packaged and exported. If packed in brine right after picking, they remain green. For white peppercorns, the berries are allowed to mature fully, becoming reddish yellow in color. After a soak in water to soften the scaly outer skin (pericarp), the skin is removed and the berries are laid in the sun to dry to a creamy ivory color.

Kuching, the capital of Sarawak, is a charming town with a rich ethnic mix, the Iban tribes constituting the majority and the Chinese, Malays, and other indigenous groups comprising the balance. Much of Kuching retains the sedate and leisurely feeling of the colonial era, and the many old cloistered government buildings, forts and towers, and the courthouse are remnants of a fascinating past.

Jimmy Choo, a well-known Kuching resident, took me to his favorite dining spot, the Hong Kong Shark's Fin Seafood Restaurant. Traditional brandy on the rocks and beer were served simultaneously before and during the meal for the men, while the women sipped tea.

The food was Chinese Chinese, not Nonya or another locally adapted style; the steamed fish, lemon chicken, stir-fried shrimp with chile sauce, barbecued pork *lo mein,* and Peking duck all tasted exactly like those I had in China.

Back in Kuala Lumpur at the end of my trip, I enjoyed a splendid buffet meal locally known as "high tea" (see the menu on page 176). Combining Malay, Indian, and Chinese dishes, it summed up the cultural and culinary diversity of beautiful Malaysia.

Selamat Menjamu Se Lera! Bon Appetit!

MALAYSIAN MENUS

Malaysian High Tea

6 to 8 people

Spicy Chicken Soup, *Soto Ayam*

◆

Chicken, Shrimp, and Rice Noodles in Coconut Sauce, *Laksa Lemak*

◆

Stir-Fried Hokkien Noodles, Nonya Style, *Hokkien Mee Meehoon*

◆

Indian Lamb-Filled Pastries, *Murtaba*

◆

Spicy Chile Sauce, *Sambal Belacan*

◆

Coconut Crepes with Coconut Sauce, *Kueh Dadar*

◆

Tea

A delightful custom in Malaysia is "high tea." Like the British high tea, this is a substantial meal, although it is served at midday or midafternoon rather than in the evening. In fact, the recipes that follow would make an impressive Malaysian buffet, perfect for a weekend brunch, lunch, or supper.

Ivo Nekvapil, general manager of the Pan Pacific Hotel in Kuala Lumpur, hosted a marvelous high tea during my visit, with a menu that drew on the various cuisines of Malaysia. Large buffet tables laden with Malay, Chinese, Indian, and Western delights were beautifully decorated with local fruits and flowers. Yet another table displayed numerous traditional sweets.

There was *Soto Ayam*, a spicy Malay chicken soup with numerous garnishes, including chicken shreds, bean threads, hot red chile peppers, and fried shallots; *Hokkien Mee Meehoon*, a delectable Chinese noodle dish blending egg noodles, rice vermicelli, vegetables, shrimp, squid, and pork in a rich pork and shrimp stock; *Laksa*

176

Lemak, an aromatic shrimp, chicken, and rice noodle soup of Malay origin; *Murtaba,* tasty Indian grilled "pastries" filled with savory spiced lamb; and deliciously sweet *Kueh Dadar,* colorful coconut crepes with coconut sauce, a perfect ending.

During the meal, the Indian *mamak roti* man entertained us by flinging dough high in the air like a pizza baker, stretching it in every direction into a paper-thin sheet of dough. He then placed the dough on a large hot griddle, filled it with a lamb combination, folded it, and served the wonderful *Murtaba* hot off the griddle. Next, he prepared *Teh Tarik,* an Indian "tea pool," by pouring a combination of condensed milk and tea from high in the air to produce a delightful tea with a tremendous foam. Our host explained that the Indians have competitions to see who can defy the laws of gravity by stretching the *Teh Tarik* the farthest between two well-used mugs.

Many of these dishes can be served alone as one-dish meals. When served together, they make a delightful combination of flavors and textures. By following the Advance Preparation directions on the individual recipes, you can serve this colorful, lavish luncheon with little last-minute preparation. The *Soto Ayam, Hokkien Mee Meehoon, Laksa Lemak,* and *Kueh Dadar* can be prepared the day before and given their final assembly just before serving. *Murtaba* can be cooked ahead and reheated in the oven. *Sambal Belacan,* a hot chile sauce, can be prepared several days in advance, or you may purchase bottled *Sambal Ulek* (page 321) instead.

KADAZAN TRIBAL FARE FROM BORNEO

4 to 6 people

Pickled Mackerel, *Hinava Tenggiri*
•
Oxtail Soup, Kadazan Style, *Asam Pedis Kadazan*
•
Grilled Beef, Kadazan Tribal Style, *Hinugu Do Daging Miampai Bavang Taagang Om Topuak*
•
Spinach with Dried Shrimp, Kadazan Style, *Napa Do Pakis*
•
Chicken Soup with Rice Wine, Kadazan Style, *Sup Manuk Om Hiing*
•
Chile Sauce Kadazan, *Chile Sambal Kadazan*
•
Rice
•
Fresh Fruit

During my writing of this book, my family has had many varied dining experiences. The night I announced that dinner would be tribal fare from Borneo, they began to mutter about going out for pizza, getting invited over to a friend's house for dinner . . . However, good sports that they are, they tried another of my unfamiliar meals— and loved it! They found Kadazan food to be light, healthy, and delicious.

The Kadazans have dwelled since time immemorial in the dense rain forest in the shadow of Southeast Asia's highest mountain, Mount Kinabalu in the state of Sabah on the north coast of Borneo. The early Kadazans lived a carefree life, enjoying the abundance of the natural world around them. Surrounded by some of the world's richest varieties and densities of plants, animals, insects, amphibians, reptiles, freshwater fish, and marine life, the Kadazans developed a wide range of natural foods and beverages as well as herbal medicinal resources.

My Kadazan guide, Robert Gailin, grew up in a traditional village of palm-thatched houses, where the women tend sago palm gardens and rice fields flooded by the monsoon rains and the men fish and hunt for the daily fare. Like many other children, he left the village to work and attend school in Kota Kinabalu, the state capital. He is now a college graduate and speaks impeccable English as well as five other languages. Robert supports his parents, who still live at the foot of Mount Kinabalu much as his ancestors did. Watching the ease and worldliness with which he made the transition to the city from the tribal village had me in complete awe.

Today, the elder Kadazans are trying to preserve their heritage and are trying to teach the children the foods of their childhood. They are very concerned that their children, after being exposed to super-market foods, will lose the ability to recognize the food resources around them. (Robert admitted to me that while he enjoys the tradi-tional dishes when he visits his parents, he prefers the foods he can obtain in the city.)

The Kadazan traditional cooking methods are pure and simple: boiling, steaming, barbecuing, pickling, and preserving. The above menu is a sampling of traditional recipes passed down from genera-tion to generation. Of course, there are many other traditional dishes made from local natural foods, which are impossible to duplicate in the United States.

Fish is abundant and loved by the Kadazan. *Hinava Tenggiri*, pickled mackerel, is a favorite fish preparation and is served on almost every occasion. Cattle are rare, so Grilled Kadazan Beef is a delicacy saved for special occasions. When a cow is slaughtered, all parts are put to good use, as in the hearty and quite delicious Oxtail Soup.

Favorite vegetables include local ferns gathered in the wild and cooked with dried shrimp. I have substituted tender young fresh spinach in this simple dish, and my children say it is the best spinach they have ever tasted. *Sup Manuk Om Hiing,* chicken soup with local rice wine, is sipped as a beverage throughout the meal. The condiments might be a local pickled sour fruit and hot red chile peppers soaked in rice vinegar or combined with lime juice. *Tapai,* rice fermented into a fiery whitish colored wine, is rarely consumed with the meal but is saved for merrymaking after dinner or for tribal dance ceremonies.

All of the dishes with the exception of the Spinach with Dried Shrimp and the Grilled Kadazan Beef can be prepared a day ahead and reheated. This reflects the tribal way of life, which is to eat when hungry rather than at a specified time. There is always a pot on the fire for snacking throughout the day. The same fire can be used for grilling within a moment's notice.

CHINESE NEW YEAR'S EVE DINNER

6 to 8 people

Raw Fish Salad, *Yee-Sang*

◆

Three Varieties Vegetables with Scallops*, *Choy Chao Yuen Bui*

◆

Five Treasure Vegetable Platter, *Gan Pun Ng Bo*

◆

Phoenix Dragon Chicken and Ham, *Shin Choy Lung Fung*

◆

Steamed Fish with Chinese Preserved Vegetables, *Dong Gou Ching Yu*

◆

Yangchow Fried Rice, *Yangchow Chao Fayn*

◆

Oranges Oriental

*double recipe

Note: Sweet and Sour Fish (page 214) may be substituted for the Steamed Fish. This is more time-consuming, but very impressive.

"Gong hay fat choy!" Happy New Year to all!

The New Year festival is one of my favorite times to be in Asia. I have had the good fortune to see in the New Year in Bangkok, Singapore, Kuala Lumpur, and Jakarta.

For a couple of weeks leading up to New Year's Eve, all the markets in the Chinese communities bustle with throngs of people. There are luscious treats, beautiful fruits, kumquat and peach blossoms, and colorful red and gold decorations from small banners to larger-than-life lions. There is a feeling of excitement in the air, much like our Christmas season. The shops and markets are at their busiest as everyone does their last-minute shopping. New Year means not only lots of food, but presents as well. The streets are full of people buying gifts for their family and friends. Fortune tellers line the streets as throngs of people surround them to learn of their good fortune for the New Year.

The beginning of the new year is not, as in the West, on the first of January. Instead, following a lunar calendar, it falls on a variable date around the end of January or the beginning of February.

The keynote of the lunar New Year is renewal: the old year goes out, taking with it old strife and misfortunes, and the new comes in, bringing with it new hope, new luck, and the renewal of harmony. Personally and in business, it is a time to pay off one's debts, tidy up all loose ends, and turn over a new leaf.

One of the more spectacular features of the New Year celebration is the lion dance. The lion dancer goes from shop to shop, shinnying up a long pole to the shop owner's window. At the top of the pole and outside the window is a leaf of green lettuce and an orange, together with a red envelope full of money for the lion. The lion eats the lettuce and the orange and collects the red envelope. The owner, who has invited the troupe of dancers to his shop, will then enjoy prosperity and good luck for the coming year. This can be a very expensive time for the shopkeeper, who may invite many lions to call upon his shop; it's also a lucrative time for the acrobatic lion dance troups.

Weeks before the first day of New Year, housewives busy themselves with spring cleaning, as the removal of the old year's dirt and dust represents getting rid of the past year's disappointments. They are also very busy preparing symbolic foods for the upcoming feasts.

A week before the New Year, the Kitchen God leaves for heaven. He is an ancient god who is closely identified with the household and acts as a kind of moral judge over members of the household. The Kitchen God makes his annual report to the God of Heaven on the behavior of "his" family. Pieces of sugar and sticky-sweet rice cakes are offered to insure that the deity's mouth is "glued" so that he will forget the family's transgressions and give a sweet report.

The reunion dinner on New Year's Eve is a very significant meal, as the whole family gathers to partake of the last meal of the old year. All disagreements are forgotten, and even in the poorest home no expense is spared to provide a lavish meal. At midnight, doors and windows are thrown open to let in all good spirits passing by. Toasts are proposed with *"Yam seng!"* meaning "Drink to success!" Firecrackers, although officially prohibited, are heard sporadically throughout the night to signify the completion of the ceremony.

On New Year's Day, everyone dresses in new clothes. Children eagerly greet their parents and elders *"Gong xi fa cai,"* "Happy New Year," knowing that they will receive *ang paws* (red envelopes filled with money) in return. All day long, relatives and visitors stream in, and there is great merrymaking. No harsh word may be spoken, for fear of marring the year's good luck. Knives and scissors should not be used, as one may cut the thread of good fortune. Sweeping is avoided, the breaking of glass or mirrors is considered a bad omen, and no cooking is done in the home. A guest in a home on New Year's Day is offered precooked delicacies such as "wax" (salted) duck and Chinese sausages, along with dried melon seeds, nuts, and a tray of assorted sweets and dried fruits, all of which have names that have good associations. Perfect, unblemished oranges are given in pairs to relatives and friends with the blessing *"Sin chia yule,"* meaning "Good luck and prosperity and may all your luck come true."

I have enjoyed many New Year's meals on my trips to Asia, but the most elegant and memorable feast was a New Year's Eve dinner hosted by the genial Karl-Heinz Zimmerman, general manager of the Regent of Kuala Lumpur. The lavishly decorated Chinese dining room was laden with red festive and symbolic ornamentation. Lucky plants were present everywhere—kumquats to bring good luck and abundance, peach blossoms for success in business and love. Pairs of red banners with bold Chinese calligraphy written in gold were at the entrance and throughout the room, carrying propitious wishes of good luck, good health, and prosperity, peace, and harmony. To add more drama to our evening, colorful lion dancers pranced among us to bring us peace and prosperity and to frighten away all evil.

For your celebration, I have selected some of the dishes from this luxurious banquet. Serve this menu during the New Year or any time you want to entertain royally in Chinese style. Because red symbolizes good luck and prosperity, try to include as much red as possible in your table setting. The guest of honor is usually seated directly across from the doorway or opening through which the food will come.

All the foods at a Chinese New Year banquet are symbolic. Take the indispensable *Yee Sang*, a delectable raw fish salad. It is believed that to start the New Year by eating raw fish will insure that one's luck will take a turn for the better. Even the ritual mixing of the salad is a symbolic act: family and friends chant *"Loh hei"* (loosely translated, "Toss to prosperity") as the sliced fish and vegetables are tossed with the sauces and seasonings. It has been fascinating to watch businessmen in restaurants during the New Year season, making merry and vigorously tossing the *Yee Sang* to great heights.

A whole steamed fish, in this case with Chinese preserved vegetables, symbolizes abundance and plenty during the New Year. There must also be at least one vegetarian dish, preferably one such as Five Treasure Vegetable Platter, which represents the five signs of prosperity. Three Varieties Vegetables with Scallops symbolizes prosperity, with the red, green, and gold colors and the coin shapes of the scallops all representing wealth in one form or another. In Phoenix Dragon Chicken and Ham, the foods represent two important mythological creatures who are embodiments of *yin* and *yang*, the two opposing forces in the universe that must be kept in harmony. Oranges are a must for dessert, since they are believed to be similar to a certain kind of fruit in heaven.

Although a multi-course Chinese meal such as this may seem daunting, the *Yee Sang*, Steamed Fish with Chinese Preserved Vegetables, and Five Treasure Vegetable Platter can be assembled ahead, covered with plastic wrap, and refrigerated. The sauce for the Oranges Oriental can be prepared 1 to 2 weeks in advance. Prepare the oranges the day before. Complete do-ahead preparations follow each recipe. I have planned your dinner so that you can both prepare and serve your feast *and* enjoy your guests without spending the evening in the kitchen.

Gong hay fat choy!

STARTERS

Spring Rolls, Penang Style, *Choon Piah*
Indian Lamb-Filled Pastries, *Murtaba*
Grilled Chicken on Skewers, *Sate Ayam*
Chicken Lollipops, Penang Style, *Penang Ayam*
Chinese New Year Fish Salad, *Yee-Sang*
Pickled Mackerel, *Hinava Tenggiri*
Shrimp Rolls, *Har Quen*

SOUPS

Spicy Chicken Soup, *Soto Ayam*
Chicken, Shrimp, and Rice Noodles in Coconut Sauce, *Laksa Lemak*
Chicken Soup with Rice Wine, Kadazan Style, *Sup Manuk Om Hiing*
Oxtail Soup, Kadazan Style, *Asam Pedas Kadazan*

MEAT

Grilled Beef, Kadazan Tribal Style, *Hinugu Do Daging Miampai Bavang Taagang Om Topuak*
Stir-Fried Beef with Oyster Sauce, *Hauyao Chao Gau*
Malay Beef Stew, *Daging Semur*
Madras Curried Beef, *Kari Daging Madras*
Lamb Curry Johore Style, *Kari Kambing, Johore*

POULTRY

Captain's Curry, *Kari Kapitan*
Grilled Chicken, Kelantan Style, *Ayam Percik, Kelantan*
Roast Sugar Cane Chicken, *Ayam Dara Bergolek Dengan Tebu*
Phoenix Dragon Chicken and Ham, *Lung Fung Ching Chang*
Phoenix Dragon Chicken and Ham with Vegetables, *Shin Choy Lung Fung*
Steamed Ginger Chicken, *Kaing Shi Ching Wat Gai*

FISH AND SEAFOOD

Steamed Fish with Chinese Preserved Vegetables, *Dong Gou Ching Yu*
Sweet and Sour Fish, *Ng Fook Chong Yee*
Grilled White Pomfret with Coconut Curry, *Ikan Bawal Panggang Dan Kari Lemak*
Three Varieties Vegetables with Scallops, *Choy Chao Yuen Bui*
Stir-Fried Shrimp in Spicy Sauce, *Sambal Udang*
Stir-Fried Scallops, Red Pepper, and Zucchini, *Hong Chiu Yuen Bui*

SALADS AND VEGETABLES

Chinese Salad, Penang Nonya Style, *Penang Rujak*
Chicken Mint Salad, *Selada Ayam*
Stir-Fried Mixed Vegetables, *Sayur Goreng*
Five Treasure Vegetable Platter, *Gan Pun Ng Bo*
Vegetables in Coconut Gravy, *Sayur Lodeh*
Spiced Green Beans, *Kacang Bendi Goreng Rempah*
Spinach with Dried Shrimp, Kadazan Style, *Napa Do Pakis*

RICE, NOODLES, OMELETS

Scented Rice, *Nasi Minyak*
Scented Rice Penang Style, *Nasi Minyak, Penang*
Fried Rice, *Nasi Goreng*
Fried Rice Noodles, Penang Style, *Penang Char Kway Teow*
Stir-Fried Hokkien Noodles, Nonya Style, *Hokkien Mee Meehoon*
Spiced Egg Noodles with Sweet Potato Gravy, *Mee Rebus*
Green Bean Omelet, *Dau Kwok Chao Dan*

SAUCES, ACCOMPANIMENTS, AND PICKLES
Peanut Sauce, *Kuah Kacang*
Savory Pineapple, *Pacri Nenas*
Baked Bananas
Cucumber and Pineapple Sambal, Penang Style, *Sambal Timun Dan Nenas*
Spicy Chile Sauce, *Sambal Belacan*
Chile Sauce Kadazan, *Chile Sambal Kadazan*

DESSERTS AND BEVERAGES
Coconut Crepes with Coconut Sauce, *Kueh Dadar*
Oranges Oriental
Papaya Fool
Spiced Tea
Ginger Fizz

STARTERS

 ## Spring Rolls, Penang Style
Choon Piah

The beautiful island of Penang offers these tasty morsels with a hint of cinnamon.

2 tablespoons oil
2 cloves minced garlic
2 teaspoons peeled, minced fresh ginger
6 ounces ground pork
6 ounces shrimp, chopped
⅓ cup chopped carrot
2 tablespoons chopped onion
10 water chestnuts, chopped
4 ounces crabmeat, cooked, flaked

SAUCE MIXTURE: Combine and set aside

3 tablespoons dark soy sauce
1 teaspoon cinnamon
1 teaspoon sugar
½ teaspoon pepper

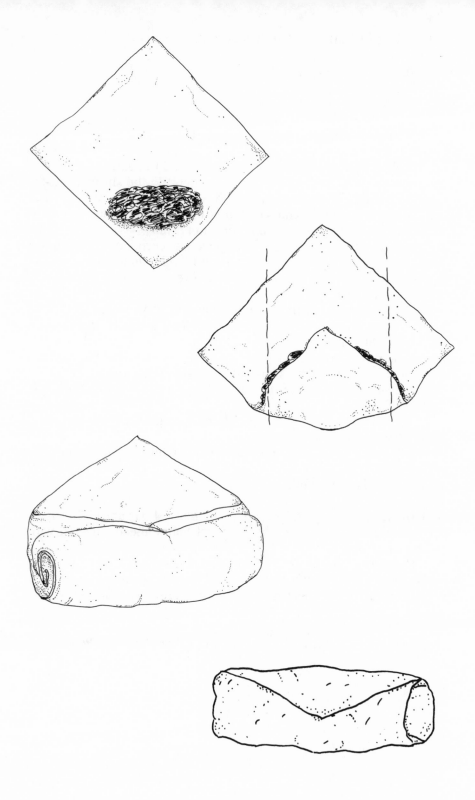

20 spring roll wrappers
1 egg, lightly beaten
3 to 4 cups oil for deep frying
½ cucumber, sliced
Violet Oon's Chile Dipping Sauce (page 164)

Heat wok. Add 2 tablespoons oil and heat. Add the garlic and ginger. Stir. Add the pork and stir-fry for 1 minute. Add the shrimp. Stir-fry until pink. Add the carrot, onion, and water chestnuts and stir until soft. Add the crabmeat and sauce mixture. Stir until the mixture is well combined and heated throughout. Let cool.

To wrap, take one spring roll wrapper, one corner pointing toward you, and spoon 2 heaping tablespoons of filling onto the lower corner of the spring roll in a sausage shape. Cover remaining spring rolls with a damp towel.

Fold the corner of the wrapper pointing at you over the filling until covered. Turn again to enclose the filling securely. Moisten the left and right corners of the triangle with beaten egg, fold over the corners and press down firmly to seal, making an envelope. Moisten the flap of the envelope with the egg and turn, rolling it into a cylinder, sealing it firmly. Set aside and repeat until all the filling has been used.

Heat oil to 375° F in a wok. Cook the spring rolls, a few at a time, until crisp and golden.

Serve with cucumbers and Violet Oon's Chile Dipping Sauce.

YIELD: 20 rolls, approximately.

ADVANCE PREPARATION: Prepare the filling 1 day ahead. Refrigerate. The rolls may be assembled several hours ahead, covered with plastic wrap and refrigerated until ready to cook.

They also may be fried ahead of time, drained, and refried at serving time, or preheat a 400° F oven. Place the spring rolls on a rack resting on a cookie sheet and heat. They are best when fried and served immediately.

Inspired by a recipe from Violet Oon, publisher, *The Food Paper.*

Indian Lamb-Filled Pastries
Murtaba

One of my many taste delights while in Kuala Lumpur and Singapore is a visit to the Indian mamak roti man, who makes quick fried envelopes of very thin dough, stuffed with savory meat and spices. Murtaba are very popular as snacks to be eaten in the open air; you can buy them from market stalls or street-side vendors who will make them especially for you, absolutely fresh and with ingredients to suit your taste.

With great skill and ease, he takes a small well-oiled ball of dough, flings it into the air tossing and stretching it in every direction until he has a paper-thin, smooth sheet of dough—all in less than a minute! He then places the dough on a large, heated, flat metal griddle, fills it with a delectable curry filling, folds it into a big square and cooks it until both sides are crispy and golden brown.

You may not be able to put on such a display at home, but it is possible to obtain the required thinness of dough by soaking the balls of well-kneaded dough in oil for an hour or more and then spreading them with your hands as thinly as possible. The dough might be a little thicker on the edges than in the center, which is all right. If you do not have a large kitchen griddle, the Murtaba may be made smaller to fit your pan. They will taste equally as good.

They are wonderful as an accompaniment with drinks, with a meal, or as a snack at any time of day.

3 cups all-purpose flour
1 teaspoon salt
1 teaspoon ghee or oil
1 cup lukewarm water
¾ cup oil, approximately

FILLING:

2 tablespoons oil or ghee
2 large onions, minced
2 garlic cloves, chopped
2 tablespoons finely minced ginger
2 teaspoons turmeric powder
1½ teaspoons red pepper powder
2 pounds ground lamb
3 teaspoons *garam masala* (page 27)
4 tablespoons finely chopped fresh coriander leaves
4 to 6 fresh red chiles, seeds removed, finely sliced
3 eggs, beaten
Salt and pepper to taste

Dough Preparation: Put the flour and salt in a large bowl and knead in the ghee or oil. Make a well in the center and pour in all of the water at once. Mix to a fairly soft dough and knead for 10 minutes or longer until dough becomes elastic and springs back. Divide the dough into 10 or 12 balls of equal size and put them in a small bowl containing ½ cup oil. Add more oil if the dough is not covered. Let rest for 1 hour.

Filling Preparation: Heat 2 tablespoons ghee or oil in a medium frying pan. Add the onion and stir-fry until soft. Add the garlic and ginger and continue stir-frying until the onion is golden brown. Add the turmeric and red pepper powder and stir. Add the lamb, and stir-fry, breaking up any large pieces, until the meat is no longer pink and is tender and quite dry. Drain off any excess oil. Do not allow the meat to become brown and crunchy. Add the *garam masala,* coriander, chiles, and eggs. Season to taste with salt and pepper. Stir. Remove from the heat and keep warm.

Cooking: Remove the dough from the bowl and knead the dough ball gently. Spread a little oil from the bowl on a smooth surface. Flatten the ball with your hand. Gently press with your fingers, spreading the dough out into a very thin crepe (as thin as possible without tearing the dough). It should be similar to strudel pastry. Place 3 to 4 tablespoons of the filling in the center of the dough. Fold over the sides of the crepe in an envelope fashion, completely enclosing the filling. Preheat a large griddle. Add oil to cover the bottom of the pan. Fry for 1 to 2 minutes, or until golden brown and crispy. Turn over and cook the other side, adding a little more ghee or oil on the griddle if necessary. Cook until crisp and golden. Serve hot or at room temperature.

YIELD: 10 to 12 *Murtaba.*

TIPS: Filo dough, purchased in American grocery stores, may be used in place of the homemade dough. Your *Murtaba* will not have the wonderful texture of the homemade dough, but you will have an easily prepared, tasty *Murtaba.*

If fresh chiles are unavailable, substitute dried chiles. Soak in warm water for 5 minutes to soften. Remove seeds, chop.

ADVANCE PREPARATION: Prepare the filling 1 to 2 days ahead. Allow it to come to room temperature before filling the dough. The dough may be kneaded and placed in the oil several hours in advance. The *Murtaba* may be cooked and frozen for 1 month. Reheat in a 425° F oven for approximately 5 minutes or until heated throughout. Some of the original crispness will be lost, but they will still be wonderful.

Inspired by a recipe from Jean Marc LaForce, head of food and beverage, Pan Pacific Hotel, Kuala Lumpur.

 ## Grilled Chicken on Skewers *Sate Ayam*

Satay, grilled meat on skewers, may be found in most Southeast Asian countries. Its origin was in Java, Indonesia, where it was adapted from the Indian kebab introduced by the Muslim traders. Satay is served at roadside stands as well as in the finest restaurants.

For an informal evening, let your guests barbecue their own pre-threaded and marinated skewers of meat. Serve the satay with Peanut Sauce (page 234), a cucumber or other vegetable salad, and hot, steaming rice. Allow 4 to 6 skewers per person. Fresh fruits make a grand finale.

½ small onion, chopped
1 clove garlic, smashed and chopped
3 tablespoons soy sauce
Juice of 1 lime
1 tablespoon palm or brown sugar
1 tablespoon oil
1 pound chicken, very thinly cut into strips ½ inch wide by 2
    inches long
Thin bamboo skewers soaked in cold water for 1 hour.
Peanut Sauce (page 234)

Combine the onion, garlic, soy sauce, lime juice, sugar, and oil in a processor or blender, and process until smooth. Place the satay in a large shallow dish and pour marinade over meat. Marinate for 30 to 60 minutes, rotating occasionally. Thread the meat strips on skewers, 3 or 4 to a stick.

Grill or broil satay about 4 inches from the heat for approximately 3 minutes per side. (If cooking with a grill, heat charcoal until the coals have a white, chalky film.) Remove and serve with Crunchy Peanut Sauce.

YIELD: 3 servings.

ADVANCE PREPARATION: Marinate satay several hours before guests arrive. Grill when serving.

VARIATION: Substitute pork or beef for chicken.

Inspired by a recipe from Lothar Winkler, executive chef, The Regent of Kuala Lumpur.

  Chicken Lollipops, Penang Style
Penang Ayam

These popular street-side snacks from Penang make wonderful appetizers.

20 large chicken wings, tips removed

MARINADE:

2 tablespoons peeled, minced fresh ginger
2 stalks lemon grass, minced, bottom 6 inches only
6 almonds, ground
1 teaspoon chili powder
1 teaspoon turmeric powder
2 teaspoons sugar
1 teaspoon salt

2 to 4 cups oil for deep frying
Lemon wedges

Remove wing tips and discard. Disjoint the upper part of the wing at the first joint and cut wing. Cut around the tip of the smaller end of the bone to release the skin and meat. Scrape and push the meat toward the thick end. Holding the meat down with the cleaver, pull the bone so the meat wraps around the thick end. You now have a "lollipop." Repeat procedure for all wings.

Pound or process the ginger, lemon grass, almonds, chili powder, turmeric, sugar, and salt to a paste, adding a little water if necessary to process. Marinate chicken for 3 hours or longer. Heat oil to 350° F over medium-high heat. Deep-fry for 3 to 4 minutes until the meat is firm and brown.

YIELD: 20 lollipops.

ADVANCE PREPARATION: The "lollipops" may be deep-fried and then frozen. Spread frozen chicken on a cookie sheet and reheat in a preheated 425° F oven until heated through, or deep-fry in hot oil.

Chinese New Year Fish Salad
Yee-Sang

Yee-Sang is a raw fish salad originating in the Chinese province of Teo Chew. It is a must during the New Year festivities in Malaysia and Singapore.

The Chinese character Yee *signifies "never ending wealth" and* Sang *means "life." The partaking of this dish is a yearly ritual for families, working people, and businessmen alike.* Yee-Sang *is traditionally eaten between the seventh and the fifteenth day of the lunar New Year. During this time, it is supposed to bring good luck and prosperity the whole of the following year.*

It is the preparation of this dish at the table that is symbolic; chopsticks are used to stir the ingredients vigorously and to toss the ingredients high. This act, symbolizing the "tossing up one's luck," Lo Hei, *is more significant than the actual eating of the dish.*

Each year the Chinese businessman who has hopes for a prosperous year will toss his heart out over Yee-Sang.

1 pound very fresh red snapper fillets, very thinly sliced
2 to 3 tablespoons white vinegar

SAUCE MIXTURE:

3 tablespoons plum sauce
2 tablespoons tomato ketchup

1 teaspoon chile sauce (optional)
5 tablespoons chicken broth or water
½ teaspoon white vinegar
½ teaspoon salt
½ teaspoon white pepper
1 tablespoon cornstarch combined with 2 tablespoons water
1½ teaspoons Chinese sesame oil

2 carrots, very finely shredded
1 cup very finely shredded Chinese white turnip (daikon, lo bok)
½ cup peeled, very finely shredded sweet potato
4 tablespoons coarsely chopped unsalted roasted peanuts
2 tablespoons shredded unsweetened coconut flakes
2 tablespoons white sesame seeds, toasted
2 green onions, finely shredded
2 tablespoons coriander leaves
2 fresh red chiles, seeds removed, finely shredded
4 teaspoons finely shredded lime zest
1½ tablespoons peeled, finely shredded fresh ginger
10 slices preserved red ginger, finely shredded
3 tablespoons Oriental mixed pickled vegetables
2 tablespoons candied orange or lemon peel
2 to 3 limes, cut into wedges

Marinate the fish in vinegar for 30 minutes, or until opaque, stirring once or twice. Place the fish in a colander and squeeze out the excess vinegar and moisture.

Prepare the sauce. Combine the plum sauce, ketchup, chile sauce, chicken broth, white vinegar, salt, and pepper in a small pan. Bring to a boil and cook until combined. Add the dissolved cornstarch mixture to the pan. Reduce the heat to simmer. Stir until the sauce is slightly thickened, translucent, and glazed. Add the sesame oil. Let cool.

Place the fish in the center of a large, round platter. Arrange the carrots, turnip, and sweet potato in neat piles in a circular fashion around the fish. Sprinkle the peanuts, coconut flakes, and sesame seeds on top. Arrange the green onions, coriander, chiles, lime zest, ginger, red ginger, mixed pickled vegetables, and candied orange peel in piles in a circular fashion around the vegetables. Pour the cooled sauce over all the shredded vegetables and fish. Serve with lime wedges.

Now comes the fun and ritualistic part! Toss with chopsticks and chant *"Lo Hei"*! Toss well for prosperity and good luck!

TIP: A short cooking in the vinegar is authentic. You may marinate the fish up to 8 hours in the refrigerator for a more complete cooking.

ADVANCE PREPARATION: Marinate the fish. Prepare the sauce 1 day ahead. Bring to room temperature before serving. Cut the vegetables 1 day ahead and wrap separately in plastic. Assemble the salad on the platter 1 to 2 hours ahead. Cover with plastic wrap. Pour the sauce over the *Yee-Sang* just before serving. Toss at the table.

Inspired by a recipe from Karl-Heinz Zimmerman, general manager, The Regent of Kuala Lumpur.

 ## Pickled Mackerel
Hinava Tenggiri

Hinava *is a colorful, classic Kadazan tribal dish from Borneo, which has a unique blending of zesty and spicy flavors. It is a favorite among the Kadazans and is always included as a first course in a meal. The fish is "cooked" in lime juice rather than using heat, which is the same technique employed in Mexican* ceviche. *A short "cooking" in the lime juice is authentic. If you prefer, you may marinate the fish for up to 8 hours for a more complete cooking.*

It is usually served at weddings and special occasions and is particularly good with Malay beer. When preparing this dish, the fish must be very fresh.

1 pound mackerel fillets
1 cup fresh lime juice
2 tablespoons finely shredded fresh ginger
3 shallots, cut in half, finely sliced
4 to 6 fresh red chiles, seeded, sliced

Rinse fish. Remove all bones and skin. Pat dry with paper towels. Using only the white flesh, cut the fish into very thin slices.

Add ¾ cup lime juice to the fish and mix well. Cover and refrigerate overnight or at least 6 hours, until the fish becomes firm and opaque. Stir occasionally. Place the fish in a colander and squeeze out all the excess liquid. Place the fish in a clean glass bowl. Add the remaining ¼ cup lime juice, ginger, shallots, and chiles. Toss to combine. Cover and marinate in the refrigerator for 1 to 2 hours. Serve cold.

ADVANCE PREPARATION: "Cook" fish in lime juice up to 8 hours prior to serving. Combine with remaining ingredients and marinate for 1 to 2 hours in the refrigerator.

Inspired by a recipe from executive chef Ralf Wiedmann, Hyatt Kinabalu International, Kota Kinabalu, Borneo.

 ## Shrimp Rolls
Har Quen

Traditionally seasoned shrimp paste is combined with carrots and black mushrooms, wrapped in a wonton skin, and lightly fried.

> 1 tablespoon finely minced, peeled, fresh ginger
> 6 water chestnuts, finely minced
> 2 green onions, finely minced
> 1 carrot, peeled, finely minced
> 6 Chinese dried black mushrooms, soaked in warm water 20 minutes or until spongy, drained, stems removed, finely minced
> 1 pound shrimp, shelled, deveined, minced into a paste
> 2 tablespoons dry sherry
> 2 teaspoons Chinese sesame oil
> 1 large egg white, lightly beaten
> 2 tablespoons cornstarch
> ½ teaspoon sugar
> ½ teaspoon salt
> ¼ teaspoon freshly ground black pepper
> 40 wonton skins
> 1 large egg yolk
> 3 cups oil
> Plum Sauce
> Chinese Hot Mustard

Combine the ginger, water chestnuts, green onions, carrot, black mushrooms, and shrimp paste. Mix in a circular motion until well blended. Add sherry, sesame oil, egg white, cornstarch, sugar, salt, and pepper. Mix well. Place 1 tablespoon of the shrimp mixture on the wonton skin and roll it evenly. Spread the filling almost to the edge. Brush one edge of the wonton skin with egg yolk. Fold the moistened edge of the skin over the roll and press lightly to seal. Repeat until all rolls have been made.

Heat wok. Add the oil and heat to 375° F. Deep-fry the shrimp rolls in batches, turning until they are golden brown. Remove. Drain on paper towels. Serve with Plum Sauce and Chinese Hot Mustard.

YIELD: 40 shrimp rolls.

ADVANCE PREPARATION: The Shrimp Rolls may be frozen for 2 months or may be cooked 1 day ahead, refrigerated, and reheated in a 350° F oven. Some flavor and texture will be lost, however.

SOUPS

 ## Spicy Chicken Soup
Soto Ayam

This zesty, refreshing Malay chicken soup is cooked with fragrant spices in the traditional manner and may be customized to your palate.

Serve as the main dish for a casual meal or as part of an elaborate banquet. Each diner assembles chicken shreds, translucent bean threads, brilliant red peppers and green onions and ladles over all an aromatic chicken broth, coriander, and other spices. Season to taste with lime juice and Chile Sambal *or prepared* Sambal Ulek.

    One 3- to 4-pound chicken, washed, cleaned, cut into large
        pieces
    1 large onion, chopped
    2 medium carrots, chopped
    2 teaspoons salt
    ½ teaspoon black peppercorns
    3 ounces bean threads, soaked in hot water 20 minutes or until
        soft, drained, cut into short lengths

PASTE INGREDIENTS:

    1 stalk lemon grass, bottom 6 inches only, chopped
    2 tablespoons minced garlic
    2 tablespoons minced ginger
    2 teaspoons coriander powder
    1 teaspoon ground cumin
    1½ teaspoons *galangal* powder
    1 teaspoon turmeric powder
    ½ teaspoon dried shrimp paste (*belacan*), optional
    5 macadamia nuts, crushed

3 tablespoons oil
1 teaspoon sugar
Salt and white pepper to taste
1 cup diced red bell pepper, or peeled, diced tomatoes

GARNISH:

2 green onions, finely sliced
4 to 5 tablespoons fried shallot flakes (page 24)
2 to 3 limes, cut into wedges

Sambal Belacan (page 237)

In a large saucepan, cover chicken with cold water and bring to a boil. Turn down to medium and cook 5 to 10 minutes, skimming the foam from the surface. When residue stops forming, add the onion, carrots, salt, and peppercorns. Simmer for 30 minutes, or until chicken is tender. Remove chicken and let cool. When cool enough to handle, remove the chicken from the bones and shred by hand. Strain and reserve broth. Skim off excess fat from broth.

Bring 3 quarts water to a boil. Add drained bean threads. Reduce heat and simmer 2 to 3 minutes, or until noodles are tender. Drain and set aside.

Pound or process the lemon grass, garlic, ginger, coriander, cumin, galangal, turmeric, shrimp paste, and macadamias to a paste. Heat 3 tablespoons oil in a pan. Add paste ingredients and fry on medium-low heat approximately 4 to 5 minutes, stirring to prevent burning. Add the strained stock. Bring to a boil. Reduce heat and simmer 10 to 20 minutes. Add sugar, salt, and white pepper to taste. Strain soup again. If stock has reduced, add water to make 6 cups.

Put the bean threads, red peppers, green onions, and fried shallot flakes in separate bowls. Place chicken on a serving dish and garnish with lime wedges. Reheat broth, and put in a serving tureen. To serve, have each guest put several spoonfuls of chicken, bean threads, and red peppers in a soup bowl. Pour very hot broth over all. Garnish with green onions and fried shallot flakes. Season with fresh lime juice and *Sambal Belacan* or bottled *Sambal Ulek,* if desired.

YIELD: 4 to 6 servings as main course, 8 to 12 as first course.

TIP: 1 packed teaspoon chopped fresh lemon zest may be substituted for the lemon grass.

ADVANCE PREPARATION: Prepare chicken and broth 1 day ahead. Cut up other ingredients and wrap in plastic wrap. Place prepared ingredients in a soup bowl as above. Reheat broth and pour hot broth on all.

VARIATION: Peeled, sliced, seeded cucumbers and bean sprouts may also be added to the soup.

Inspired by a recipe from Jean Marc LaForce, head of food and beverage, Pan Pacific Hotel, Kuala Lumpur.

 ## Chicken, Shrimp, and Rice Noodles in Coconut Sauce
Laksa Lemak

Thin rice noodles swimming in a subtly seasoned coconut milk sauce with chicken, shrimp, bean sprouts and tofu is one of the most popular dishes in Malaysia and Singapore.

2½ cups water
1 chicken breast
1 teaspoon salt
Freshly ground black pepper
2 cloves garlic, minced
1 tablespoon minced fresh ginger
4 to 6 dried red chiles, soaked in hot water until softened, minced
1 stalk lemon grass, bottom 6 inches only, sliced or thinly peeled
    rind of 1 lemon
1 medium onion, minced
3 macadamia nuts, minced (optional)
1 teaspoon ground turmeric
2 teaspoons ground coriander
6 tablespoons oil
2 teaspoons dried shrimp, soaked in hot water until soft, about 10
    minutes
6 ounces shrimp, shelled, deveined
12 ounces dried rice noodles, soaked in hot water to soften, about
    10 minutes, drained
1¼ cups thick coconut milk
6 ounces tofu, (bean curd) cut into small cubes
2 cups bean sprouts

GARNISH:

3 hard-boiled eggs, quartered (optional)

5 fresh red chiles, chopped
4 green onions, chopped
2 limes, cut into wedges

Bring water to a boil in a pan. Add chicken, salt, and pepper. Cover and simmer for 30 minutes. Strain and reserve the cooking liquid. Cut the chicken into bite-size cubes. Pound or blend garlic, ginger, chiles, lemon grass, onion, macadamia nuts, turmeric, and coriander until a fine paste is formed. Pound or blend dried shrimp separately until fine. (If necessary, add 1 to 2 tablespoons coconut milk to blender or processor to aid in blending mixture.) Heat 2 tablespoons oil. Add dried shrimp and fry shrimp for 1 minute. Add pounded spices and fry for 1 to 2 minutes. Add 2 tablespoons oil. Heat. Add the shrimp and chicken and stir-fry 1 minute. Add the reserved cooking liquid and simmer for 25 minutes. Add the drained rice noodles and coconut milk and bring very slowly to a boil, stirring gently to prevent the coconut milk from curdling. Add the tofu and bean sprouts, and simmer for 5 minutes, stirring occasionally. Top with a hard-boiled egg quarter. Serve with separate bowls of chiles and green onions and halved limes for those who prefer a more piquant flavor.

YIELD: 6 servings.

Inspired by a recipe from Jean Marc LaForce, head of food and beverage, Pan Pacific Hotel, Kuala Lumpur.

Chicken Soup with Rice Wine, Kadazan Style
Sup Manuk Om Hiing

A delicately flavored soup, which is served during a Kadazan tribal meal as a beverage and palate refresher. Chef Roslan says the flavors will have a chance to mellow if prepared a day ahead.

One 2½-pound chicken, cleaned, excess fat removed
2 inches ginger, cut into thin slices, smashed with the side of a cleaver
2 green onions, smashed with the side of a cleaver
Water to cover chicken
½ cup rice wine
Salt and pepper to taste
Watercress leaves

Place chicken breast-side down in a deep heavy pan into which the chicken fits snugly. Add ginger, green onions, and water to cover. Heat to boiling. Reduce heat. Simmer, skimming off residue that rises to the surface. When there is no remaining residue (about 10 minutes), cover and let the chicken simmer gently for 25 minutes. Remove the pan from the heat. Let the chicken steep, covered, for 45 minutes. Remove the chicken and cut the meat into bite-size pieces. Strain the stock. Wash the pan. Put the chicken and the stock into the clean pan. Reheat the soup. Add the wine. Season with salt and pepper to taste. Garnish with watercress. Serve.

YIELD: 4 to 6 servings.

TIP: Dry sherry or vodka may be substituted for rice wine.

ADVANCE PREPARATION: Prepare completely one day in advance. Reheat at serving time.

Inspired by Sous Chef Roslan, Tanjung Aru Beach Hotel, Kota Kinabalu, Borneo.

 ## Oxtail Soup, Kadazan Style
Asam Pedas Kadazan

A delightful blending of hot and sour, this traditional Kadazan tribal soup tastes better when made a day ahead.

3½ pounds oxtails, cut into 1-inch pieces
4 shallots, chopped
4 cloves garlic, chopped
1 tablespoon chopped fresh ginger
5 stalks lemon grass, bottom 6 inches only, sliced
1 tablespoon minced galangal
3 ounces candlenuts or macadamia nuts
5 dried red chiles, soaked in hot water for 5 minutes to soften, drained
3 tablespoons oil
1 teaspoon turmeric powder
5 Kaffir limes leaves, sliced finely (optional)
1 tablespoon plus 2 teaspoons tamarind soaked in ⅓ cup warm water for 10 minutes, strained
Salt to taste

Have your butcher cut the oxtails into 1-inch pieces. Put in a pan. Cover with water. Bring to a boil. Cook 5 minutes. Remove and drain the oxtails. Discard cooking water. Blend shallots, garlic, ginger, lemon grass, galangal, and nuts to a paste, adding some of the tamarind water if necessary for processing. Pound or process chiles to a coarse paste. Heat the oil on moderate heat in a frying pan. Add blended paste and stir until lightly browned. Add turmeric, Kaffir lime leaves, and chile paste mixture. Stir for 1 minute. Add strained tamarind water, oxtails, and water to cover. Bring to a boil. Reduce heat and simmer for 2 to 4 hours, stirring every 15 minutes, until oxtail becomes very tender and sauce becomes thick. Season with salt if desired. Serve hot with steamed rice.

YIELD: 4 servings.

ADVANCE PREPARATION: Cook one day ahead. Refrigerate. Reheat before serving.

Inspired by a recipe from Ralf Wiedmann, executive chef Hyatt Kinabalu, Kota Kinabalu, Borneo.

MEAT

 ## Grilled Beef, Kadazan Tribal Style
Hinugu Do Daging Miampai Bavang Taagang Om Topuak

The lightly seasoned marinade brings out the best natural flavors of beef in this Kadazan tribal favorite from Borneo. You may find that this is one of your preferred grilled beef dishes, and you will want to use the marinade when grilling a steak.

1 pound trimmed top sirloin or other tender beef cut
5 shallots, chopped
3 cloves garlic, chopped
1½ tablespoons peeled, chopped fresh ginger
½ teaspoon salt
2 tablespoons oil
Bamboo skewers, soaked in water for 1 to 2 hours to prevent
    burning during cooking

Cut the beef into ¼- by 2- by 1-inch strips. Pound or process the shallots, garlic, ginger, and salt to a smooth paste. Add the oil and mix. Put the beef in the paste mixture and combine together thoroughly. Let marinate for 2 hours, refrigerated. Thread the meat strips on the skewers. Grill over charcoal or broil in the oven, about 5 minutes on each side or to desired doneness, basting occasionally with the marinade. Serve with rice and Spinach with Dried Shrimp, Kadazan Style (page 225) and Chile Sauce Kadazan (page 238).

YIELD: 3 to 4 servings.

 ## Stir-Fried Beef with Oyster Sauce
Hauyao Chao Gau

A subtly flavored Chinese stir-fry.

¾ pound boneless lean beef (flank steak)
1 tablespoon light soy sauce
2 teaspoons rice wine or dry sherry
2 teaspoons sugar
2 teaspoons Chinese sesame oil
2 teaspoons cornstarch
4 tablespoons oil
8 Chinese dried black mushrooms, soaked in warm water until
    soft, about 20 minutes, stems removed
1 green bell pepper, cut into 1-inch squares
1 red bell pepper, cut into 1-inch squares
3 green onions, cut into 1½-inch lengths

SAUCE: Combine and set aside.

2 tablespoons oyster sauce
⅓ cup chicken stock
2 teaspoons cornstarch combined with 1 tablespoon water

Marinate beef in soy sauce, wine, sugar, sesame oil, and cornstarch for 20 minutes.

Heat 2 tablespoons of oil in a wok. Add pepper and green onions, and stir-fry for about 2 minutes. Remove and set aside. Add 2 tablespoons oil. Heat. Add the beef and stir-fry until browned. Add the cooked vegetables and stir. Add the sauce mixture, and stir until slightly thickened and translucent. Serve hot.

YIELD: 3 to 4 servings.

Malay Beef Stew
Daging Semur

Here is a hearty beef stew that is marvelous for family meals. Wonderful on a winter's night or after a busy day, this dish tastes even better when prepared a day ahead and the flavors are allowed to mellow.

2 pounds lean, boneless chuck, trimmed, cut into 1½-inch cubes
3 tablespoons light soy sauce
3 tablespoons dark soy sauce
3 tablespoons white vinegar
1 teaspoon black pepper
⅓ cup oil
3 cloves garlic, crushed
3 cups thinly sliced onions
3 cups beef stock or water
3 whole cardamoms, bruised
3 cloves
1½-inch piece cinnamon stick
½ teaspoon freshly ground nutmeg
3 medium potatoes, cut in half lengthwise, sliced into ¼-inch
    pieces
2 medium carrots, sliced on the diagonal into ¼-inch pieces
12 small white onions, peeled
Salt and pepper to taste
2 green onions, finely chopped (optional)

In a bowl, combine the beef, soy sauces, vinegar, and black pepper. Combine well and let marinate for 1 hour.

In a wok or heavy-bottom pan, heat oil. Add the garlic and onions, and sauté over moderate heat until soft and transparent. Do not brown. Add the beef, reserving the marinade. Cook, stirring, until the beef is lightly browned on all sides. Pour off any excess oil. Add the stock, reserved marinade, cardamom, cloves, cinnamon, and nutmeg. Bring to a boil. Reduce the heat to simmer, cover, and cook for 1½ to 2 hours or until the meat is tender and can be easily pierced with a fork. If necessary, replenish the liquid during the cooking. Add the potatoes, carrots, and onions and cook for 30 minutes longer, or until the vegetables are tender. Skim off any excess fat. Add salt and pepper to taste. Garnish with green onions. Serve hot with rice.

YIELD: 8 to 10 servings.

ADVANCE PREPARATION: Prepare completely 1 to 2 days in advance and refrigerate or freeze for 1 to 2 months.

Inspired by a recipe from sous chef Saw Siew Sim, Golden Sands Hotel, Penang.

 Madras Curried Beef
Kari Daging Madras

Brother Gerard Koe Soon Boon, a Malaysian student at Lewis University, Romeoville, Illinois, prepared this tasty, easily prepared curry for me. He used venison in his preparation, and it was excellent. He says you may also use lamb if you wish. It is also an excellent filling for Murtaba *(page 187) or other stuffed savories.*

> 2 tablespoons oil
> 1 large onion, diced into ¼-inch cubes
> 3 to 4 tablespoons Madras curry powder
> 1½ pounds ground beef
> 2 large potatoes, peeled, diced into ¼-inch cubes
> 1 cup water
> Salt to taste
> 2 tablespoons coriander leaves

Heat 2 tablespoons oil in a wok over moderate heat. Add the onion and stir-fry until soft and translucent, about 2 minutes. Add the curry powder and fry until the flavors are released, about 3 to 4 minutes, stirring to prevent burning. Add the ground meat and potatoes, and stir-fry about 3 minutes. Add 1 cup water. Stir. Reduce the heat to simmer and cook, stirring occasionally, until almost all of the water has reduced, and the dish is almost dry. Add salt to taste. Garnish with coriander. Serve with rice.

YIELD: 3 to 4 servings.

ADVANCE PREPARATION: The dish may be prepared ahead completely and reheated on the stove or in the microwave on medium heat.

Lamb Curry, Johore Style
Kari Kambing, Johore

A rich, luxurious lamb curry from southern Malaysia. It is perfect for a buffet as it can easily be doubled or tripled and be prepared a day ahead as the flavors improve upon standing.

8 shallots or 1 small onion, chopped
3 garlic cloves, chopped
1-inch piece fresh ginger, chopped
3 tablespoons ground coriander
1 teaspoon ground cumin
1 teaspoon turmeric powder
½ teaspoon nutmeg
1½ teaspoons ground chili powder (optional)
½ teaspoon black pepper
5 tablespoons oil
1-inch stick cinnamon
3 cardamom pods
8 whole cloves
3 sections star anise
2 pounds lean lamb, boned, cut into bite-size pieces
2½ cups thin coconut milk
4 potatoes, peeled, cut into bite-size pieces
3 medium tomatoes, cut into 6 wedges each
1 cup thick coconut milk
Salt to taste
Sambal Belacan (page 237), (optional)

Combine shallots, garlic, ginger, coriander, cumin, turmeric, nutmeg, chili powder, and pepper, and pound or process to a paste. Remove and set aside. Heat 3 tablespoons oil in a pan. Add cinnamon, cardamom, cloves, and star anise, and fry on moderate heat, stirring, for about 1 minute. Be careful not to burn the ingredients. Add paste ingredients, and fry on medium-low heat about 4 to 5 minutes, until fragrant. Stir often to prevent the mixture from burning. Add 2 tablespoons oil. Increase the heat. Add lamb and stir-fry until coated with spice mixture and no longer pink, about 3 to 5 minutes.

Add thin coconut milk. Bring to a boil. Reduce heat to simmer. Cover, and simmer for 30 minutes, or until meat is almost tender, stirring occasionally. Add the potatoes and tomatoes. Add the thick coconut milk. Bring to a boil. Reduce heat and simmer, uncovered, stirring occasionally until lamb is tender and potatoes are cooked, about 30 to 40 minutes. Season to taste with salt. Serve with rice and *Sambal Belacan* or purchased *sambal ulek,* if desired.

YIELD: 4 to 6 servings with other dishes.

ADVANCE PREPARATION: Prepare ahead, and refrigerate for 1 to 2 days or freeze. Reheat on medium heat in the microwave or on top of stove. If sauce is too thick, add more coconut milk or water.

Inspired by a recipe from Karl-Heinz Zimmerman, general manager, The Regent of Kuala Lumpur.

POULTRY

 ## Captain's Curry
Kari Kapitan

This thick, rich curry with the typical Nonya sour tang of tamarind is a classic Penang/Nonya dish. The Indian influence is also reflected in the use of turmeric. It was first served to me at the charming Dragon King Restaurant, a Nonya restaurant in Georgetown, Penang, by the owner, Mr. Khor Cheang Kee. His version had small potatoes in the curry. If you wish a heartier curry, you may add potatoes to the pan after adding the thin coconut milk.

Kari Kapitan is marvelous for a buffet as it can be doubled or tripled, and can be prepared ahead and reheated.

> 2 cloves garlic, minced
> 12 macadamia nuts, chopped
> 2 stalks lemon grass, bottom 6 inches only, minced
> 6 to 8 fresh red chiles, seeds removed, minced
> 4 tablespoons oil
> 16 shallots, minced
> One 2½- to 3-pound chicken, cut into bite-size pieces
> 2 teaspoons turmeric powder
> ½ teaspoon salt
> 2 cups thin coconut milk
> ⅓ cup thick coconut milk
> Juice of 1 to 2 limes

In a mortar, blender, or mini-processor, pound or process the garlic, macadamias, lemon grass, and chiles to a smooth paste, adding thin coconut milk to processor if necessary. Heat 2 tablespoons oil. Add shallots and cook until lightly browned. Add paste ingredients and fry over moderate heat until dry, about 4 to 5 minutes, adding more oil to prevent burning, if necessary. Add 2 tablespoons oil and the chicken. Stir-fry until all pieces are evenly browned. Add the turmeric, salt, and thin coconut milk. Bring to a boil, then reduce heat and simmer until the chicken is tender, about 30 minutes. Add the thick coconut milk. When gravy comes to a boil, add lime juice to taste. Serve with rice.

YIELD: 3 to 4 servings.

TIPS: Chicken breasts may be substituted for the whole chicken.

The amount of lime used is dependent upon the piquancy desired to balance the hotness of the chiles. If you reduce the amount of chiles, reduce the amount of lime juice. The flavors should be balanced to have an even amount of hot and sour.

ADVANCE PREPARATION: Prepare 1 to 2 days ahead and refrigerate or freeze for 2 months. Reheat in a microwave or on top of the stove on medium heat. If sauce is too thick, add more coconut milk or water.

Inspired by a recipe from sous chef Saw Siew Sim, Golden Sands Hotel, Penang.

 ## Grilled Chicken, Kelantan Style
Ayam Percik, Kelantan

The Regent of Kuala Lumpur serves this famous grilled chicken from the east coast of Malaysia. The aromatic, succulent chicken, enlivened with chiles and shallots, is mildly spiced and slightly sweet.

> ½ teaspoon dried shrimp paste (*belacan*)
> 3 tablespoons chopped fresh ginger
> 4 cloves garlic, chopped
> 1½ teaspoons salt
> 4 to 8 dried red chiles, soaked in hot water for 5 minutes to
>   soften, chopped
> 8 shallots or 1 small onion, chopped
> 1 tablespoon tamarind paste mixed with 3 tablespoons water,
>   soaked for 20 minutes, drained
> 3 cups coconut milk

1½ tablespoons rice flour
1 teaspoon sugar
One 2½-pound frying chicken, cut into pieces

Wrap the shrimp paste in foil. Toast over moderate heat in a dry pan for 2 minutes on each side. Remove and let cool.

Pound or process half the ginger, the garlic, and 1 teaspoon salt to a coarse paste. Rub the chicken with the mixture and let stand for 1 hour.

Pound or process chiles, shallots, remaining ginger, and toasted shrimp paste to a smooth paste. Strain the tamarind water. Combine the coconut milk with the rice flour, chile paste mixture, and tamarind water, and bring to a slow boil. Add ½ teaspoon salt and sugar, and stir over moderate heat for 10 to 15 minutes, or until thickened.

Dip the chicken into the thick coconut sauce. Grill over charcoal or in oven, basting frequently with coconut mixture, for approximately 15 minutes, or until both sides are browned and chicken is cooked. When done, the chicken should be moist from the repeated basting with the coconut mixture.

YIELD: 4 servings.

ADVANCE PREPARATION: Prepare the coconut sauce 1 day ahead. Marinate the chicken up to 6 hours ahead. Grill chicken before serving.

Inspired by a recipe from Karl-Heinz Zimmerman, general manager, The Regent of Kuala Lumpur.

 ## Roast Sugar Cane Chicken
Ayam Dara Bergolek Dengan Tebu

The delicate sweetness of sugar cane juice complements the lightly spiced seasonings in this succulent roast chicken. In Malaysia, the chicken is traditionally prepared by grilling the chicken over hot charcoal to dry it out and then baking it in the oven. I have used an easier method, which is simply to roast the chicken in an oven.

2 teaspoons chopped galangal
2 tablespoons chopped lemon grass, bottom 6 inches only
6 garlic cloves, chopped
2 shallots, chopped
2 to 3 fresh red chiles, seeds removed, chopped

3 tablespoons oil
½ teaspoon turmeric powder
¼ teaspoon fennel powder
¾ teaspoon cumin powder
2 bay leaves
2 tablespoons fresh lime juice
1 cup sugar cane juice
One 2- to 2½-pound chicken
Fried shallot flakes (page 24)

Pound or process the galangal, lemon grass, garlic, shallots, and chiles to a smooth paste. Heat the oil in a pan. Add the paste mixture and stir-fry for 3 to 4 minutes on moderate heat. Be careful not to allow the mixture to burn. Add the turmeric, fennel, cumin, bay leaves, lime juice, and sugar cane juice. Bring to a boil. Cook for 10 minutes to reduce the sauce by half, stirring occasionally. Remove from heat and let cool slightly. Rub the chicken inside and out with the cooked sauce, reserving any extra sauce. Preheat oven to 425° F. Place the chicken breast-side down on a rack in a roasting pan. Roast for 10 minutes. Brush the chicken with the sauce and turn the chicken over. Baste the breast with the sauce and roast for 10 minutes. Reduce the oven temperature to 350° F. Brush the chicken with the sauce. Cook the chicken for 15 minutes. Turn over the chicken and brush with the sauce. Continue cooking the chicken for another 15 minutes or until tender and the juices run clear when the chicken is pierced by a fork. Serve with rice and garnish with fried shallot flakes.

YIELD: 3 to 4 servings.

TIP: Sugar cane juice is available in cans in Asian markets. You may substitute sugar syrup prepared from 3½ tablespoons raw sugar dissolved in 1 cup water. Raw sugar is best, but you may substitute granulated sugar.

ADVANCE PREPARATION: Cook the sauce one day ahead and refrigerate.

Inspired by a recipe from executive chef August Werhle, Hyatt Kuantan.

Phoenix Dragon Chicken and Ham
Lung Fung Ching Chang

In this dish, the dragon (ham) represents Yang *power, which stands for heaven, the sun, and the positive male principle of light, warmth, and activity. The chicken,* Yin, *stands for the opposite: the earth, the moon, and the negative or female principle of shade, cold, and inactivity. This dish is an example of the Chinese belief that all good and harmonious things in the universe are produced by the interaction of these two opposing principles or forces. Because of its symbolism, Phoenix Dragon Chicken, which joins the female beauty of the chicken and the male virility of the ham in perfect harmony, is a perfect dish to serve on the Chinese New Year.*

The ham is put between two layers of chicken, then enclosed in a crunchy batter, deep-fried, and served with a sprinkling of roasted Szechuan peppercorn salt. It is wonderful for a party as it stands well on a buffet table.

4 large chicken breasts, skinned, boned
8 ⅛-inch-thick slices cooked Smithfield ham or 8 slices
    baked ham

BATTER:

    1 cup all-purpose flour
    2 teaspoons baking powder
    ¼ teaspoon salt
    1 egg
    ¾ cup water

    4 cups oil
    Szechuan peppercorn salt (page 27)

For easier handling, freeze the chicken breasts until firm, about 2 hours. Remove the fillets and cut off the thin tapered ends of the breasts. Place a piece of chicken on a cutting board. Starting at the thicker side of the breast, slice horizontally through the middle of the meat to within ½ inch of the far end, yielding two flaps of meat with the end attached to form a pocket. Repeat with the remaining breast halves.

Open the flap of each chicken breast, line the breast neatly with a slice of ham, and press the breast together to close.

Prepare the batter. Combine the flour, baking powder, and salt. Lightly beat the egg and water together. Add the egg mixture to the flour, gradually stirring, until it is as smooth as a thin pancake batter. Set aside.

Add 4 cups oil to a wok. Heat the oil to 350° F. Stir the batter. Dip a chicken breast into the batter, holding together the open end and allowing the excess batter to drip off. Quickly slip the breast into the hot oil. Repeat with the remaining breasts. Fry them for 1 minute, then turn. Reduce the heat to medium and fry for 3 minutes, turning constantly until they are crisp and brown. To test for doneness, press the breast to see if it is firm. If not, cook again until firm to the touch. Drain the chicken. Coat and fry the remaining breasts. Reheat the oil to 350° F. Refry all the chicken together for 1 to 2 minutes. Remove. Drain on paper towels. Slice diagonally into ½-inch pieces. Serve with Szechuan peppercorn salt.

YIELD: 6 to 8 servings with other dishes.

ADVANCE PREPARATION: The ham-filled chicken breasts may be refrigerated 1 day or frozen 1 to 2 months.

The chicken may be prepared ahead and fried the first time earlier in the day. Refry for the second time at serving time.

 ## Phoenix Dragon Chicken and Ham with Vegetables
Shin Choy Lung Fung

Crispy chicken served on a bed of vegetables imparts an interesting contrast of tastes and textures.

The Chinese believe that chicken served on special occasions must be plump and succulent: you risk shrinking your luck with one that is scrawny.

1 recipe Phoenix Dragon Chicken (page 209)
3 tablespoons oil
2 slices ginger, the size of a quarter, peeled, minced
1 garlic clove, minced
½ cup shredded bambo shoots
4 water chestnuts, sliced
4 green onions, shredded into 2-inch lengths

SAUCE MIXTURE: Combine and set aside

¾ cup chicken broth
1 tablespoon dry sherry
1 tablespoon soy sauce
Pinch freshly ground white pepper

1 tablespoon cornstarch dissolved in 2 tablespoons cold water
1 teaspoon Chinese sesame oil

Prepare the Phoenix Dragon Chicken through the first frying. Reserve the deep-frying oil. Heat the wok. Add 3 tablespoons oil and heat. Add the ginger and garlic, and cook until fragrant, about 10 seconds. Add the bamboo shoots, water chestnuts, and green onions. Stir rapidly for 30 seconds. Add the sauce mixture. When the liquid comes to a boil, stir in the dissolved cornstarch mixture and stir until translucent and a glaze has formed. Add the Chinese sesame oil. Stir.

Reheat the deep-frying oil for the Phoenix Dragon Chicken to 350° F. Refry all the chicken together for 1 to 2 minutes. Turn the chicken until it is very crisp and brown. Remove and drain on paper towels. Slice the chicken diagonally into ½-inch pieces.

Reheat the sauce. Spread the vegetable sauce on a platter, making a bed for the cooked chicken. Place the chicken on top of the vegetables. Serve.

YIELD: 6 to 8 servings with other dishes.

ADVANCE PREPARATION: Fry the chicken and prepare the vegetable sauce earlier in the day. Fry the chicken a second time and reheat the sauce at serving time.

 ## Steamed Ginger Chicken
Kaing Shi Ching Wat Gai

Easily prepared and low in calories, this chicken is wonderful hot or cold!

½ cup chicken stock
2 tablespoons dark soy sauce
2 tablespoons white vinegar
1 teaspoon sugar
1 teaspoon Chinese sesame oil

Salt and pepper to taste
One 2½-pound chicken, cut into 6 pieces
5 teaspoons peeled, minced fresh ginger
2 green onions, shredded into 1½-inch lengths
6 Chinese dried black mushrooms, soaked in warm water to
   soften, about 20 minutes, stems removed

Combine the chicken stock, soy sauce, vinegar, sugar, sesame oil, salt, and pepper. Fill a steamer with 2 to 3 inches of water, or put a rack into a wok or large deep pan and fill it with water almost to the rack. Bring the water to a boil.

In a shallow heatproof container, arrange the chicken pieces with breasts on the bottom and joints on the top. Pour the soy sauce mixture over the chicken. Sprinkle the ginger, green onions, and Chinese black mushrooms on the chicken. Gently lower the bowl into the steamer. Cover the pan tightly and lower the heat. Steam for approximately 45 minutes, or until tender and cooked throughout. Check the water level of the steamer occasionally and replenish with water if necessary. Serve hot or cold.

YIELD: 3 to 4 servings.

VARIATION: Add 1 sliced Chinese sausage when steaming.

Two whole boned chicken breasts, cut in half, may be substituted for the whole chicken. Steam for approximately 15 minutes or until done. If using boned chicken breasts, reduce the amount of minced ginger to 4 teaspoons.

FISH AND SEAFOOD

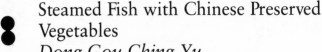 **Steamed Fish with Chinese Preserved
Vegetables
*Dong Gou Ching Yu***

Like all steamed fish prepared in the Chinese manner, this dish is very versatile. It is wonderfully simple for a meal for two or equally fitting as a finale for an elegant dinner. The sweetness of the Chinese preserved vegetables and the zip of the chiles are combined with the purity and texture of the fresh fish. A whole fish is symbolic of abundance and plenty to the Chinese and is the perfect ending to a Chinese banquet.

The preparation and steaming of the fish takes only 30 minutes and requires little care.

    One 1½- to 2-pound fish (sea bass, whitefish, pike), cleaned,
        scaled, with head and tail intact
    4 Chinese dried black mushrooms, soaked in hot water for 20
        minutes until spongy, drained, stems removed, shredded
    3 tablespoons finely shredded Chinese preserved vegetables
    1 to 2 fresh red chiles, seeded, finely sliced
    1 tablespoon light soy sauce
    2 tablespoons dry sherry
    ¼ teaspoon freshly ground black pepper
    2 green onions, finely sliced
    2 tablespoons coriander leaves

Wash and pat the fish dry with paper towels. Make 3 diagonal slashes 1 inch apart on each side of fish. Place the fish on a heatproof platter. Place the mushrooms, preserved vegetables, and chiles on top of fish. Combine the soy sauce, sherry, and black pepper, and pour on top of fish.

    Place the fish on a heatproof plate on a rack in a steamer or large roasting pan. Fill the steamer with boiling water to within 1 inch of top of rack. Cover, turn heat to medium-high, and steam the fish, allowing 10 minutes per inch of thickness of the fish. Add more boiling water to the pan if necessary. The fish is done when a skewer or thin knife easily penetrates the thickest part and comes out clean. Keep steamer covered until ready to serve. Remove the platter from the steamer. Garnish with green onions and coriander. Serve.

YIELD: 2 to 3 servings.

TIPS: Canned Chinese preserved vegetables are available in Asian grocery stores.

Four quarter-sized pieces of ginger, shredded, may be substituted for the preserved vegetables.

ADVANCE PREPARATION: Assemble the fish and ingredients on a heatproof platter several hours before cooking. Cover with plastic wrap. Refrigerate. Steam just before serving.

Inspired by a recipe from Karl-Heinz Zimmerman, general manager, The Regent of Kuala Lumpur.

Sweet and Sour Fish
Ng Fook Chong Yee

This fish dish, consisting of five shredded vegetables, represents the five signs of prosperity, Ng Fook. A popular dish among the Cantonese, this is usually served for a family reunion.

It is an impressive presentation, which is deep-fried and glazed with a colorful vegetable sauce.

One 2- to 2½-pound whole fish (red snapper, pike), scaled,
    cleaned, head and tail intact
4 cups plus 3 tablespoons oil
2 to 3 fresh red chiles, seeds removed, thinly sliced
1 green bell pepper, shredded into 1½-inch lengths
1 cucumber, peeled, cut in half, seeds removed, shredded into
    1½-inch lengths
1 medium onion, cut into quarters, thinly sliced
1 medium tomato, cut into quarters, thinly sliced
¼ cup cornstarch
¼ cup all-purpose flour

SAUCE MIXTURE: Combine and set aside

6 tablespoons tomato ketchup
2 tablespoons chile sauce *(sambal ulek)*
2 tablespoons plum sauce
5 tablespoons sugar
2 tablespoons white vinegar
½ cup chicken broth
1 tablespoon cornstarch dissolved in 2 tablespoons water

Coriander or parsley for garnish (optional)

Make deep scores diagonally an inch apart across the body of the fish. Turn the fish over and repeat on the other side.

Heat 3 tablespoons oil in the wok. Add the chiles, green pepper, cucumber, onion, and tomatoes and stir-fry for 1 to 2 minutes or until the vegetables are crunchy, but not soft. Stir the sauce mixture and add to the wok. Stir until the mixture boils and thickens. Set aside.

Heat oil in a wok to 350° F. Combine the cornstarch and flour. Coat the fish completely with the mixture. Slowly lower the fish into the oil head first and immerse it in the oil. Ladle the hot oil over the fish. Deep-fry the fish 5 to 7 minutes, or just long enough to brown lightly on each side, basting and shifting it occasionally. Gently remove the fish with a slotted spoon. Place on paper towers to drain. Place on a large, heated serving platter. Reheat the sauce and pour over the fish. Garnish with coriander. Serve hot.

YIELD: 3 to 4 servings with other dishes.

ADVANCE PREPARATION: The sauce may be prepared ahead. Deep-fry the fish the first time several hours before serving. Refry a second time in hot oil when ready to serve. Reheat the sauce and pour over the fish.

Inspired by a recipe from Karl-Heinz Zimmerman, general manager, The Regent of Kuala Lumpur.

 Grilled White Pomfret with Coconut Curry
Ikan Bawal Panggang Dan Kari Lemak

Delicate flavors of the grilled pomfret are combined with a tangy sauce.

2 to 4 fresh red chiles, seeded, minced
1 clove garlic, minced
2 shallots, minced
2 teaspoons peeled minced fresh ginger
1 stalk lemon grass, bottom 6 inches only, finely minced
½ teaspoon turmeric powder
One 1½-pound white pomfret, pompano, or red snapper
4 tablespoons oil
Salt and white pepper to taste
½ cup thin coconut milk

Pound or process chiles, garlic, shallots, ginger, and lemon grass to a coarse paste. Add the turmeric and mix.

Rinse the fish and drain well. Score the fish with diagonal cuts spaced 1 to 2 inches apart across the body. Stuff the fish with half of the paste, oil, and season with salt and pepper to taste. Grill over charcoal or broil in the oven, allowing approximately 10 minutes per inch of thickness of fish.

To prepare coconut curry, heat 2 tablespoons oil in a medium saucepan. Add the remaining paste mixture and fry on moderate heat for 2 to 3 minutes, stirring to prevent burning. Add the coconut milk. Season to taste with salt and pepper. On moderate heat, bring to a slow boil. Reduce the heat to simmer and continue cooking for 5 minutes. Pour the coconut curry into a serving container. Serve immediately with the grilled fish. Serve with rice and vegetables.

YIELD: 2 to 3 servings with other dishes.

TIP: White pomfret is available frozen in some Asian markets. It is a very highly regarded fish in Southeast Asia.

ADVANCE PREPARATION: Stuff the fish and prepare the sauce several hours ahead. Grill at serving time.

Inspired by a recipe from Karl Moser, executive chef, Hyatt Saujana, Petaling Jaya, Malaysia.

 ## Three Varieties Vegetables with Scallops
Choy Chao Yuen Bui

All is harmonious in this symbolic, easily prepared Chinese stir-fry. Good luck is represented by red peppers, and wealth and prosperity by golden baby corn and the green bok choy.

8 ounces scallops, washed and drained
4 tablespoons oil
1 slice fresh ginger, the size of a quarter, chopped
1 clove garlic, chopped
One 8-ounce can baby corn, drained
8 ounces bok choy, tough stems removed, cut into 1½-inch
    pieces
12 snow peas, stringed
1 small red bell pepper, cut into 1-inch squares
6 large dried Chinese black mushrooms, soaked in warm water
    for 20 minutes to soften, tough stems removed

SAUCE MIXTURE: Combine and set aside

1 tablespoon oyster sauce
1 tablespoon light soy sauce
1 tablespoon dry sherry
½ teaspoon sugar
½ teaspoon white pepper
1 tablespoon cornstarch dissolved in 2 tablespoons cold water

1 teaspoon Chinese sesame oil (optional)

If using large sea scallops, cut each crosswise into 2 pieces. Heat 2 tablespoons oil in wok or heavy skillet. Add ginger and garlic and stir 5 to 10 seconds. Add scallops and stir-fry until scallops are opaque and cooked throughout, about 2 to 3 minutes. Remove and set aside. Add 2 tablespoons oil to wok. Add baby corn, bok choy, snow peas, red peppers, and black mushrooms. Stir-fry for 1 to 2 minutes or until vegetables are tender. Return cooked scallops to pan. Stir. Add sauce mixture and cook until sauce thickens slightly and has a glaze. Add the sesame oil. Stir. Pour into a hot serving dish. Serve immediately with rice.

YIELD: 3 to 4 servings.

ADVANCE PREPARATION: Vegetables and scallops may be prepared in advance and refrigerated in self-sealing plastic bags. Sauce may be prepared several hours ahead. Cook at serving time.

VARIATION: Substitute sliced bamboo shoots for baby corn or an 8-ounce can straw mushrooms, drained, for Chinese dried black mushrooms.

Inspired by a recipe from Karl-Heinz Zimmerman, general manager, The Regent of Kuala Lumpur.

 ### Stir-Fried Shrimp in Spicy Sauce
Sambal Udang

Hot, sour, and easily prepared, this dish can be just as hot as you desire. Adjust the amount of chiles to your liking. If you wish to dine as the Malays, use 10 chiles. It will be hot!

4 to 10 dried, hot red chiles, soaked in warm water to soften,
    about 10 minutes
8 cashew nuts
7 shallots, chopped
¾ teaspoon dried shrimp paste *(belacan)*
1 medium onion, coarsely sliced
1 pound medium shrimp, shelled, deveined
6 tablespoons oil
2 tablespoons tamarind water (page 25)
½ teaspoon salt
2 teaspoons sugar

Pound or process the chiles, cashews, shallots, and shrimp paste to a smooth paste. Heat oil in a wok or skillet on moderate heat. Add the paste mixture and stir-fry 3 to 4 minutes. Add the onions and stir-fry for 1 minute. Add the shrimp and stir-fry an additional minute. Add the tamarind water, salt, and sugar. Stir-fry 3 to 5 minutes, or until the shrimp and onions are cooked and tender. Serve hot with rice.

YIELD. 4 servings with other dishes.

TIP: 4 teaspoons lime or lemon juice may be substituted for the tamarind water.

ADVANCE PREPARATION: Prepare ahead completely. Reheat on moderate heat at serving time.

Inspired by a recipe from executive chef Puan Noor Ha Yati Shafir, The Shangri-La Hotel, Kuala Lumpur.

 ## Stir-Fried Scallops, Red Peppers, and Zucchini
Hong Chiu Yuen Bui

An easily prepared, colorful Chinese stir-fry.

    4 tablespoons oil
    1 red bell pepper, cored, seeded, cut into ¼-inchy cubes
    1 small zucchini, quartered lengthwise, cut crosswise into ¼-
        inch cubes
    3 green onions, shredded into 1-inch shreds
    2 tablespoons minced fresh ginger
    1 garlic clove, peeled, minced
    ¾ pound bay scallops

SAUCE MIXTURE: Combine and set aside

    1 tablespoon ketchup
    2 tablespoons oyster sauce
    1 tablespoon light soy sauce
    1 tablespoon dry sherry
    ¾ teaspoon sugar
    1 teaspoon Chinese sesame oil
    ¼ teaspoon freshly ground white pepper

Heat wok. Add 2 tablespoons oil. Heat. Add red pepper, zucchini, and green onions. Stir-fry for 1 minute. Remove from wok. Add 2 tablespoons oil to the wok. Heat. Add the ginger and garlic. Stir-fry for 5 seconds. Add the scallops and stir until they become opaque, about 1 minute. Add the cooked vegetables. Stir. Stir the sauce mixture. Add to the wok. Stir until heated throughout. Serve.

YIELD: 2 to 3 servings.

SALADS AND VEGETABLES

 ### Chinese Salad, Penang Nonya Style
Penang Rujak

Mr. Khor Cheang Kee, owner of the Dragon King Restaurant, Penang, serves this special salad, which may be served as an appetizer, a snack, a side dish, or even as a meal in itself. Mr. Khor said the Nonya/Penang version of Rujak is made predominantly with fruit. The Nonyas have their own name for this type of dish, Chia Thit Tho, *meaning literally "eating for complete enjoyment" whatever the time of day or whatever the occasion. The tasty combination of flavors—sour, sweet, spicy— found in the sauce make this salad a perfect accompaniment for curries.*

In other areas of Malaysia, Rujak is prepared with vegetables and garnished with hard-boiled eggs.

SAUCE INGREDIENTS:

2 to 3 fresh red chiles, seeds removed, minced
½ teaspoon dried shrimp paste toasted (*belacan*)
3 tablespoons brown sugar
4 tablespoons ground unsalted roasted peanuts
1½ tablespoons tamarind paste dissolved in ½ cup water,
    strained, pulp discarded
Salt to taste

1 medium sweet potato, cooked, peeled, cut into thin slices
½ cucumber, cut in half, seeds removed, sliced
½ fresh pineapple, sliced into wedges, ½ inch by ¾ inch
2 fresh mangoes, sliced (optional)
4 ounces fresh bean sprouts, blanced in boiling water for 30
    seconds
1 cup Chinese turnip (*daikon, lo bok*), peeled, sliced

GARNISH:

2 tablespoons unsalted dry roasted peanuts, chopped
2 teaspoons toasted sesame seeds
2 limes, cut into wedges

In a blender or processor, process chiles, toasted shrimp paste, sugar, ground peanuts, and tamarind water together to make a paste. Add salt to taste. Pour sauce into a small bowl. Arrange salad ingredients around the sauce and let each guest spoon the sauce on the Rujak— or toss all together before serving. Serve garnished with peanuts, sesame seeds, and lime wedges. For a more tangy taste, squeeze the juice of limes over the salad.

YIELD: 4 to 6 servings.

TIPS: For a more interesting flavor, substitute 1 cup of pounded peanut brittle instead of brown sugar and roasted peanuts.

If sauce is too thick, dilute with water.

ADVANCE PREPARATION: Prepare ingredients and sauce 1 day ahead. Wrap separately in plastic wrap. Combine salad when serving.

 ## Chicken Mint Salad
Selada Ayam

A cool, refreshing salad with a hint of mint!

2 whole chicken breasts, boned, skinned
Salt and pepper to taste
½ teaspoon shrimp paste (*belacan*)
1 medium onion, chopped
1 tablespoon chopped ginger
2 fresh red chiles, seeded, chopped
½ teaspoon salt or to taste
1½ tablespoons brown sugar
1 cup coconut milk
1 cucumber, peeled, halved, seeded, shredded
¾ cup fresh mint leaves

Season chicken with salt and pepper. Grill over charcoal or broil in oven until done. Let cool. Cut into bite-size, 1½-inch shreds.

Wrap shrimp paste in foil. Toast over moderate heat in a dry pan for approximately 2 minutes on each side.

Pound or process the onion, ginger, chiles, shrimp paste, and salt to a smooth paste. Add brown sugar and mix. In a bowl, combine the coconut milk with the paste mixture. Add the cucumber, chicken, and half the mint to the coconut mixture. Toss to combine ingredients. Add salt to taste. Chill. Serve garnished with remaining mint leaves.

YIELD: 3 to 4 servings with other dishes.

ADVANCE PREPARATION: Prepare ahead completely. Chill.

 ## Stir-Fried Mixed Vegetables
Sayur Goreng

An easily prepared, colorful, zesty vegetable dish.

- 1 small onion, minced
- 2 shallots, minced
- 1 clove garlic, minced
- 4 tablespoons oil
- 15 green beans, sliced into 1½-inch lengths
- 2 carrots, sliced
- 1 green bell pepper, cut into 1½-inch strips
- ½ small head cauliflower, cut into small flowerets
- 12 ears canned baby corn
- 2 fresh red chiles, seeded, shredded
- 3 tablespoons ketchup
- 1½ tablespoons chile sauce
- Salt to taste
- ⅛ teaspoon freshly ground pepper

Combine onion, shallots, and garlic. Pound or process to a smooth paste. Add 2 tablespoons oil to the wok or frying pan. Heat. Add the paste to the wok and sauté until golden brown, about 3 minutes. Add 2 tablespoons oil. Add green beans, carrots, green pepper, cauliflower, baby corn, and chiles. Stir-fry until done, about 5 to 6 minutes. Add ketchup and chile sauce. Stir for 1 minute until well combined. Season with salt and pepper to taste. Serve.

YIELD: 4 servings.

Five Treasure Vegetable Platter
Gan Pun Ng Bo

Vegetables, delicately seasoned and attractively presented, make this dish perfect for an elegant banquet. The five treasures represent the Chinese five signs of prosperity.

You may use your own creativity in choosing the vegetables. Be sure to have complementary colors of the vegetables arranged in a decorative pattern on the platter. I prefer to serve the vegetables at room temperature, giving me plenty of time to arrange the food presentation. I then reheat the sauce and pour the hot sauce over the vegetables at serving time. This recipe may easily be doubled or tripled.

1 pound asparagus, stems peeled, tough ends removed
1 pound baby carrots, peeled, trimmed
One 15-ounce can straw mushrooms, drained
One 15-ounce can baby corn
3 medium tomatoes

SAUCE MIXTURE:

2 cups chicken stock
1 tablespoon dry sherry
1 tablespoon light soy sauce
1 teaspoon sugar

2 tablespoons cornstarch dissolved in 4 tablespoons cold water
½ teaspoon Chinese sesame oil

Steam the asparagus and carrots separately over boiling water until barely tender. Drain in a colander. Run under cold water. Drain. Blanch the drained mushrooms and corn separately in boiling water for 15 seconds. Drain. Run under cold water. Drain. Blanch the tomatoes in boiling water for 30 seconds to loosen the skins. Remove and peel the tomatoes. Cut the tomatoes into quarters. Remove the seeds.

Combine the sauce ingredients. Heat and stir until the sugar is dissolved. Reheat the vegetables individually in the sauce mixture. Drain the vegetables into the pan. Place the mushrooms in the center of the platter. Place the other vegetables in a pinwheel design around the edge of the mushrooms. Heat the sauce mixture to boiling. Add the dissolved cornstarch and stir until thickened. Add the sesame oil. Stir. Pour the sauce over the vegetables.

YIELD: 6 to 8 servings with other dishes.

ADVANCE PREPARATION: Cook the vegetables ahead. Prepare the sauce. If you wish to serve the vegetables hot, reheat the vegetables in the sauce or by steaming or microwaving on moderate heat, being careful not to overcook the vegetables. Reheat the sauce and pour it over the vegetables.

 ## Vegetables in Coconut Gravy
Sayur Lodeh

Executive Chef Puan Noor Ha Yati Shafir, the Indonesian-born chef of the Shangri-La Hotel, Kuala Lumpur, introduced me to this wonderful "vegetable stew." She explained that there are many variations; her version reflects her Indonesian heritage. The word Sayur *means "vegetables," and* Lodeh, *"cooked until soft." In Malaysia and Indonesia, it is served with rice as part of a meal. It is ideal for a buffet and an interesting vegetable dish to serve during a Western dinner.*

    1 small onion, chopped
    1 fresh red chile, chopped
    1 fresh green chile, chopped
    2 garlic cloves, minced
    1 teaspoon shrimp paste (*belacan*)
    2 tablespoons oil
    2 cups coconut milk
    ¾ teaspoon coriander powder
    2 bay leaves
    10 long Chinese green beans or 15 string beans, tips removed,
        cut into 1½-inch lengths
    2 medium carrots, cut into 1½-inch shreds
    1 cup cauliflowerets
    ¼ pound cabbage, coarsely shredded
    2 ounces dried rice sticks, soaked in warm water for 20 minutes
        or until pliable, drained, cut into 1½-inch lengths
    ½ teaspoon brown sugar
    6 sprigs watercress (optional)
    Salt and pepper to taste

Pound or process onion, chiles, garlic, and shrimp paste to a coarse paste. Heat 2 tablespoons oil over moderate heat. Fry the paste, stirring to prevent burning, 2 to 3 minutes. Add the coconut milk and bring to the simmering point. Add the coriander and bay leaves. Add the beans, carrots, and cauliflower, and simmer until almost tender, about 5 to 7 minutes. Add the cabbage and simmer another 2 to 3 minutes. The vegetables should be tender but still crisp. Add the rice sticks and brown sugar. Bring slowly to a simmer, stirring constantly and cook about 1 minute. Add salt and pepper to taste.

YIELD: 4 servings with other dishes.

ADVANCE PREPARATION: Cook the vegetables and coconut milk ahead. Add the rice sticks and brown sugar when reheating. Season to taste.

VARIATION: Add shelled, cooked shrimp, and cook for 2 to 3 minutes at the end of the cooking time. If desired, omit the rice sticks.

 Spiced Green Beans
Kacang Bendi Goreng Rempah

Green beans and shrimp are combined with spices to produce a flavorful, spirited dish.

6 dried red chiles, soaked in warm water for 20 minutes to soften, chopped
2 medium onions, chopped
6 macadamia nuts, chopped
½ teaspoon shrimp paste (*belacan*)
3 tablespoons oil
½ pound small shrimp, peeled, deveined
1 pound green beans, tips removed, cut into 1½-inch pieces
4 tablespoons water
Salt to taste

Pound or process the chiles, onions, nuts, and shrimp paste to a coarse paste. Heat oil in a skillet on moderate heat. Add the paste mixture and fry for 2 to 3 minutes. Add the shrimp and stir-fry for 1 minute. Add the green beans. Stir. Add the water and salt to taste. Bring to a boil. Reduce heat and simmer until the beans are cooked, but still crunchy.

YIELD: 6 servings with other dishes.

VARIATION: Substitute sliced zucchini for the green beans.

Spinach with Dried Shrimp, Kadazan Style
Napa Do Pakis

This traditional Kadazan dish was first served to me during a tribal dinner at the Tanjung Aru Beach Hotel. For their preparation, they used local ferns. I have substituted tender, young spinach.

My children say that spinach has never tasted so good because it doesn't taste like spinach! They feel this is a dish you must try.

12 ounces fresh young spinach, tough part of stems removed
1 teaspoon dried shrimp, soaked in hot water until softened, drained
3 shallots, cut in half, thinly sliced
2 tablespoons oil
Salt to taste
Dash white pepper
1 fresh red chile, seeds removed, chopped, (optional)

Wash and drain spinach. Pound or process the presoaked dried shrimp to a fine powder. In a wok, heat 2 tablespoons oil. Add the shallots and stir-fry until very lightly browned. Add the shrimp powder. Stir. Add spinach and cook until just wilted. Do not overcook. Season with salt and pepper. Garnish with chile if desired. Serve immediately.

YIELD: 2 to 3 servings with other dishes.

TIP: Substitute ferns or watercress for the spinach.

Inspired by a recipe from sous chef Roslan, Tanjung Aru Beach Hotel, Kota Kinabalu, Borneo.

RICE, NOODLES, AND OMELETS

 Scented Rice
Nasi Minyak

Nasi Minyak is served on festive occasions, such as a wedding, when it has special garnishes such as candied flowers.

T. Kemala Intan, who is from the Malay tribe in Medan, North Sumatra, taught me this dish. She explained that on the wedding day, a chicken is buried inside the Nasi Minyak. *The bride feeds the groom and then the groom feeds the bride. It is said that if the bride pulls out the chicken, she will rule the family. If the groom does, he will. If they pull it out together, they will rule the family jointly.*

> 2 cups long-grain rice
> 2 tablespoons ghee or oil
> 2-inch stick cinnamon
> 2 whole cloves
> ¼ teaspoon cardamom seeds
> 6 shallots, finely sliced
> 2 cloves garlic, minced
> 1 tablespoon shredded fresh ginger
> ½ teaspoon turmeric
> 3 cups chicken stock or water
> Salt to taste

GARNISH:

> ½ cup golden raisins
> Fried shallot flakes (page 23)

Wash rice until water runs clear. Place in a colander and let drain for 1 hour.

Heat ghee or oil in a deep pan. On medium-high heat, fry cinnamon, cloves, and cardamom for 1 minute, stirring. Add shallots, garlic, ginger, and turmeric, and cook over moderate heat until lightly browned, about 1 minute.

Add the drained rice and fry 2 to 3 minutes, until each grain is coated with ghee. Add chicken stock and salt to taste. Bring to a boil. Reduce heat. Cover the pan and allow rice to cook on lowest heat until all liquid is absorbed, about 15 to 18 minutes. Lift cover only long enough to check that rice has absorbed the water. Cover again. Remove from heat. Let stand for 10 minutes before fluffing the rice. Garnish with raisins and fried shallot flakes. Serve hot.

YIELD: 3 to 4 servings.

 ## Scented Rice, Penang Style
Nasi Minyak, Penang

A potpourri of spices is combined in this fragrant rice dish.

> 2 cups long-grain rice, soaked in water for 1 hour, drained in colander for 1 hour
> 2 tablespoons ghee or oil
> 6 shallots, finely sliced
> 2 cloves garlic, minced
> 1 tablespoon shredded fresh ginger
> 2-inch piece of cinnamon stick
> 4 cloves
> 2 star anise pods
> ⅓ cup cashews
> ½ cup raisins
> 3 tablespoons tomato ketchup
> Pinch salt
> 3 cups water
> Fried shallot flakes (page 23), optional

Heat ghee or oil in a 3 to 4 quart saucepan. On medium-high heat, fry the shallots, garlic, ginger, cinnamon, cloves, and star anise, stirring until the shallots are translucent. Add the cashew nuts, raisins, and drained rice, and fry for 2 to 3 minutes, or until each grain of rice is covered with ghee. Add the ketchup, salt, and water. Bring to a boil, stirring occasionally. Reduce the heat. Cover the pan and let the rice cook on the lowest heat until all the liquid is absorbed, about 15 to 18 minutes. Lift the cover only long enough to check to see if the rice has absorbed the water. Remove from the heat. Let stand for 10 minutes before fluffing the rice. Garnish with fried shallot flakes, if desired.

YIELDS 4 to 6 servings.

Fried Rice
Nasi Goreng

More than any other dish in Southeast Asia, the content of Nasi Goreng *depends upon ingredients available, the tastes of an individual area, as well as the mood of the cook. It is a favorite in Singapore, Malaysia, and Indonesia. No two versions are ever the same.*

This version was served to me for breakfast at the Royal Sands Hotel in Penang. Accompaniments were chicken and beef satay.

Nasi Goreng *can be served alone or accompanied by a meat or fish curry and a vegetable dish.*

2 medium onions, minced
2 cloves garlic, minced
2 to 4 fresh red chiles, minced
½ teaspoon dried shrimp paste *(belacan)*
4 tablespoons oil
8 ounces small shrimp, cleaned, deveined
8 ounces beef or pork, cut into fine shreds
4 cups cold cooked rice
2 tablespoons soy sauce

GARNISH:

Fried egg (optional)
2 tomato wedges (optional)
3 cucumber slices (optional)
1 fresh red chile, shredded
1 green onion, shredded
3 tablespoons fried shallot flakes (page 24)

Pound or process onions, garlic, chiles, and shrimp paste together to a form a smooth paste. Heat 2 tablespoons oil in a wok or pan. Add the paste and fry until soft, about 5 minutes. Add 2 more tablespoons oil. Add the shrimp and beef. Stir-fry until cooked. Add the rice and stir to mix thoroughly. Add the soy sauce. Stir until the grains are evenly coated and the rice is heated throughout. Garnish with fried egg, tomato wedges, cucumbers, chile, green onions, and shallot flakes. Serve with *Sambal belacan* (page 237) or *sambal ulek.*

YIELD: 4 to 6 servings.

TIP: The secret to good *Nasi Goreng* is to start with cold cooked rice. Otherwise, you will have a "mushy" dish.

Southeast Asian Spices and chart with spice names.
Courtesy of The Thai Cooking School at The Oriental, Bangkok, Thailand

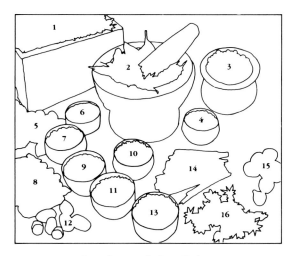

Southeast Asian Spices

1. Dried Chiles
2. Bay/Cassia Leaves
3. Cardamom
4. Chili powder
5. Garlic
6. White sesame seeds
7. Cloves
8. Mace
9. Black sesame seeds
10. Peppercorns
11. Cumin
12. Nutmeg
13. Coriander seeds
14. Cinnamon
15. Shallots
16. Star Anise

Southeast Asian Herbs and chart with herb names.

Courtesy of The Thai Cooking School at The Oriental, Bangkok, Thailand

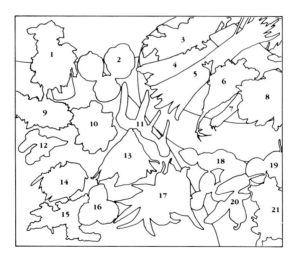

Southeast Asian Herbs

1. Basil leaves
2. Green peppers
3. Chinese celery
4. Pandanus Leaves
5. Lemon Grass
6. Coriander
7. Green onions

8. Balsam Leaves
9. Sweet Balsam Leaves
10. Ginger
11. Galangal
12. Fresh turmeric
13. Lesser ginger
14. Bird Chiles

15. Pepper
16. Kaffir lime
17. Chiles
18. Kaffir lime leaves
19. Lime
20. Banana peppers
21. Mint leaves

Southeast Asian Vegetables and chart with vegetable names.

Courtesy of The Thai Cooking School at The Oriental, Bangkok, Thailand

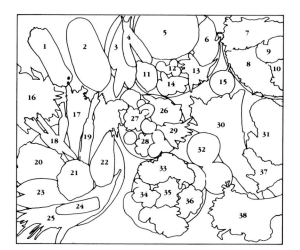

Southeast Asian Vegetables

1. Asparagus
2. Winter melon
3. Ribbed gourd
4. Asian Eggplants
5. Pumpkin
6. Eggplants
7. Water spinach
8. Bean sprouts
9. Tamarind
10. Pea Eggplants
11. Taro
12. Thai Eggplants
13. Okra
14. Cucumber
15. Squash
16. Water spinach
17. Thai greens
18. Carrots
19. Chinese turnip, Icicle radish
20. Lettuce
21. Cabbage
22. Banana Blossom
23. Bitter melon
24. Corn
25. Chinese yard-long green beans
26. Gourd
27. Eggplants
28. Tomatoes
29. Corn
30. Bok choy sum
31. Chinese broccoli
32. Coconut
33. Mushrooms
34. Straw mushrooms
35. Cloud ears
36. Chinese dried black mushrooms
37. Water Spinach
38. Chinese celery

Shrimp Rolls, Prataad Lom
Courtesy of The Thai Cooking School at The Oriental, Bangkok, Thailand

Pork in Golden Threads, Moo Sarong
Courtesy of The Thai Cooking School at The Oriental, Bangkok, Thailand

Lamb Satay, Satai Kambing
Hyatt Bumi Surabaya, Surabaya, Indonesia

Fried Noodles with Pork, Chicken and Shrimp, Mee Krob
Courtesy of The Thai Cooking School at The Oriental, Bangkok, Thailand

Spiced Seafood Salad, Pla Talay
Courtesy of The Thai Cooking School
at The Oriental, Bangkok, Thailand

Aromatic Steamed Fish, Pla Nueng
Courtesy of The Thai Cooking School at
The Oriental, Bangkok, Thailand

**Spicy Chicken and Rice Noodles
with Coconut Sauce, Laksa Lemak**
Pan Pacific Hotel, Kuala Lumpur, Malaysia

Grilled Pomfret with Coconut Curry
Hyatt Suajana, Suajana, Malaysia

Roast Sugar Cane Chicken, Ayam Dara Bergolek Dengan Tebu
Hyatt Kuantan, Kuantan, Malaysia

Grilled Chicken with Spicy Sauce, Ayam Panggang Rica-Rica

Hyatt Bumi Surabaya, Surabaya, Indonesia

Stir Fried Squab with Asparagus

Hyatt Regency, Singapore

Fried Rice Noodles, Penang Style
Penang Char Kway Teow

Here is a favorite noodle dish, often served by the street vendors on the beautiful island of Penang. This recipe is very special to me because it was given to me by a good friend, Brother Gerard Koe Soo Boon, a Malaysian student at Lewis University, in Romeoville, Illinois.

4 tablespoons oil
3 cloves garlic, minced
6 fresh red chiles, seeded, ground
3 Chinese sausages *(lap cheong)*, thinly sliced
4 ounces shrimp, shelled, deveined
4 ounces squid, cleaned, thinly sliced (optional)
¾ pound ¼- to ½-inch-wide fresh rice noodles
6 tablespoons plus 1 teaspoon soy sauce
4 eggs, lightly beaten
¼ teaspoon freshly ground black pepper
2 ounces bean sprouts
2 green onions, green part only, shredded into 1-inch lengths

Heat wok on medium heat. Add 2 tablespoons oil. Heat. Add garlic, and stir-fry until fragrant, about 10 seconds. Add chiles. Stir-fry about 30 seconds. Add sliced Chinese sausage, shrimp, and squid. Stir-fry 1 to 2 minutes or until squid and shrimp are cooked. Turn heat to high. Add 2 tablespoons oil. Heat. Add the rice noodles, separating them as you put them into the wok. Stir-fry, tossing the noodles so they will not stick to the bottom, about 1½ minutes. Sprinkle 6 tablespoons soy sauce lightly over the noodles. Continue stir-frying for 2 additional minutes. Add 2 tablespoons oil to wok and heat. Make a well in the center of the wok. Add the eggs, 1 teaspoon soy sauce, and ground pepper, stirring with chopsticks. When they have a soft-scrambled consistency, start incorporating the noodle mixture, stirring and tossing. Add the bean sprouts and green onions. Stir-fry until the mixture is heated through. Season to taste with additional soy sauce and black pepper if desired. Serve immediately.

YIELD: 4 to 6 servings.

TIP: ½ pound dried rice noodles may be substituted. Soak in hot water for 20 minutes or until pliable. Drain. Cook as directed.

Stir-Fried Hokkien Noodles, Nonya Style
Hokkien Mee Meehoon

The Hokkien Chinese traveled from South China down the Malay peninsula and brought this favorite of both the Malaysians and Singaporeans. It is often sold in the hawkers' stands along the streets.

Hokkien Mee combines egg noodles and rice vermicelli, which are fried with shrimp, squid, pork, and bean sprouts in a small amount of rich pork and shrimp stock. Nonya cooks use smoking hot lard and streaky pork and serve it with Sambal Belacan and a wedge of lime to squeeze on the noodles.

To the Chinese, eating noodles is a symbol of longevity because noodles never seem to end!

> 5 tablespoons lard or oil for frying
> ¾ pound medium shrimp, shelled and deveined, heads and shells reserved
> 3 to 4 cups water
> 4 tablespoons soy sauce
> 1 teaspoon sugar
> ½ pound pork butt or streaky pork
> ¼ pound squid, center bone and ink bag removed (optional)
> 3 cloves garlic, minced
> 3 shallots, minced
> 8 ounces fresh, thick Chinese egg noodles, blanched in boiling water to cover for 1 minute, drained well
> 2½ ounces thin dried rice sticks, soaked in hot water 20 minutes or until softened, drained well
> 2 eggs, lightly beaten
> ¾ pound bean sprouts
> 2 tablespoons lime juice
> Black pepper to taste

GARNISHES:

> 2 green onions, shredded into 2-inch lengths
> 1 cucumber, peeled, seeded, shredded into 2-inch lengths
> 2 fresh red chiles, finely shredded
> 2 limes cut into wedges
> Fried Shallot Flakes (page 24)

Heat wok over high heat. Add 2 tablespoons lard or oil. Heat. Add shrimp heads and shells, and stir-fry 3 to 4 minutes, until bright red. Remove from wok.

In a saucepan, bring water to a boil. Add 2 tablespoons soy sauce, sugar, and the pork. Bring to a boil. Add the shrimp and boil, stirring for 2 minutes or until cooked. Remove with a slotted spoon. Add the squid to the boiling liquid and cook, turning for 1 minute. Transfer to a bowl with a slotted spoon. When cool, cut into ¼-inch rings. Cover the pork and simmer over medium heat until tender, about 30 minutes. Remove pork, drain, and set aside to cool. When cool, cut lengthwise into thin strips, about 3⁄16 inch by 2 inches. Add stir-fried shrimp shells to the stock and boil for 10 minutes until the liquid has been reduced to about 1 cup. Strain liquid.

Heat 3 tablespoons lard or oil in a wok or large skillet. Add garlic and shallots. Stir-fry until fragrant. Add blanched noodles and rice sticks. Stir-fry until lightly browned in places. Make a well in the center of the noodles. Add the eggs and let them set as they cook, then toss with the noodles. Add pork, squid, shrimp, and bean sprouts. Add the reduced stock and 2 tablespoons soy sauce. Stir gently. Cover and cook 2 minutes, or until noodles have absorbed most of the liquid. Season with pepper. Transfer to a serving platter. Sprinkle with lime juice. Garnish with green onions, cucumber, chiles, and lime quarters. Serve with *Sambal Belacan* (page 237).

YIELD: 4 to 6 servings.

TIP: If substituting dried egg noodles, use 6 ounces. Cook in boiling water until tender. Drain. Use as directed.

ADVANCE PREPARATION: Cook the shrimp shells, pork, shrimp, and squid 1 day ahead. Cook the noodles 1 day ahead. Drain. Toss with 1 teaspoon oil. Put in plastic bag and refrigerate. Finish cooking one hour before serving. Reheat at serving time.

Inspired by a recipe from Jean Marc LaForce, head of food and beverage The Pan Pacific Hotel, Kuala Lumpur.

Spiced Egg Noodles with Sweet Potato Gravy
Mee Rebus

Mee Rebus *is popular in the many street-side stalls. It has an unusual combination of flavors and textures and a rich spicy sauce. Serve it as part of a meal or for a light supper with a salad or vegetable.*

ACCOMPANIMENTS:

> ½ pound bean sprouts, blanched in boiling water for 30 seconds
> 3 fresh red chiles, seeded, shredded
> 2 hard-boiled eggs, shelled, cut into wedges
> 2 limes, cut into wedges
> Fried shallot flakes (page 24)

> 6 to 8 dried red chiles, soaked in water to soften, about 5
>   minutes, seeded, chopped
> 2 cloves garlic, chopped
> 12 almonds, chopped
> 1 medium onion, chopped
> 2 tablespoons minced fresh ginger
> 1½ tablespoons coriander powder
> ½ teaspoon turmeric powder
> 1 tablespoon yellow bean paste (optional)
> 2 tablespoons oil
> 2 whole boned, skinless chicken breasts, thinly sliced
> 4 cups chicken stock
> 2 large sweet potatoes, boiled, peeled, mashed
> 10 ounces fresh [¼-inch-thin] egg noodles, cooked *al dente*
> Fresh coriander leaves for garnish (optional)

Prepare the accompaniments. Place the bean sprouts, chiles, egg wedges, limes, and fried shallot flakes in separate serving bowls.

Pound or process chiles, garlic, almonds, onion, ginger, coriander, turmeric, and yellow bean paste to a coarse paste. Heat 2 tablespoons oil over moderate heat. Add the paste ingredients and stir for 2 to 3 minutes, being careful not to burn. Add the chicken and stir to combine it with the paste. Stir-fry until the chicken is lightly browned on all sides. Add the stock. Bring to a boil. Reduce the heat to simmer and simmer for 10 minutes. Add the sweet potato, one half at a time, stirring until smooth. Cook stirring, until heated throughout. Remove from the heat.

To serve, place noodles in individual bowls. Reheat the sauce and pour it into the bowls. Garnish with coriander. Serve hot with accompaniments.

YIELD: 4 to 6 servings.

VARIATION: Green onions may be substituted for coriander. If substituting dried egg noodles, use 7 ounces. Cook according to package directions.

 ## Green Bean Omelet
Dau Kwok Chao Dan

A simple Malay snack, combining crunchy green beans, hot chiles, and eggs. It is an unusual and tasty addition to a Western brunch and can easily be doubled or tripled.

3 eggs
½ teaspoon salt
¼ teaspoon white pepper
3 tablespoons oil
5 green beans, tips removed, chopped into ¼-inch pieces
1 to 2 fresh red chiles, seeds removed, finely chopped
½ teaspoon minced garlic
2 tablespoons chopped fresh coriander (optional)

Beat eggs with salt and pepper. Heat a 7-inch skillet. Heat 2 tablespoons oil, add the beans, and stir-fry for 2 minutes until just softened. Add the chiles. Stir for 10 seconds. Remove and add to the beaten egg. Stir. Wipe the pan with a paper towel, leaving a small residue of oil. Add the egg mixture and sprinkle with coriander. Cook until firm. When the underside is golden, turn and cook the other side. Cut into wedges and serve at once with cucumber slices.

YIELD: 2 to 3 servings with other dishes.

VARIATION: Sliced green onions may be substituted for the green beans.

SAUCES, ACCOMPANIMENTS AND PICKLES

 ## Peanut Sauce
Kuah Kacang

The flavor of this robust peanut sauce will improve if prepared ahead. It makes a very tasty sauce for satay as well as a dipping sauce for vegetables.

⅓ cup oil
1 teaspoon dried garlic flakes
1 tablespoon dried onion flakes
2 to 4 dried red chiles
1 teaspoon shrimp paste (*belacan*), (optional)
1 tablespoon lime juice
1 tablespoon dark soy sauce
1 cup crunchy peanut butter
1½ tablespoons palm or brown sugar
Coconut milk or water to thin to desired consistency

Heat oil to moderate in a small wok or pan. Place garlic and onion flakes in a fine wire strainer and lower into the oil. Cook until golden. Drain on paper towels. Fry whole chiles until puffed and crisp, about 40 seconds. Remove. Drain on paper towels. Let cool. Discard chile seeds. Fry shrimp paste in oil remaining in pan, crushing with the back of a spoon. Add lime juice and soy sauce. Remove from heat. Add peanut butter and sugar. Stir to blend well. Cool. Crumble garlic flakes, onion flakes, and chiles into small pieces and add to mixture. Combine well. Serve at room temperature.

YIELD: 1⅓ cups, approximately.

ADVANCE PREPARATION: Prepare 1 week in advance. Store in a tightly covered glass container in refrigerator. If sauce is too thick, add coconut milk or water to the desired consistency.

Inspired by Lothar Winkler, executive chef, The Regent of Kuala Lumpur.

Savory Pineapple
Pacri Nenas

Sweet and tangy, Pacri Nenas *is an interesting palate refresher with any meal. It is equally good served hot or chilled.*

This is one of many dishes traditionally served at Malay weddings.

¼ cup oil
3 whole cardamom pods
1 star anise
2 cloves
1 medium onion, thinly sliced
1 tablespoon finely minced fresh ginger
2 cloves garlic, finely minced
½ teaspoon red pepper powder
½ teaspoon white pepper
½ teaspoon ground cumin
½ teaspoon coriander powder
1 tablespoon sugar
1 ¾-ripe pineapple, peeled, quartered, core removed, cut into ½-inch wedges
2 fresh red chiles, seeds removed, shredded
Salt to taste

Heat oil on moderate heat in a heavy saucepan. Add the cardamom, star anise, and cloves. Stir for about 15 seconds. Add the onion and stir for 1 minute. Add the ginger and garlic and stir for an additional minute, or until the onion is soft and translucent, but not browned. Add the red pepper powder, pepper, cumin, coriander, and sugar and fry until the sugar dissolves and the oil separates, about 30 to 60 seconds. Add the pineapple wedges and chiles and stir-fry about 4 minutes. Add water to cover. Bring to the boil. Reduce the heat to simmer and cook, covered, for 10 minutes. Remove the cover and continue to simmer until the oil separates. Add salt to taste. Serve hot or cold.

YIELD: 4 to 6 servings with other dishes.

Baked Bananas

Bananas are delicately flavored with brown sugar and citrus in this Malay delight. They are commonly served as an accompaniment during the meal. For a wonderful dessert, sprinkle the bananas with coconut flakes.

4 tablespoons butter
⅓ cup tightly packed light brown sugar
¼ teaspoon ground cloves
1½ tablespoons orange or pineapple juice
1½ tablespoons lime juice
1 teaspoon peeled, minced fresh ginger
6 small firm bananas, sliced in half lengthwise

Preheat the oven to 375°F. In a bowl, cream the butter and sugar together until the mixture is pale and soft. Beat in the cloves, orange juice, lime juice, and ginger.

Place the bananas in a well-greased medium baking dish and spread the seasoned butter mixture over them. Bake for 10 to 15 minutes, or until the top is bubbling and the bananas are cooked through and tender. Serve at once.

YIELD: 6 servings.

ADVANCE PREPARATION: Prepare and place in the baking dish several hours ahead. Bake just before serving.

Cucumber and Pineapple Sambal, Penang Style
Penang Sambal Timun Dan Nenas

A refreshing and easily prepared accompaniment to any meal.

1½ teaspoons dried shrimp paste, toasted (belacan),
4 to 6 fresh red chiles, seeded, chopped
1 tablespoon dark soy sauce
2 tablespoons sugar
1 cucumber, seeded, cut into ¼-inch cubes
½ pineapple, peeled, cored, cut into ½-inch by ¾-inch wedges

Combine toasted shrimp paste, chiles, soy sauce, and sugar, and pound or process to a paste, adding water if necessary. Put cucumber and pineapple in a bowl. Add pounded mixture and combine well. Let *sambal* stand, covered and chilled for at least 1 hour and up to 2 hours.

YIELD: 2 cups, approximately.

 ## Spicy Chile Sauce
Sambal Belacan

Sambal Belacan, *a pounded mixture of two ingredients (chiles and dried shrimp paste,* belacan) *is seldom missing from a Nonya or Malay meal. The* sambal *is fiery and fragrant with a slight sour tang from the juice of* limau kasturi *(small limes available in Southeast Asia), which are squeezed in for good measure. It is a complement that goes with any and every dish.*

Cooks prepare their sambals *in the traditional manner using the mortar and pestle. Chiles should go into the mortar first, then the toasted shrimp paste should be added to the chiles and pounded into them while it is still hot. This way, the chiles will absorb the belacan taste and give that distinctive fragrance and sharp smack.*

Sambal Belacan *is quite often combined with fresh vegetables or fried ingredients and becomes an instant and convenient seasoning for many meals.*

> 2 teaspoons dried shrimp paste (*belacan*)
> 16 fresh red chiles, seeded, chopped
> Juice of 1 lime
> Salt to taste
> 1 teaspoon shredded lime

Wrap the shrimp paste in foil. Toast in a dry skillet on moderate heat for approximately 1 minute on each side. Remove from the heat.

Pound or process chiles and shrimp paste to a paste. Mix in the lime juice. Serve in a small bowl, garnished with lime zest.

YIELD: ½ cup.

TIP: The amount of dried shrimp paste has been reduced to suit Western tastes. If you prefer to serve the *sambal* as the Malays, use two 1-inch cubes of dried shrimp paste.

Sambal Belacan will keep refrigerated for 1 week in an airtight container.

VARIATION: Sambal Ulek may be substituted for the homemade *Sambal Belacan*. It may be purchased in jars in Asian grocery stores.

 ## Chile Sauce Kadazan
Chile Sambal Kadazan

An easily prepared chile sauce.

> 6 to 10 fresh red chiles, seeded, chopped
> ¼ teaspoon salt
> 4 teaspoons fresh lime juice

Pound or process the chiles and salt to a smooth paste. Add the lime juice and mix. Serve.

TIP: If fresh chiles are unavailable, add the lime juice to purchased *Sambal Ulek.*

ADVANCE PREPARATION: The chile sauce will keep for 1 week in a tightly covered glass jar in the refrigerator.

DESSERTS

 ## Coconut Crepes with Coconut Sauce
Kueh Dadar

These delicious, brightly colored green crepes will be the highlight of your dinner! They were first served to me during "high tea" at the Pan Pacific Hotel in Kuala Lumpur and are very popular throughout Southeast Asia.

CREPES:

> ½ cup all-purpose flour
> Pinch salt
> 2 eggs, lightly beaten

¾ cup thin coconut milk or water
Few drops green food coloring
Oil for cooking crepes

COCONUT FILLING:

½ cup tightly packed palm or dark brown sugar
⅓ cup water
1½ cups dried unsweetened coconut flakes
Pinch of ground cinnamon
Pinch of ground nutmeg
Pinch of salt
1 teaspoon lemon juice

COCONUT SAUCE:

⅓ cup granulated sugar
2 tablespoons cornstarch
Pinch salt
2 cups coconut milk

OPTIONAL GARNISH:

½ cup toasted, unsweetened dried coconut flakes
4 to 6 tablespoons toasted, slivered almonds

For the crepes: Sift the flour and the salt. Beat the eggs in a medium-size bowl. Beat in the coconut milk, flour, and salt, producing a smooth batter. Add the green food coloring and mix. Cover and let stand at room temperature for 30 minutes.

Processor method: Process to a rapid sift the flour and salt with 2 five-second pulses. Add the eggs to the container. With the machine running, pour the coconut milk through the chute within 8 seconds. Process 5 seconds. Scrape down the sides of the container. Process 10 seconds. Stop the motor and scrape down the sides of the container. Process a few seconds longer. Allow the batter to rest for 30 minutes. (If there is froth on top of the batter when ready to cook the wrappers, remove before cooking.)

Heat a 6-inch skillet, preferably non-stick, over medium-high heat. Lightly oil the pan with a piece of paper toweling dipped in the oil and rubbed over the heated pan. Add a scant ¼ cup of the batter to the pan and swirl very quickly to coat the bottom of the pan evenly. Cook until the top of the crepe appears dry and the edges begin to curl, about 20 to 30 seconds. Be careful not to brown the crepes. Turn and cook briefly, about 2 to 3 seconds, on the other side. Remove and stack on a plate. Continue cooking until all the batter is used. Cover the crepes while preparing the filling.

Filling preparation: Gently heat the sugar and water in a small saucepan, stirring until the sugar has dissolved. Add the coconut, cinnamon, nutmeg, and salt. Mix well. Cook, stirring until almost dry. Cool, stirring occasionally. Add the lemon juice. Stir.

For the sauce: Combine the sugar, cornstarch, and salt in a small saucepan. Gradually stir in the coconut milk over medium heat. Bring the mixture slowly to a boil, stirring until the sugar dissolves and the mixture thickens slightly. Set aside. Serve warm or at room temperature.

To serve: Place 1 slightly rounded tablespoon of the filling in a strip on the lower third of the crepe. Roll up tightly to form a firm cylinder, continuing until all the crepes have been filled. Top with the Coconut Creme Sauce and garnish with toasted coconut and toasted almonds if desired. Serve 2 crepes per person.

YIELD: 4 to 5 servings.

TIP: If desired, 1 tablespoon of amaretto or kahlua liqueur may be added to the sauce.

ADVANCE PREPARATION: Prepare the crepes ahead. Place waxed paper between the crepes and freeze or refrigerate. Prepare the filling and sauce 1 day ahead. Fill the crepes 1 to 2 hours ahead. Reheat the sauce or serve at room temperature. Pour sauce over crepes when serving. The crepes should be served at room temperature.

Inspired by a recipe from Jean Marc LaForce, head of food and beverage, Pan Pacific Hotel, Kuala Lumpur.

Oranges Oriental

In Chinese symbolism, Mandarin oranges and kumquats mean good luck and prosperity. They are often given in pairs to relatives and friends during the Chinese New Year celebration.

This light, refreshing dessert is easily prepared in advance and is a perfect ending to a Southeast Asian light supper or elegant dinner.

8 oranges
2 cups water
2 cups sugar
½ teaspoon cream of tartar
½ cup Cointreau
1 to 2 tablespoons cognac
Mint leaves for garnish (optional)

Peel the orange rind as thinly as possible, being careful not to include any of the white part of the orange. Reserve the fruit. Cut the peel into very fine shreds. Combine the orange shreds, water, sugar, and cream of tartar in a saucepan. Heat to boiling and reduce heat enough to maintain a rolling boil. Boil until the mixture is a thin syrup. Continue cooking until the mixture is reduced by one-third and has thickened slightly. Remove from the heat. Let cool. Stir in the Cointreau and cognac. Refrigerate.

Remove all of the white membrane from the oranges and cut them into sections, removing the seeds. Place in a bowl and refrigerate for 2 hours or longer.

To serve, place several orange slices in a glass serving dish. Pour the chilled syrup over the oranges. Garnish with the shredded peel and mint leaves.

YIELD: 6 to 8 servings.

TIP: The orange-flavored syrup is wonderful as a topping on coconut or vanilla ice cream.

ADVANCE PREPARATION: Prepare the syrup several weeks in advance. Refrigerate. Prepare the oranges 1 day in advance. Store covered, in the refrigerator.

Papaya Fool

Pure comfort food after an exotic meal!

> 3 egg yolks
> 1 cup evaporated or coconut milk
> 3 pounds papayas, peeled, seeded
> 2 tablespoons lime juice
> 3 egg whites
> ¼ cup sugar
> Mint leaves (optional)

Stir the egg yolks into the milk. In a heavy pan, bring slowly to a boil over low heat, stirring constantly. Remove from heat and let cool. Beat until frothy.

Blend or process the papaya and lime juice to a puree. Beat the egg whites until stiff, but not dry.

Combine the beaten egg yolk mixture and pureed papaya mixture and sugar. Fold in the egg whites. Check for sweetness. Add more sugar if desired. Chill. Serve cold in chilled glasses. Garnish with mint leaves.

YIELD: 8 to 10 servings.

TIP: Substitute 2¾ pounds of bananas for the papaya. Fresh blueberries may be added for garnish.

ADVANCE PREPARATION: Prepare completely 1 day in advance. Put mixture into serving dishes. Cover with plastic wrap. Refrigerate.

 ## Spiced Tea

Fragrant and aromatic, this tea is a delight!

> 4 cups boiling water
> 4 heaping teaspoons fresh tea
> 4 cardamom pods, bruised
> 1 small piece cinnamon stick
> 2 tablespoons finely flaked almonds
> Sugar to taste

Prepare tea, add the cardamom and cinnamon, and let steep for 5 minutes. Place a teaspoon of flaked almonds into each tea cup. Pour the tea over the almonds and sweeten with sugar if desired. Serve hot.

YIELD: 4 servings.

TIP: Try adding cardamom and cinnamon after tea has brewed.

 ## Ginger Fizz

Delicious for a hot summer day.

1½ cups water
1 cup sugar
½ cup sliced fresh ginger, crushed with the side of a cleaver
1 teaspoon lemon zest
3 tablespoons lemon juice
Club soda
Lemon slices for garnish

Combine water, sugar, ginger, and lemon zest in a saucepan. Stir to mix. Bring to boil slowly over low heat. Boil 5 minutes. Remove from heat. Cover and let steep until cool. Strain, removing lemon zest and ginger. Add lemon juice and stir. To serve, mix 2½ tablespoons of mixture with 1 cup soda or water. Ice cubes may be used if desired. Garnish with a lemon slice.

YIELD: 2 cups ginger syrup.

TIP: The ginger must be very fresh for this beverage.

ADVANCE PREPARATION: Prepare ginger syrup several days in advance and refrigerate in a tightly covered glass container.

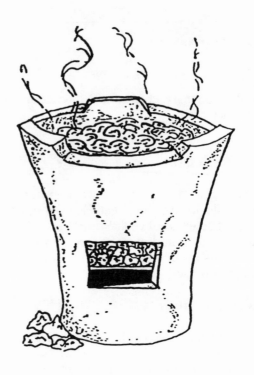

INDONESIA

Selamat Datang! Welcome!

Located at the crossroads of the great trade route between the Middle East and Asia, Indonesia has, through the centuries, lured traders, pirates, and immigrants, all eager to share in the riches of the Spice Islands. The culinary influences of the Indians, Chinese, Arabs, and Dutch colonists, added to the Indonesians' ability to combine spices and local herbs, have emerged in a distinctively Indonesian blend that is unquestionably one of the world's great cuisines.

Indonesian cuisine is as varied as the inhabitants of the country, which consists of more than 13,000 islands stretching a distance of 3,200 miles from Sumatra in the west to the wild coast of Irian Jaya (New Guinea) in the east. The kaleidoscopic array of peoples, languages, customs, and material cultures found in Indonesia is truly outstanding, for living here are approximately 300 ethnic groups with about 200 different languages, many of which are spoken in different dialects. There is now one official language for the whole country, Bahasa Indonesia, but in the rural areas, other languages and dialects are still spoken, making it very hard to communicate at times.

My travels, starting in Medan, North Sumatra, and ending in Biak, Irian Jaya, made me aware of the enormous physical and cultural differences exhibited by the peoples from one end of this archipelago to the other. The largest ethnic group in Indonesia is the Malay. They include the Achenese, Minangkabau, and Malays of Sumatra, the Sundanese and Javanese of Java, the Sasaks of Lombok, the Makassarese and Buginese of Sulawesi, and the Balinese and Madurese of their respective islands. These groups monopolize the

245

best agricultural lands and most strategic river ports. It is foods from these people from which my recipes originate.

Within these groups the old school regarded cooking as a craft to be practiced communally, but with the observance of a strict hierarchy of roles and jobs. The Javanese and Minangkabau, in particular, put great emphasis on cooperative and social attitudes, even in the kitchen. *Rukun,* harmony, is the primary goal, which is achieved by knowing one's place in society. To be *sopan-santun,* well-mannered, is the rigid social norm.

As elsewhere in Southeast Asia, rice is the main course in every meal. A *sambal* made from chiles and spices is always on the table to allow each person to season his food to the desired degree of spiciness. The failure of Westerners to understand the practice of eating almost everything mixed with rice has many people believing that Indonesian foods are terribly hot and spicy. Hot they may be, but almost every dish is meant to be spread over a large quantity of rice. Still, knowing the eating habits of the West, I have toned down most of the recipes in this chapter. If you desire to dine as the Indonesians, increase the amount of chiles when cooking, or simply add some *sambal* to your dishes at the table.

My culinary tour of Indonesia was designed by Hidayat, consul of information and cultural affairs, Consulate General of the Republic of Indonesia, Chicago. He felt that to understand Indonesian cuisine I should learn the customs and appreciate the vastness of the country. To do this, he arranged for many of the wonderful visits to Indonesian homes I made to acquire my knowledge firsthand from prominent citizens of each area. All were eager to share both their recipes and their homes, and were well prepared to teach me as much as possible about their life-style and culture. As Hidayat says, "It is the Indonesian way!"

Starting in the far northwestern part of Indonesia, in Medan, North Sumatra, I was greeted by Jansen Nababan of the Batak group. This very closely knit clan were the infamous "headhunters of Sumatra" in tales of yore. Today, they are Christians, better known for hunting higher education than heads (Jansen's son would soon begin graduate studies at the University of Illinois). Many Bataks are well placed in government, academia, and business circles.

Jansen's wife had prepared a traditional Batak dinner for me. A pig had been slaughtered for the occasion. The barbecued pork was served with *Andaliman Sauce,* a dark brown, slightly spicy sauce made from freshly drained pig's blood combined with local andaliman dried berries with a lemon pepper flavor, fried coconut, tangy tamarind, salt, and black pepper. I must admit that if I were not the guest of honor I might not have tried this dish, but it turned out to be wonderful! The same was true of *Sang Sang,* small pieces of pork combined with ginger, laos (galangal), chiles, fried coconut, salt, and black pepper, and cooked in fresh pig's blood.

For *Naniura,* a Batak fish specialty, local goldenfish was marinated in tamarind, turmeric, and crushed peanuts, then left to "cook" in this marinade for 3 to 4 hours to produce a tangy fish with a creamy yellow sauce. It's the same technique used in Latin America to make ceviche. A side dish of what looked like spinach turned out to be manioc (cassava) cooked with turmeric, salt, and black pepper. The greens of this wonderful vegetable, which I was to see all over Indonesia, taste like a cross between mustard greens and spinach, and the starchy root is used to make tapioca. Rice and fresh bananas completed the meal, and each glass of water had a perfect square of red chile centered in the bottom.

In Medan, my next visit was to T. Kemala Intan of the Deli tribe, known to be among the most aristocratic of the Malay ethnic groups. Intan is a medical doctor, and her husband, also a professor, attended graduate school in Australia. Her parents, both lawyers, are professors at the University of North Sumatra. Intan and her sister-in-law, Zita Nelliza, also a professor of English at the university, were totally prepared for my visit. All the ingredients for each dish were neatly arranged in beautiful china bowls on individual trays as if I were attending a professional cooking school. They explained they do this often for foreign field-service students and had invited some for lunch after the class.

Intan's home was large, with beautiful furnishings that combined Malay and Chinese influences. There were two separate kitchens. One, for the family, contained a food processor, a mini-food processor, a kitchen scale, an ice-cream maker, a moderate-size countertop toaster/oven, a pressure cooker, a refrigerator, and china and glassware. She explained that this was the family kitchen for light meals.

In a separate wing away from the main house, there was a second, "working," kitchen where her helpers did all of the hot cooking. In it, there was a charcoal grill, where satay was being grilled for lunch. Three large gas-flamed burners were lined up side-by-side on the outside wall. On two were Chinese woks and on the third was a pot in which fragrant Beef Rendang was cooking. A large two-door refrigerator/freezer was at the end of the kitchen.

As I sipped *markisa* juice, a sweet, pale yellow, refreshing drink made from the concentrated juice of a large passion fruit, Zita demonstrated the preparation of *Nasi Minyak,* a traditional Malay wedding dish of scented rice flavored with ginger, shredded coconut, shallots, cloves, cardamom, cinnamon, and turmeric (see recipe in Malaysia chapter, page 226). Placing the rice in the bottom of a very large glass bowl, she arranged beautifully carved green papayas on top. Candied flowers prepared from local fruits were attached to long green floral stems and placed in the papaya to form a beautiful bouquet. Next she prepared two spectacular desserts: *Serikaya,* a local "pumpkin" stuffed with palm sugar, coconut milk, and beaten eggs, and then steamed, and *Serikaya Telur,* a steamed pudding of coconut milk, eggs, and sugar tinted green with pandan leaves. An unexpected delight was *Manisan,* tasty and colorful candied long red chiles, which combined both sweet and hot flavors.

Lunch followed, with barbecued chicken, *Gado-Gado* (a cooked vegetable salad with peanut dressing), Tamarind Prawns, Beef Rendang, fried *tempeh* (a form of fermented tofu), plain rice, and the two desserts surrounding the *Nasi Minyak.* (Many of her recipes are included in this chapter; others, being traditional Malay dishes, are found in the chapter on Malaysia.)

West Sumatra, especially the capital city of Padang and the nearby market town of Bukit Tinggi, is the land of the matriarchal Minangkabau society. In contrast to the rest of Indonesia, the mother is the controlling and guiding force, and the women own the land and the businesses (although the men run them). The Minangkabaus are adaptable, intelligent, and one of the most successful ethnic groups in the country. They are also known for turning out some of the best cooks in Indonesia.

Padang or Minang food is beloved throughout the country, but the heart of the cuisine is in Bukit Tinggi. In this lovely and fascinating town, where pompadoured horsecarts provide transportation and beautiful scenery and flowers abound, the food is the hottest in all of Indonesia. Sampling a Beef Satay laced with a thick, peppery peanut sauce, I thought for a moment that my throat had suffered third-degree burns. The same was true of a Beef Rendang, the distinctive local style of curry in which the coconut milk is reduced to the point where the oil separates.

A visit to Bukit Tinggi would not be complete without a visit to the huge market on a Wednesday or Saturday. Everyone from the countryside appears in the city, and the sprawling market covers a whole hill. To get to the market, one has to climb a 300-step stairway or use twisting cart lanes. This market is like no other market I have encountered while in Asia; its vastness is hard to take in on one visit. Everything is sold, from local crafts to antiques to produce, spices, and kitchen utensils. There is an abundance of magnificent aromas, colors, and sounds. Excitement is everywhere. Produce vendors display a spectacular array of fruits and vegetables, including huge piles of many varieties of chiles, small pale-green pea-sized eggplants, lemons, limes, cabbages, papayas, mangoes, guavas, coconuts, and assorted varieties of bananas, from fat red ones to tiny fingerlike yellow types. You can find meat stalls with piles of red meat, intestines, brains, liver, hearts, and probably every other part of the cow. Sweets also abound, including *Lemang* (rice and palm sugar cooked in banana leaves), sweet coconut cakes, wonderful dried-banana and other fruit chips. Featured in other stalls are bowls upon bowls of traditional Padang foods, and even over fifty kinds of rice. Many of the items had come to market upon someone's head, the traditional manner to carry everything; I watched one woman carry twenty coconuts on top of head, another with an enormous stack of bananas.

Padang restaurants offer not only some of the best food in Indonesia, but the quickest. Once you are seated, the waiters bring a cold napkin with which to freshen up, a glass of hot tea, a glass of hot water to hold your utensils, and a lit candle to keep away the flies. No menu is provided; instead, like Chinese *dim sum,* an overwhelming array of foods arrives at your table by waiters carrying up to twenty dishes of food on both arms. They are all placed on the table, and you choose those desired. When the meal is over, you pay only for those dishes you eat. There are usually about ten varieties of curries, fried fish, fresh vegetables cooked in coconut sauce, eggs with chiles, and a great variety of goat, chicken, and beef dishes plus a large bowl of rice. For dessert, bananas and fresh pineapple are served.

Among my many encounters with Padang food, I have enjoyed some wonderful dishes and have turned away a few others untasted. A few favorites stand out: *Dendeng Belado,* a chewy beef with a red chile sauce; *Gulai Sumsum,* a bone-marrow curry seasoned with chiles, turmeric, and coconut milk (in West Sumatra, *gulai* means any dish cooked with coconut milk that retains its sauce); *Cubadak,* a local fruit combined with chiles and young bamboo shoots; Beef *Kalio,* a half-cooked version of Beef Rendang; *Pechal,* a *gulai* of manioc, green beans, papaya leaves, and chiles, and another *gulai* of tender fish fillets, with tangy tamarind and a touch of chile. All of these were accompanied by the famous *Sambal Lado,* a fiery hot chile sauce, which varied in each restaurant, depending upon the amount of hot chiles used in preparing the sauce. At times, it was even too hot for my guides! For dessert, bananas and pineapples were served.

Admittedly, there were some Padang foods that didn't tempt me in the least. Maybe on a future visit I'll try such specialties as scrawny smoked eels, all tied up in a dried-up bunch, *Rabu* (fried beef lungs, cooked so long they looked like shoe leather), *Gulai Gajebo* (buffalo back side in a hot green chile sauce), or beef brain steamed in a huge triangle of banana leaves. On the other hand, maybe I won't.

Bustling Jakarta, the capital of Indonesia, is the melting pot of many Indonesian cuisines. It also has excellent seafood and ethnic restaurants such as Thai, Indian, and Korean, but what I remember most is the fried chicken.

Indonesians love fried chicken, and it is available in a multitude of styles (including Kentucky!). But the pilgrimage points for fried-chicken lovers from all over Java are the "Mbok Berek" restaurants, named after the woman who invented their chicken recipe. *Ayam Goreng Jawa* originated in Yogyakarta in central Java, and restaurants specializing in the dish have spread throughout Java. Ny. Umi owns six of them in Jakarta, each of which can serve 300 at a time, and it was in one of these that she showed me the process. To tenderize the free-ranging Javanese chickens, which are full of flavor but rather tough in comparison to our chickens, they are first boiled for a couple of hours in a mixture of rich spices and coconut cream, then cooled. When a chicken is ordered, it is fried crisp for a short time in very hot oil. The flavor is incomparable.

In addition to our aromatic fried chicken, she served many specialties of Yogyakarta: *Sayur Buncis* (green beans in a spicy coconut milk sauce), *tahu* (bean curd), and *tempeh* (fried fermented soybean cake), a fresh vegetable platter consisting of green beans, eggplant, cabbage, lettuce, tomatoes, cucumbers, and *Gado-Gado,* the famous vegetable salad with peanut sauce. It was topped with *krupuk udang,* large crunchy wafers made from shrimp paste and rice flour, which puff up dramatically when deep-fried. *Gudeg,* a specialty of Yogyakarta, consists of young jackfruit cooked in coconut cream with chiles, onions, coriander, salam, laos, palm sugar, and salt; it is topped with a gelatinous slice of *krecek* (buffalo hide boiled in chile sauce) and a piece of chicken. I became a fan immediately of this dark colored, slightly sweet but spicy dish. (In Yogyakarta, it was served three times in one day!)

Ratna Etchika (Etty), Hidayat's niece, invited me into her Jakarta kitchen to learn about more Javanese specialties. Perhaps because of an American influence (she had just returned to Jakarta after receiving her master's degree from the University of Iowa), her dishes are all easy to prepare, in many cases using a food processor. Her recipes for *Lapis Daging,* a quick steak stir-fry, *Oseng-Oseng,* stir-fried vegetables, *Slada Huzar,* a tasty salad with a creamy egg dressing, and *Orak-Arik,* stir-fried Chinese cabbage with eggs, are presented in this chapter. After dinner, we had delicious *Asinan,* fresh mangoes and papaya marinated in a vinegar, sugar, and chile sauce.

Yogyakarta, called "Yogya" by most Indonesians, is Java's second largest city and the cradle of the island's culture. It is rich in tradition and history and is said to have the most sophisticated cuisine in Indonesia.

A little before nine one evening, I was in a jewelry shop on Jalan Malioboro, one of the main streets, when a parade of tables and buckets of food, woks, and cooking utensils appeared from the rear of the store. Many young Indonesians marched through the jewelry store and out to the street. I was about to see the famous *warung,* the makeshift food stalls that appear nightly in many parts of Indonesia (indeed, all over Southeast Asia).

In no time all was set up, including a large white banner covering the storefront, which said "Putri Solo Restaurant" and listed the menu: *Mie Goreng* (fried noodles), *Ayam Goreng* (fried chicken), *Pecel* (boiled spinach, beans, and cabbage in a peanut sauce), *Rempeyek Kacang* (peanut fritters), the ubiquitous *satay,* and even *Burung Dara Goreng,* deep-fried dove!

Promptly at nine, the hungry locals pulled up on motorcycles, on foot, or by *bechak* (trishaw) to enjoy this street-side feast, which is the pure cuisine of the area. Mats were laid on the sidewalk, upon which had been placed low tables. Everyone walked from stall to stall to choose the evening meal and returned to sit on a mat, enjoy the food, and exchange the gossip of the day. Meanwhile, strolling guitar players sang Indonesian tunes. I sampled the dove, which was spicy-sweet from palm sugar and chiles and was wonderful. *Mie Goreng,* fried noodles with chicken and vegetables and topped with a fried egg and crispy fried shallots, was another delight. Promptly at midnight, everything closed. The next day it would be business as usual at the jewelry store.

Yogya food struck me as distinctly different, more sophisticated and complex than I had had elsewhere in Indonesia. A fuller spectrum of flavors appeared in some of the same dishes I had had in Jakarta. In particular, the food was much sweeter from the addition of lots of palm sugar, which balanced the chiles and spices and subdued their fire. I was told in Yogya that they feel the sweets combat the high temperatures in the humid climate.

I sampled more formal Yogya cuisine at the home of Soedarso, president of the Indonesian Institute of Arts Yogyakarta and former cultural attache to the Netherlands. He and his wife live above ordinary Indonesian standards in the International Village, in a lovely house furnished with a harmonious blend of modern and traditional pieces. An extensive art collection, with traditional Balinese paintings, Dutch graphic art, and modern Indonesian paintings based on traditional elements, decorates the walls. A successful sculptor, Soedarso was in the midst of a monumental statue of a horse commissioned by a famous building in Yogyakarta.

I was greeted at the door by Ibu (Mother) Soedarso, who teaches *Bahasa Indonesia,* the national language, at a local junior high school. In traditional Indonesian manner, she served *Nasgithel,* a hot, sweet Javanese tea, and a couple of sweet appetizers. *Klepon,* a delicious sweet ball prepared from rice flour, enclosed a palm sugar center; *Kue Cara Bikang,* sweet cakes prepared from flour, sugar, tapioca, and coconut milk, were colored in pretty light-pink and green.

The kitchen housed a gas stove with an oven, the first I had seen in an Indonesian kitchen. (In most homes, grilling is done outside on a charcoal fire, and there is no oven.) Ibu Soedarso demonstrated the preparation of *Bakmie Goreng,* Javanese fried noodles, and *Tahu Telur,* a wonderful egg and bean-curd omelet topped with sweet *kecap manis,* tart vinegar, bean sprouts, green onions, and chiles. An elaborate dinner followed, beginning with a clear corn-and-chicken soup with lots of pepper, reminiscent of one I had in China. The *Gudeg* was a sweeter and more refined version than I had had in Jakarta. There were two very different *satays*—chicken with a sweet peanut sauce and lamb marinated in the sweet soy sauce, *kecap manis*—plus *Sayur Lodeh,* mixed vegetables in a chile and spice coconut sauce, and *Rempeyek Kacang,* crisp and spicy peanut fritters. *Gado-Gado* came with a peanut sauce that was definitely sweeter than in Jakarta, but with sour tamarind added to keep it from being simply too sweet. For dessert, we had delicate young coconut, its sweet flesh still soft enough to scoop out with a spoon, sprinkled with palm sugar. All this was clearly more of a selection than would traditionally be served at one sitting, but my hosts wanted me to taste as many Yogya dishes as possible. Many of the dishes, in fact, had not been made in the home as they were too time-consuming.

Although the island of Bali lies only a short distance off the eastern tip of Java, it might as well be another country. Not only are the language and religion different, there is just a different feeling that is hard to describe. To the ever-growing numbers of tourists, Bali's beaches fit the expectations of a tropical paradise, but I found the real Bali farther inland, away from the beaches and the modern hotels. Traditional Balinese culture survives along the back roads and in the villages, where religion and everyday life are inextricably woven together as they have been for centuries. Religious symbolism and ritual is everywhere and dictates every act of every day.

Bali is unique among the Indonesian islands in being predominantly Hindu; thus the Balinese, unlike the Muslim majority in the country, regularly eat pork. Even so, they are not large meat eaters except during festivals, when *satays* and *Babi Guling* (roast suckling pig) are very often required in the offerings.

There are few days in the year without incense, glamour, and feasting in some part of Bali. The Balinese year consists of 210 days, many of which are temple festivals, special religious holy days, or just propitious days for such important jobs as planting and harvesting rice, laying foundations, cutting bamboo, mating the pigs, or even eloping. The most spectacular of all Bali's life-cycle ceremonies is the cremation ceremony. Large ornate funeral pyres, feasts, and offerings make cremations extremely lavish and expensive affairs. A cremation is often postponed until enough money has been saved. Sometimes a whole village may organize a mass cremation for long-buried dead.

Along the roadsides in Bali are thousands of Hindu temples decorated with ornate carvings and sometimes piled high with *gebogan* (food and flower offerings). As we drove along, girls transported towering *gebogans* on their heads to a nearby temple. These offerings, which take days to make, are absolutely awesome in their size and intricate, artistic arrangement. Some were towers made totally of flowers, but most were made of food. On the base was a bamboo basket, upon which were placed layers of fruits—apples, mangoes, papayas, oranges, bananas—all topped with pink and green sweet rice cakes and decorated with flowers. The girls were on the way to the temple where their offerings were made to the chanting priests, who blessed them and dedicated them to the spirits. Afterward, they would be consumed at a ceremonial feast.

The natural beauty and cultural charm of Bali have made the island a major tourist destination, and the Bali Hotel and Tourism Training Institute is developing a staff to run the growing hospitality business. The beautiful campus, with one-story buildings in the ornate Balinese architectural style set among a lush tropical garden of flowers and palms, gives little clue that inside is an up-to-date kitchen like that of any first-class urban restaurant.

Here, young chefs practice their trade under the direction of Head Chef I. Wayan Arcana, learning both international cuisine and traditional Balinese dishes such as *Sate Empol Ikan* (minced fish combined with chiles, shrimp paste, garlic, shallots, tamarind, and palm sugar). A long "Bali *satay* stick," made from the hollowed-out stem of a young banana tree, was stuffed with the fish combination and baked in the oven, which made a wonderful presentation at the table.

Every part of Indonesia has at least one exceptional chicken dish, and *Betutu Ayam* (chicken marinated with chiles and spices, wrapped in a banana leaf, and baked in the oven) was a masterpiece. I also enjoyed *Jukut Mekalis* (green beans, carrots, and ground beef in a spicy coconut milk sauce), *Lawar Nangka* (young jackfruit and coconut in a hot chile paste and coconut milk mixture), and *Sayur Ares Ala Balung* (the peeled, sliced trunk of a very young banana palm, boiled with fiery Balinese spices and coconut milk, and rice). For dessert, we had one of my favorite desserts, *Bubur Injin*, a reddish-black rice cooked for a long period until very soft, sweetened with palm sugar, served like a thick soup, and topped with rich, thick coconut cream. The meal was served on a creatively decorated table with lovely, whimsical Balinese statues amid many pyramids of flowers.

The lure of the famous Spice Islands, fought over by the Spanish, Portuguese, British, and Dutch merchant fleets for nutmeg and cloves, brought me to the Moluccas. The trade in these spices goes back at least to 300 B.C., and it was their wealth that motivated Columbus to sail west across the Atlantic, discovering America in his search for a shortcut to the "Indies." Today, the 999 islands that make up the Moluccas are the most undiscovered and least developed part of Indonesia, constituting less than four percent of the country's land area.

Arnold Stephanus Tomasoa had invited me to his village on the small but lush coral island of Saparua, a short distance from Ambon, the provincial capital of Maluku Province. A large clove plantation still exists on the island. It was October, the clove-picking season, and the cloves were scattered on the tiny village streets to dry. The buds of the clove must be picked before the flower opens, and it is a very busy time within the village. Surprisingly, nutmeg and cloves are not used in the cooking of the Moluccas; instead, most of the clove crop is combined with tobacco to produce *Kretek,* Indonesia's aromatic, sweet-smelling cigarettes. The natives also chew on whole cloves, saying that they will keep you awake if you are sleepy.

Like many other islands of eastern Indonesia, the terrain of Saparua cannot support rice cultivation. Staples of the island diet include *sago,* a starch from the trunk of the sago palm, and cassava, the tuberous root also known as tapioca, manioc, or yucca. Mr. Tomasoa showed me the preparation of the daily staple, *Papeda.* Pulverizing and straining the pulp of the sago palm, then boiling the extract with water, produces a bland, whitish, gluelike mass. More interesting than the flavor of *Papeda* is the method of eating it—by bending directly over your plate and slurping it up as best you can. I found that this takes great practice, otherwise you will end up with a face of the paste.

Sago is also made into a sort of bread. A sago dough is placed in bricklike molds and set out in the sun to bake, resulting in a hard and tasteless bread that must be dipped in water to soften before eating. The other major starch is cassava, which when steamed resembles a bland, pale sweet potato.

To balance out the blandness of these staples, the remaining dishes are generally sweet, sour, and spicy. By Southeast Asian standards, very little chile is used, a definite Dutch influence; instead, the dishes rely on local herbs, giving the food a delicious flavor but one totally different from any other I tasted throughout Indonesia. My first meal of *Papeda* was accompanied by a freshly caught grilled tuna and *Colo Colo* sauce, a sweet-sour mixture of lime, red onion, and sugar with a touch of chile. *Sayur Santen,* a vegetable dish combining green papaya, chiles, garlic, onion, shrimp paste, lime, and coconut milk was also sweet, sour, and slightly spicy. *Kenari* nuts, similar to almonds, always appear at the end of meals and are used as the basis of many dishes. Steamed bananas and pineapples in cardamom-flavored syrup are the desserts.

My visit to Saparua ended on a definite sweet note with a delightful breakfast amid the beautiful flowers, palms, and parrots. Sweet sticky rice *(ketan)* was topped with a combination of freshly grated palm sugar and coconut. A sweet palm sugar sauce, the consistency of warm maple syrup, was poured on top. More delicate, freshly grated coconut was the final topping. This was accompanied by fried bananas. It was a wonderful combination of tastes and textures.

"Selamat makan," or "Good eating," as the Indonesians say at the start of every meal!

►INDONESIAN TRADITIONAL MENUS◄

A JAVANESE *SLAMETAN*

6 to 8 people

Festive Yellow Rice Cone, *Nasi Tumpeng Kuning Lengkap*

◆

Beef and Potato Balls, *Perkedel Goreng*

◆

Coconut Beef Balls, *Rempah*

◆

Fried Chicken, *Ayam Goreng*

◆

Coconut-Flavored Vegetables, *Urap*

◆

Grilled Shrimp, Javanese, *Udang Panggang Jawa*

◆

Crunchy Peanut Fritters, *Rempeyek Kacang*

◆

Toasted Spiced Coconut with Peanuts, *Serundeng Kacang*

◆

Marbled Eggs, *Telur Berwarna*

◆

Pickled Vegetables, *Acar Kuning*

◆

Chile Sauce, *Sambal Ulek*

◆

Shrimp Crackers, *Krupuk Udang*

◆

Sweet Coconut Rice Balls, *Klepon*

◆

Fresh Fruits

Whether the occasion is an open house or a New Year's Eve party, a selection of Javanese dishes will make for a truly memorable buffet.

A *Slametan,* the traditional special-event feast of Java, may be held at any time and for almost any reason. The most common occasions are to celebrate a birth, a marriage, a circumcision, or an anniversary; or it may be held to commemorate a death, to dispel bad luck, or to invite good fortune. Today, a *Slametan* is also served for a gathering of friends and can have no religious aspects.

The centerpiece and the most important dish in a *Slametan* is the *tumpeng,* a giant cone of steamed rice. Unlike many ceremonial dishes that are designed for appearance only, the *tumpeng* is also delicious. It can be garnished in a variety of ways. I have seen *tumpengs* topped with a banana leaf cap, or a chile pepper flower, garnished with large flowers carved from white Chinese turnips that have been dyed red, carrots, tomato roses, and delicate yellow egg shreds. Often, long Chinese green beans are placed on the *tumpeng,* to signify long life.

Nasi Tumpeng is central to Islamic religious rituals. The white of the rice signifies purity. The beautifully adorned cone rests on a blue and white cloth, which is intended to ward off evil spirits and disease. As long as the whiteness of the rice is balanced by these colors, the *tumpeng* is believed to assure the mastery of reason over passion. (In ancient ceremonies, there were two *tumpengs,* one larger and one smaller: the men served themselves from the larger, which the women were not allowed to touch. Today, everyone is served from the same cone.)

Nasi Tumpeng Kuning Lengkap, a yellow rice cone, is also served on festive occasions but has different ceremonial meanings. The yellow color (from turmeric) signifies happiness, and the dish is used for weddings and births. Traditionally, the ingredients in the *tumpeng* were strictly determined by the nature of the occasion. Today, this is an all-purpose festive dish, and there are many variations, one of which is included here.

The rest of the dishes in a *Slametan* are designed to complement the *tumpeng,* providing a contrast of flavors and textures. Most can be prepared in advance. The Crunchy Peanut Fritters, *Serundeng Kacang,* Pickled Vegetables, and Shrimp Crackers can be prepared several days ahead; the Beef and Potato Balls, *Rempah,* Fried Chicken, Grilled Shrimp, Javanese; Marbled Eggs, and *Klepon* a day ahead. You can reheat the fritters, *Rempah,* and chicken before serving if you like, but it is equally appropriate to serve them at room temperature. The fruit can be prepared and the Urap cooked in the morning, then reheated in the evening, if desired; it too is delicious at room temperature. The only last-minute preparation is to assemble and garnish the rice cone. Complete advance preparation tips are included with the individual recipes.

Enhance your celebrations with this Javanese tradition!

PADANG PANACHE

6 people

Beef Rendang, *Daging Rendang*
♦
Spicy Grilled Chicken, *Ayam Panggang Padang*
♦
Spinach in Coconut Milk, *Gulai Daun Bayem*
♦
Padang Vegetable Salad, *Slada Padang*
♦
Chile Sauce, Pandang Style, *Sambal Lado*
♦
Rice
♦
Bananas

Here is a menu of Padang or Minang fare from West Sumatra, as enjoyed by the Minangkabau people of Bukit Tinggi and Padang. Known for its fire, Padang food is equally welcome in summertime (as everyone in the tropics knows, chile-hot food has a cooling effect in the heat) or winter (when it warms the body from within).

A typical Padang menu consists of several dishes, each cooked by a different method. There is usually at least one grilled item, one *Gulai* (a broad category of dishes cooked with coconut milk, which retain their sauces), a *slada* (salad), and as often as not, the robust Beef Rendang, a highly spiced stew simmered until the coconut milk is reduced to oil. A fiery *sambal* is always on hand, to be added judiciously to other dishes or to season a bite of rice.

In the home of Mrs. Tity Yulisman, a Minangkabau, I watched her helper pound all of the fresh ingredients for the Beef Rendang on a flat-bottom stone called the *ulekan*. First, coarse salt was added to the stone to aid in the blending. Each ingredient was added and pounded completely to a paste before the next ingredient was added. Next the chiles were crushed and pounded, then the shallots, garlic, *laos (galangal)*, and finally, fresh turmeric, producing a thick, tantalizingly aromatic paste. She added this fragrant paste to the coconut milk along with a bouquet of aromatic leaves (fresh lime, turmeric, and *daun salam*) and then the beef. The kitchen was full of wonderful fragrances, and I could hardly wait for the Beef Rendang to be cooked so that we could sample it.

When everything was ready, we dined in true Muslim fashion, without silverware. The rice was cooked on the dry side, and Mrs.

Yulisman demonstrated how to combine a little rice with the sauces and other dishes, roll it up the right hand into a neat handful, and place it on her tongue without losing a single grain of rice. (The left hand is never used for eating as it is considered unclean and impolite.) I must admit that eating with the right hand requires a little practice, but after a while I mastered the technique.

True Pandang food is among the hottest in Indonesia. In these recipes I have reduced the amount of spices for the American palate. If you wish to dine as they do in Padang, increase the amount of chile peppers used.

In true home-cooking style, Mrs. Yulisman's classic Padang dishes may be made ahead of time and served at leisure. The *Rendang* tastes even better when prepared several days in advance so the flavors mellow. The Fried Chicken and the *Sambal Lado* can also be made ahead. Serve the Spicy Grilled Chicken at room temperature as Tity Yulisman did, or reheat it before serving. *Slada Padang* can be prepared a day ahead and combined before serving. The *Gulai Daun Bayem* can be reheated when serving.

Enjoy your adventuresome Padang Panache!

A BALINESE BARBECUE

Spicy Grilled Chicken Balinese, *Ayam Bali*
♦
Grilled Fish in Banana Leaves Balinese, *Ikan Panggang Bali*
♦
Spiced Eggs, Balinese Style, *Telur Bumbu Bali*
♦
Green Beans and Carrots in Coconut Sauce, *Jukut*
♦
Chile Sauce, *Sambal Ulek*
♦
Rice
♦
Fresh Fruits

Bali has its own special cuisine and language. The food is highly artistic and vivid with chiles, spices, coconut, and other exciting flavors. The atmosphere is relaxed and casual. In this menu, I have tried to recreate the true spirit of this fascinating island. All of the dishes can be prepared ahead and grilled or reheated before serving.

To understand Balinese cuisine, Nyoman Bagiarta, director of the Bali Hotel and Tourism Institute, took me on a tour of the back roads of this fascinating Hindu island. The food of Bali is based on recipes and traditions that have changed little throughout the centuries. The Hindu religion is the force that meshes every force of Balinese life with everything else, including food. The special artistic and cultural life of the Balinese revolves almost entirely around their religion.

We visited a traditional house along the roadside, where several related families live within the same walled enclosure. The wall is to divide the family from the outside world and to keep out the evil spirits. Inside, there was a garden, and small separate buildings for each household function—one for cooking, one to sleep, and even a small family temple. Balinese society is an intensely communal one; the organization of the villages, the cultivation of the farmlands, and even the creative arts are communal efforts. The houses, however, separate village families from one another.

The amazingly simple kitchen consisted of a thatched roof supported by four to six posts. A bamboo platform that served as a kitchen table stood at one end, and a primitive mud stove at the other. On the stove was a clay rinsing-soaking pot for rice, a clay rice-boiling pot, a steaming pot (also clay) with a woven basket for rice on top of the pot, a wok, and a grinding stone and pestle. The only utensils were two coconut graters—coarse and fine—a vegetable ladle, a split-bamboo skimmer for removing food from the wok, tongs, a knife, and a cleaver. A wooden chopping board, clay drinking-water jug, a large clay water jug and ladle, and coconut shell bowls completed the kitchen. This particular family used plates, but banana leaves often serve the same function.

Surprisingly, everyday eating is not a social act for the Balinese; instead, meals at home are taken individually to be eaten in the privacy of a corner of the kitchen, uninterrupted by talking or watching people. However, they love to eat out at the *warung* (roadside stands). But festival and ceremonial meals are definitely social; in fact, the entire family, neighbors, and villagers may be called upon to assist in the preparation.

Your Balinese Barbecue won't require the help of your neighbors, as many of the dishes lend themselves to advance preparation. You can prepare the *Sambal Ulek* several days ahead or purchase it. The *Jukut, Telur Bumbu Bali,* and *Ayam Bali* can be partially prepared a day ahead. On the morning of the barbecue, marinate the fish and wrap it in banana leaves or foil, and refrigerate. Before serving, grill the chicken and fish, and cook the rice. Reheat the *Telur Bumbu Bali* and the *Jukut* just before serving, then relax and enjoy!

STARTERS

Coconut Beef Balls, *Rempah,*
Beef and Potato Balls, *Perkedel Goreng*
Cruncy Peanut Fritters, *Rempeyek Kacang*
Crunchy Anchovy Fritters, *Rempeyek Teri*
Shrimp Chips, *Krupuk Udang*

SOUPS

Indonesian Chicken Soup, *Soto Ayam*
Cream of Spinach and Coconut Soup, *Bayem Dengan Kelapa Muda*

MEAT

Beef Rendang, Padang Style, *Daging Rendang*
Beef in Coconut Gravy, *Kalio*
Crisp Chile-Beef Slices, Padang Style, *Dendeng Belado*
Stir-Fried Beef, *Lapis Daging*
Borneo Ribs
Grilled Lamb on Skewers, *Satai Kambing*

POULTRY

Grilled Chicken on Skewers, *Satai Ayam*
Grilled Chicken with Coconut Sauce, *Ayam Panggang Mesanten*
Grilled Chicken with Chile Sauce, *Ayam Panggang Bumbu Rujak*
Spicy Grilled Chicken, *Ayam Panggang Padang*
Grilled Chicken, Balinese Style, *Ayam Bali*
Roast Chicken in Banana Leaves, *Betutu Ayam*
Grilled Chicken with Spicy Sauce, *Ayam Panggang Rica-Rica*
Tamarind Chicken, *Ayam Goreng*
Javanese Fried Chicken, *Ayam Goreng Jawa*

FISH AND SEAFOOD

Grilled Fish in Banana Leaves, Balinese Style, *Ikan Panggang Bali*
Grilled Fish with Balinese Sauce, *Pepes Bumbu Bali*
Grilled Shrimp, Javanese, *Udang Panggang Jawa*

SALADS AND VEGETABLES

Mixed Vegetable Salad with Peanut Dressing, *Gado-Gado*
Spicy Fruit Salad, *Rujak*
Padang Vegetable Salad, *Slada Padang*
Fruit and Vegetable Salad, *Slada Huzar*
Stir-Fried Vegetables, *Oseng-Oseng*
Spinach in Coconut Milk, *Gulai Daun Bayem,*
Stir-Fried Cabbage and Shrimp, *Orak-Arik*

Stir-Fried Eggplant and Tomatoes, *Semur Terong Tomat*
Coconut-Flavored Vegetables, *Urap*
Green Beans, Carrots, and Beef in Coconut Sauce, *Jukut Mekalis*
Green Beans and Carrots in Coconut Sauce, *Jukut*
Spiced Tomato Sambal, *Sambal Goreng Tomat*
Spiced Beans and Tomatoes, *Sambal Goreng Buncis Tomat*
Spiced Cucumbers, *Sayur Timun*

RICE, NOODLES, EGGS

Festive Yellow Rice Cone, *Nasi Tumpeng Kuning Lengkap*
Festive Yellow Rice, *Nasi Kuning*
Rice Rolls in Banana Leaves, *Lontong*
Pressed Rice Squares, *Ketupat*
Javanese Fried Noodles, *Bakmie Goreng Jawa*
Spicy Tofu Omelet, *Tahu Telur*

ACCOMPANIMENTS, PICKLES, AND SAUCES

Fried Bananas, *Pisang Goreng*
Marbled Eggs, *Telur Berwarna*
Crisp Fried Beef, *Dendeng Ragi*
Toasted Spiced Coconut with Peanuts, *Serundeng Kacang*
Javanese Pickled Cucumbers, *Acar Ketimun Jawa*
Pickled Vegetables, *Acar Kuning*
Spiced Eggs, Balinese Style, *Telur Bumbu Bali*
Satay Sauce, Surabaya Style, *Sambal Kacang Surabaya*
Indonesian Sweet Soy Sauce, *Kecap Manis*
Chile Sauce, *Sambal Ulek*
Chile Sauce, Padang Style, *Sambal Lado*

DESSERTS, BEVERAGES

Sweet Coconut Rice Balls, *Klepon*
Pandan Refresher

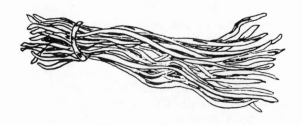

STARTERS

 ## Coconut Beef Balls
Rempah

These tasty morsels are often served with a tumpeng *(rice cone) during a ceremonial dinner. They are a delicious accompaniment for cocktails or for a buffet table.*

1 small onion, minced
1 clove garlic, minced
¼ teaspoon shrimp paste *(terasi)*
1 teaspoon ground coriander
1 teaspoon brown sugar
1 teaspoon salt
½ teaspoon black pepper
½ pound ground beef
1 cup freshly grated coconut
2 eggs, lightly beaten
2 cups oil for frying

Combine the onion, garlic, shrimp paste, coriander, sugar, salt, and black pepper in a bowl, making sure the shrimp paste is completely combined with the remaining ingredients. Add the beef, and coconut. Knead well with your hands. Add the eggs and mix thoroughly. Shape into 1-inch balls.

Heat oil in a wok. Add the meatballs to the oil, a few at a time, and fry until medium brown and cooked throughout. Remove. Drain on paper towels. Serve hot or at room temperature.

YIELD: 20 meatballs.

TIP: If fresh coconut is unavailable, use ½ cup unsweetened dried coconut flakes. Refresh it by soaking briefly in cold water. Drain well, pressing down in a sieve to squeeze out most of the water.

ADVANCE PREPARATION: Prepare 1 day ahead or freeze fried meatballs for 2 months. Reheat in a moderate oven or in a microwave until heated through. Serve hot or at room temperature.

From the kitchen of Soedarso Sp., president of the Indonesian Institute of Arts Yogyakarta, and Ibu Soedarso.

Beef and Potato Balls
Perkedel Goreng

This tasty beef and potato ball is usually served as a garnish for the traditional tumpeng *during a* Slametan. *Chiles are not a traditional ingredient in Javanese* Perkedel. *I have added them to give the dish a more vivacious spirit.*

They are delightful as an accompaniment to Western cocktails, and are equally delightful on a buffet table or even a summer picnic.

2 cloves garlic, finely chopped
2 fresh red chiles, seeded, or 1 teaspoon *Sambal Ulek* (page 321).
    optional
3 cups oil for frying
1 small onion, finely chopped
4 medium potatoes, boiled in skins, peeled, mashed
4 green onions, chopped
2 teaspoons chopped parsley
¼ teaspoon ground nutmeg
Salt and pepper to taste
½ pound finely minced lean beef
1 egg, beaten

Pound or process the garlic and chiles to a smooth paste. Heat 1 tablespoon oil and fry the onion until translucent. Combine the potatoes with the paste mixture. Add the green onions, parsley, nutmeg, salt, and pepper. Add the beef. Knead the potato mixture and the meat thoroughly. (If using a food processor, process for a few seconds with several pulses. Do not overprocess.) Add the beaten egg. Mix well with a fork. Shape 1 heaping teaspoon of the mixture into a small meatball. Flatten the balls slightly with the side of a spoon—or if you are garnishing another dish, make smaller balls, the size of a marble. When all of the balls have been made, heat the oil to 350° F in a wok. Reduce the heat to medium and deep-fry 6 to 8 at a time until they are cooked and brown, approximately 3 to 4 minutes. Drain on paper towels.

If the *Perkedel* are served by themselves, they are usually served hot. As a garnish, as in *Nasi Tumpeng Kuning Lengkap* (page 305), they are usually served at room temperature.

YIELD: approximately 40 balls.

TIP: The mashed potatoes should be firm and dry when mashed so they will not disintegrate in the frying.

ADVANCE PREPARATION: Prepare ahead completely. Serve at room temperature or reheat on moderate heat in the microwave or in the oven.

Inspired by Hidayat, consul of information and cultural affairs, Consulate General, Republic of Indonesia, Chicago.

 ## Crunchy Peanut Fritters
Rempeyek Kacang

Here is a crisp, spiced fritter of irregular shape and unusual flavor, which can be served as an accompaniment for cocktails, or as a snack.

In Yogyakarta, they were served in the home of Professor and Ibu Soedarso with rice and curries as part of our meal. Ibu Soedarso said the secret to making these fritters is to slide the peanut batter around the sides of the wok just above the level of the hot oil.

1 cup rice flour
1 cup thin coconut milk or water
1 egg, beaten
1½ teaspoons coriander powder
¾ teaspoon turmeric
½ teaspoon salt
¼ teaspoon sugar
1 clove garlic, finely minced
½ cup dry roasted unsalted peanuts, broken in half
2 to 3 cups oil for deep frying

Prepare a batter by combining the rice flour, thin coconut milk, egg, coriander, turmeric, salt, sugar, and garlic. Mix well, making sure the batter is completely combined and there are no lumps. Add the peanuts and stir. This will be a thin batter.

Heat oil in a wok over medium-high heat to 350° F. Pour 1 tablespoon of the batter quickly against the side of the wok just above the level of the hot oil. Do this in tablespoons all around the wok. You will be able to make approximately 4 to 5 fritters at a time, as they will spread into approximately 3-inch rounds. Let fry 1 minute, scraping the edges as they set. Then, let them float and fry in the oil for about 2 minutes. Turn them with a slotted spoon for 30 seconds more, or until they are crisp and golden on both sides. Be sure to stir the mixture each time you add it to the wok, as the peanuts will settle to the bottom of the bowl as it stands. The fritters should be thin, lightly browned, and crispy. Remove and drain on paper towels. Store in an airtight container.

YIELD: 20 to 25 fritters.

ADVANCE PREPARATION: The fritters will keep in an airtight container for 1 to 2 weeks.

From the kitchen of Soedarso Sp., president of the Indonesian Institute of Arts Yogyakarta, and Ibu Soedarso.

 ## Crunchy Anchovy Fritters
Rempeyek Teri

Ibu Zaenuddien, the famous television personality and caterer, showed me how to prepare crisp, tasty Rempeyek Teri *using small* teri, *dried anchovies. They are served on many festive occasions as part of a ceremony. Don't fear, they won't blink at you when eating!*
They make an unusual cocktail or dinner accompaniment.

3 macadamia nuts, chopped
1 clove garlic, chopped
2 teaspoons coriander powder
½ teaspoon salt
1 cup rice flour
1 cup thin coconut milk or water
1 egg, beaten
1 ounce (1 to 2 tablespoons) dried anchovies

Pound or process macadamias, garlic, coriander, and salt to a smooth paste in a mortar, blender, or food processor.

Prepare a batter by combining the rice flour, thin coconut milk, egg, and the paste. Mix well, making sure the batter is completely combined and there are no lumps. Add the anchovies and stir. This will be a thin batter.

Heat oil in a wok over medium-high heat to 350° F. Pour 1 tablespoon of the batter quickly against the side of the wok just above the level of the hot oil. Repeat this all around the wok. You will be able to make approximately 4 to 5 fritters at a time, as they will spread into approximately 3-inch rounds. Let fry 1 minute, scraping the edges as they set, and let them float and fry in the oil for about 2 minutes. Turn them with a slotted spoon for 30 seconds more, or until they are crisp and golden on both sides. Be sure to stir the mixture each time you add it to the wok, as the anchovies will settle to the bottom of the bowl as the batter stands. The fritters should be thin, lightly browned, and crispy. Remove and drain on paper towels. Store in an airtight container.

YIELD: 20 to 25 fritters.

TIP: Ibu kept the heads on the anchovies, which I found very interesting. If you wish, you may cut them off before adding them to the batter.

ADVANCE PREPARATION: Rempeyek Teri will keep in an airtight container for 1 to 2 weeks.

Inspired by Ibu Zaenuddien, television cooking show hostess, caterer, owner, Ibu Zaenuddien's Sweet Shops, Yogyakarta.

 ## Shrimp Chips
Krupuk Udang

Uncooked shrimp chips come in many shapes and sizes. The most flavorful type is from Indonesia and is pale-pink in color with a distinct shrimp flavor. Another variety, popular in Chinese cooking, comes in multi-colors. When deep fried in hot oil, they become light, crisp and crunchy, and swell to more than twice their size within seconds.

    Oil for deep frying
    Dried shrimp chips

Heat oil in a wok or deep frying pan to 360° F. Fry the chips, a few at a time. if the oil is hot enough, they will puff up within 2 to 3 seconds. Fry until lightly colored, approximately 15 seconds. Remove. Drain on paper towels. Cool and store in an airtight container. The chips will keep for 2 to 3 days.

TIP: If the shrimp chips become soft due to moisture, dry them in a low oven for 10 to 15 minutes before frying.

SOUPS

 ## Indonesian Chicken Soup
Soto Ayam

When I visited Nila Chandra, the famous Jakarta cooking school owner, she taught me her grandmother's version of this favorite Indonesian soup. It is nourishing, filling, and attractive, and makes a festive luncheon or party dish. Many Indonesians use turmeric in place of Nila's saffron in this soup.

If you prefer a spicier version, you may serve the soup as Nila Chandra does with a side dish of Sambal Ulek (page 321). Each diner adds the sambal to his Soto Ayam according to his taste.

For a more filling meal, she serves it with sliced rice rolls (Lontong), page 309, and Peanut Fritters (Rempeyek Kacang), page 265.

    10 shallots or 1 medium onion, chopped
    3 cloves garlic, chopped
    4 macadamia nuts, chopped
    ½ teaspoon shrimp paste *(terasi)* (optional)
    1 teaspoon chopped fresh ginger
    1 teaspoon coriander seeds
    1 tablespoon oil
    One 2- to 3-pound chicken, quartered
    1½ teaspoons salt
    1 stalk lemon grass, bottom 6 inches only, crushed, or 1 teaspoon
        grated lemon rind
    1 teaspoon saffron
    2 ounces thin rice noodles, soaked in warm water for 20 minutes,
        drained, cut into 2-inch lengths
    Salt and pepper to taste
    1 medium potato, boiled, peeled, thinly sliced, cut in half
        (optional)

GARNISHES:

    2 hard-boiled eggs, sliced
    Fried Shallot Flakes (page 24)
    Parsley leaves
    2 limes, cut into wedges

Pound or process shallots, garlic, macadamias, shrimp paste, ginger, and coriander seeds to a paste. Heat oil in a pan over moderate heat. Add paste and cook, stirring, for 1 to 2 minutes.

Place the chicken in a pan. Add water to cover the chicken. Add salt, lemon grass, saffron, and the cooked paste mixture. Stir. Bring to a boil. Reduce heat. Cook, covered, over medium heat for 30 minutes or until chicken is tender. Remove from heat and let chicken stand in the broth for 15 minutes to absorb flavors. Remove the chicken. Strain and reserve the broth. If stock has reduced, add water to make 6 cups. Cut or pull the chicken meat into strips about ⅛ inch wide and 1 to 1½ inches long.

Bring 3 quarts of water to a boil. Add the drained noodles and simmer for 2 to 3 minutes, or until noodles are tender. Drain and set aside. Taste the stock for seasoning, adding salt and pepper if desired.

To serve, distribute chicken pieces, sliced potato, and noodles into each of 8 individual soup plates. Reheat the broth and ladle the very hot broth over all. Garnish the top with egg slices, fried shallot flakes and parsley leaves. Serve with lime wedges and a side dish of *Sambal Ulek*.

YIELD: 8 servings.

VARIATIONS: Cooked rice may be used in place of the boiled potato.

Five minutes before the end of cooking time, 4 ounces of peeled, washed shrimp may be added to the cooking chicken broth. Remove from broth with chicken. At serving time, place in soup platters with the chicken pieces.

ADVANCE PREPARATION: Prepare ingredients 1 day ahead. Serve as directed. Reheat broth when serving.

Inspired by a recipe from Nila Chandra, cookbook author, cooking school owner, and holder of the 1989 Guinness Book of Records for the creation of the most complicated and unique cake house.

Cream of Spinach and Coconut Soup
Bayem Dengan Kelapa Muda

Executive Chef Hubert Lorenz of the Bali Hyatt shared his recipe for this attractive soup, which has a delightful coconut flavor. He serves it hot. I enjoy it chilled as well.

  2 tablespoons oil
  2 tablespoons chopped red onions
  1 stalk lemon grass, bottom 6 inches only, crushed
  1 tablespoon brown sugar
  3 cups chicken stock
  1⅓ cups coconut milk
  1 pound spinach leaves, stems removed
  5 ounces young coconut meat, diced
  Salt and pepper to taste

Heat oil in a heavy soup pot and sauté the onions over moderate heat, being careful not to brown. Add the lemon grass and brown sugar and sauté until the sugar has dissolved, about 10 to 20 seconds. Add the chicken stock and coconut milk. Stir. Bring to a boil. Reduce heat and simmer for approximately 10 minutes, stirring frequently. Add spinach leaves and half of the coconut meat. Bring to a boil. Reduce heat and simmer for approximately 10 minutes. Season with salt and pepper. Remove from the heat. Discard the lemon grass. Pour the soup into a blender or food processor and puree for 1 to 2 minutes. Return to pan and reheat soup.

Serve in a soup tureen or individual soup bowls. Garnish with remaining coconut meat.

YIELD: 4 servings.

TIP: If fresh coconut is unavailable, use 6 tablespoons unsweetened dried coconut flakes. Refresh it by soaking briefly in cold water. Drain well, pressing down in the sieve to squeeze out most of the water.

ADVANCE PREPARATION: Prepare completely in advance. Reheat or serve cold.

MEAT

 ## Beef Rendang, Padang Style
Daging Rendang

Padang food, also known as Minang food, is a favorite among Indonesians. It is originally from the district in west central Sumatra known as Minangkabau, which means "Victorious Buffalo." The people of this beautiful area eat buffalo more than beef as cows are not plentiful. While the buffalo meat is delicious, it must be cooked for many, many hours as it is very tough.

Mrs. Tity Yulisman, a well-known Padang cook, taught me this dish in her kitchen. She substituted beef for this classic Sumatran specialty and said that once it is cooked, this heavily spiced dish will keep for 3 or 4 days. She said that years ago the Minangkabau traders would carry it on their long trips through the jungles and eat it with Lontong rolls of steamed rice wrapped in banana leaves (page 309).

I have recreated in my kitchen a version using modern methods and ingredients available here. It tastes remarkably similar to Mrs. Yulisman's. She served it with Gulai Daun Bayem (page 297), Sambal Lado (page 322), and rice. She said she usually makes a large quantity of the Beef Rendang because it freezes well.

This Rendang differs from Singapore Chef Joe Yap's Nonya Beef Rendang (page 127) in that this is a more robust dish using Sumatran spices and has no sauce. In his Nonya version of Beef Rendang, the coconut milk is not reduced and produces a rich sauce for rice.

It is wonderful for a Western buffet or dinner as it can be made ahead, doubled or tripled, and is equally delicious hot or at room temperature.

½ teaspoon chopped laos (*galangal*)
2 teaspoons chopped fresh ginger root
2 to 4 fresh hot red or green chiles, chopped
3 cloves garlic, chopped
2 tablespoons coriander powder
¼ teaspoon turmeric powder
4 cups thick coconut milk
1 stalk lemon grass, bottom 6 inches only, crushed
1 *daun salam* leaf or substitute bay leaf
1 Kaffir lime leaf
2 small green tomatoes, chopped

2 pounds lean beef chuck, trimmed of excess fat, sliced 1 inch
  thick and cut into 2½- by 1-inch pieces
Salt and freshly ground black pepper to taste

Pound or process the laos, ginger, chiles, and garlic to a coarse paste. Add the coriander and turmeric, and blend. In a wok, add the coconut milk, paste mixture, lemon grass, *daun salam,* Kaffir lime leaves, and tomatoes. Bring to a boil. Reduce the heat and simmer for 5 to 10 minutes to allow ingredients to blend. Add the beef. Bring to a boil and reduce heat. Let the mixture bubble gently, stirring frequently, until it becomes thick and the meat is tender. This should take about 2 to 2½ hours. Add salt and pepper to taste. At the end of this time, the meat should be tender and the oil will separate from the gravy. Turn the heat to high. Fry the meat, stirring. (It is very important to stir constantly at this point, to prevent the mixture from burning.) The beef should be nicely browned, but not scorched. Serve with rice, a vegetable, and *Sambal Lado* (page 322)

YIELD: 8 servings with other dishes.

TIP: For a less spicy version, remove the seeds from the chiles. In Padang, they are not removed.

VARIATIONS: Substitute red tomatoes for the green tomatoes.

Substitute ½ teaspoon grated lemon zest for Kaffir lime leaf.

ADVANCE PREPARATION: The Rendang may be prepared ahead, and refrigerated or frozen for 2 months. Reheat in a moderate oven or in a microwave on medium heat at serving time.

 Beef in Coconut Gravy
Kalio

Kalio *is a version of Beef Rendang. The coconut milk has not cooked away and the beef is served in the coconut milk gravy.*

½ teaspoon laos (*galangal*), chopped
2 teaspoons chopped fresh ginger root
2 to 3 fresh hot red or green chiles, chopped
3 cloves garlic, chopped
2 tablespoons coriander powder

¼ teaspoon turmeric powder
4½ cups coconut milk
1 stalk lemon grass, bottom 6 inches only, crushed
1 *daun salam* leaf or bay leaf
1 Kaffir lime leaf (optional)
2 small green tomatoes, chopped (optional)
2 pounds lean beef chuck, trimmed of excess fat, sliced 1 inch
    thick and cut into 2½- by 1-inch pieces
Salt and freshly ground black pepper to taste

Pound or process the laos, ginger, chiles, and garlic to a coarse paste. Add the coriander and turmeric, and blend. In a wok, add the coconut milk, paste, lemon grass, *daun salam*, Kaffir lime leaf, and tomatoes. Bring to a boil. Reduce the heat and simmer for 5 to 10 minutes to allow ingredients to blend. Add the beef. Bring to a boil and reduce heat. Let mixture bubble gently, stirring frequently, until it becomes thick and the meat is tender. If the sauce becomes too thick during the cooking, add more coconut milk or water. This should take about 2 to 2½ hours. Taste. Add salt and pepper to taste. At the end of this time, the meat should be tender.

YIELD: 8 servings with other dishes.

TIP: The meat may be prepared ahead, refrigerated, and reheated at serving time.

VARIATIONS: Chicken may be used instead of beef. Cook the chicken for approximately 40 minutes or until tender.

Red tomatoes may be used as a substitute for the green tomatoes.

From the kitchen of Mrs. Tity Yulisman, a Minangkabau, Padang, West Sumatra.

 ## Crisp, Chile-Beef Slices, Padang Style
Dendeng Belado

Well-done beef slices give an unexpected chewy texture to this exciting form of the Chinese beef jerky. Mrs. Tity Yulisman of Padang says to make your sauce less pungent, pound or process an additional ¼ cup red tomatoes with the hot red chiles. The red tomatoes provide the bright red color characteristic of this dish but lessen the intensity of the chiles.

3 cups water
2 pounds beef round steak or boneless chuck, trimmed
7 tablespoons oil
¾ cup chopped onions
3 to 4 fresh red chiles, chopped
½ cup cubed red, ripe tomatoes
1 teaspoon salt
3 to 4 tomato slices for garnish

Bring the water to a boil. Add the beef and cook in the water for 15 minutes. Remove. Drain. Slice into thin 2-inch squares. Heat pan. Add ¼ cup oil and heat. Fry the beef in batches, turning. This will take approximately 4 to 5 minutes. The beef should be brown, dry, and crisp on both sides. Remove and set aside to drain on paper towels.

Pound or process the onions, chiles, tomatoes, and salt to a coarse paste. Heat 3 tablespoons oil in a wok and fry the paste for 3 to 4 minutes over moderate heat. Add the beef and stir-fry for approximately 2 minutes to coat the slices and distribute the flavors. Add the sliced tomatoes and cook for approximately 1 minute or until softened. Serve with rice.

YIELD: 8 servings with other dishes.

TIP: The beef and sauce may be prepared ahead and refrigerated. When serving, reheat the sauce, add the beef, and continue cooking as above. Do not combine the beef and sauce ahead of serving time. The beef will soften, and you will lose the unusual texture of the dish.

 ## Stir-Fried Beef *Lapis Daging*

While in Jakarta, Ratna Etchika, the niece of Hidayat, Consulate of the Republic of Indonesia, taught me this simply prepared, spirited, colorful dish.

1 medium ripe tomato
½ teaspoon nutmeg
1 egg, beaten
½ pound flank steak, sliced thinly into 2- to 3-inch lengths
1 tablespoon oil
¼ cup thinly sliced onion

1 clove garlic, thinly sliced
1 tablespoon sweet soy sauce, *kecap manus*
One 1-inch piece cinnamon stick
2 cloves
Dash pepper
Fried shallot flakes (page 24, optional)

Bring 4 cups water to a boil. Immerse the tomato in the water for about 15 seconds or until skin just loosens. Remove. Peel skin.

Combine the nutmeg with the egg. Coat the steak slices with the beaten egg and nutmeg. Add the oil to a skillet and fry the onion and garlic over moderate heat until softened, about 2 minutes. Drain the egg from the steak and fry in batches for 2 minutes on each side or until it is no longer pink. Combine the sweet soy sauce, cinnamon, cloves, pepper, and tomato. Add to the cooked steak. Mix well. Fry for about 5 minutes, or until the sauce has thickened slightly. Add a little water during the final cooking, if necessary, to prevent burning. Sprinkle with fried shallot flakes. Serve immediately with rice and *Sambal Goreng Buncis* (page 304).

YIELD: 2 to 4 servings with other dishes.

 Borneo Ribs

A simple and delicious dish, which can be easily prepared ahead and reheated.

2 large cloves garlic, minced
2 tablespoons minced fresh ginger
¾ teaspoon ground nutmeg
½ teaspoon ground cloves
½ teaspoon five-spice powder
½ teaspoon black pepper
1 tablespoon brown sugar
3 tablespoons soy sauce
3 tablespoons oil
1½ pounds meaty spare ribs, chopped by your butcher into
    1-inch pieces, fat removed
1 to 2 cups boiling water

Combine the garlic, ginger, nutmeg, cloves, five-spice powder, black pepper, brown sugar, soy sauce, and 1 tablespoon oil in a large bowl. Add the ribs to the mixture and let marinate for 1 hour.

Heat wok over high heat. Add 2 tablespoons oil and heat. Add the ribs and stir-fry, turning until each piece is lightly browned. Add the boiling water to cover. When the liquid comes to a boil, turn the heat to low to maintain a gentle simmer. Cover and simmer for 45 minutes or until tender, stirring occasionally. Turn heat to medium-high. Stir vigorously until most of the liquid has evaporated. Serve.

YIELD: 3 to 4 servings with other dishes.

 ## Grilled Lamb on Skewers
Satai Kambing

Satay, grilled meat on a skewer, originated centuries ago in Java. It is thought its true origination might be from the Indian kebab. In Java, a predominantly Muslim area, the most common meat is lamb, goat, chicken, and beef. You may use any of these meats for this recipe.

Satay is found in many variations throughout Indonesia as well as throughout Southeast Asia. It is eaten as part of a meal, as a snack, and is wonderful as an appetizer for a Western cocktail party.

> 2 tablespoons sweet soy sauce, *kecap manis*
> 2 cloves garlic, chopped
> Pinch cumin powder
> 1 pound boneless lamb, cut into 1-inch cubes
> Long metal skewers, or bamboo skewers soaked in water for 1
>   hour

Combine the sweet soy sauce, garlic, and cumin in a bowl. Add the lamb and let marinate for 30 minutes to 1 hour.

Place 3 to 4 cubes of lamb on each skewer, and broil over charcoal or in the oven for about 3 minutes on each side. Serve the satay with Satay Sauce, Hyatt Bumi Surabaya Style (page 320), rice or Lontong (page 309), and sliced cucumbers.

YIELD: 4 servings with other dishes.

TIP: If grilling the satay on a gas grill or gas broiler, cover the handles of the bamboo skewers with aluminum foil to prevent burning.

Inspired by a recipe from executive chef Gerd Sankowski, Hyatt Bumi Surabaya.

POULTRY

 ## Grilled Chicken on Skewers
Satai Ayam

A rich, creamy sauce provides a nice balance for the aromatic satay. This is one of the most popular Indonesian satays.

1 to 2 fresh red chiles, seeded, chopped
2 small onions, chopped
1 tablespoon chopped fresh ginger
2 tablespoons lemon juice
4 tablespoons soy sauce
2 tablespoons Chinese sesame oil
2 tablespoons brown sugar
1 pound chicken breast, boned, skinned, cut into thin strips
Bamboo skewers, soaked in cold water for one hour
Oil for grilling
½ cup coconut milk
Fried shallot flakes (page 24) (optional)

Pound or process the chiles, onions, ginger, lemon juice, and soy sauce to a smooth paste. Add the sesame oil and sugar. Blend to combine. Place chicken in a bowl. Add paste mixture and rub it into the chicken. Cover and let marinate for 1 to 2 hours or overnight in refrigerator.

Thread pieces of chicken on the skewers. Grill over charcoal or under preheated broiler for 5 minutes. Turn over and cook the other side. Brush each side once with oil during grilling.

Pour remaining marinade into a small saucepan. Add the coconut milk and simmer over low heat until smooth and thickened, stirring constantly. Pour into a serving bowl. Serve with the cooked satay. Garnish with fried shallot flakes, if desired.

YIELD: 4 to 6 servings.

ADVANCE PREPARATION: Marinate the chicken for several hours or overnight in refrigerator. Thread the skewers and prepare the sauce several hours before serving. Refrigerate. Grill the satay and reheat the sauce before serving.

Grilled Chicken with Coconut Sauce
Ayam Panggang Mesanten

The exotic Bali Hyatt has shared their recipe for this grilled chicken topped with an appealing, flavorful savory sauce. Lovers of fiery foods might like to add Sambal Ulek *(page 321) to the sauce.*

1 chicken, about 2 to 3 pounds
1 teaspoon salt
1 cup oil
1 teaspoon dried shrimp paste *(terasi)*
4 shallots, chopped
3 cloves garlic, chopped
2 to 3 fresh red chiles, seeds removed, finely shredded
2⅓ cups coconut milk
2 bay leaves
1 stalk lemon grass, crushed with the side of a cleaver
1 tablespoon lime juice
1 fresh red chile, finely shredded into 1½-inch lengths

Cut the chicken in half. Wash and pat dry. Rub with salt and oil. Grill over hot coals or broil in the oven for approximately 10 to 15 minutes on each side, or until done. Slice the cooked chicken into bite-size pieces.

Wrap the shrimp paste in foil and toast on each side over moderate heat about 2 minutes. Pound or process in a mortar, blender, or small processor the shallots, garlic, chiles, and toasted shrimp paste into a paste.

Heat 2 tablespoons oil in a frying pan. Add the paste and fry on moderate heat, stirring, for about 4 to 5 minutes, or until fairly dry, being careful not to burn. Add the coconut milk gradually, stirring after each addition. Add the bay leaves and lemon grass. Bring to a boil. Reduce heat to simmer and simmer for 5 minutes to allow flavors to blend. Add lime juice. Stir. Add the cooked chicken and reheat in the sauce. Garnish with chile shreds. Serve with rice and *Sambal Ulek* (page 321).

YIELD: 4 servings.

VARIATION: Chicken legs or breasts, or 2 Rock Cornish hens may be substituted. If using Cornish hens, cut in half after grilling to prevent drying out of breast meat.

ADVANCE PREPARATION: Grill chicken and prepare sauce 1 day in advance. Reheat chicken in the sauce at serving time.

Inspired by a recipe from executive chef Hubert Lorenz, Bali Hyatt.

 Grilled Chicken with Chile Sauce
Ayam Panggang Bumbu Rujak

Nila Chandra shared her grandmother's recipe for this festive, fiery chicken. This makes a tasty, aromatic buffet dish.

    1 medium onion, chopped
    2 cloves garlic, chopped
    4 macadamia nuts, chopped
    4 to 6 teaspoons chili powder
    ½ teaspoon dried shrimp paste (*terasi*), (optional)
    4 tablespoons oil
    1 chicken, about 2 to 3 pounds, washed, dried, cut into 4 pieces
    2⅔ cups thin coconut milk
    1 tablespoon tamarind water (page 25)
    6 teaspoons dark brown sugar
    Salt and pepper to taste

In a mortar, blender, or processor, pound or blend the onion, garlic, macadamias, chili powder, and shrimp paste to a coarse paste.

In a frying pan, heat 2 tablespoons oil over moderate heat. Add the paste and sauté, stirring, for approximately 2 minutes or until fragrant. Be careful not to burn the paste mixture. Add the chicken pieces, and cook the chicken in the paste mixture on both sides until golden. Gradually add the coconut milk, tamarind water, and brown sugar. Stir to blend spices. Bring to a boil. Reduce heat to simmer and cook for 30 minutes, stirring occasionally. Remove the chicken pieces from the frying pan. Drain. Brush the chicken lightly with oil and grill over charcoal or under the broiler until nicely browned on both sides. Reheat the sauce. Add salt and pepper to taste. Serve the chicken, placing the sauce in a separate bowl. Serve with rice and a vegetable.

YIELD: 3 to 4 servings with other dishes.

TIP: If the sauce is too thin after cooking the chicken, cook until it has reduced to a slightly thick consistency.

ADVANCE PREPARATION: Chicken and sauce may be prepared ahead. Reheat the grilled chicken in a moderate oven. Reheat the sauce on medium heat on top of the stove or in a microwave. The chicken and sauce may be frozen before grilling.

Inspired by a recipe from Nila Chandra, cookbook author, cooking school owner, and holder of the 1989 Guinness Book of Records for the creation of the most complicated and unique cake house.

 ## Spicy Grilled Chicken
Ayam Panggang Padang

Mrs. Tity Yulisman, a Minangkabau, prepared this do-ahead aromatic chicken dish in her kitchen. She said it is a staple and is served with many Padang meals. It is ideal for a buffet or a summer barbecue, as it can be prepared completely in advance.
If you wish a less spicy chicken, reduce the amount of white pepper.

1 2- to 3-pound chicken, washed, dried, cut into 4 pieces
2 teaspoons chopped fresh ginger
2 teaspoons chopped laos (*galangal*), (optional)
6 macadamia nuts, chopped
½ teaspoon turmeric
1 to 2 tablespoons freshly ground white pepper
1 tablespoon soy sauce
2 tablespoons tamarind water (page 25)

Add chicken parts to a pan. Cover with water. Bring to a boil. Reduce heat to simmer and cook for 15 minutes. Remove. Drain.

In a mortar or processor, combine the ginger, laos, and macadamia nuts, and process to a paste. Add the turmeric, white pepper, soy sauce, and tamarind water, and blend. Rub this mixture into the chicken and let the chicken marinate in a bowl for 15 to 30 minutes. Grill over a hot charcoal fire or under the broiler, basting frequently with the marinade. Serve hot or cold.

YIELD: 3 to 4 servings.

ADVANCE PREPARATION: The chicken may be grilled 1 day ahead. Serve at room temperature or reheat in a moderate oven.

 ## Grilled Chicken, Balinese Style
Ayam Bali

Easily prepared, this colorful, lightly spiced, savory chicken is delectable hot or cold. It is a perfect addition to a Western dinner or a picnic.

One 2- to 3-pound chicken, washed, dried, cut into 4 pieces
1 teaspoon salt
2 teaspoons pepper
4 tablespoons oil
4 shallots, chopped
2 cloves garlic, chopped
3 fresh red chile, chopped
1 tablespoon chopped fresh ginger
6 macadamia nuts, chopped
2 tablespoons ketchup
1 tablespoon brown sugar
1 tablespoon soy sauce
Lemon or lime wedges

Rub chicken with salt and pepper and set aside for 10 minutes. In a mortar, blender, or processor, pound or process the shallots, garlic, chiles, ginger, and macadamia nuts to a coarse paste. Heat a frying pan. Add the oil and heat. Add the chicken and fry until lightly browned. Remove. Drain on paper towels. Pour off all but 1 tablespoon oil. Add the paste mixture and fry for 2 minutes, stirring. Add the ketchup, brown sugar, and soy sauce. Stir until sugar is dissolved. Remove from the heat. Let cool. Rub the cooked mixture into the chicken and let the chicken marinate for 1 hour. Broil or grill the chicken until cooked throughout, basting often with the marinade. Serve with lime wedges, rice, and a vegetable or salad.

YIELD: 3 servings.

ADVANCE PREPARATION: Cook 1 day ahead. Refrigerate. Bring to room temperature when serving.

Inspired by a recipe from executive chef Hubert Lorenz, Bali Hyatt.

Roast Chicken in Banana Leaves
Betutu Ayam

This tender chicken is coated with spices and wrapped in banana leaves. It has a stimulating combination of spices and is featured at many festive occasions in Bali.

The Balinese prefer the chickens that roam the housing compounds and village streets. They feel these chickens have a better flavor than our commercial chickens, which is attributed to the great variety of foods obtained in their daily scavenging. These chickens are not as tender, and require longer cooking.

When Executive Chef I. Wayan Arcana of the Bali Hotel and Tourism Training Institute Cooking School taught me this recipe, he prepared it in the traditional manner by boiling the chicken first before roasting it. Our chickens do not need this step.

> 2 fresh red chiles, chopped
> 4 shallots or 1 small onion, chopped
> 1 tablespoon chopped fresh ginger
> 2 teaspoons laos *(galangal)*, chopped
> 3 cloves garlic, chopped
> ½ teaspoon dried shrimp paste *(terasi)*
> 2 *daun salam* or bay leaves
> 5 teaspoons white sesame seeds
> 2 tablespoons tomato ketchup
> 2 teaspoons coriander powder
> ½ teaspoon turmeric powder
> 1 teaspoon black pepper
> ½ teaspoon nutmeg
> 2 tablespoons tamarind water (page 25)
> 2 tablespoons brown sugar
> One 2½- to 3-pound chicken, washed and dried
> Banana leaves or heavy duty aluminum foil (page 26)

In a mortar, blender, or processor, pound or process the chiles, shallots, ginger, laos, garlic, shrimp paste, *daun salam,* and sesame seeds to a coarse paste. Add the ketchup, coriander, turmeric, black pepper, nutmeg, tamarind, and brown sugar. Mix well. Rub the chicken with the paste mixture, putting any remaining mixture in the cavity of the chicken. Truss the chicken. Let marinate for 30 minutes.

Preheat the oven to 350° F. Pour boiling water over the banana leaves to make them pliable. Wrap the chicken with the banana leaves or foil. Place the chicken in a shallow pan and roast for approximately

1 hour or until tender. Serve in the banana leaf. Carve at the table. Serve with rice and other vegetables such as *Jukut Mekalis* (page 00).

YIELD: 4 to 6 servings.

TIP: The chefs at the school wrapped the chicken first in the banana leaves and then placed aluminum foil on top of the banana leaves. The fragrance of the banana leaves was imparted, but none of the juices were lost.

ADVANCE PREPARATION: Wrap the chicken completely ahead and refrigerate.

 Grilled Chicken with Spicy Sauce
Ayam Panggang Rica-Rica

This dish comes from Menado, which lies at the tip of the lovely, mountainous Minchasa region. Literally translated in Mandonese, rica-rica means "a lot of chile." Actually, rica-rica means dishes seasoned with a lot of spices (lemon grass, ginger, basil leaves) and a lot of chile.

Traditionally, this grilled chicken is served with a very spicy sauce with a complex combination of flavors. For the American palate, I have toned down the amount of chiles used. If you prefer to dine as the Indonesians, add 10 chiles to the sauce. You will enjoy a very spirited chicken!

    3 shallots, chopped
    4 cloves garlic, chopped
    4 to 10 fresh red chiles, seeds removed, chopped
    1 medium ripe tomato, chopped
    4 fresh basil leaves
    ½ teaspoon dried shrimp paste *(terasi)*
    ¾ teaspoon turmeric powder
    5 teaspoons tamarind water (page 25)
    2 tablespoons oil
    2 stalks fresh lemon grass, bottom 6 inches only, crushed with
        the side of a cleaver
    2 pieces ginger, each the size of a quarter, crushed with the side
        of a cleaver
    3 Kaffir lime leaves
    2 whole chicken breasts

GARNISH:

 1 fresh red chile (optional)
 Fresh basil leaves (optional)

Pound or process the shallots, garlic, chiles, tomato, basil leaves, and shrimp paste to a coarse paste. Add the turmeric and tamarind water and mix well.

 Heat oil in a frying pan over moderate heat. Add the paste mixture, lemon grass, ginger, and Kaffir lime, and cook for 2 to 3 minutes. Add the chicken and continue cooking for approximately 6 minutes or until three-quarters done, turning once. Remove the chicken from the pan. Continue to reduce the spices until the sauce just coats the back of a spoon. (If the paste mixture becomes too thick, add a little water). The sauce should be fairly thick and spicy. Remove the lemon grass, ginger, and Kaffir lime leaves. Set aside.

 Meanwhile, grill the chicken on both sides over charcoal or under the broiler until done. Reheat sauce. Cover the chicken partly with the sauce. Serve with rice and a vegetable.

YIELD: 4 servings.

TIP: If the tomatoes are not sweet and ripe, add brown sugar to the sauce.

ADVANCE PREPARATION: Cook chicken in the sauce one day in advance. At serving time, remove the chicken from the sauce, grill the chicken, and reheat sauce.

Inspired by a recipe from executive chef Gerd Sankowski, Hyatt Bumi Surabaya.

 Tamarind Chicken
Ayam Goreng

An easily prepared chicken with the subtle, tangy flavors of tamarind, which makes a great picnic or buffet dish.

 2 shallots, minced
 3 garlic cloves, minced
 1½ teaspoons salt
 1 teaspoon freshly ground black pepper
 1 teaspoon sugar

2 teaspoons coriander powder
½ teaspoon turmeric powder
1½ tablespoons tamarind dissolved in ½ cup hot water
One 2½-pound chicken, cut up for frying into approximately 10
     pieces
½ cup oil for frying, approximately

Pound or process to a paste, in a mortar, blender, or processor, the shallots, garlic, salt, pepper, sugar, coriander, and turmeric. Strain tamarind water, discarding the pulp, and blend the liquid into paste. Add the chicken and turn the pieces until they are well coated with the marinade. Marinate chicken for at least 1 hour or refrigerate overnight, turning pieces occasionally.

Heat oil to 375° F in a large frying pan. Add chicken, approximately four pieces at a time, and cook, turning, for about 15 minutes or until done and all the pieces are brown and crispy. Remove. Drain well on paper towels. Serve hot or at room temperature.

YIELD: 3 to 4 servings.

ADVANCE PREPARATION: Prepare 1 to 2 days in advance. Refrigerate, covered with plastic wrap. Serve at room temperature or reheat in a moderate oven.

Inspired by a recipe from executive chef Gerd Sankowski, Hyatt Bumi Surabaya.

 Javanese Fried Chicken
Ayam Goreng Jawa

The Javanese tenderize their chickens by boiling them first in water or coconut milk until partially done. They are then fried, producing tender pieces of crisp, tasty chicken. The chicken is great hot or cold and is wonderful for a picnic.

During a Javanese Slametan *(celebration), this chicken is almost always served with the* tumpeng *(page 305).*

One 2½- to 3-pound frying chicken
1 medium onion, finely minced
1 to 3 fresh or dried red chiles, finely minced
½ teaspoon ground turmeric
2 teaspoons ground coriander
1 teaspoon laos powder *(galangal),* (optional)

2½ cups coconut milk
1 daun salam or bay leaf
1 piece lemon grass, bottom 6 inches only, crushed with the side
   of a cleaver
Salt to taste
3 to 4 cups oil for frying

If using a whole chicken, cut the chicken at the joints. Separate the drumsticks from the thighs, wings from the breast, and cut the breast in half lengthwise.

Pound or process the onion and chiles to a coarse paste. Add the turmeric, coriander, and laos, and mix. In a pan, add the coconut milk, the paste mixture, salam leaf, and lemon grass. Mix. Add the chicken pieces and bring slowly to a boil, stirring. (The liquid should cover the chicken.) Reduce the heat and cook, uncovered, until the chicken is tender, about 20 to 30 minutes. Remove the chicken and drain the sauce from the chicken. Continue cooking the sauce until it has thickened to a thin gravy consistency. Season the sauce with salt to taste.

In the meantime, heat the oil in a wok to 350° F. Add the chicken pieces, three or four at a time, and deep-fry on both sides until golden brown. Remove and drain on paper towels. Continue cooking until all the pieces have been fried.

Reheat the sauce when serving. Serve the chicken hot, room temperature, or cold. Serve with rice, a vegetable dish such as *Urap* (page 299), and *Acar Kuning* (page 318).

YIELD: 3 to 4 servings.

TIP: If red chiles are unavailable, substitute ½ to ¾ teaspoon red pepper powder. Substitute 3 strips thinly sliced, peeled lemon zest for the lemon grass.

ADVANCE PREPARATION: Cook the chicken one day ahead. Serve cold or reheat on moderate heat in the microwave or oven. Reheat the sauce at serving time.

Inspired by Soedarso Sp., president of the Indonesian Institute of Arts Yogyakarta, and Ibu Soedarso.

FISH AND SEAFOOD

 ## Grilled Fish in Banana Leaves, Balinese Style
Ikan Panggang Bali

The fragrant aroma of fish cooked in a banana leaf is always exciting. Fresh fish is combined with the spiciness of Sambal Ulek *and the tartness of lime in this attractive presentation.*

One 2½-pound mackerel, red snapper, or sea bass, cleaned and
  scaled, with head and tail intact
2 teaspoons salt
2 teaspoons *Sambal Ulek*
½ onion, chopped
½ ripe tomato, peeled, chopped
1 tablespoon thin coconut milk
½ teaspoon turmeric
1 lime, thinly sliced
Fresh coriander sprigs (optional)
Banana leaves or aluminum foil (page 26)

Wash and dry fish. Score both sides of the fish with diagonal cuts almost to the bone, 1 to 2 inches apart. Rub fish inside and out with salt.

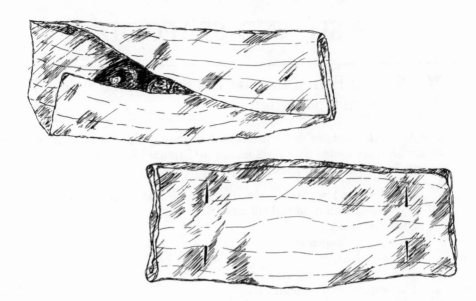

In a blender or processor, combine *Sambal Ulek*, onion, and tomato, and process to a paste. Add coconut milk and turmeric, and blend well. Place fish in the middle of a large square of banana leaf or aluminum foil. Rub the paste onto the fish, putting any extra paste inside the cavity. Place lime slices on top of fish. Garnish with coriander. Wrap in banana leaf in envelope style into a neat parcel. Secure with a metal skewer or toothpick. Let marinate for 30 minutes.

Preheat oven to 450° F. Measure fish at its thickest part and bake the package on a sheet pan, allowing 10 to 12 minutes per inch of thickness. Turn fish over halfway through cooking process. Open the banana leaf and broil the fish for 1 or 2 minutes until the top is crispy. Serve the fish in the banana leaves with rice, vegetables, and a *sambal*.

VARIATIONS: Fish may be grilled over glowing coals, allowing 10 minutes per inch of thickness of fish.

Fish may be prepared by dry-frying the fish in a frying pan on medium heat on top of the stove, pressing down on fish while cooking. Cook one side, then turn oven and cook the other side, allowing 10 minutes per inch of thickness of fish.

ADVANCE PREPARATION: Wrap fish in banana leaves several hours before cooking. Refrigerate. Cook at serving time.

Inspired by a recipe from executive chef Hubert Lorenz, Bali Hyatt.

Grilled Fish with Balinese Sauce
Pepes Bumbu Bali

Here is a beautiful presentation for this tangy, citrus-flavored fish with a touch of spice.

    1-pound fillet of haddock, flounder, or sole
    2 to 3 fresh red chiles, seeded, minced
    1 tablespoon minced fresh ginger
    2 teaspoons laos (*galangal*), (optional)
    5 shallots, minced
    2 cloves garlic, minced
    2 tablespoons palm or brown sugar
    1 tablespoon tomato ketchup
    Banana leaves (page 26')

GARNISH:

    1 lemon or lime, peeled, thinly sliced
    1 fresh red chile, seeded, sliced
    Fresh coriander sprigs (optional)

Rinse fish well and pat dry. Cut into small pieces. In a blender or processor, process chiles, ginger, laos, shallots, garlic, sugar, and ketchup to a coarse paste. Marinate the fish in the paste for 30 minutes. Pour boiling water over the banana leaf to soften and prevent splitting. Place fish overlapping in the middle of a large square of banana leaf. (You will probably have to make two banana leaf packets.) Place the lemon slices, chiles, and coriander sprigs on top of fish. Wrap envelope style into a neat parcel, keeping seam side on top. Secure with a metal skewer, toothpick, or staples.

Grill fish over glowing coals, allowing 10 minutes per inch of thickness of fish. Cut open the banana leaves. Serve the fish in the banana leaves with rice, vegetables, and a sambal.

YIELD: 3 servings.

TIP: The fish may be prepared by dry-frying the fish in a frying pan on top of the stove. Cook on one side, pressing down as it cooks, and then turn over and cook the other side.

ADVANCE PREPARATION: The fish may be wrapped several hours ahead and refrigerated. Grill at serving time.

Inspired by a recipe from Executive Chef Hubert Lorenz, Bali Hyatt.

Grilled Shrimp, Javanese Style
Udang Panggang Jawa

Easily prepared, grilled shrimp are wonderful hot off the grill or when served at room temperature.

> 1 pound large shrimp, peeled and deveined
> 3 tablespoons soy sauce
> 2 tablespoons lime juice
> 2 cloves garlic, minced
> ¼ to ½ teaspoon chili powder
> 2 teaspoons brown sugar
> 1 tablespoon oil
> 12-inch bamboo skewers soaked in cold water for 1 hour

In a bowl, combine shrimp, soy sauce, lime juice, garlic, chili powder, brown sugar and oil. Marinate for 30 minutes. Thread shrimp on a skewer, allowing 2 to 4 shrimp per skewer. Grill over medium-hot fire until shrimp are opaque, about 4 minutes. Turn once during the grilling and brush with remaining marinade. Serve hot or at room temperature.

YIELD: 4 servings with other dishes.

SALADS AND VEGETABLES

Mixed Vegetable Salad with Peanut Dressing
Gado-Gado

Gado-Gado is the foremost Indonesian salad and is universally admired. As I traveled throughout the archipelago, I found the seasonings to vary greatly. The love of sweets was very apparent in Yogyakarta as the sauce was much sweeter than other parts of the country. You may vary your sauce and adjust the amount of sugar to fit your tastes.

It should be presented attractively on a large round or oval serving dish. Gado-Gado is an excellent buffet presentation. The Gado-Gado can accompany a full meal, or if you wish to try Indonesian style, serve the salad as an appetizer or after the main course as a palate refresher.

1 package firm bean curd (tofu) (8 ounces)
1 teaspoon sweet soy sauce, *kecap manis* (optional)
⅓ cup oil
1 cup carrots, shredded into 2-inch lengths
1 cup green beans, cut into 2-inch pieces
2 cups shredded cabbage
1½ cups fresh bean sprouts
½ pound small boiling potatoes

SAUCE:

1 to 2 fresh red chiles, minced
1 clove garlic, minced,
2 shallots minced
¼ teaspoon shrimp paste *(terasi)*
1 cup coconut milk
1 tablespoon brown sugar
¼ cup smooth or crunchy-style peanut butter
Juice of ½ lime or to taste
Salt to taste

1 small cucumber, seeded, cut into thin slices
1 tomato, sliced
2 hard-boiled eggs, sliced
¼ cup fried shallot flakes (page 24)
Shrimp crackers *(Krupuk Udang)* (optional)

Drain tofu. Rinse and cut in half. Place on a plate. Top with another plate. Place a weight of about 1 to 2 pounds on top. Let stand 30 minutes. Discard liquid. Pat the tofu dry with paper towels. Sprinkle with *kecap manis*. In a large frying pan, heat the oil over moderately high heat until it is hot but not smoking. Fry tofu for 3 to 4 minutes, or until it is golden. Transfer to paper towels to drain. Cut the tofu into ½-inch cubes. Heat oil in a wok to 350 degrees. Fry until golden brown and puffy, about 3 to 4 minutes. Remove and drain on paper towels. Set aside. Boil the potatoes, peel, and cut into ¼-inch slices.

In a large saucepan of boiling water, blanch carrots, green beans, and cabbage separately for 1 to 2 minutes. Drain. Refresh with cold water. Drain. Set aside. Blanch the bean sprouts in boiling water for 30 seconds. Rinse under cold water. Drain well. Set aside. Boil the potatoes, and cut into ¼-inch slices.

Pound or process chiles, garlic, shallots, and shrimp paste to a paste. Add the coconut milk, sugar, and peanut butter. Blend well. Cook the sauce over medium-low heat, stirring, for 5 minutes or until it has thickened. Add lime juice and salt to taste. Set aside. Reheat when ready to serve.

Arrange the various vegetables in separate sections on a large platter. Surround with slices of cucumber and tomatoes. Put hard-boiled eggs in center. Pour the warm peanut sauce over the salad and sprinkle with fried shallot flakes. *Gado-Gado* is served at room temperature.

YIELD: 8 servings.

TIP: If you wish, you may serve the *Gado-Gado* in salad-bar style and let each guest select vegetables of their choice. Serve the *Gado-Gado* sauce in a separate container.

VARIATIONS: Water may be substituted for the coconut milk if desired.

ADVANCE PREPARATION: Prepare sauce completely ahead. Vegetables may be prepared ahead and refrigerated in plastic wrap. Bring sauce and vegetables to room temperature when serving.

Inspired by the kitchen of Dr. T. Kemala Intan, Medan, North Sumatra.

 Spicy Fruit Salad
Rujak

The Javanese have combined conventional fruits with tamarind and chile to produce an exciting contrast of tangy, spicy, and sweet flavors.

Prepare Rujak *with fruit, as I have done, or with vegetables, such as green beans, carrots, potatoes, and bean sprouts.*

> 1 green pear, peeled, cored, quartered, cut into ⅛-inch slices
> 1 firm green apple (Granny Smith), peeled, cored, quartered, cut into ⅛-inch slices
> 1 cucumber, peeled, halved, seeds removed, cut into ⅛-inch slices
> 2 small oranges, peeled, sectioned, tough membrane removed
> 1 firm mango, peeled, cut into bite-size pieces (optional)
> ½ fresh pineapple, peeled, cut into ½-inch wedges

DRESSING:

> ½ teaspoon dried shrimp paste (*terasi*) (optional)
> ½ teaspoon *Sambal Ulek,* or ½ teaspoon dried chili flakes soaked
>   in 1 teaspoon water for 20 minutes
> 3 tablespoons dark brown sugar
> 1 tablespoon soy sauce
> 1 tablespoon tamarind dissolved in 4 tablespoons warm water

Combine fruits and vegetables in a large bowl. Wrap shrimp paste in foil. Cook over moderate heat for 2 minutes on each side. Remove foil. Mix together the dressing ingredients in a blender or small processor. Pour over salad. Mix well. Serve at room temperature.

YIELD: 6 servings with other dishes.

ADVANCE PREPARATION: Prepare sauce 1 to 2 days ahead. Refrigerate. Bring to room temperature before serving. Combine salad ingredients when serving.

    ## Padang Vegetable Salad
    Slada Padang

An interesting salad from Padang, West Sumatra, which combines a full range of textures from crunchy to creamy.

> 2 medium potatoes, thinly sliced into ⅜-inch slices
> 3 cups oil
> 3 hard-boiled eggs
> 1 medium potato, boiled, chopped coarsely
> 7 tablespoons melted butter
> 1 tablespoon sugar
> 1 tablespoon white vinegar
> Salt and pepper to taste
> 1 cucumber, peeled, seeded, sliced
> 10 to 12 Romaine lettuce leaves
> 1 ripe tomato, sliced
> Parsley leaves for garnish

Crisp the potatoes in ice water for one hour. Drain and dry between towels or paper toweling. (Potatoes may be wrapped in a dry towel and stored in refrigerator until ready to fry.) Heat oil in a wok to 375° F. Fry slices, a few at a time, turning with a slotted spoon until potatoes are light golden brown. Drain on paper toweling. Let cool. This may be done hours in advance of serving.

Separate egg whites from yolks. Slice the egg whites. To prepare the sauce, mash the egg yolks and the boiled potatoes together. Add the melted butter gradually, stirring. Blend until smooth. Add the sugar, vinegar, and salt. Mix well.

Food processor method for sauce: Using metal blade, add egg yolks, boiled potatoes, sugar, white vinegar, salt, and pepper. Process 30 seconds until slightly fluffy. With machine running, very slowly drizzle the butter through the food chute until the mixture begins to thicken. Remaining butter may be poured in a slow steady stream. All of the melted butter should be added within 1 minute.

To serve, combine the fried potatoes, cucumbers, and two-thirds of the sliced egg whites with the sauce. Line a flat serving dish with the lettuce leaves. Garnish with remaining egg whites, tomato slices, and parsley leaves.

YIELD: 4 servings.

TIP: The secret to emulisified sauces is to add the sauce within the time specified in the recipes. If the butter is added too rapidly, the sauce will be thin. If added too slowly, the sauce will be thicker than desired. If sauce is too thick, add more melted butter or oil.

ADVANCE PREPARATION: The sauce and salad ingredients may be prepared 1 day ahead. Wrap ingredients in plastic wrap and refrigerate.

Inspired by the kitchen of Mrs. Tity Yulisman, Padang, West Sumatra.

Fruit and Vegetable Salad
Slada Huzar

A slightly spicy egg sauce is combined with many tantalizing textures in this surprising salad. Ratna Etchika, the niece of Hidayat of the Consulate of the Republic of Indonesia, taught this to me in her Jakarta kitchen.

> 5 medium potatoes, peeled
> 3 cups oil
> 5 hard-boiled eggs
> 1½ tablespoons sugar
> ¼ teaspoon dry mustard
> 1½ tablespoons white vinegar
> ¼ cup warm water, approximately
> Salt and pepper to taste
> ½ pineapple, peeled, sliced, cut into bite-size wedges
> 1 cucumber, peeled, sliced, cut in half
> 2 carrcts, parboiled, sliced
> 1 to 2 fresh red chiles, seeds removed, thinly sliced
> 10 to 12 romaine lettuce leaves

Cut 2 of the potatoes into small cubes. Cut the remaining 3 potatoes into thin slices. Crisp the sliced potatoes in ice water for one hour. Drain and dry between towels or paper toweling. Wrap in a dry towel and store in the refrigerator until ready to fry.

Heat oil in a wok or deep pan to 375° F. Add potatoes, a few at a time, turning with a slotted spoon until potatoes are light golden brown. Drain on paper toweling. Let cool.

Separate egg yolks from whites. Chop whites and set aside.

To prepare sauce, mash the egg yolks with a fork until a smooth paste is formed. Add sugar, mustard, and vinegar. Stir. Add warm water gradually to make a smooth sauce of fairly thick consistency. Add salt and pepper to taste. If mixture is too thick, add more water.

Line a flat serving plate with lettuce leaves. Arrange the pineapple, cucumber, carrots, and fried potatoes in a decorative fashion on the platter. Garnish with chopped egg white and chiles. Serve with sauce mixture in a separate dish. The sauce may also be combined with the salad and mixed completely.

YIELD: 4 to 6 servings.

TIPS: The secret to crisp, fried potatoes is the second frying. The potatoes may be fried hours ahead and set aside or refrigerated, covered with plastic wrap.

For a richer sauce, you may cream 3 to 4 tablespoons of butter into the eggs.

ADVANCE PREPARATION: Assemble the salad several hours before serving. Cover with plastic wrap and refrigerate. Pour sauce on salad at serving time.

 ## Stir-Fried Vegetables
Oseng-Oseng

An easily prepared, colorful stir-fry.

2 tablespoons oil
3 dried red chile peppers
⅓ cup thinly sliced onion
3 cloves garlic, minced
16 string beans, tips removed, cut into 2-inch lengths
3 carrots, peeled, thinly sliced on the diagonal
1 green bell pepper, sliced into ⅓- by 2-inch shreds
2 cups shredded cabbage
½ teaspoon salt
1 teaspoon sugar
1½ tablespoons sweet soy sauce, *(kecap manis)*

In a wok or skillet, heat oil. Add chiles and fry until darkened. Add onion and garlic and fry until softened and transparent. Add beans, carrots, and pepper. Stir-fry for 3 to 4 minutes. Add cabbage and stir until wilted. Add salt, sugar, and *kecap manis*. Stir-fry for 30 seconds.

YIELD: 4 servings.

Spinach in Coconut Milk
Gulai Daun Bayem

In her Padang kitchen, Mrs. Tity Yulisman, a Minangkabau, prepared this popular, slightly spicy dish using fresh cassava or manioc leaves. Because they are hard to obtain, I have substituted spinach. Hearts of bok choy, Chinese choy sum, or mustard greens, tough stems removed, may also be used.

This dish often accompanies a Padang meal. Serve it with Beef Rendang (page 271) rice, and Sambal Lado *(page 322).*

2 cups thin coconut milk
2 small green tomatoes, chopped (optional)
2 fresh green chiles, chopped
1 clove garlic
4 shallots, sliced
1 pound fresh young spinach or bok choy hearts, tough part of
 stems removed, washed, drained, sliced thinly into 1-inch
 slices
Salt to taste

In a wok or pan, add coconut milk, green tomatoes, chiles, garlic, and shallots. Bring to a boil and cook for 2 to 3 minutes to distribute flavors. Add the drained spinach to the pan. Cook, uncovered, until spinach is tender. Add salt to taste. Remove and place in serving dish. Serve hot or at room temperature.

YIELD: 3 to 4 servings.

TIP: For a milder version, remove seeds of chiles. However, this is not done in Padang!

ADVANCE PREPARATION: Prepare completely in advance. Reheat on medium heat in microwave or on top of the stove before serving. Serve hot or at room temperature.

Stir-Fried Cabbage and Shrimp
Orak-Arik

This easily prepared, delicious stir-fry was taught to me by Ratna Etchika, niece of Hidayat of the Consulate General of the Republic of Indonesia, Chicago, in her Jakarta kitchen.

2 tablespoons oil
1 medium onion, cut in half and finely sliced
¼ pound small shrimp, peeled, cleaned, washed, dried
2 bay leaves
8 ounces finely shredded cabbage or Chinese cabbage
¼ teaspoon chili powder
Salt and pepper to taste
2 eggs, lightly beaten

Heat oil in a wok. Add onion and fry until softened. Add the shrimp and cook until pink. Add bay leaves. Stir for 30 seconds. Add the shredded cabbage, chili powder, salt, and pepper, and stir-fry for 2 to 3 minutes or until cabbage has wilted. Cover the wok and cook the mixture over low heat for 5 minutes. Uncover. Stir in the beaten eggs and scramble them with the cabbage. As soon as the egg has set, serve immediately.

YIELD: 3 to 4 servings.

Stir-Fried Eggplant and Tomatoes
Semur Terong Tomat

A piquant, delicious, and easily prepared vegetable dish.

1 pound eggplant, preferably long Chinese, cut into ½-inch
    slices, then each slice cut in half
Salt
2 tablespoons oil

1 small onion, sliced
2 cloves garlic, sliced
2 ripe tomatoes, chopped
2 tablespoons dark soy sauce
2 teaspoons dark brown sugar
¼ teaspoon nutmeg
½ teaspoon chili powder
Salt and pepper to taste

Sprinkle the eggplant slices lightly with salt and let stand in a colander for 30 minutes. Heat oil in a skillet. Add onion and garlic, and sauté until onion is softened. Add the eggplant, and stir-fry for 2 to 3 minutes. Be careful not to mash the eggplant. Add the tomatoes, soy sauce, sugar, nutmeg, and chili powder. Cover the pan and simmer for 10 minutes. Add salt and pepper to taste. Serve hot or at room temperature.

YIELD: 4 servings with other dishes.

TIP: Canned tomatoes may be substituted for fresh tomatoes.

Coconut-Flavored Vegetables
Urap

Crunchy vegetables are prepared in a light, coconut-flavored sauce.
Urap is excellent for a buffet and entertaining as it can easily be doubled
or tripled and prepared with almost any combination of vegetables.
Quite often, Urap is served only with greens and bean sprouts. Urap is
usually served hot or at room temperature.

Urap is an ancient recipe served with a tumpeng (rice cone) during
traditional ceremonies such as childbirth, the remembrance of the dead,
and a Javanese Slametan. Long Chinese string beans are a part of this
dish, as they signify long life. Traditionally, the Indonesians would leave
whole at least one Chinese bean for symbolism.

2 cups fresh bean sprouts
¼ pound fresh spinach, shredded
¼ pound Chinese cabbage, shredded
½ cup long Chinese string beans or ½ cup string beans, cut into
   ½-inch pieces on the diagonal

2 medium carrots, shredded, cut into ½-inch lengths (optional)
½ teaspoon dried shrimp paste (*terasi*)
1 clove garlic, minced
½ teaspoon red chili powder
1 tablespoon tamarind water (page 25) or juice of ½ lime
½ teaspoon sugar
½ cup freshly grated coconut
Salt to taste
Parsley leaves

In a large saucepan, blanch bean sprouts, spinach and cabbage separately in boiling water for approximately 30 seconds. Drain. Refresh with cold water. Drain. Set aside. Blanch string beans and carrots separately in boiling water for 2 minutes. Drain. Refresh in cold water. Drain. Combine the vegetables.

Wrap the shrimp paste in aluminum foil and toast 1 to 2 minutes in a skillet over medium heat, turning once. Unwrap. In a mortar, blender, or processor, combine the shrimp paste, garlic, and chili powder. Pound or process to a paste. Add the tamarind water and sugar. Mix. (If using a blender or miniprocessor, add the tamarind water and sugar to the above ingredients and process to a smooth paste.) Remove and put into a container. Add the coconut and mix well. Add the mixture to the vegetables and toss until well mixed. Garnish with parsley. Serve with *Sambal Ulek* as an accompaniment to a main course of rice and meat.

YIELD: 6 servings.

TIP: This dish relies heavily on the flavor and texture of the grated coconut. Dried unsweetened coconut flakes can be used. It will not be as flavorful as the freshly grated coconut.

If using dried coconut flakes, combine all paste ingredients with ⅓ cup dry coconut flakes in a pan. Add 1 cup water. Bring to a boil. Stir continuously until it boils, then cook for 5 minutes. Add the cooked vegetables to the pan and stir well. Let cook for 1 to 2 minutes longer to blend flavors.

ADVANCE PREPARATION: Cook the vegetables and sauce ahead. Combine 1 hour before serving. The flavor of the sauce will improve upon standing.

Inspired by Hidayat, consul of information and cultural affairs, Consulate General of the Republic of Indonesia, Chicago.

Green Beans, Carrots, and Beef in Coconut Sauce
Jukut Mekalis

This colorful, spicy, coconut-flavored Balinese dish is a perfect accompaniment to a meal. It can also be a meal in itself by adding cooked rice sticks.

1 pound long Chinese green beans, tips removed
3 carrots, peeled
1 cup bean sprouts
3 cloves garlic, chopped
1 slice laos *(galangal)*, the size of a quarter, minced
1 slice fresh ginger, the size of a quarter, peeled, minced
3 to 4 fresh red chiles, seeds removed, chopped
1 teaspoon white sesame seeds
½ teaspoon dried shrimp paste *(terasi)*
1 teaspoon salt
½ teaspoon pepper
2 tablespoons oil
8 ounces ground beef
2 *daun salam* or bay leaves
2 cups thick coconut milk
2 tablespoons lime juice
2 tablespoons palm or brown sugar
Fried shallot flakes (page 24) (optional)

Cook the green beans and carrots separately until tender. Drain. Cut the beans into ½-inch pieces. Cut the carrots into ½-inch slices, then cut each slice into quarters. Blanch the bean sprouts in boiling water for 30 seconds. Drain. Refresh in cold water.

Pound or process the garlic, laos, ginger, chiles, sesame seeds, and shrimp paste to a smooth paste. Add salt and pepper. Mix well. Heat a skillet. Add the oil and fry the ground paste mixture over moderate heat for 2 minutes, stirring. Add the beef and sauté, chopping to separate, until it is no longer pink. Do not brown. Add *daun salam* and coconut milk. Stir.

Cook on a gentle simmer for 5 to 6 minutes, stirring, being careful not to allow the coconut milk to come to a boil. Add the cooked vegetables to the pan. Bring almost to a boil. Reduce heat to a gentle simmer. Cook for 2 to 3 minutes. Add the lime juice and palm sugar.

Stir. Check seasonings, adding more lime and palm sugar if necessary. Serve warm, garnished with Fried Shallot Flakes.

YIELD: 4 to 6 servings.

ADVANCE PREPARATION: Prepare completely in advance. Refrigerate covered with plastic wrap. Reheat on medium heat in microwave or on top of stove.

Inspired by a recipe from executive chef I. Wayan Arcana, Bali Hotel and Tourism Training Institute Cooking School.

 ## Green Beans and Carrots in Coconut Sauce
Jukut

A colorful, spicy, coconut-flavored Balinese vegetable dish.

> 1 pound long Chinese green beans, tips removed
> 4 carrots, peeled
> 1 cup bean sprouts
> 3 cloves garlic, chopped
> 1 slice laos *(galangal),* the size of a quarter, minced
> 1 slice ginger, the size of a quarter, minced
> 3 to 4 fresh red chiles, seeds removed, chopped
> 1 teaspoon white sesame seeds
> ½ teaspoon dried shrimp paste *(terasi)*
> 1 teaspoon salt
> ½ teaspoon pepper
> 2 tablespoons oil
> 2 *daun salam* or bay leaves
> 1½ cups coconut milk
> 2 tablespoons lime juice
> 2 tablespoons palm or brown sugar

Cook the green beans and carrots separately until tender. Drain. Cut the beans into ½-inch pieces. Cut the carrots into ½-inch slices. Cut each carrot slice into quarters. Blanch the bean sprouts in boiling water for 30 seconds. Drain. Refresh in cold water.

Pound or process the garlic, laos, ginger, chiles, sesame seeds, and shrimp paste to a smooth paste. Add salt and pepper. Mix well. Heat a skillet. Add the oil and fry the ground paste mixture over moderate heat for 2 minutes, stirring. Add *daun salam* and coconut milk. Stir. Cook on a gentle simmer for 5 to 6 minutes, stirring, being careful not to allow the coconut milk to come to a boil. Add the cooked vegetables to the pan. Bring almost to a boil. Reduce heat to a gentle simmer. Cook for 2 to 3 minutes. Add the lime juice and palm sugar. Stir. Check seasonings, adding more lime and palm sugar if necessary. Serve warm.

YIELD: 4 to 6 servings.

ADVANCE PREPARATION: Prepare completely in advance. Refrigerate covered with plastic wrap. Reheat on medium heat in microwave or on top of the stove until heated throughout.

Inspired by a recipe from executive chef I. Wayan Arcana, Bali Hotel and Tourism Training Institute Cooking School.

 ## Spiced Tomato Sambal
Sambal Goreng Tomat

This enticing sambal is a colorful addition to any meal.

- 1 tablespoon oil
- 1 small onion, minced
- 2 cloves garlic, minced
- 1 teaspoon minced fresh ginger
- 1 to 3 fresh red chiles, seeds removed, minced
- 1 cup coconut milk
- 1 tablespoon brown sugar
- 1 tablespoon tamarind water (page 25)
- 2 bay leaves
- ½ teaspoon salt
- 6 firm large tomatoes, skins removed, cubed

Heat oil in a medium skillet. Add onion, garlic, ginger, and chiles, and sauté over moderate heat for 2 minutes, stirring to avoid burning. Add coconut milk, sugar, tamarind water, bay leaves, and salt. Bring to a boil. Reduce heat to simmer and let cook for 5 minutes, stirring occasionally. Add the tomatoes. Bring to a boil. Reduce heat to simmer and simmer approximately 4 to 5 minutes. Do not overcook. The tomatoes should remain firm and retain their shape. Serve hot or at room temperature.

YIELD: 4 servings.

ADVANCE PREPARATION: Prepare ahead completely. If desired, reheat when serving or serve at room temperature.

 ## Spiced Beans and Tomatoes
Sambal Goreng Buncis Tomat

A unique, colorful, easily prepared vegetable dish with intricate, palate-tantalizing flavors.

Chinese long string beans are usually used in Indonesia. They are more tender and need less cooking time. This dish was served many times during my travels and is sure to be one of your favorites.

> 2 tablespoons oil
> 1 medium onion, cut in half, thinly sliced
> 3 cloves garlic, sliced
> 2 fresh red or green chiles, seeds removed, thinly sliced
> ½ teaspoon dried shrimp paste *(terasi)*
> 1 pound green beans, cut diagonally into ¼-inch slices
> 2 cups cubed tomatoes
> 1½ cups coconut milk
> 1 teaspoon salt
> 1 teaspoon tamarind water (page 25)
> 2 bay leaves
> 2 slices laos *(galangal)*, each the size of a quarter, crushed

Heat oil. Over moderate heat, sauté onion, garlic, chiles, and shrimp paste for 1 to 2 minutes, stirring occasionally. Add beans and tomatoes and stir-fry for 2 minutes. Add coconut milk, salt, tamarind water, and laos. Cook over medium heat, stirring frequently, for approximately 10 minutes, or until green beans are soft but still crunchy.

YIELD: 4 servings.

TIP: If using dried laos, use 1 slice. Soak in hot water for 30 minutes until soft. Chop the laos.

ADVANCE PREPARATION: Prepare ahead completely. Refrigerate. Serve hot or at room temperature or reheat on medium heat in microwave or on top of the stove before serving.

Spiced Cucumbers
Sayur Timun

Cucumbers with a new twist!

2 tablespoons oil
6 shallots, thinly sliced
8 garlic cloves, sliced
3 fresh green chiles, sliced, seeded
¼ teaspoon dried shrimp paste *(terasi)*
1½ cups coconut milk
2 medium cucumbers, peeled, cut in half, sliced
Salt to taste
Fried shallot flakes (page 24)

Heat oil. Add shallots, garlic, chiles, and shrimp paste. Cook on moderate heat, stirring, for 1 to 2 minutes, being careful not to brown. Add the coconut milk. Bring to a boil. Reduce heat and simmer for 10 minutes, stirring occasionally. Add cucumbers and cook for 2 to 3 minutes. Season with salt. To serve, garnish with Fried Shallot Flakes.

YIELD: 3 to 4 servings.

Inspired by a recipe from executive chef Hubert Lorenz, Bali Hyatt.

RICE, NOODLES, AND EGGS

Festive Yellow Rice Cone
Nasi Tumpeng Kuning Lengkap

Ibu Zaenuddien, the famous Yogyakarta television personality and food-store owner, showed lme the preparation of tumpeng (rice cone), Indonesia's famous ceremonial dish. Nasi Tumpeng Kuning Lengkap makes an outstanding centerpiece for a lavish meal.

The yellow in Nasi Tumpeng Kuning Lengkap signifies happiness, and the dish is used for weddings, births, and other festive occasions. Traditionally, the ingredients were strictly determined by the nature of the occasion. Today, this is an all-purpose festive dish, and there are many variations.

During the preparation of the cone, Ibu Zainuddien's love for the beauty and color of the tumpeng *was very apparent. She placed it on a round banana leaf tray and completely surrounded it with triangular pieces of banana leaf, which were attached to the central circular leaf. Ibu Zaenuddien smiled as she fondly decorated the* tumpeng *with tomato flavors, delicate egg shreds, and parsley, and surrounded the base with halved hard-boiled eggs, an assortment of shredded vegetables, and other traditional cooked dishes. She was most pleased when her exquisite masterpiece was completed. I have simplified her rice preparation and used ingredients available in America.*

Accompaniments to this lavish rice cone can be as few or as many as you wish. The traditional menu featured in the Javanese Slametan *(page 256) provides a contrast of flowers and textures and may be prepared in advance.*

½ cup oil
1 large onion, minced
1 tablespoon minced garlic
2 stalks lemon grass, cut into 2-inch pieces, crushed
3 bay leaves
4 Kaffir lime leaves (optional)
4 teaspoons turmeric powder
1 tablespoon salt
3 cups long-grain rice, washed, drained for 1 hour
6 cups thin coconut milk

GARNISHES:

2 eggs, lightly beaten
1 head romaine lettuce, washed, separated into leaves, trimmed
¾ cup bean sprouts, blanched
2 cups parboiled or steamed green beans, cut into ½-inch pieces
2 cups Chinese cabbage, parboiled or steamed, finely shredded
2 cups carrots, parboiled or steamed, shredded into ½-inch
    lengths
1 cucumber, scored lengthwise with tines of a fork, sliced
4 hard-boiled eggs, shells removed, quartered
Parsley springs
3 to 4 tomatoes, made into flowers (optional)
6 fresh red chiles, chopped
4 tablespoons fried shallot flakes

Preheat oven to 350° F. Heat oil in a heavy 4- to 5-quart casserole over moderate heat. Add onions and garlic and stir-fry for 2 to 3 minutes, or until soft and transparent, being careful not to brown. Add lemon grass, bay leaves, Kaffir lime, turmeric, and salt. Cook for 1 minute, stirring. Add drained rice, and fry until the rice is evenly coated, about 2 to 3 minutes. Do not let the rice brown. Add coconut milk and cook over moderate heat until small bubbles appear around edge of pan. Do not allow the coconut milk to boil. Cover tightly. Bake in the middle of the oven for approximately 35 minutes, or until the liquid is absorbed and the rice is tender. Remove lemon grass, bay and Kaffir lime leaves.

While hot, pack the rice tightly, one cup at a time, into a cone mold or a conical sieve, about 8 inches deep and 7½ inches in diameter. It is very important to pack the rice when it is hot and to pack it tightly. Place a large serving plate upside down over the mold. Hold together and invert the cone and plate. Tap the plate on a flat surface to allow the rice cone to slide out.

While the rice is cooking, prepare the garnish. In a heavy 12-inch skillet, heat 1 scant teaspoon oil over moderate heat. Add the beaten egg, swirl around to make an even pancake. Let set for 1 minute or until bottom is very lightly browned. Turn the pancake over and cook for another minute. Remove and let cool. Cut into strips ¼ inch by 2 inches.

To assemble: Arrange the lettuce in a spoke-like pattern around the cone. Arrange the vegetables around the rice cone in the following order: bean sprouts, beans, cabbage, and carrots. Alternate the cucumber slices and hard-boiled eggs around the rim of the plate. Sprinkle some of the egg shreds over the rice cone. Decorate the cone with parsley sprigs and tomato roses. Serve remaining egg shreds, chiles, and fried shallots in separate dishes.

To serve, cut off the top of the cone horizontally and serve to the guest of honor. Cut the remaining cone horizontally and then into pie-shaped pieces.

YIELD: 10 to 12 servings.

ADVANCE PREPARATION: Make the egg pancake 1 day ahead. Cook the beans, cabbage, carrots, and eggs ahead. Prepare the garnishes. The rice may be cooked and packed several hours ahead. Unmold and garnish the cone when serving.

Inspired by Ibu Zaenuddien, television cooking-show hostess, caterer, and owner of Ibu Zaenuddien's Sweet Shops, Yogyakarta.

Festive Yellow Rice
Nasi Kuning

Nasi Kuning *was originally a ceremonial food prepared according to strict protocol to celebrate happy occasions, such as weddings, wedding anniversaries, birthdays, and the birth of children.*

The marriage ceremony of the Minangkabau people of Sumatra has its own rice custom. The bride's family prepares a huge nasi kuning. *Within the* nasi kuning *they hide two wedding rings for which the bride and groom must search at the end of the ceremony—a rite symbolizing the search for fortune during married life. Whoever finds a ring first establishes moral superiority over the other. Naturally, the groom digs deeper and more frantically than his bride.*

Today, the nasi kuning *appears throughout Indonesia as part of a festive meal.*

While in Yogyakarta, Ibu Zaenuddien, the renowned cooking personality, showed me her version of this famous dish. I have adapted her methods for you.

To serve the nasi kuning, *she cut a circular banana leaf and placed it in the center of a large round bamboo plate and stapled triangular pieces of banana leaf around the entire edge of the circle. The rice was then mounded in the center. She garnished the rice with thin egg strips and fried shallots. Around the outer rim of the rice, she scattered* Dendeng Ragi *(page 315), dried coconut-flavored shredded meat. Tomato roses, halved hard-boiled eggs, and parsley sprigs were used for garnishes. A circular rim of tined cucumber halves outlined her beautiful creation. Instead of using tomato flowers, you may use chile flowers for a variation—or if you wish, serve it with no garnishes.*

    1 cup long-grain rice
    1¾ cups coconut milk
    1 stalk lemon grass, bottom 6 inches only
    2 daun salam leaves (bay leaves may be substituted)
    ½ teaspoon turmeric powder
    ¼ teaspoon salt

GARNISHES:

    Egg omelet strips (page 25)
    Fried shallot flakes (page 24)
    Dendeng Ragi (page 315)
    Tomato roses
    Hard-boiled eggs, halved

Parsley sprigs
Chile flowers (optional)

Wash and drain the rice several times until the water runs clear. Add
the coconut milk to a heavy saucepan. Add the rice, lemon grass,
daun salam, turmeric, and salt, and stir. Bring slowly to a boil. Cook,
covered, over low heat for approximately 10 minutes, or until the
liquid is absorbed by the rice.

Place the partially cooked rice in a rice steamer or on aluminum
foil in a Chinese steamer. Steam for approximately 20 minutes or
until it is quite soft and ready to eat. Remove the daun salam and
lemon grass. Serve hot or at room temperature with optional garnishes.

YIELD: 4 to 6 servings.

ADVANCE PREPARATION: Prepare the optional garnishes a day
ahead. The rice will keep warm in the steamer for approximately 20
minutes.

Inspired by Ibu Zaenuddien, television cooking-show host, caterer,
and owner of Ibu Zaenuddien's Sweet Shops, Yogyakarta.

 ## Rice Rolls in Banana Leaves
Lontong

---

*This traditional food travels well and was carried by the traders during
their long journeys.*

*Lontong are consumed at picnics and as an accompaniment to
meals, usually cold or at room temperature. They can be made several
days in advance and refrigerated.*

*In Indonesia, they are wrapped with banana leaves, which can be
purchased here fresh or frozen in Asian markets. If unavailable, aluminum foil may be used. However, the special fragrance of the banana
leaves will not be present. They are especially good with satay and
soups.*

1 cup long-grain rice
3 cups water
3 pieces banana leaves (see page 26)

Rinse the rice in cold water 2 or 3 times, or until the water runs clear.
Drain. Add the rice and water to a pan. Bring the water to a boil.

Reduce the heat to simmer and cook, covered, over medium heat for 15 minutes. Remove the covered saucepan from the heat and allow the rice to rest for 15 minutes, covered.

Pour boiling water over the banana leaf to prevent splitting. Place 1 cup cooked warm rice near the edge of the banana leaf. Press the rice firmly into a 6- to 7-inch by 1½-inch sausage shape. Tightly roll the banana leaf over the rice and seal the ends carefully with string, a toothpick, skewer, or staples.

Place the rolls in boiling water to cover. Reduce the heat and simmer for 1 hour. Drain. Let cool at least 4 to 6 hours or overnight in the refrigerator. To serve, remove the banana leaf and cut into ½-inch-thick slices. Serve at room temperature.

YIELD: 3 rolls.

TIPS: If the banana leaves split, wrap the leaves with aluminum foil before boiling.

The *Lontong* may also be steamed for 2 hours over low heat.

ADVANCE PREPARATION: Prepare ahead completely 1 to 2 days before serving. Bring to room temperature when serving.

 ## Pressed Rice Squares
Ketupat

Ketupat *is prepared in the same manner as* Lontong *(page 309). The* Ketupat *is filled with the cooked rice and placed into a shell made of banana or coconut leaves woven into the shape of a square, then boiled as in* Lontong. *The result is a square rice cake.*

It is a traditional Javanese food served during Idulfitri, *the Muslim New Year, or Idul Adha. After a long month of fasting, the Muslim celebrates the New Year, called* Lebaran. *On the first morning of* Lebaran, *all family members gather around to break the fast and Ketupat Lebaran is served.*

Javanese Fried Noodles
Bakmie Goreng Jawa

Chinese in origin, this easily prepared, colorful dish appears in many versions throughout Southeast Asia. Because pork is forbidden in the Islam religion, this Javanese version substitutes beef for pork, which would be used in China. Noodles are often served at birthday celebrations, as they symbolize long life.

Professor and Ibu Soedarso taught me this delightful version when I visited them in Yogyakarta. Ibu Soedarso is very health conscious and uses safflower oil instead of the usual coconut oil.

This very popular dish can be a complete family meal or can be served with other dishes when entertaining. When served as a complete meal, it is usually topped with a fried egg.

4 ounces fine Chinese egg noodles
½ cup safflower oil
5 shallots, minced

2 garlic cloves, minced
3 ounces beef fillet or flank steak, shredded into 1½-inch pieces
3 ounces shrimp, peeled, deveined, cut into ½-inch pieces
2 or 3 romaine or other green lettuce leaves, shredded
2 carrots, peeled, shredded
½ cup bean sprouts
4 green onions, sliced
2 tablespoons light soy sauce
Salt and freshly ground pepper to taste

GARNISH:

Parsley sprigs
Fried shallot flakes (page 24)

Cook the noodles in boiling water until just tender, but firm to the bite. Drain. Rinse in cold water and drain again. In a wok or heavy skillet, heat 2 tablespoons oil over medium high heat. Add shallots and garlic, and stir-fry until fragrant. Add beef and shrimp. Stir-fry for about 2 minutes or until done. Add lettuce and carrots. Stir for 1 minute. Add noodles and bean sprouts, and stir until noodles are heated through. Add green onions and soy sauce. Stir. Season with salt and pepper. Garnish with and parsley and Fried Shallot Flakes.

YIELD: 3 to 4 servings.

ADVANCE PREPARATION: Cook noodles 1 day ahead. Toss with 1 tablespoon oil. Cut up remaining ingredients. Store all ingredients separately in self-locking plastic bags in refrigerator. Cook 1 hour before serving. Reheat at serving time.

From the kitchen of Soedarso Sp., president of the Indonesian Institute of Arts Yogyakarta, and Ibu Soedarso.

 Spicy Tofu Omelet
Tahu Telur

Ibu Soedarso taught me this delicious omelet, which combines tofu, eggs, kecap manis, tart vinegar, and hot chiles. It is easily prepared and perfect for a brunch or supper. Because she is very health conscious, she uses safflower oil in most of her cooking.

In Yogyakarta, Tahu Telur is a popular snack sold by the street vendors.

2 ounces fresh bean sprouts
6 ounces Chinese tofu (fresh bean curd), drained
4 eggs, beaten with ¼ teaspoon salt
½ teaspoon salt
1 teaspoon safflower oil
2 fresh red or green chiles, seeds removed, finely sliced
2 tablespoons sweet soy sauce *(kecap manis)* (page 321)
1 tablespoon white vinegar
2 to 3 tablespoons fried crushed peanuts
3 tablespoons Fried Shallot Flakes (page 24)
1 tablespoon fresh parsley leaves

Blanch the bean sprouts in boiling water for 30 seconds. Drain. Refresh with cold water. Drain. Cut the tofu into tiny pieces or mash with a fork. Combine eggs, tofu, and salt in a bowl.

Heat oil in a 10-inch non-stick or heavy cast-iron frying pan, and lightly oil the pan with a paper towel. Add half the egg mixture, tilting the pan to make a thin omelet. Cook over moderate heat until set and lightly browned. Carefully turn over the omelet. Remove and place on a large heated plate. Repeat to make the second omelet. Scatter bean sprouts and chiles over each omelet. Combine *kecap manis* and vinegar, and drizzle over the omelets. Garnish with peanuts, Fried Shallot Flakes, and parsley leaves. To serve, cut into wedges.

YIELD: 3 to 4 servings.

From the kitchen of Soedarso Sp., president of the Indonesian Institute of Arts Yogyakarta, and Ibu Soedarso.

ACCOMPANIMENTS, PICKLES, AND SAUCES

 Fried Bananas
Pisang Goreng

This popular Indonesian snack food is a delightful combination of bananas with sweet and tart flavors. It is served as part of a meal or as a dessert. Many variations appear throughout Southeast Asia.

4 firm bananas, peeled, halved, sliced in half lengthwise
2 tablespoons brown sugar
Juice of 1 lemon
2 tablespoons oil

Combine sugar and lemon juice and sprinkle over bananas. Cover and allow bananas to marinate for 30 minutes, turning several times during marination.

Heat oil in a frying pan. Add bananas, and fry over medium heat until they are lightly browned all over. Turn carefully, as the bananas will break easily when hot. Drain on paper towels. Serve warm or at room temperature.

YIELD: 4 to 6 servings.

 Marbled Eggs
Telur Berwarna

Colorful, hard-boiled eggs are often served as an accompaniment or as garnish for a celebration dish such as Nasi Tumpeng *(page 305).*

6 small eggs
Red, green, and yellow food coloring

Rinse the eggs carefully to remove any blemishes. Place the eggs in a saucepan and run cold water over them. Slowly heat eggs to simmer over low heat, stirring gently to insure yolks are centered. Simmer about 7 minutes. Remove eggs, and cool under running water.

Put water into three small saucepans. Add red, green, and yellow food colorings separately to pans. Bring to a boil. Tap each egg lightly with a spoon until it is covered with many fine cracks, but do not remove any part of the shell. Put 2 eggs into each pan and simmer 5 minutes. Turn off heat and allow eggs to cool in pan of colored water for at least 2 hours. If serving immediately, remove the shell from each egg and cut into quarters, lengthwise.

ADVANCE PREPARATION: Prepare 1 day ahead. Remove shell just before serving.

 ## Crisp Fried Beef
Dendeng Ragi

Dendeng is a popular style of meat preservation. The meat is sliced, seasoned with spices, herbs, and salt, and set out in the sun to dry. It can be kept almost indefinitely. This type of preservation is known as spicy, dry refrigeration.

While in Yogyakarta, Ibu Zaenuddien taught me this popular co-conut-flavored beef condiment, which she served as a garnish for Nasi Kuning (page 308). It will keep refrigerated for several days or can be eaten at room temperature. It is also good when reheated.

8 ounces of flank steak, trimmed, sliced very thinly into 2-inch
   strips
3 shallots, chopped
2 cloves garlic, chopped
1 teaspoon ground laos *(galangal)*
1 teaspoon ground coriander
1 daun salam or bay leaf
1½ teaspoons brown sugar
2 tablespoons tamarind water (page 25)
2 Kaffir lime leaves or 1½-inch square of lemon zest
1½ cups water
1 cup (8 ounces) freshly grated coconut
1 tablespoon oil

Put the beef, shallots, garlic, laos, coriander, daun salam, sugar, tamarind, Kaffir lime, and water in a wok. Bring to a boil. Reduce the heat to medium and boil gently, covered, for approximately 40 minutes. Add the coconut. Stir. Let the mixture cook until all the water has been absorbed by the coconut, then stir continuously until dry. Remove the salam and Kaffir lime leaves. Add the oil and stir-fry over moderate heat until the coconut is golden brown, being careful not to burn. Serve hot or cold as a side dish.

TIP: For a more robust version, add 1 to 2 teaspoons red chili powder when cooking. You will then be making *Dendeng Ragi, Sumatran style*.

One-half cup of dried unsweetened coconut flakes may be substituted for the freshly grated coconut. Soak the coconut for 5 minutes in 1 cup of water to absorb moisture before cooking. Let it simmer until all the water has been soaked up by the coconut before starting to stir.

ADVANCE PREPARATION: Prepare 2 to 3 days in advance. Serve cold, at room temperature, or reheat at serving time.

Inspired by Ibu Zaenuddien, television cooking personality, bakery owner, and caterer, Yogyakarta.

 ## Toasted Spiced Coconut with Peanuts
Serundeng Kacang

Easily prepared, Serundeng Kacang *is an intrinsic part of the Indonesian meal, as it can be sprinkled over practically any dish to give added texture and flavor. It is almost always served with* Nasi Tumpeng *during a* Slametan *(page 256).*

> 5 shallots, chopped
> 3 cloves garlic, chopped
> 2 tablespoons oil
> 1 teaspoon ground coriander
> ½ teaspoon ground cumin
> ½ teaspoon ground laos (*galangal*)
> 1 tablespoon tamarind water (page 25)
> 1 teaspoon brown sugar
> ½ teaspoon salt
> 1 cup freshly grated coconut
> ½ cup unsalted roasted peanuts

Pound or process shallots and garlic to a smooth paste. Heat oil in a wok or frying pan and stir-fry the paste mixture over moderate heat for approximately 2 minutes, or until translucent, being careful not to brown. Add the coriander, cumin, laos, tamarind water, brown sugar, and salt. Stir-fry for one minute on low heat to blend the flavors. Add the coconut and mix well. Cook over low heat, stirring frequently, until the coconut is nearly dry and medium brown in color, about 20 to 30 minutes. This takes quite a while and cannot be hurried by raising the heat. Add the peanuts and toast for approximately 5 minutes longer, stirring continuously until the coconut is golden brown. Be very careful not to allow the mixture to burn. Remove from the heat and let cool before serving.

TIP: One-half cup of dried unsweetened coconut flakes may be substituted for the freshly grated coconut. Soak the coconut for 5 minutes in 1 cup of water to absorb moisture before cooking. Let it simmer until all the water has been soaked up by the coconut before starting to stir.

ADVANCE PREPARATION: Serundeng Kacang will keep in an airtight container for approximately one month.

 ## Javanese Pickled Cucumbers
Acar Ketimun Jawa

Pickled cucumbers are quite often served as a palate refresher during the meal. To obtain the best flavor, make them three days in advance.

1 large cucumber, peeled, cut into bite-size pieces
2 teaspoon salt
¼ cup water
⅓ cup distilled white vinegar
¼ cup sugar
3 black peppercorns
3 whole cloves

Place the cucumbers in an earthen pot or heatproof jar. Combine the salt, water, vinegar, sugar, peppercorns, and cloves in a pan. Bring to a boil. Reduce the heat to simmer and cook for 5 minutes. Pour the liquid over the cucumbers. Cool and cover tightly. Allow to stand for 3 days before serving.

ADVANCE PREPARATION: Javanese Pickled Cucumbers will keep refrigerated in a tightly covered glass container for 2 weeks.

▼ Pickled Vegetables ▼
▲ Acar Kuning ▲

Seasoned with turmeric, this fresh, crunchy salad pickle is one of my favorite accompaniments to many meals. It is extremely colorful, tasty, and refreshing. You may choose any assortment of vegetables such as sliced cucumbers, celery, bean sprouts, and green peppers. Be sure to choose an attractive blending of colors. For a more spirited dish, add about ten fresh red or green chiles.

Acar Kuning *can be served right away or will keep up to one week refrigerated. It is quite often served with* Nasi Tumpeng Kuning Lengkap *(page 305).*

> 2 tablespoons oil
> 2 cloves garlic, finely minced
> 2 teaspoons finely minced fresh ginger
> ½ teaspoon powdered turmeric
> 2 fresh or dried red chiles
> ½ teaspoon ground cumin
> ¼ cup distilled white vinegar
> ¾ cup water
> 2 teaspoons sugar
> ½ teaspoon salt
> 1 medium onion, cut in half, finely sliced
> ¾ cup carrots, peeled, cut into 1½- by ¼-inch sticks
> ¾ cup green beans, tips removed, cut in half, then cut on the
> diagonal into 1½-inch lengths
> 1 medium red bell pepper, seeded, cut lengthwise into 1½-by ¼-
> inch strips
> ¾ cup caulifloweret, stems trimmed, cut into bite-size pieces

In a heavy 3-quart saucepan, heat oil over moderate heat. Add garlic and ginger, and stir until fragrant, about 5 seconds. Add the turmeric, chiles, and cumin, and cook, stirring, for 1 minute. Add the vegetables, vinegar, water, sugar, and salt. Cook over low heat, stirring, until the vegetables are just tender, but still crisp to the bite. Remove from the pan and cool to room temperature before serving. For a more piquant flavor, put in a tightly covered glass jar. Let the *Acar* marinate in the refrigerator for 24 hours before serving, stirring it occasionally. Serve at room temperature.

YIELD: 8 servings.

ADVANCE PREPARATION: Prepare ahead. Refrigerate up to one week.

Spiced Eggs, Balinese Style
Telur Bumbu Bali

Vivacious red and yellow Telur Bambu Bali *makes a spirited and attractive accompaniment to any meal. It is an excellent with a Western brunch or supper and is a dish I serve often.*

5 tablespoons oil
4 hard-boiled eggs, peeled
1 clove garlic, minced
¼ cup minced onion
1 red bell pepper, minced
1 to 2 teaspoons Chile Sauce, *Sambal Ulek* (page 321)
½ cup water
1 teaspoon tamarind pulp dissolved in 1 hot tablespoon water,
    strained, pulp discarded
½ teaspoon sugar
½ teaspoon salt
2 teaspoons sweet soy sauce, *kecap manis* (page 321)
1 teaspoon minced fresh ginger
Fried shallot flakes (page 24)
Parsley leaves

Heat 4 tablespoons oil in a small pan. Fry eggs on all sides for 5 minutes, or until brown all over. Remove and set aside.

In a processor or blender, process the garlic, onion, pepper, and *Sambal Ulek* into a coarse paste. Add water, and mix well. Add 1 tablespoon oil to a skillet and heat. Add the mixture to the pan and fry for 2 minutes. Add tamarind water, sugar, salt, *kecap manis,* and ginger. Stir. Add the eggs and stir. Turn the heat to medium-low. Continue cooking, about 5 minutes until sauce thickens, stirring to baste eggs. Cut eggs in half and pour sauce over eggs. Garnish with fried shallot flakes and parsley leaves. Serve at room temperature.

ADVANCE PREPARATION: Prepare eggs and sauce separately. Do not combine eggs with sauce. Refrigerate. At serving time, reheat sauce with eggs. Serve at room temperature.

Inspired by a recipe from Ny. Tanzil, one of Jakarta's foremost cooking teachers and restaurant owners.

Satay Sauce, Surabaya Style
Sambal Kacang Surabaya

A vivacious, easily prepared peanut sauce from Surabaya, Java's northeast coast. It is full of spirit and can be prepared several days in advance. Serve with Lamb Satay (page 276).

> 2 tablespoons oil
> 1 cup unsalted, dry-roasted peanuts
> 2 shallots, minced
> 2 garlic cloves, minced
> 1 tablespoon minced fresh ginger
> 4 to 6 fresh red chiles, seeded, minced
> 2 tablespoons sweet soy sauce, *kecap manis*
> ¼ teaspoon shrimp paste, *terasi*, (optional)
> 1½ cups water
> Salt to taste

Heat oil in a 10-inch frying pan over moderate heat. Add the peanuts, shallots, garlic, ginger, and chiles. Cook, stirring, until the shallots are translucent, about 3 to 4 minutes. Do not brown. Remove and let cool. Pound or process the mixture in a mortar, blender, or processor to a coarse paste. Add the *kecap manis*, shrimp paste, and water. Process to mix. Put the mixture in a saucepan or wok. Bring to a boil. Reduce heat to simmer and simmer on very low heat, stirring occasionally, for 10 minutes or until a thick dipping-sauce consistency. Add salt to taste.

YIELD: 2 cups, approximately.

ADVANCE PREPARATION: The peanut sauce may be prepared ahead 1 to 2 days in advance and refrigerated. If sauce is too thick, reheat and add more water to the sauce to make it a thick dipping-sauce consistency.

Inspired by a recipe from executive chef Gerd Sankowski, Hyatt Bumi Surabaya.

Indonesian Sweet Soy Sauce
Kecap Manis

Kecap Manis is like a dark, sweet soy sauce and can be purchased in Asian grocery stores. It has a rich, mellow flavor and is the essential flavoring in Indonesian cuisine. It is much sweeter than Chinese soy sauce.

If it is unobtainable, you can make it yourself. Once made, it will keep in a tightly covered glass container for two to three months.

1 cup dark brown sugar
1 cup water
¾ cups Japanese soy sauce
⅓ cup plus 2 tablespoons dark molasses
¼ teaspoon ground laos (*galangal*)
¼ teaspoon ground coriander
¼ teaspoon freshly ground black pepper
1 star anise (optional)

Combine the sugar and water in a heavy 1-quart saucepan and simmer over low heat, stirring frequently, until the sugar dissolves. Increase the heat to high and boil until the syrup reaches 200° F on a candy thermometer, approximately 5 minutes. Reduce heat to low, add the remaining ingredients, and simmer 3 minutes. Remove from the heat. Let cool. Pour the sauce into a tightly covered glass jar.

YIELD: 1½ cups, approximately.

ADVANCE PREPARATION: You may remove the star anise after cooking. I prefer to leave it in, as it will continue to provide flavor.

Chile Sauce
Sambal Ulek

This hot chile sauce is served during most meals to season soup, meat, and fish dishes. Each diner adds Sambal Ulek to his dishes to suit his desired degree of spiciness. It is quite highly spiced, so use sparingly at first. There are many variations of Sambal Ulek.

Prepared Sambal Ulek may be purchased in jars in Asian grocery stores.

½ teaspoon salt
8 to 12 fresh hot red chiles, thinly sliced
½ teaspoon shrimp paste *(terasi)*
½ teaspoon sugar
¾ cup cubed ripe tomato

Pound or process salt, chiles, shrimp paste, and sugar in a mortar or processor to form a coarse paste. Add the tomato cubes and crush slightly to blend flavors.

YIELD: ¾ cup, approximately.

TIP: In Indonesia, quite often the tomatoes might not be added to the *Sambal Ulek.* I have added them to suit American tastes. If you prefer a spicier paste, do not add the tomatoes. Add 1 tablespoon lime juice to the paste in place of the tomatoes. For a less spicy paste, reduce the chiles or add more tomatoes.

ADVANCE PREPARATION: Prepare 1 week ahead and keep tightly covered in refrigerator.

 Chile Sauce, Padang Style
Sambal Lado

This fiery sambal was taught to me by Mrs. Tity Yulisman, a Minangkabau. It is served with most Padang meals as a condiment or is added to one's dish as a seasoning. If your sambal is too spicy, reduce the amount of chiles. She used long green chiles when preparing it for me, but many Padang restaurants use red chiles and red tomatoes.

3 shallots
3 small green tomatoes, cut into chunks
15 fresh long green chiles

Place shallots and tomatoes in a small heatproof dish. Put in the center of a medium-size pan. Place the green chiles in the pan surrounding the dish. Add enough water just to cover the chiles, being careful not to allow the water to enter the dish containing the shallots and tomatoes. Boil on moderate heat for 10 minutes. Drain the chiles. Pound or process the chiles, shallots, and green tomatoes to make a paste.

TIP: If using red chiles, use red tomatoes for a more attractive *Sambal Lado.*

ADVANCE PREPARATION: Prepare ahead. Keep in a tightly covered glass container in the refrigerator for 1 to 2 weeks.

DESSERTS

 ## Sweet Coconut Rice Balls
Klepon

Ibu Soedarso served these delectable sweets during afternoon tea in her home in Yogyakarta. They are usually green in color from the juice of green pandan leaves. If you wish, you may substitute green food coloring.

Yogyakarta is the heart of sweet food in Indonesia. Professor Soedarso, her husband, had his aromatic Javanese tea, Nasgithel, *with three spoonfuls of their wonderful coarsely grained sugar! Not to be outdone, I tried it myself, and it was delightful.*

1½ cup glutinous rice flour
¾ cup lukewarm thin coconut milk or water
Pinch of salt
2 drops green food coloring (optional)
4 tablespoons palm or dark brown sugar (approximately)
1 cup fresh coconut flakes

Mix the glutinous rice flour, coconut milk, salt, and green food coloring in a bowl. Stir together until the mixture becomes a firm but flexible dough.

If using a food processor, process the above ingredients approximately 30 seconds. Remove and mix by hand to avoid overprocessing, which will toughen the dough.

To shape the balls, take about 1 heaping teaspoon of the dough and roll it into a ball about 1 inch in diameter. With your finger, make a well in the center of the dough. Place ¼ teaspoon of the sugar in the well. Pinch the opening together to enclose the sugar completely. Roll the ball in the palm of your hands. Prepare the remaining balls and set aside.

In a saucepan, bring 8 cups of water to a boil. Drop about 10 balls at a time into the water and let cook for approximately 2 minutes, or until the balls float to the surface. With a slotted spoon, transfer the balls to a paper towel to drain. While they are still warm, roll them in the shredded coconut flakes. Cool to room temperature and serve.

YIELD: 20 *Klepon,* approximately.

TIP: If using dried unsweetened coconut flakes, reduce the amount of coconut to one cup. Allow the coconut flakes to stand in water for a few minutes. Drain and squeeze out the excess water.

ADVANCE PREPARATION: Prepare 1 to 2 days ahead. Store in an airtight container.

Inspired by the kitchen of Soedarso Sp., president of the Indonesia Institute of Arts Yogyakarta, and Ibu Soedarso.

 Pandan Refresher

This cool, refreshing, bright green beverage served to me by Padang's Mrs. Tity Yulisman is wonderful on a hot day.

    3 cups water
    2 cups sugar
    10 fresh or frozen pandan leaves
    Green food coloring

Combine water and sugar in a saucepan. Bring to a boil slowly over low heat. Boil 5 minutes. Add pandan leaves. Cover and continue cooking another 5 minutes. Remove from heat. Let cool, covered, or pandan fragrance will escape. Pour into a tightly covered glass container. Refrigerate until ready to use. To serve, add pandan mixture to cold water.

YIELD: 6 to 8 servings.

TIP: Prepared pandan syrup may be purchased in some Asian grocery stores.

◇ THE PHILIPPINES ◇

Mabuhay! Welcome!

Warm, friendly, easygoing, and fun-loving, the Filipinos are an extremely hospitable and happy people who are always ready to smile. They enjoy the philosophy that a good meal, like all other aspects of life, should be enjoyed to the fullest.

An archipelago of 7,107 islands lying between the Pacific Ocean and the China Sea, the Philippines are a crossroads of many cultures. Malay, Hindu, Moslem, Chinese, and later Spanish and American influences have formed a unique blend that has resulted in the very adaptable Filipinos of today.

The multicultural heritage of the Philippines is carried into their food, which is influenced for the most part by Chinese and Spanish, with some remaining Malay touches. Monina A. Mercado describes it in *The Culinary Culture of the Philippines:* "Drawing origins from various cultures but displaying regional characteristics, Filipino food was prepared by the Malay settlers, spiced by commercial relations with Chinese traders, stewed in 300 years of Spanish rule and hamburgered by American influence on the Philippine way of life. The multiracial features of the Filipino—a Chinese-Malayan face, a Spanish name, and an American nickname—thusly inform Philippine cuisine, producing dishes of oriental and occidental extraction."*

While rice is the mainstay of the Filipino diet, the Chinese, who first came as traders, have been responsible for the immense popularity of noodles. Two of the most popular forms of noodle are *bihon,* rice sticks, and *sotanghon,* bean threads, transparent noodles made from soy beans. They are thoroughly absorbed into Philippine cuisine

*The Culinary Culture of the Philippines, edited by Gilda Cordero-Fernando. Vera-Reyes, Inc., Philippines, 1976.

325

and virtually no region is without a *pancit,* noodle dish, of its own, using local ingredients. From the Chinese, they have learned various ways to serve noodles—in broth, braised, or stir-fried, topped with sauces made from locally available foods such as fish and shellfish, Chinese sausages, chorizos, and vegetables.

The same foods that garnish noodles are also stuffed inside noodlelike doughs to form other popular foods, the best known of which is the stuffed thin crepes known as *lumpia.* There are also Filipino versions of the Chinese noodle-wrapped dumplings, *shao mai.* Because all these noodle-based foods are relatively inexpensive, they are common to the lower and middle class, but they are also a favorite with all classes during *merienda,* afternoon snack time, and are equally at home on an elegant fiesta table.

The Spanish, who came as conquerors, exercised their culinary influence mostly on the elite, and this food became fiesta fare. Its basic ingredients and processes are from a different material and ethnic world. The upper-class families wished to imitate the Spanish and soon were serving elegant *Lengua al Bodeguero,* ox tongue with cheese and tomato sauce, *Morcon,* stuffed rolled steak, and *Caldereta,* a delectable beef or goat stew.

The dishes and cooking methods introduced by the Spanish have spread throughout Filipino cuisine, to the point that many dishes, even those which are of Chinese origin, have Spanish names. The basic techniques are simple sautéing and stewing. Most typical of this style are the dishes known as *guisado* (sautéed). They begin with garlic, sautéed in oil until brown, then add onions, which are cooked until soft and transparent. Sometimes tomatoes are sautéed before the meat or other ingredients are added. This preliminary base (and the flavor of olive oil, which is not native to Asia and is not used anywhere else) can make almost anything taste uniquely "Filipino" as opposed to similar Asian dishes.

The native food from the Malays, sister to the cuisines of other Southeast Asian countries, is served at all levels but is the principal fare of the lower classes. A family meal is often a one-dish combination of meat and vegetables in broth (plus rice, of course). A more elaborate meal may include one dish with broth, some sautéed vegetables, and a "dry" dish such as a grilled fish. The broth is spooned over the rice to season it. All dishes are served on the table at the same time, family style. Traditional Filipinos eat with their hand, rolling up the rice into small neat parcels before putting it into their mouths. Today, a spoon and fork are used, which is practical for eating the rice, broth, meat, or sauce. A sweet dessert is always part of a meal. In fact, the skill of the cook is often judged more on the basis of the desserts she prepares than on the main course.

As in other cultures, there are many variations in cooking, and each region has its own favorite. For example, on the northern island of Luzon, where the capital city of Manila is located, rice is the everyday staple, while Visayans in the southern island of Cebu prefer the more readily available corn.

After the chile-hot curries and spicy sauces of the Malays and Thais, I found Filipino food bland at first. Glenda Barretto, owner of Via Mare, one of Manila's best restaurants, soon changed my mind. In her elegant restaurant in the posh Makati district, she set out on a mission to introduce me to the best of Philippine cuisine.

Among the traditional Philippine favorites she served were *Ukoy,* crispy shrimp fritters, *Caldereta,* a tasty goat stew, *Adobong Sugpo,* a delicately flavored yet piquant shrimp dish, and *Pancit Luglug,* rice noodles topped with a heavenly shrimp sauce. Unlike in French cuisine, she explained, it is understood that the chef and the diner join together, the final product being a communal effort. The diner takes an active part in the creation of the food by preparing the final *sawsawan* (sauce), to be added to taste to each dish. Principal to these sauces are two ingredients: thin fish sauce *(patis)* and a thicker, more pungent fish or shrimp sauce *(bagoong). Patis,* like the Thai *nam pla* and the Vietnamese *nuoc mam,* is the salty amber liquid decanted from fermented small fish or shrimp. *Bagoong balayan,* prepared by fermenting small fish in a large stone jar, is of pouring consistency. *Bagoong alamang,* made from minute shrimp, is pale pink and of a drier, lumpier consistency.

Sawsawan is not a single mixture; it embraces a vast array of dipping sauces, each one usually mixed by the diner to go with a specific dish. During a meal, many saucers appear, as different dishes call for different combinations of seasonings. *Calamansi,* a small local variety of lime, is automatically squeezed over noodles. Next a little *patis* is added, along with some pepper. There may be vinegar with crushed garlic to accompany roast pork, *bagoong* and *calamansi* for grilled fish, *patis* and *calamansi* for broiled chicken, and there is always a bottle of vinegar and tiny, red hot chile peppers for spice lovers. The correct *sawsawan* is so important to Filipinos that when traveling, they will often pack a bottle of *patis* and some *bagoong.*

Glenda explained that the Filipinos have changed and adapted the foods of other countries to make them unmistakably their own. As elsewhere in Asia, ginger, garlic, and onion are among the dominant flavoring ingredients, but the Filipino taste also calls for dramatic contrasts and distinct flavors. Bitter, sour, salty, meaty, and fishy flavors are often combined.

The famous *lumpia* is clearly related to the Chinese spring roll, but it has become distinctly Filipino in its two main forms, as well as in its accompanying sauces, which are completely unlike the original Chinese sauces. Fried *Lumpia Shanghai,* containing ground pork, shrimp, and vegetables, is served with a *sawsawan* of cooked vinegar, soy sauce, tomato ketchup, crushed garlic, and pepper. For fresh *Lumpia Ubod,* the soft crepe is wrapped around a cooked filling and eaten without any further cooking, along with a precooked brown sugar, vinegar, and garlic dipping sauce.

Glenda also introduced me to a favorite Filipino institution, *halo-halo*. After a few bites of this wonderful, towering concoction, served in a tall, fluted glass filled with crushed ice, I became a *halo-halo* addict!

Halo-halo is the epitome of the Filipino fondness for throwing all kinds of foods together (the name means "mix-mix" in Tagalog). It is a potpourri of colorful diced seasonal fruits (pineapple, mangoes, melons, sweet jackfruit), shredded sweetened coconut, red beans, cubes of colored gelatin, sugar palm seeds, chickpeas, gelatinous purple yams called *ube*, evaporated milk . . . the list goes on and on and almost anything goes. For extra richness, it may be topped with a scoop of *ube* ice cream, or perhaps another flavor, such as *buco,* made from young coconut. Like jewels in a glass, *halo-halo* is rich, sweet, flamboyant, and indigenously Filipino. It is a delight to eat, pleasing to the eye and palate, and the ultimate refreshment.

The same Filipino flamboyance is seen in the overly decorated "jeepneys," the public transport vehicles which flourish in the streets. Barely recognizable as army-surplus jeeps, they are Filipino art on wheels. The exterior is an explosion of pop-art design. Painted on the body are names of movie stars and girlfriends, declarations of love, splashes of mythology, and religious slogans. Adorning the hood are silver horses, multicolored lights, and mirrors. Inside may be a portrait of the Virgin Mary pasted on the dashboard, leis made of sampaguita, the national flower, religious medals, plastic-covered prayer cards, multicolored plastic streamers, and much more.

At the Maya Kitchens Culinary Arts Center, director Lourdes Fajardo invited me to have dinner with Sandy and Mariles Daza, popular television cooking personalities and cookbook authors. She served an elegant feast of Filipino favorites: delicate *Lumpia Ubod* with a hearts of palm filling, *Chicken Binakol,* a tasty chicken dish seasoned with garlic, ginger, fish sauce, and young coconut meat and steamed in a bamboo tube, *Rellenong Bangus,* delicious boned milkfish stuffed with its own flaked meat, ground pork, tomatoes, and red bell peppers and seasoned with *calamansi* and soy sauce, and a tangy Chicken and Pork Adobo. Dessert was a beautifully decorated *Leche Flan,* a pure delight of a creamy custard topped with *macapuno,* the sweetened meat of a young coconut.

If there is a Philippine national dish, it may be Chicken and Pork

Adobo. It's just one of many variations on a cooking style imported from Spain and popular throughout Philippine cooking. Chunks of meat are marinated in local palm vinegar, crushed garlic, bay leaves, salt, and pepper. The meat is boiled in its marinade, fried until lightly browned, and finally simmered in its cooking stock, along with soy sauce, until the liquids turn to a thick sauce. There are many other variations—dry or moist, whole or shredded, meat or seafood—but they all share the subtle sourness that makes *adobo* unique.

Lourdes explained that the Filipinos have retained their love of sour foods, even when modern refrigeration makes preservation with vinegar and other sour ingredients unnecessary. Because of the flexibility and imagination of the Filipino, there are no hard and fast combinations or proportions. This same imagination is found in the souring of other dishes. Where lime or vinegar might be considered too obvious, Filipino cooks might use mashed tamarind, *camias* (a local acidic fruit), or green pineapple or guava to obtain more interesting results.

While in Manila, I stayed at the historic and elegant Manila Hotel, one of the best and most sophisticated in Asia. In the hotel's spectacular Maynila restaurant, a splendid meal was made more so by the graceful, natural movements of the Bayanihan Dance Company's performance. The dances, like the food, reflect early Malay, Muslim, and Spanish influences.

A shrimp and mango salad was attractively presented in the form of a crab, the large shrimp forming the legs around the mango body. *Bistek Filipino*, tenderloin smothered in onions and served with a *calamansi*-juice and soy-sauce topping, followed, along with *Atsara*, a tangy shredded and pickled green-papaya and carrot palate refresher similar to the Acars of Malaysia and Indonesia. *Guisadong Sitaw*, sautéed green beans, included shrimp, pork, and coconut in a style reminiscent of Chinese vegetable dishes.

Philippine meals don't necessarily follow our three-a-day pattern. Since Spanish times, a favorite breakfast has been a chocolate-flavored porridge of glutinous rice served with dried smoked fish and sweetened rice cake topped with coconut flakes. Next comes a midmorning snack such as *Pancit Mami Guisado* (fried noodles), followed by a complete lunch, possibly *Caldereta* or another stew. If the period between lunch and dinner is too long, a midafternoon *merienda* is in order. (Please see the menu on page 334.) In the evening, they might go to a simple *turo-turo* cafeteria (the name, literally translated, means point-point, as you indicate your preference by pointing at the foods), or to an elegant restaurant and enjoy a full dinner from soup to nuts!

Food is a token of good will. It is always shared, and anyone who enters the home should be fed. If it is not mealtime, a *babingka*, rice cake topped with slivers of local water buffalo cheese or salted egg, or *sapin-sapin*, an elaborately layered sticky rice cake, painstakingly made in different-colored layers, might be offered. If a guest arrives during dinner he is always invited to join the meal in progress. A Filipino mother might take away other privileges when a child misbehaves, but she will never send the child to bed without food! Food gifts, often elaborately prepared and wrapped, are always welcome.

The beautiful northern resort of Baguio, the summer capital of the Philippines, lies about a hundred miles north of Manila. The road to Baguio zigzags upward through rugged mountains with breathtaking views of gorges and waterfalls into a world of fog and pine. There is a sense of leisure and frivolity in the brisk mountain air.

In his high-spirited canary-yellow Volkswagen, which played "Happy Birthday" when in reverse, the ebullient executive chef Michael Oberle of the Baguio Hyatt Terraces took me on a tour through the brilliant flower-lined maze of streets to visit the large, two-story market. Its gaily covered awnings and buntings gave it the vivacious air of a fiesta. Stalls upon stalls of fresh fruit and produce lined the alleys, and various types of meat and poultry hung from hooks. Members of the Igorot tribe, the men in G-string loincloths and the women more colorfully and extensively attired, sold a treasure-trove of tribal textiles, woven baskets, swords, and jewelry.

The longest line was at the "banana-cue." A short, sweetish local banana known as *saba* was deep-fried in sugar syrup and skewered on a stick, like a barbecue. Other treats are boiled and roasted corn, *ube*, jam, *bikang-bikang*, sweet strips of sweet potato, and *bokayo*, sweet grated coconut patties.

We stopped in the pine-filled forest to visit an Igorot tribal ceremony. The men were as minimally clothed as in the village, while the women were bedecked in colorful tribal home-loomed wrap-around skirts of red, black, yellow, and white, shell and agate beads, and bronze earrings with fertility motifs. They were preparing for *canao*, the traditional tribal feast. A socio-religious ceremony, *canao* is held to appease the spirits during the various stages of rice production; that day's observance was to thank the gods for a bountiful harvest.

A chicken and a pot of rice were taken to the site of a sacred tree. The chicken was slaughtered, and some of the feathers were plucked and attached to the sacred tree. Care was taken to leave the inner organs intact as the chicken was singed and defeathered. The tribesmen opened the chicken and checked the position of the liver. It was in the correct position and the bile was a healthy color, indicating that the rice harvest would have a favorable outcome and the festival could continue.

After the chicken was split into parts, it was boiled with other meats, sweet potatoes, and plantains in a large cauldron over a wood fire. While the stew cooked, men and women danced to the beat of gongs. Rice was served in plates made from banana trunks, and the chicken and meats were served in wooden bowls. Before eating, the eldest in the group said a prayer, and the group leader invited the spirits. A jug of the local rice wine *(tapuy)* was brought out, and a little wine was spilled on the ground for the spirits. The rest of the day was spent in a haze of sheer enjoyment.

The jubilant Volkswagen wound its way back to the Hyatt Terraces, nestled on a promontory surrounded by lush pine forests. The decor of tribal swords, masks, antiques, and intricate weavings created an atmosphere that evoked the fascinating history of this captivating area.

Graciously flamboyant, Chef Michael invited me to his chef's table to sample local favorites; we began with *Kinilaw na Isda,* a ceviche of delicately flavored local fish fillet marinated in *calamansi* with onions, garlic, ginger, and pepper, all topped with coconut dressing. *Camaron Rebosado*—shrimp lightly coated with butter dough, deep-fried, and dipped in a tasty sweet and sour sauce—had an exquisite delicate balance of flavors. *Inihaw na Baboy*—pork chops marinated in a typically Filipino mixture of vinegar, garlic, pepper, soy sauce, and salt and then roasted over charcoal—were combined with grilled sliced eggplant and pickled papaya. Corn *Maja,* made from coconut milk, glutinous rice flour, sweet palm sugar, corn kernels, and topped with toasted grated coconut, provided a sweet finale (I thought) to my food tour of the Philippines. Then, in a spectacular gesture of Philippine exuberance and hospitality, a glacial *halo-halo* appeared.

Halina't magsalu-salo tayo! Let's share our meal!

◇ PHILIPPINE TRADITIONAL MENUS ◇

A PHILIPPINE FIESTA BUFFET

12 to 14 people

Roast Pork Loin, *Lechon*

◆

Liver Sauce, *Lechon Sauce*

◆

Stuffed Rolled Steak, *Morcon*

◆

Goat Casserole, *Goat Caldereta*

◆

Oxtail Stew, *Kare-Kare*

◆

Green Beans, Philippine Style[†], *Guisadong Sitaw*

◆

Bean Thread Noodles with Shrimp and Pork[*],
Sotanghon Guisado II

◆

Rice

◆

Leche Flan[*]

◆

Tea, Coffee, Hot Chocolate

[*] double recipe   [†]triple recipe

The exuberance of the Filipino spirit is best seen in the fiesta. A fiesta may be held to honor a saint, to give thanks for a good harvest, to spread good will, for a family reunion, wedding, birthday, or graduation, or just any time you want to invite friends to eat, sing, dance, and be merry. In the Philippines, practically any time of the year is fiesta time!

332

At the fiesta table the Spanish influence is very strong, and only the best, classiest, most expensive foods are served. The favorite centerpiece dish is *Lechon,* a whole suckling pig stuffed with rice, tamarind, and aromatic leaves, roasted over hot coals until golden. The first pinch of the pig must be with the bare fingers. There are two spots to obtain the skin, one around the ears and the other around the tail. The guest of honor gently removes the ear of the pig. The skin comes off and the rest of the party takes turns pinching off the delectable golden, brown skin until the pig is completely skinned. Now the carver appears to serve the succulent meat. A sweet-sour liver *sawsawan* (sauce), spiced with lots of garlic, onions, and peppercorns, is typically served with the roast pig. (I haven't included a recipe for *Lechon* in the book, as few of us are likely to tackle roasting a whole pig; however, roast suckling pigs and cuts from larger pigs are available from Chinese and Filipino shops in many cities. The sauce is equally good on pork loin roasted at home.)

No Filipino fiesta is complete without a great variety of laboriously made sweets. *Pastillas,* sweets wrapped in multicolored paper with long tails of delicately cut-out designs of hearts and flowers, grace the festive table. Often they are arranged in three-tiered centerpieces, and the delicate wrappers, which take days to make, are thrown away as soon as the sweet is eaten.

Abrillantadas, fresh fruits in season; pomelo, native limes; soursops, breadfruit; and other local fruits are made into sweets, glazed with sugar, and carved into flowers, fish, swans, and folk-art designs. Apples, pears, and guavas are candied and molded back into the shape of the fruit out of which it was made. All are pierced on individually carved toothpicks and assembled into an overwhelming tiered centerpiece.

Rows of fruit preserves—pomelo, jackfruit, mango, makapuno (a delicate type of coconut meat), and chick peas—are carved into rosettes so exquisite that nobody has the heart to eat them. A fiesta ends with a bang of desserts—and often the bang of fireworks!

For this fiesta menu, I have chosen an assortment of favorite Filipino dishes. (A fiesta table is usually laden with meat dishes, vegetables being more of an everyday food; I have added the green-bean dish to suit American tastes.) *Kare-Kare* is a robust oxtail dish with peanut sauce. *Caldereta* is a flavorful, typically sour stew of beef or goat. *Morcon,* a stuffed and rolled steak, comes out in picture-perfect slices. All three, plus the green beans, can be prepared a day ahead and reheated.

The Filipinos have adopted the Chinese belief that long, uncut noodles symbolize long life and prosperity, so at least one noodle dish must be served at a proper fiesta for good luck. Here it is *Sotanghon*

Guisado, stir-fried bean threads with shrimp and pork. Plain white rice absorbs the flavorful sauces of the many dishes. Dessert is *Leche Flan,* a delicious caramel custard of European origin that is as popular in the Philippines as it is in Latin America.

Your elegant fiesta buffet can be prepared ahead with little last-minute preparation. To serve it in true Filipino style, garnish the table with assorted fruits and flowers; if you are artistically inclined, try your hand at carved fruit and vegetable garnishes like those described above. The various stews and green beans can be made a day ahead and reheated. Rice can be prepared and kept warm in a rice cooker for several hours. *Leche Flan* is best when prepared the day before. Even the pork and shrimp topping for the *Sotanghon Guisado* can be made ahead and combined with the noodles just before serving. Purchase your pork or prepare a roast pork the day of your fiesta. Enjoy the festivities with your guests!

MERIENDA
A delectable brunch or light supper.

6 people

Fresh Spring Rolls with Hearts of Palm, *Lumpia Ubod*
•
Shrimp and Vegetable Fritters, *Ukoy*
•
Rice Noodles with Shrimp Sauce, *Pancit Luglug*
•
Cheese Roll, *Ensaymada*
•
Coconut Sweets, *Maja Blanca*
•
Tea, coffee, *Salabat,* or hot chocolate

Merienda in the Philippines is as traditional as four o'clock tea in England. Late in the afternoon, after siesta time, the Filipino wanders into the kitchen for a snack. Friends may stop by for a friendly chat and, of course, some of whatever is freshly cooked.

Merienda can be very substantial or just sweets. Today almost anything is served during *merienda* except rice (once rice appears, it is considered a full meal). For those of us not bound by tradition, this menu can make an excellent brunch or Sunday-night buffet.

Pancit Luglug, a favorite and impressive noodle dish, consists of boiled rice noodles topped with shrimp, pork, and various toppings. *Ukoy* are crispy shrimp and vegetable fritters. *Lumpia Ubod,* fresh spring rolls with hearts of palm, are a delicious alternative to the better-known fried variety. There are usually several sweets; *Ensaymada*, a Spanish-derived sweet bread, and *Maja Blanca*, a lime-flavored creamy custard with coconut topping, are two favorites.

To minimize last-minute preparations, you can prepare the *Ensaymada*, *Maja Blanca*, the *Pancit Luglug* sauce, and the *Lumpia Ubod* filling and sauce a day ahead. Assemble the *Lumpia Ubod* several hours before serving and cover with plastic wrap. The *Ukoy* can be fried ahead of time and reheated in the oven along with the *Ensaymada*. Only the beverages and the final dipping and saucing of the noodles need be done at the last minute.

STARTERS
Fresh Spring Rolls with Hearts of Palm, *Lumpia Ubod*
Fried Spring Rolls, *Lumpia Shanghai*
Fresh Spring Rolls with Pork and Shrimp, *Lumpiang Sariwa*
Shrimp and Vegetable Fritters, *Ukoy*

SOUPS
Ginger Chicken Soup, *Chicken Tinola*
Chicken Macaroni Soup, *Sopas*

MEAT
Stuffed Rolled Steak, *Morcon*
Steak, Philippine Style, *Bistek Filipino*
Stuffed Tenderloin, *Lomo Basilan*
Beef Casserole, *Beef Caldereta*
Oxtail Stew, *Kare-Kare*
Ox Tongue with Cheese and Tomato Sauce, *Lengua Al Bodeguero*
Roast Pork Loin, *Lechon*
Braised Pork, *Humba*
Steamed Pork Loaf, *Embutido*
Goat Casserole, *Goat Caldereta*

POULTRY
Chicken and Pork Adobo, *Adobong Manok at Baboy*
Grilled Chicken, Philippine Style, *Inihaw na Manok*

FISH AND SEAFOOD
Catfish in Coconut Sauce, *Guinataang Hito*
Milkfish with Black Beans, *Tocho*
Piquant Shrimp, *Adobong Sugpo*

SALADS AND VEGETABLES

Bean Salad, *Enchasadang Sitaw*
Green Beans, Philippine Style, *Guisadong Sitaw*
Steamed Asparagus, *Pinasingawang Asparagus*
Snow Peas with Shrimp, *Guisadong Chicharo*

RICE, NOODLES, AND WRAPPERS

Fried Noodles with Pork, Shrimp, and Vegetables, *Pancit Mami Guisado*
Bean Thread Noodles with Chicken, *Sotanghon Guisado I*
Bean Thread Noodles with Shrimp and Pork, *Sotanghon Guisado II*
Rice Noodles with Shrimp Sauce, *Pancit Luglug*
Fresh Spring Roll Wrappers, *Lumpia Wrappers*

SAUCES

Liver Sauce, *Lechon Sauce*
Sweet and Sour Sauce, *Agre Dulce*
Garlic Sauce, *Paalat*

DESSERTS, SWEETS, AND SNACKS

Cheese Roll, *Ensaymada*
Coconut Sweets, *Maja Blanca*
Creme Caramel, *Leche Flan*
Banana Rolls, *Turon*
Tropical Fruit Potpourri, *Halo-Halo*
Ginger Tea, *Salabat*

STARTERS

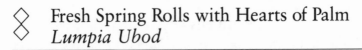

◇ Fresh Spring Rolls with Hearts of Palm ◇
Lumpia Ubod

Here is a very popular, refreshing Filipino treat. It is perfect as an appetizer or for a light luncheon or supper.

Lumpia Ubod, *prepared from the heart of the coconut palm, is highly regarded, as a whole tree has to be sacrificed to obtain the tender, creamy, nutty white heart of the palm* (ubod). Ubod *can be purchased in jars in Asian markets.*

4 tablespoons oil
2 cloves garlic, finely minced
1 small onion, finely minced
6 ounces pork, minced
6 ounces shrimp, shelled, deveined, minced
8-ounce jar hearts of palm (*ubod*), drained, cut into 2-inch
    matchstick strips
½ teaspoon salt
1 teaspoon pepper
12 fresh *lumpia* wrappers (page 366)
12 Boston or romaine lettuce leaves, washed, dried, separated
2 green onions, chopped
Garlic Sauce (page 368)

Heat wok. Add 2 tablespoons oil. Heat. Add garlic and onion, and stir-fry until onion becomes translucent. Add pork and shrimp and stir-fry for 1 minute. Add the hearts of palm and stir-fry for an additional 2 minutes. Season with salt and pepper. Cool in a colander, allowing liquid to drain.

Place a wrapper on a plate. Put a lettuce leaf on the wrapper and about 2 tablespoons of filling on the lettuce. Roll the wrapper and fold it at one end, leaving lettuce protruding from the other. Pour a little sauce on top. Garnish with green onions. Serve at room temperature with Garlic Sauce.

YIELD: 12 rolls.

TIP: Shredded bamboo shoots may be substituted for hearts of palm. Frozen *lumpia* or spring roll wrappers are available at Asian grocery stores.

ADVANCE PREPARATION: Prepare filling 1 day in advance. Refrigerate, covered with plastic wrap. Assemble the *Lumpia Ubod* 1 hour before serving.

Inspired by a recipe from the Maynila Room, Manila Hotel.

Fried Spring Rolls
Lumpia Shanghai

This Philippine version of the Chinese spring roll is a favorite snack.

3 cups oil
2 cloves garlic, minced
½ pound lean pork, ground
½ pound shrimp, shelled, deveined, minced
¾ cup minced water chestnuts
2 carrots, minced
1 cup minced celery
½ cup green onions, cut very finely
2 tablespoons soy sauce
1 teaspoon salt (optional)
½ teaspoon freshly ground pepper
Lumpia or spring roll wrappers, 8 inches in diameter
Sweet and Sour Sauce (page 368)

In a wok or pan, heat 2 tablespoons oil. Add garlic and stir until fragrant, about 5 seconds. Add the pork and shrimp and stir-fry for 1 minute. Add the water chestnuts, carrots, celery, and green onions. Stir-fry for approximately 2 minutes, or until the vegetables are tender but still crunchy. Add the soy sauce, salt, and pepper. Stir. Remove from heat. Drain excess moisture from pan.

To assemble the *lumpia,* place about ⅓ cup of the filling on the lower third of the wrapper. Fold the portion of the wrapper nearest you over the filling until just covered. Turn the wrapper again to enclose the filling securely. Moisten the edges of the wrapper with water or a mixture of cornstarch and water. Fold over the corners and press down firmly to seal, making an envelope. Moisten the flap of the envelope with water and turn, rolling firmly into a 1-inch cylinder. Seal firmly. Set aside, seam side down. Repeat until all the filling has been used.

Heat oil in a wok to 375° F. Place 4 or 5 lumpia at a time in the hot oil. Deep-fry until crisp and golden. Remove with a skimmer and drain on paper towels. Serve hot with Sweet and Sour Sauce (page 368).

YIELD: 30 *lumpia,* approximately.

ADVANCE PREPARATION: The rolls may be prepared ahead and frozen for 1 to 2 months. Deep-fry at serving time, or deep-fry ahead and reheat in a moderate oven on a rack resting on a shallow roasting pan or cookie sheet. They are best when fried and served immediately.

Inspired by a recipe from Tiyang DiGregorio, wife of David Di-Gregorio, executive chef, The 95th Restaurant, Chicago, Illinois.

 ## Fresh Spring Rolls with Pork and Shrimp
Lumpiang Sariwa

A crisp, refreshing appetizer or snack.

> 1 recipe cooked filling mixture for Lumpia Shanghai (page 338)
> 1 head romaine lettuce, separated into leaves, washed, dried
> Fresh *Lumpia* wrappers (page 366)
> Garlic Sauce (page 368)

Place a leaf of romaine on a Lumpia Wrapper. Put 2 tablespoons of the filling on the lettuce leaf. Roll up the wrapper, turning in the sides so that the filling is enclosed.

If you prefer, you may serve the ingredients in separate dishes and let your guests prepare the *Lumpiang Sariwa* at the table. Serve at room temperature with warm Garlic Sauce.

YIELD: 14 rolls.

TIP: Prepared frozen lumpia or spring roll wrappers are available at Asian grocery stores. However, the homemade wrappers are superior.

ADVANCE PREPARATION: Assemble 1 hour ahead. Cover with plastic wrap. Refrigerate. Bring to room temperature before serving.

 ## Shrimp and Vegetable Fritters
Ukoy

One of the most popular and attractive Filipino snack foods, Ukoy is quite often served on a merienda table, an afternoon mini-meal of cakes, tarts, and sweet fritters, although this is not a sweet. In the Philippines, the shrimp shell is left intact. If you wish, remove the shell, leaving the tail on the shrimp. There are many variations. For a Western or Filipino dinner, it makes a very tasty appetizer.

GARLIC SAUCE:

> 1 tablespoon finely minced garlic
> 1 teaspoon salt
> 1 cup distilled white vinegar
> 1 cup cornstarch
> 1 cup flour
> 1 teaspoon salt
> ¾ cup water, approximately
> 1 teaspoon annatto seeds soaked in 2 tablespoons hot water for
>   20 minutes, rubbed occasionally to exude color, strained,
>   drained, reserving the liquid
> 1 to 2 large sweet potatoes (approximately 1 pound), peeled,
>   coarsely grated
> 12 medium shrimp, shells intact
> 2 cups oil
> 3 green onion tops, finely chopped

Prepare Garlic Sauce. With the back of a spoon or in a miniprocessor, crush garlic and salt together to a smooth paste. Add vinegar and stir until thoroughly mixed. Set aside.

In a bowl, combine cornstarch, flour, and salt. Add water and strained annatto liquid. Knead until liquid is absorbed. Add the grated sweet potato and beat vigorously with a spoon until the mixture is well combined.

Heat oil to 375° F in a 10- to 12-inch skillet. The oil should be about ½ inch deep. Spoon 2 tablespoons of the batter onto an oiled saucer. Sprinkle 1 teaspoon green onions on top. Lightly press a shrimp in the center. Holding saucer close to the surface of the oil, slide the *ukoy* into it. Fry the cakes 2 or 3 at a time for about 3 minutes, spooning oil over each cake. Turn carefully and fry another 3 minutes, turning the heat down if necessary to prevent burning. Remove and drain on paper towels.

Arrange shrimp-side up. Brush each cake with garlic sauce and serve with remaining sauce on the side. Serve immediately or keep warm in the oven.

YIELD: 10 to 12 *Ukoy*.

TIP: If annatto seeds are unavailable, use yellow food coloring to color the dough if you wish a brighter color.

ADVANCE PREPARATION: The *Ukoy* freeze well and can be reheated in a moderate oven. Prepare the sauce 1 day in advance.

Inspired by a recipe from Glenda Barretto, Via Mare, Manila.

SOUPS

◇ Ginger Chicken Soup
◇ *Chicken Tinola*

Sautéed chicken in broth seasoned with ginger and topped with fresh spinach.

In the Philippines, this is traditionally made with green papaya. Lourdes Fajardo has suggested substituting fresh spinach.

4 tablespoons oil
2 cloves garlic, chopped
1 tablespoon minced fresh ginger
1 medium onion, sliced
2 to 2½ pounds chicken, cut into 10 to 12 serving pieces
1 quart water
½ cup shredded green papaya, or fresh young spinach, tough
    stems removed, cut into 2-inch shreds
Fish sauce *(patis)* to taste
Pepper to taste

In a heavy 5- or 6-quart casserole, heat 2 tablespoons oil over moderate heat. Sauté garlic and ginger until lightly browned. Add onion and stir-fry until soft and transparent, but not brown. Remove and set aside. Heat 2 tablespoons oil. Add chicken pieces in batches and stir-fry until all the pieces are very lightly browned. Return the garlic, ginger, and onion to the pan. Add water. Bring to a boil over high heat. Reduce heat to low and simmer, partially covered, for 20 to 30 minutes, or until chicken is just tender but not falling off the bone. Add papaya or spinach leaves. Stir. Add fish sauce and pepper to taste. Serve immediately from a heated tureen.

YIELD: 4 to 6 servings.

TIP: Prepare soup ahead. Add papaya or spinach just before serving.

Inspired by a recipe from Lourdes Fajardo, director, Maya Culinary Arts Center, Manila.

Chicken Macaroni Soup
Sopas

Rene Cortez, Thai Airways International Ltd., has shared his favorite childhood soup. His mother prepared this often for him in the Philippines. He says Sopas *is a good way to start a hearty family meal.*

½ pound chicken breast
5 cups homemade chicken broth, or one 14½-ounce can
    condensed unsalted chicken broth plus water to make 5
    cups
2 tablespoons oil
2 cloves garlic, chopped
1 small onion, chopped
2 frankfurters, sliced thin (optional)
2 tablespoons fish sauce *(patis)*, or to taste
1 cup elbow macaroni
1 small carrot, cut into thin 1½-inch matchstick strips
½ cup fresh or evaporated milk
¾ cup shredded cabbage, cut into 1½-inch lengths
Salt and freshly ground black pepper to taste
Dash of Chinese sesame oil

Put chicken breast and broth in a pan. Cover. Bring to a boil. Reduce the heat to simmer and cook until the chicken is tender, about 30 minutes. Remove the chicken and let cool. Discard the chicken bones and skin. Shred the chicken meat and set aside. Strain the broth and set aside. Clean the saucepan.

Heat 2 tablespoons oil in a pan. Sauté the garlic and onion and cook over moderate heat until the onion is soft and translucent. Add the chicken and frankfurters. Stir-fry for 2 minutes. Add the chicken broth. Cover and bring to a boil. Reduce the heat and simmer for 2 minutes. Add the fish sauce to taste. Add the macaroni and simmer until just tender. Add the carrots and milk. Simmer until the carrots are crispy and tender. Add the cabbage. Stir-fry for 1 minute longer. Season to taste with salt and pepper, if desired. Add sesame oil. Serve hot.

YIELD: 4 to 6 servings.

MEAT

 ## Stuffed Rolled Steak
Morcon

You will find a strong Spanish influence in this delicious and spectacular Philippine dish. It is perfect for a buffet, as it can be made ahead and reheated at serving time.

One 2½- to 3-pound flank steak
2 to 3 cloves garlic, crushed
3 tablespoons soy sauce
1 tablespoon plus 2 teaspoons fresh lemon juice
2 medium carrots, peeled, cut lengthwise into 6 strips
1 canned *chorizo de Bilbao,* cut lengthwise into 8 thin strips
4 slices lean bacon, cut lengthwise into strips
3 dill pickles, about 5 inches long, cut lengthwise into 6 strips
3 hard-boiled eggs, cut lengthwise into quarters
4 tablespoons oil
3 cups water
2 ripe medium tomatoes, chopped
1 medium onion, chopped
1 bay leaf
Salt and freshly ground pepper to taste
Parsley for garnish

Ask your butcher to butterfly the flank steak or do it yourself, using the following method.

Chill or partially freeze the flank steak. Holding 1 hand on top of the chilled steak, with a long, very sharp knife, cut the flank steak in half horizontally from one long side to within ¾ inch of the far end. Be very careful not to cut through the steak. This will give you a large, flat steak, about double its original size. Spread the steak open to a long strip. Pound the joining seam to make it lie flat. Continue pounding the entire length of the steak with the side of a cleaver or kitchen mallet to flatten the steak into a thin sheet. Trim the gristle and fat.

Place the butterflied steak, cut-side up, on a large jelly roll pan. Rub the surface of the meat with the garlic, soy sauce, and lemon juice. Let the steak marinate for 30 minutes. Starting at the smaller end of the steak, arrange the carrots, chorizo, bacon, pickles, and hard-boiled eggs perpendicular to the grain of the meat in neat,

evenly spaced parallel rows. Carefully roll the steak into a long, thick cylinder. Cut about an 8- to 10-foot length of kitchen string. Wrap one end of the string around the steak about 1 inch from the end of the roll and tie with a knot. Spiral the remaining string around the beef roll to within 1 inch of the opposite end. Wrap the end of the spiral around the opposite end and tie securely.

Heat 4 tablespoons oil in a large, deep casserole, and brown the meat on all sides, turning it gently. Be careful not to burn the meat. Remove the roll from the pan. Pour off all but a thin layer of fat from the pan. Add the water, tomatoes, onion, and bay leaf to the pan. Bring to a boil. Reduce the heat to medium-low. Add the browned roll to the pan. When the liquid returns to a boil, cover. Reduce the heat to low and simmer the meat for 1¼ to 1½ hours or until tender. Turn the meat several times during cooking. Remove the cooked roll from the pan. When cool enough to handle, remove the string.

Put the contents of the pan in a food processor or blender. Process for a few seconds to make a smooth sauce. Check for seasonings, adding salt and pepper if desired. (If the sauce is not thick enough, return it to the pan and reduce it by boiling, until it is a gravy consistency. If it is too thick, add water.)

Carve the *Morcon* crosswise into ¾-inch slices. Arrange the slices decoratively on a heated platter. Serve the sauce separately.

YIELD: 6 to 8 servings.

TIPS: Olives and sharp cheddar cheese slices may be added to the filling. Two cups of canned tomatoes may be substituted for the fresh tomatoes.

VARIATION: Substitute one 6-ounce precooked chorizo or other highly seasoned garlic-flavored sausage cut lengthwise into strips for *chorizo de Bilbao.*

ADVANCE PREPARATION: Cook the roll one day ahead and refrigerate in the sauce. Cover with foil. Reheat in the foil in a slow oven. Process, and reheat the sauce when serving.

Inspired by a recipe from Tiyang DiGregorio, wife of David Di-Gregorio, executive chef, The 95th Restaurant, Chicago, Illinois.

 ## Steak, Philippine Style
Bistek Filipino

The Filipinos have taken steak and added onions, soy sauce, and lime to make it their own. It is an easily prepared, elegant entree.

    one 8-ounce fillet of beef tenderloin
    Salt and pepper to taste
    4 tablespoons lime juice
    3 tablespoons soy sauce
    1 to 2 tablespoons oil
    1 small white onion, sliced into rings
    2 cloves garlic, minced

Pound the beef slightly to flatten. Season with salt and pepper. Add 1 tablespoon of lime juice and 2 teaspoons soy sauce. Rub into the steak. Let marinate for 20 minutes or longer. Heat pan. Add oil and sear the beef on both sides. Remove from the pan. Add the onion rings and garlic, and sauté until light brown. Add the remaining soy sauce and lime juice. Simmer for 30 seconds. Add the beef and toss gently. Pour the onions and sauce over the beef. Serve with sautéed vegetables such as baby carrots, green beans, or okra.

YIELD: 1 serving.

Inspired by a recipe from Executive Chef Martin Allies, Hyatt Regency, Manila.

Stuffed Tenderloin
Lomo Basilan

A delicious, easily prepared entree from the elegant Maynila Room of the famed Manila Hotel, where it is garnished with sautéed cauliflower, tomato, and carrots. Local kesong puti, cheese made from carabao milk, is used for this dish. They have suggested substituting Edam cheese.

One 6- to 8-ounce fillet of beef
½ ounce lobster meat
1 small fresh mushroom, sliced
½ ounce Edam cheese
Oil
Salt and pepper to taste

Trim the beef. Make a small cut in the steak and insert the lobster meat, mushroom slices, and Edam cheese. Rub the beef with oil. Season with salt and pepper. Broil. Serve the juice of the meat as the sauce.

YIELD: 1 serving.

TIP: Chopped shrimp may be substituted for the lobster meat.

Beef Casserole
Beef Caldereta

Braised beef and potatoes seasoned with herbs and onions, and served in a slightly spicy tomato sauce, is perfect for entertaining or on a cool winter's evening. This tastes even better when prepared one day before serving.

1 ½ pounds stewing beef, cut into 1½-inch cubes
½ cup cider vinegar
6 whole black peppercorns, crushed
3 cloves garlic, crushed
4 tablespoons oil
2 medium potatoes, peeled, cut into ½-inch cubes
1 medium onion, cut in half, thinly sliced
1 cup beef broth
1 cup tomato sauce
1 bay leaf

½ red bell pepper cut into ¼-inch strips
½ green bell pepper cut into ¼-inch strips
2 ounces liver sausage (optional)
1 teaspoon hot pepper sauce
Salt to taste
Garnish
¼ cup stuffed olives, sliced
2 hard-boiled eggs, sliced (optional)

Marinate beef in vinegar, peppercorns, and garlic for at least 30 minutes. Drain well. In 2 tablespoons oil, fry beef in batches until browned on all sides. Remove and set aside. Add 2 tablespoons oil. Add potatoes and fry until lightly browned. Remove and set aside. Add onion and more oil if necessary. Sauté on moderate heat, about 5 minutes, until soft but not browned. Add beef, beef broth, tomato sauce, and bay leaf. Bring to a boil. Reduce heat and simmer, covered, for 1½ hours. Add potatoes, and red and green peppers. Continue cooking until potato is soft but not overcooked. Add liver sausage and hot pepper sauce. Simmer another 2 minutes. Season to taste with salt if desired. Put in serving dish. Garnish with sliced stuffed olives and hard-boiled eggs. Serve with rice.

YIELD: 4 servings.

ADVANCE PREPARATION: The Caldereta may be prepared ahead and reheated at serving time.

 Oxtail Stew
Kare-Kare

Kare-kare *is one of the most traditional Filipino fiesta dishes and is usually served at the table in an earthenware pot simmering over a charcoal brazier. Serve the tender chunks of oxtail with the peanut sauce over rice. For a heartier dish, stew beef is sometimes added to the oxtails.*

2½ pounds oxtail, cut into 2- to 3-inch lengths, excess fat trimmed
½ pound stew beef, cut into 2-inch cubes (optional)
3 tablespoons oil
1 medium onion, sliced into paper-thin slices
2 teaspoons minced garlic
2 tablespoons annatto seeds crushed in ⅓ cup water, soaked for 20 minutes, strained

½ cup uncooked rice
⅓ cup creamy peanut butter
½ pound green beans, washed, trimmed
One ¾-pound Oriental eggplant, washed, stemmed, cut into 1-
    inch pieces
½ small cabbage, core removed, cut into 3-inch wedges
2 tablespoons fish sauce (patis), or to taste
Salt and pepper to taste

GARNISH:

1 green onion, sliced into thin slices
2 tablespoons celery leaves, chopped (optional)

Wipe oxtail pieces with a dampened towel. Place the oxtail in a large pot. Add enough water to cover. Bring to a boil and cook for 10 minutes. Drain oxtail and discard water. Wash oxtail under running water. Wash pan. Return oxtail to pan. Add beef if desired, and add water to cover. Bring to a boil. Lower the heat and simmer, partially covered, for 1½ hours or until meat is tender. Remove meat with slotted spoon. Set aside.

Add 2 tablespoons oil to a pan and heat on moderate heat. Add onion and garlic, and sauté on moderate heat until soft and translucent. Add the annatto water. Stir. Add the meat and 2 cups of the cooking liquid to the pan. Bring to a boil. Reduce the heat to low and simmer for 15 minutes.

Meanwhile, toast the rice in a dry pan over medium heat, shaking pan to allow grains to color evenly. Allow to cool and blend rice to a very fine powder in a processor or blender. Add the rice powder and peanut butter, stirring until smooth and well combined. Add the green beans, eggplant, and cabbage. Bring to a boil. Reduce heat to simmer and cook, uncovered, stirring occasionally, for 10 minutes or until vegetables are tender but not mushy. Add fish sauce (patis) and salt and pepper to taste. Serve from the casserole or from a deep heated bowl. Garnish with scallions and celery leaves. Serve with rice. Kare Kare is usually accompanied with extra fish sauce (patis), a hot sambal sauce, and Binagoongan Sauce.

YIELD: 6 servings.

TIPS: If Oriental eggplant is unavailable, substitute regular eggplant, cut into 1-inch pieces.

ADVANCE PREPARATION: The oxtails and beef may be cooked a day ahead and refrigerated. Add the rice, peanut butter, and vegetables several hours before serving. The flavors will improve upon standing.

Ox Tongue with Cheese and Tomato Sauce
Lengua al Bodeguero

Glenda Barretto, owner of the marvelous Via Mare Restaurants in Manila and Los Angeles, has provided an interesting dish. The Spanish influence, in the use of tomato paste, olives, and pimentos, is very much apparent. It is a dish loved by Filipinos and one that can be prepared ahead and reheated before serving.

    One 2½- to 3-pound ox or beef tongue
    ¼ cup soy sauce
    Oil for frying
    2 tablespoons olive oil
    1 tablespoon minced garlic
    2 tablespoons minced onion
    ½ cup tomato sauce
    ¼ cup tomato paste
    3 cups beef broth
    ½ cup white wine
    ¼ teaspoon crushed black peppercorns
    2 bay leaves
    ½ teaspoon fennel seeds
    1 cup grated Edam cheese
    1 cup sliced mushrooms
    ½ cup stuffed green olives
    1 teaspoon salt
    1 teaspoon pepper

When choosing tongue, the smaller tongues are preferable. Scrub the tongue well. In a pot, cover the tongue with boiling water. Simmer the tongue, skimming off any residue after the first 5 minutes. Simmer the tongue uncovered for 15 minutes. Remove the tongue. Peel off or scrape the outer skin. Remove the root ends, small bones, and gristle. Wash tongue thoroughly. Return the tongue to the pan and cook until tender, about 50 minutes per pound. Drain. Cool.

Rub the tongue with soy sauce. Cover the bottom of a skillet with oil, and heat. Fry the tongue until golden brown on all sides. Remove. Drain on paper towels. Cut into ¼-inch slices.

Heat 2 tablespoons olive oil on moderate heat. Sauté the garlic and onion until the onion is soft and translucent. Add the tomato sauce, tomato paste, beef broth, white wine, peppercorns, bay leaves, and fennel. Add the tongue and simmer for 10 to 15 minutes. Add the grated cheese, mushrooms, and green olives. Continue to simmer for

5 minutes longer. Season with salt and pepper to taste. Garnish with chopped parsley.

YIELD: 6 servings.

ADVANCE PREPARATION: Cook 1 to 2 days ahead. Refrigerate. Add the cheese, mushrooms, and olives, and finish cooking ½ hour before serving.

 ## Roast Pork Loin
Lechon

During a fiesta, a whole roast suckling pig is often served with a liver sauce. This is time-consuming to prepare, and I suggest you purchase your roast pig from an Asian grocery store.

Preparing a pork shoulder or loin with the skin intact is a simpler, easier-to-manage entree.

One 7-pound pork shoulder or loin with skin intact
2 cloves garlic, crushed
5 teaspoons salt
1 cup freshly ground black pepper

Rub the pork with garlic, salt, and pepper. Let stand for 1 hour, refrigerated. Preheat the oven to 500° F. Put the pork on a rack in a large roasting pan. Roast uncovered for 10 minutes. Reduce the heat to 300° F. Add 1 cup water to the pan, and roast the loin until tender, about 3½ hours. Transfer to a platter. Serve with *Lechon Sauce* (page 367).

YIELD: 12 servings.

TIP: The pork may also be roasted in a moderate oven, 325° F to 350° F for 35 to 40 minutes per pound.

 ## Braised Pork
Humba

Glenda Barretto, owner of Via Mare in Manila and Los Angeles, serves this sweet and sour, flavorful dish, which is excellent for a buffet, as it stands well and can be prepared several days in advance. It is an absolute winner!

> 2½ to 3 pounds pork shank, cut by your butcher into 2-inch
>   pieces
> ½ cup soy sauce
> 1 cup cider vinegar
> 2 tablespoons salted black beans (*tausi*)
> ½ cup whole peanuts, shelled, uncooked
> 2 teaspoons minced garlic
> 2 pieces bay leaves
> 1 teaspoon crushed black peppercorns
> 1 cup dark brown sugar
> 1½ tablespoons salted bean curd (optional)
> Parsley or coriander sprigs for garnish

Remove the tough skin and fat from the pork hock. (The Filipinos love the fat and would not remove all of the fat.) Cut the pork into 1½-inch cubes. Boil in water to cover for 10 minutes. Remove the pork and let drain in a colander. Reserve the boiling liquid for use as pork stock. Place the pork in a deep casserole. Combine the soy sauce, vinegar, black beans, peanuts, garlic, bay leaves, peppercorns, brown sugar, and bean curd. Add to the pork, and turn several times to cover pork with the marinade. Let marinate, refrigerated, overnight. Transfer the marinated pork and any remaining marinade to a pan. Add 4 cups of the reserved pork stock. Bring to a boil. Reduce the heat and let simmer for 2 hours, or until the pork is tender. Remove the pork. Reduce the sauce until slightly thickened. Pour over the pork. Garnish with parsley or coriander leaves.

YIELD: 6 servings.

VARIATION: 2 pounds pork loin may be substituted for pork shank.

TIPS: Glenda Barretto used pork belly, which contains a fair amount of fat. After the first boiling she removes the pork and cuts it into 1½-inch cubes. After this step, continue cooking as above.

Inspired by a recipe from Glenda Barretto, Via Mare, Manila.

Steamed Pork Loaf
Embutido

Philippine-style meat loaf topped with a tasty tomato sauce makes an easy family meal.

2 pounds ground pork
4 tablespoons chopped red bell pepper
4 tablespoons chopped green bell pepper
1 medium onion, chopped
2 tablespoons fine breadcrumbs
3 eggs, beaten
Salt and pepper to taste
6 pieces bacon

SAUCE:

1 tablespoon butter or oil
2 tablespoons olive oil
1 teaspoon minced garlic
¼ cup minced onion
1 cup tomato sauce
1 teaspoon brown sugar
Salt and pepper to taste

Combine the pork, peppers, onion, breadcrumbs, egg, and salt and pepper to taste. Shape the mixture into a loaf and wrap the bacon pieces around the loaf. Wrap the pork loaf with cheesecloth and secure with string. Steam over boiling water for approximately 45 minutes. Cool slightly. Cut into 1-inch slices. Arrange on a serving platter.

To prepare the sauce, melt butter and olive oil in a saucepan. Add the minced garlic and onion, and sauté until soft and translucent. Add the tomato sauce and brown sugar. Season to taste. Simmer until the sugar is dissolved and the sauce is slightly thickened. Pour over the Embutido.

YIELD: 4 servings.

VARIATION: Roll the meatloaf into a log shape, omitting the bacon. Wrap with aluminum foil, securing the ends. Bake in a 350° F oven for 1 hour.

ADVANCE PREPARATION: Prepare ahead completely. Reheat at serving time.

Inspired by a recipe from Glenda Barretto, Via Mare, Manila and Los Angeles.

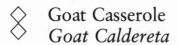

Goat Casserole
Goat Caldereta

The Ilocos region is an arid stretch in the north, where it is difficult to grow food. Daily food is simple, seasoned with lots of pungent bagoong. For feasting, a Caldereta, *magnificently cooked in rich sauce, is a favorite.*

Glenda Barretto, owner of the top-rated Via Mare restaurant in Manila, cooks to perfection! Her version of Caldereta is exciting, spicy, colorful, and tastes as good as it looks. It is a festive buffet dish that tastes even better when prepared one day ahead.

2 large ripe tomatoes, approximately 1 pound
2 pounds goat or lamb
2 teaspoons salt
½ cup lemon or lime juice
⅔ cup brandy
5 tablespoons olive oil
4 to 6 chicken livers or 1 small can liver spread
⅓ to ½ cup pitted green olives
5 cloves garlic, chopped
1 large onion, chopped
One 8-ounce can tomato sauce
1 tablespoon flour
2 cups beef stock
1 cup pimento, shredded into thin 1½-inch strips
2 to 3 fresh red chile peppers, seeded, minced
3 tablespoons grated cheddar cheese

Boil 3 cups water. Plunge the tomatoes into the water for about 30 seconds to loosen skins. Peel. Remove seeds. Chop.

Remove all the fat from the meat. Cut into 3-inch chunks. Combine salt and lemon juice and rub into the meat. Let marinate for 30 minutes to 1 hour. Run water over the meat and drain in a colander. Pour ⅓ cup brandy over the meat.

Heat a pan. Add 3 tablespoons olive oil and heat. Add the meat and fry, stirring, until it is lightly browned on all sides. Discard excess oil. Add enough water to cover the meat. Bring to a boil. Reduce the heat to simmer and cook until the meat is tender.

In the meantime, heat 2 tablespoons oil in a skillet. Add the liver, and sauté until cooked. (If using canned liver spread, this step is not necessary.) Remove and mash the liver. Set aside. Add the olives and fry just enough to seal the olives. Remove. Set aside. To the oil in the pan, add the garlic and onion, and sauté until the onion is soft and translucent. Add the tomatoes and tomato sauce and simmer for 5 minutes. Add the cooked meat, mashed liver, flour, and stock. Bring to a boil. Reduce the heat and simmer for 15 to 20 minutes. Add the pimentos, olives, chile pepper, and cheese. Simmer for another 2 to 3 minutes, stirring. Before serving, add remaining ⅓ cup brandy. Serve hot.

YIELD: 8 servings.

VARIATION: Beef or lamb may be substituted for goat's meat.

ADVANCE PREPARATION: Prepare 1 day ahead, refrigerate. Add the brandy when serving.

POULTRY

 ## Chicken and Pork Adobo

Adobo *might be considered the Philippine national dish. Many varia-tions of* adobo *exist, but the combination of chicken and pork is a favorite. It should have a subtle sourness from the vinegar, which also acts as a preservative.*

    2½ to 3 pounds chicken, cut into serving pieces
    2 garlic cloves, crushed
    1 bay leaf
    ½ cup palm or white vinegar
    1 teaspoon salt
    1 cup water
    1 pound boneless lean pork, cut in 1-inch cubes
    2 tablespoons oil
    2 tablespoons soy sauce

GARNISH:

Tomato wedges
Parsley sprigs

Remove wing tips, excess skin, and fat from chicken. Separate drumsticks and thighs. Cut the breast in half crosswise. In a pan, combine garlic, bay leaf, vinegar, salt, and water. Stir to mix. Add the chicken and pork. Stir to mix.

Bring the mixture to a boil. Reduce the heat and simmer for 30 minutes. Add ½ cup water and continue simmering until the chicken and pork are tender. Remove the garlic from the pan. Heat 2 tablespoons oil in a skillet. Add the garlic, and sauté until fragrant. Add the chicken and pork, about 6 pieces at a time, and fry until lightly browned on all sides, adding more oil if necessary. Add the soy sauce and cooking stock to the meat, and let simmer 5 minutes. To serve, pour the sauce over the chicken and pork. Garnish with tomato wedges and parsley sprigs. Serve hot with rice.

YIELD: 4 to 6 servings.

ADVANCE PREPARATION: Cook the chicken and pork 1 to 2 days ahead. Refrigerate in sauce mixture. Reheat in sauce at serving time.

Inspired by a recipe from Lourdes Fajardo, director, Maya Culinary Arts Center, Manila.

 ## Grilled Chicken, Philippine Style

A delicate balance of sweet and sour is found in this superb grilled chicken. Great for a barbecue!

½ cup pineapple juice
½ cup brown sugar
¼ cup soy sauce
2 teaspoons distilled white vinegar
1 teaspoon minced garlic
1 teaspoon minced ginger
1 tablespoon honey
¼ teaspoon freshly ground black pepper
2½ to 3 pounds chicken, cut into serving pieces

Combine pineapple juice, brown sugar, soy sauce, vinegar, garlic, ginger, honey, and black pepper. Marinate the chicken in the mixture for 4 hours, or overnight in refrigerator. Grill over charcoal or broil in oven until both sides are golden brown and the chicken is cooked. Baste both sides frequently with marinade.

YIELD: 3 to 4 servings.

FISH AND SEAFOOD

 ## Catfish in Coconut Sauce
Guinataang Hito

Tender, moist fish in a smooth coconut sauce with a hint of chile.

  2½ pounds catfish fillets
  Oil for frying
  2 tablespoons olive oil
  1 tablespoon chopped garlic
  1½ tablespoons chopped onion
  5 tablespoons cider vinegar
  1½ tablespoons soy sauce
  1 bay leaf
  2½ cups coconut milk
  1 to 2 chile peppers, seeds removed, thinly sliced
  Salt and pepper to taste

Wash catfish and pat dry. Heat oil to cover the bottom of the pan. Fry the catfish on both sides until golden brown. Remove and let drain on paper towels. Heat 2 tablespoons olive oil. Add the garlic and onion. Sauté over moderate heat until soft and transparent. Add the vinegar, soy sauce, bay leaf, and coconut milk. Bring to a boil and cook for 3 to 4 minutes. Add the fried catfish and chiles. Season to taste with salt and pepper. Simmer for 2 to 3 minutes to allow flavors to blend. Serve hot with rice.

YIELD: 6 servings with other dishes.

Inspired by a recipe from Glenda Barretto, Via Mare, Manila and Los Angeles.

Milkfish with Black Beans
Tocho

This is a family recipe from Rene Cortez of Thai Airways International Limited, which uses milkfish, the national fish of the Philippines. He says that "although there are many ways to savor the delicacy of the bangus (milkfish), the Tocho is one of the most original, being a favorite among the fishing villagers around the country." He suggests substituting Canadian whitefish for the traditional milkfish, although milkfish is available frozen in Asian markets.

⅓ cup oil
1 pound milkfish or Canadian whitefish fillets, cleaned, cut into
    1-inch pieces
2 cloves garlic, minced
2 teaspoons chopped ginger
1 medium onion, thinly sliced
1 small ripe tomato, finely chopped
1 tablespoon salted black beans (*tausi*), drained
1 tablespoon vinegar
¾ cup water
2 teaspoons sugar or to taste
Salt to taste

Heat oil in a skillet, and fry the fish until golden brown. Remove. Drain on paper towels. Discard all but 2 tablespoons of cooking oil. Heat on moderate temperature. Add the garlic, ginger, and onion, and sauté until the onion is soft and translucent. Add the tomato and cook until soft. Add the salted black beans, vinegar, ¾ cup water, and sugar. Simmer for 2 minutes. Add the fish and simmer another 3 minutes. Add salt to taste. Serve with rice.

YIELD: 3 to 4 servings.

Piquant Shrimp
Adobong Sugpo

Easily prepared tangy shrimp are quite often served by Glenda Barretto as a light luncheon or dinner dish in her Via Mare restaurants.

2 pounds shrimp, shelled, deveined
3 cloves garlic, chopped
1 cup wine vinegar
1 cup water
½ teaspoon freshly ground black pepper
Salt to taste
1 bay leaf
½ cup plus 2 tablespoons oil
¼ cup flour

Put the shrimp, garlic, vinegar, water, black pepper, salt, and bay leaf in a casserole. Bring to a boil. Reduce heat. Let simmer for 2 minutes. Remove the shrimp and strain the liquid.

Add ½ cup of oil to a pan. Heat over low flame. Add the flour, and stir constantly until the mixture is golden brown, being very careful not to burn. Add the strained liquid gradually, beating constantly with a wire wisk until the sauce is smooth. In another skillet, melt the remaining 2 tablespoons oil. Add the shrimp, and stir-fry for 1 to 2 minutes or until very lightly browned. Remove the shrimp and place on a serving plate. Pour the hot sauce over the shrimp. Serve immediately over hot rice.

YIELD: 4 to 6 servings.

SALADS AND VEGETABLES

 ## Bean Salad

½ pound fresh green beans, tips removed
1 small onion, thinly sliced
2 tablespoons light soy sauce
1 tablespoon lemon juice

1 teaspoon olive oil
Few drops hot pepper sauce
Salt and freshly ground pepper to taste
3 teaspoons chopped fresh mint
Mint leaves for garnish

Heat water to boiling. Add beans and cook until crisp-tender. Drain. Rinse with cold water. Drain. Place in a salad bowl. Add the onion. Combine the soy sauce, lemon, oil, hot pepper sauce, salt, and pepper. Add to the vegetables. Toss until all are coated. Refrigerate for 1 hour. When serving, sprinkle with chopped mint and garnish with mint leaves.

YIELD: 3 servings.

 ## Green Beans, Philippine Style
Guisadong Sitaw

Green beans are elevated to a new level in this hearty, colorful dish.

¼ pound boneless pork with some fat, cut into strips
½ cup water
1 clove garlic, minced
1 small onion, sliced
1 medium tomato, coarsely chopped
1 tablespoon fish sauce (*patis*)
½ teaspoon sugar
½ teaspoon salt
⅛ teaspoon freshly ground black pepper
¼ pound shrimp, peeled, deveined, cut into ⅓-inch pieces
¾ cup chicken stock or water
½ pound julienned green beans

Simmer pork with ½ cup water in a skillet over medium heat until all the water evaporates and the pork fat appears. Stir for 1 to 2 minutes. Remove the pork and set aside. Add garlic and onion, and cook on medium heat, stirring, until onion is transparent. Add tomatoes. Sauté until the mixture is soft and mushy. Add the pork, fish sauce, sugar, salt, and pepper. Add the shrimp, and cook, stirring, for 1 minute. Add the stock, and let come to a boil. Add the green beans, and cook, covered, stirring occasionally, until the beans are done, about 7 minutes. Serve hot.

YIELD: 3 to 4 servings.

Steamed Asparagus

An easily prepared vegetable dish that can be steamed or microwaved.

1 pound fresh asparagus
2 tablespoons butter
1 teaspoon fresh lemon juice
Salt to taste

Wash asparagus. Snap off the lower part of the stalks where they break easily. Tie the asparagus in serving bunches with kitchen string. Place them upright in an asparagus steamer or in a deep pan such as the bottom of a double boiler. Add boiling water to cover the bottom of the stalks about 1 inch. Cover and cook for 8 to 10 minutes, or until tender. Add butter, lemon juice, and salt. Serve.

Microwave Method: Snap off asparagus tips. Wash, leaving residual water. Place in a 1-quart casserole, turning half of the spears in the opposite direction to ensure even cooking. Cover and cook at high for 4 to 6 minutes or until done. Add butter, lemon juice, and salt.

YIELD: 4 servings.

Snow Peas with Shrimp
Guisadong Chicharo

An easily prepared, colorful stir-fry combining crispy green snow peas with delicate shrimp.

3 tablespoons oil
3 garlic cloves, minced
1 small onion, chopped
6 medium shrimp, shelled, deveined
1 pound snow peas, strings removed
2 tablespoons soy sauce
2 tablespoons rice wine or dry sherry
Freshly ground black pepper to taste

Heat oil in a wok or frying pan. Add garlic and onion, and stir-fry until onion is light brown. Add the shrimp. Stir-fry 45 seconds. Add the snow peas, and stir-fry 45 seconds. Add the soy sauce and rice wine. Cover. Cook on medium-high heat for 1½ minutes, or until snow peas are crisp-tender. Add black pepper. Mix. Serve.

YIELD: 4 servings.

RICE, NOODLES, AND WRAPPERS

Fried Noodles with Pork, Shrimp, and Vegetables
Pancit Mami Guisado

While in Manila, I always look forward to enjoying soul-satisfying Pancit *in neighborhood restaurants.* Pancit *is a much loved noodle dish that can be made with egg or rice noodles and cooked in many variations.*

Pancit Mami Guisado, *made with egg noodles, can be a hearty one-dish meal or part of a buffet. It is attractive and colorful and makes a beautiful presentation. Philippine San Miguel beer is tasty with this dish.*

½ pound boneless pork
1 chicken breast, skinned
2 Chinese sausages
1 teaspoon salt
1 pound fresh thin Chinese egg noodles
5 tablespoons oil
2 cloves garlic, minced
1 small onion, peeled, chopped
2 carrots, cut into 1½-inch shreds
2 celery stalks, leaves discarded, thinly sliced on the diagonal
1 teaspoon paprika
¼ pound shrimp, shelled, deveined, cut into ¼-inch cubes
2 to 4 tablespoons fish sauce *(patis)*

GARNISH:

2 hard-boiled eggs, quartered lengthwise
½ cup bean sprouts, blanched in boiling water 15 seconds, drained
6 snow peas, blanched in boiling water for 1½ minutes, drained

¼ cup finely sliced green onions
2 lemons or limes cut into 6 wedges

In a heavy 3- to 4-quart saucepan, add pork, chicken, sausage, and salt. Add water to cover by at least 1 inch. Bring to a boil. Reduce heat. Cover and simmer 15 to 20 minutes or until chicken is done. Remove chicken and set aside. Continue cooking pork and sausage until pork is tender, approximately 20 minutes longer. Remove meats with a slotted spoon, reserving cooking liquid. Cut pork into 1½-inch julienne strips. Cut 1 sausage into ¼-inch cubes. Cut the second sausage on the diagonal into ⅛-inch slices. Set aside for garnish. Remove the bones from the chicken and tear into 1½-inch-thin shreds.

In a large pan, bring reserved cooking liquid to a boil. If the amount of water is insufficient to cook the noodles, add more hot water. Add the noodles, stirring constantly to prevent them from sticking to the pan. When the water returns to a boil, cook for 1 minute or until the noodles are *al dente* (tender to the bite). Be careful not to overcook. Remove the noodles, drain, and rinse with cold water to prevent further cooking. Toss with 1 tablespoon oil. Set aside.

Heat 2 tablespoons oil in a pan over moderate heat. Add garlic and onion and cook, stirring frequently, until soft but not brown. Add the carrot and celery, and stir-fry for 1 minute. Remove. Add 1 tablespoon oil. Add the paprika, shrimp, pork, sausage, and chicken. Stir-fry for 1 minute or until the shrimp is firm and pink. Add cooked vegetables, and stir-fry until heated throughout. Cover and remove pan from heat.

Heat 1 tablespoon oil in a heavy 10- or 12-inch skillet. Add the noodles, and toss until heated through, about 2 to 3 minutes. Add the fish sauce *(patis)* to taste, and stir until evenly mixed.

To serve, mound the noodles on a heated platter. Reheat the chicken and vegetable topping, and spoon over the noodles. Garnish the edge of the platter with alternating egg wedges, clusters of bean sprouts, and snow peas. Sprinkle the green onions over the top. Arrange sausage slices and lemon wedges over the green onions.

YIELD: 6 to 8 servings.

TIP: If fresh Chinese egg noodles are unavailable, ½ pound of dried thin egg noodles or fettucine may be substituted. Cook according to package directions.

ADVANCE PREPARATIONS: The sauce may be prepared one day in advance. Reheat at serving time. The noodles may be cooked one day ahead, tossed with 1 tablespoon oil, placed in a plastic bag, and refrigerated. Reheat the noodles in boiling water at serving time. Prepare garnishes and refrigerate, covered. If desired, the *Pancit* may be prepared ahead, covered with foil, and kept warm in a 250° F oven for approximately 30 minutes. Garnish when serving.

Inspired by a recipe from Tiyang DiGregorio, wife of David Di-Gregorio, executive chef, The 95th Restaurant, Chicago, Illinois.

 ## Bean Thread Noodles with Chicken
Sotanghon Guisado I

Rene Cortez shares his mother's recipe for this delicate treat combining interesting textures and tastes.

One 2½-pound chicken, trimmed of fat
2 tablespoons oil
2 cloves garlic, minced
1 small onion, minced
6 ounces peeled, deveined small shrimp
1 teaspoon paprika
1 carrot, cut into 1½-inch shreds
8 snow peas, cut on the diagonal into shreds
½ pound bean threads (*sotanghon*), soaked in warm water for 10
    to 20 minutes or until soft, drained, cut into 4-inch lengths
2 teaspoons soy sauce
2 tablespoons fish sauce (*patis*)
Salt and pepper to taste
1 green onion, shredded into 1½-inch lengths

Place chicken in a pot and cover with water by about 2 inches. Bring the water to a boil. Reduce the heat to a simmer. Cook the chicken, skimming off any foam that comes to the surface, until the chicken is tender, about 30 to 35 minutes. Remove the chicken from the pot. Let cool. Strain the broth. Set aside. Remove all the meat from the cooked chicken. Discard the skin, and cut the chicken meat into thin strips.

In a wok or frying pan, heat the oil. Sauté the garlic and onion until the onion is soft and transparent. Add the shrimp, and cook until pink. Add the chicken meat, and stir-fry for 30 seconds. Add the paprika and 2 cups of the reserved chicken broth, and bring to a boil over high heat. Stir in the carrot and snow peas, and cook until the vegetables are crispy tender, about 2 minutes. Add the bean threads. Season to taste with soy sauce and fish sauce. Simmer until the noodles are heated through, about 1 minute. Add salt and pepper if desired. Remove and place in a large bowl. Garnish with green onion.

YIELD: 4 to 6 servings.

Inspired by a recipe from Rene Cortez, area sales manager, Pacific Northwest–Central USA, Thai Airways International Ltd.

Bean Thread Noodles with Shrimp and Pork
Sotanghon Guisado II

Another winner from Glenda Barretto, who combines shrimp, pork, and vegetables in this tasty noodle dish.

3 tablespoons oil
1 tablespoon annatto seeds (optional)
1 tablespoon chopped garlic
1 small onion, sliced
½ pound lean boneless pork, shredded into 1½-inch pieces
½ pound shrimp, shelled, deveined
2½ cups chicken stock
¼ cup celery, shredded into 1½-inch pieces
½ cup shredded cabbage
2 carrots, shredded into 1½-inch lengths
6 ounces bean threads (*sotanghon*), soaked in warm water until
    soft, about 20 minutes, drained, cut into 4-inch lengths
2 to 3 tablespoons fish sauce (*patis*), or salt and pepper to taste
1 green onion, shredded into 1½-inch lengths
Coriander leaves for garnish
2 hard-boiled eggs, sliced

Heat oil on medium heat. Add annatto seeds and fry 15 seconds. Remove the annatto seeds with a spatula and discard. Add the garlic and onion, and sauté until golden. Add the shredded pork, shrimp, and chicken stock. Bring to a boil. Reduce heat. Simmer for 2 to 3 minutes, or until pork and shrimp are almost cooked. Add celery, cabbage, and carrots, and cook for 2 minutes or until crispy tender. Add the bean threads and stir until heated through. Season to taste with fish sauce or salt and pepper. Serve garnished with green onions, coriander, and sliced eggs.

YIELD: 6 servings.

Inspired by a recipe from Glenda Barretto, Via Mare Restaurant, Manila.

Rice Noodles with Shrimp Sauce
Pancit Luglug

In this attractive, aromatic Philippine dish, rice noodles are elevated to a higher level! Rice noodles are dipped into boiling water, drained, placed on a serving dish, covered with a luscious shrimp sauce, and topped with sautéed pork, smoked fish, coriander, green onions, and egg slices.

2 pounds shrimp, shelled, deveined (reserve shells)
¼ cup annatto seeds (optional)
½ pound pork loin
3 tablespoons oil
1 tablespoon finely minced garlic
1 cup finely minced onion
1 tablespoon fish sauce *(patis)*
Salt and freshly ground black pepper to taste
2 tablespoons cornstarch dissolved in 4 tablespoons water
8 ounces rice sticks, soaked about 20 minutes in boiling water
        until softened, drained
1 cup finely flaked smoked fish (optional)
1 cup pork cracklings, pounded to a powder (optional)
6 tablespoons chopped coriander or parsley leaves
6 tablespoons finely sliced green onions
2 hard-boiled eggs, sliced
6 lime wedges

Puree shrimp shells in a food processor. Add ¾ cup water, and process for 1 to 2 minutes. Strain and reserve the juice. Add annatto seeds to 1 cup hot water. Let stand for 20 minutes. Press the seeds between the fingers to release the red color. Strain the water and discard the seeds. Set aside.

Boil the pork in water to cover until tender. Remove and cut into ½-inch cubes. Reserve the cooking liquid. In a wok or large skillet, heat oil. Add garlic and onion, and sauté until the onion is soft. Add the pork cubes and shrimp. Stir to mix. Add the shrimp juice, reserved pork stock, annatto water, and fish sauce. Season to taste with salt and pepper. Bring to a boil. Recombine cornstarch mixture and cook, stirring, until thickened. Remove from the heat. Set aside.

Bring 5 quarts water to a boil. Add rice noodles. Stir to separate. When water returns to a boil, remove. Drain. Place on a large platter. Arrange shrimp and pork mixture on top of the noodles. This may also be served in separate bowls, if desired. Garnish with smoked fish flakes, pork cracklings, coriander, green onions, and egg slices. Serve hot with lime wedges and fish sauce.

YIELD: 6 to 8 servings.

TIP: Substitute ½ cup shrimp bisque for shrimp juice, and smoked oysters for smoked fish.

ADVANCE PREPARATION: Prepare the shrimp sauce and garnish ahead. Reheat shrimp sauce and boil noodles when serving.

Inspired by a recipe from Glenda Barretto, Via Mare Restaurant, Manila.

 ## Fresh Spring Roll Wrappers
Lumpia Wrappers

---

2 eggs, lightly beaten
2 cups flour
Pinch of salt
2 cups water
2 tablespoons oil
Flour for waxed paper

Combine eggs, flour, salt, and water in a bowl, and stir until a smooth batter is formed.

Processor method: Process to a rapid sift the flour and salt. Add the eggs and oil. With the machine running, pour cold water through the food chute within 8 seconds. Process 5 seconds. Scrape down the sides of the container. Process 10 seconds. Stop the motor and scrape down the sides of the container. Process a few seconds longer. Allow the batter to rest for 30 minutes. (If there is froth on top of the batter when ready to cook the wrappers, remove before cooking.)

Heat an 8-inch skillet, preferably nonstick, over moderate heat. Lightly oil the frying pan with a piece of paper toweling dipped in oil and rubbed over the heated pan. Using a ladle, pour in just enough batter to cover the bottom of the pan, about 2 tablespoons. Swirl the pan very quickly to make a very thin coating over the bottom of the pan. Cook the wrapper for a few seconds until it begins to curl away from the edges of the pan. Turn over and cook the other side for a few seconds. Remove the wrapper and transfer it to lightly floured waxed paper. Continue the process until all of the batter is used. The wrappers may be stacked between the layers of waxed paper, flour side down, and wrapped with foil and refrigerated, or frozen for up to one month.

YIELD: Twenty-four 8-inch-diameter wrappers, approximately.

TIP: *Lumpia* or spring roll wrappers may be purchased frozen in Asian markets.

SAUCES

 ## Liver Sauce
Lechon Sauce

2 cups liver paté, mashed
1 cup cider vinegar
2 cups water
1½ cups fine bread crumbs
1 cup sugar
2 bay leaves, crushed
2 teaspoons salt
½ teaspoon black pepper
2 tablespoons oil
6 tablespoons finely minced garlic
2 cups finely minced onion

Combine liver paté, vinegar, water, bread crumbs, sugar, bay leaf, salt, and pepper. Mix well. Set aside.

Heat 2 tablespoons oil in a pan. Add garlic and onion, and sauté until onion is soft and translucent. Add the liver mixture. Cook over medium heat until thickened, stirring frequently. Serve with *Lechon*.

YIELD: 8 cups, approximately.

TIP: The amount of sauce is for a 7-pound roast pork shoulder or loin.

ADVANCE PREPARATION: Prepare 1 day ahead. Reheat when serving.

Sweet and Sour Sauce
Agre Dulce

A tangy, sweet sauce usually served with Lumpia Shanghai.

1 cup chicken broth
¼ cup white vinegar
¼ cup sugar
1 teaspoon soy sauce
1 tablespoon tomato ketchup
¼ teaspoon freshly ground black pepper
1½ tablespoons cornstarch dissolved in 3 tablespoons water

In a pan, combine chicken broth, white vinegar, sugar, soy sauce, ketchup, and black pepper. Bring to a boil. Add cornstarch mixture, and stir until sauce has thickened and is translucent. Serve warm with *Lumpia Shanghai* (page 368).

YIELD: 1½ cups, approximately.

TIP: If you prefer a Hot and Sour Sauce, add 1 teaspoon of red pepper sauce as a substitute for the black pepper.

ADVANCE PREPARATION: Prepare sauce 1 to 2 days ahead. Reheat at serving time.

Garlic Sauce

¼ cup tightly packed brown sugar
¼ cup light soy sauce
1½ cups chicken stock
2 tablespoons cornstarch dissolved in 4 tablespoons water
2 cloves garlic, minced

Combine the sugar, soy sauce, and stock. Cook for 2 minutes. Add the dissolved cornstarch, and cook, stirring constantly, over high heat until sauce thickens. Serve the sauce hot, sprinkled with minced garlic.

Inspired by a recipe from the Maynila Room, Manila Hotel.

DESSERTS, SWEETS, AND SNACKS

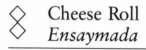

Cheese Roll
Ensaymada

Here is a popular Philippine treat, topped with cheese and sugar, which is often served during afternoon tea or merienda. *It is one of my family's favorite breakfast treats!*

Glenda Barretto prepares this in individual Ensaymada *molds. I have substituted one large layer pan.*

⅓ cup warm water (105–115°F)
½ cup sugar
1 package active dry yeast
2½ to 2¾ cups sifted flour
½ teaspoon salt
3 eggs
¾ cup soft butter
½ cup grated Edam cheese
1 tablespoon sugar for topping

Warm ⅓ cup water and ½ teaspoon sugar in a pan until the temperature reaches between 105° F and 115° F. Stir to dissolve sugar. Sprinkle the yeast on top of the water mixture, and let it proof until a light brown frothy head appears, approximately 5 minutes.

In a large bowl, mix 1½ cups flour, salt, and remaining sugar. Then mix in the proofed yeast mixture. Add eggs, one at a time, mixing with a wooden spoon after each egg. Mix in the remaining flour with a wooden spoon until well combined. Turn out the dough on a lightly floured smooth surface and knead for 5 to 10 minutes. (The dough should have a smooth satin finish. Gradually add a little flour if dough is too wet.) Put dough in a lightly greased large bowl. Cover with a dry towel or plastic wrap, and let it rise slowly at room temperature, free from drafts, until it doubles in bulk (about 1½ hours).

Generously butter the bottom and sides of an 8-inch layer pan. Turn out the dough onto a lightly floured surface. Roll out the dough into a ³⁄₁₆-inch-thick sheet, about 8 inches wide and 26 inches long. Spread with ¼ cup of the softened butter, and sprinkle with half of the grated cheese. Roll, jelly-roll fashion, from the long edge into a thin log shape. Form into snakelike coils or twists. Starting at the outside edge of the buttered pan, leaving spaces in between, turn dough into a coil twisting it at the same time. Cover with a dry cloth. Let rise in a warm place until double in bulk, about 1 hour. Preheat oven to 350° F. Bake for 25 to 30 minutes or until golden brown. Remove. While hot, brush with remaining softened butter and sprinkle with remaining 1 tablespoon sugar and grated cheese. Serve *Ensaymada* warm or at room temperature.

YIELD: 4 to 6 servings or 1 large Ensaymada.

Inspired by a recipe from Glenda Barretto, Via Mare Restaurant, Manila.

 ### Coconut Sweets
Maja Blanca

A delicately flavored, creamy dessert or snack—comfort food at its best!

½ cup unsweetened coconut flakes
1½ cups sugar
1 cup cornstarch
½ cup water
Two 14-ounce cans coconut milk
2 cups evaporated milk
1 tablespoon grated lemon or lime rind

In a skillet, brown coconut flakes on low heat. Remove. Set aside.

In a bowl, combine sugar, cornstarch, and water. Mix until cornstarch is dissolved and a smooth mixture is formed. Set aside. In a pan, combine coconut milk, evaporated milk, and lemon or lime. Boil for 5 minutes. Gradually add cornstarch mixture, stirring constantly. Cook, stirring over medium heat, until sugar is dissolved and the mixture has thickened, about 2 to 3 minutes. Pour into an oiled 12½ by 8½-inch pan. Allow to cool and set. Sprinkle toasted coconut on top. To serve, cut into squares.

YIELD: 8 servings.

Inspired by a recipe from Glenda Barretto, Via Mare Restaurant, Manila.

◇ Creme Caramel
Leche Flan

Here is Spanish-influenced comfort food at its best!

CARAMEL:

> 1 cup sugar
> ⅓ cup water

CUSTARD:

> Two 12-ounce cans evaporated milk
> One 14-ounce can sweetened condensed milk
> 12 egg yolks, lightly beaten
> 1 teaspoon vanilla, or 1 tablespoon finely grated fresh lemon or
>   lime rind

Prepare the caramel: Place sugar and water in a saucepan and swirl (shake pan with circular motion) over moderately high heat until the sugar has completely dissolved. Then let the sugar boil, swirling the pan occasionally, until the syrup turns a molasses brown. This will take approximately 10 minutes. Remove saucepan from the heat as soon as the desired color is reached. If you let it darken too much, it will have a bitter taste. Pour the carmelized syrup into a flan mold or individual heatproof small bowls or cups, tilting and swirling the molds to evenly coat the entire bottom. Be very careful not to burn yourself, as the syrup is very hot.

Preheat the oven to 325° F. To prepare the custard, combine the evaporated and condensed milks, egg yolks, and vanilla or grated lemon or lime rind. Stir lightly to prevent bubbles or foam from forming. Strain through a fine sieve into the caramel-coated flan mold. Place the filled mold into a large baking pan and place on the middle shelf of the oven. Pour boiling water into the baking pan to come halfway up the mold. Bake for 40 minutes to 1 hour, or until a knife inserted in the center of the custard comes out clean. (Do not allow the baking water to come to a boil or the outer perimeter of the custard will cook too fast.) Remove from the oven and cool to room temperature. When cool, cover with plastic wrap or aluminum foil and refrigerate until thoroughly chilled, preferably for 8 hours.

To serve, run a knife around the edge of the mold. Holding the mold and the plate firmly together, turn them over. Tap the plate on a flat surface to allow the custard to slide out onto the serving plate. Serve chilled.

YIELD: 6 to 8 servings.

ADVANCE PREPARATION: Prepare 1 to 2 days ahead. Refrigerate covered. Unmold just before serving.

Inspired by a recipe from Lourdes Fajardo, director, The Maya Culinary Arts Center, Manila.

 ## Banana Rolls
Turon

A favorite snack served during afternoon merienda *in the Philippines. It is a perfect ending to dinner.*

4 tablespoons sugar
4 tablespoons sesame seeds
4 large ripe plantain bananas, sliced lengthwise ¼ inch thick
8 *lumpia* wrappers
1 egg, lightly beaten
3 to 4 cups oil
½ cup powdered sugar

Sprinkle sugar and sesame seeds on a banana slice. Place a second banana slice on top of the sugar and sesame seed mixture. Repeat with remaining banana slices.

To assemble, place a filled banana on the lower third of the wrapper. Fold the portion of the wrapper nearest you over the filling until just covered. Turn the wrapper again to enclose the banana securely. Moisten the left and right hand edges of the wrapper with egg. Fold over the corners and press down firmly to seal, making an envelope. Moisten the flap of the envelope with egg and turn, rolling firmly into a cylinder. Seal firmly. Set aside, seam side down. Repeat with remaining slices.

Heat oil in a wok to 375° F. Place 4 or 5 *turon* at a time in the hot oil. Fry until crisp and golden. Remove with a skimmer and drain on paper towels. Serve hot, sprinkled with powdered sugar.

YIELD: 8 banana rolls.

ADVANCE PREPARATION: The rolls may be prepared ahead and refrigerated, covered with plastic wrap. Fry at serving time.

Tropical Fruit Potpourri
Halo-Halo

While in the Philippines, I enjoyed this cool, refreshing delight many times. It represents the Filipino's desire to make a pleasant concoction by combining many favorites. This is a suggested recipe, but you may use any fruits or sweetened canned fruits you desire.

A prepared Halo-Halo *mixture is available in Asian markets. If you wish to be truly Filipino, you will add your own ingredients to the prepared mix to make your own concoction. This is a refresher in which almost anything goes!*

> 1 tablespoon sugar palm seeds *(kaong)*
> 1 tablespoon jackfruit
> 1 tablespoon coconut flesh *(macapuno)*
> 1 tablespoon sweet kidney beans
> 1 tablespoon sweet garbanzos
> 1 tablespoon sweetened plantain or yam *(ube)*
> 1 tablespoon sweetened corn kernels
> 1 tablespoon *Leche Flan* (page 00)
> Crushed ice to fill tall glass
> ⅓ cup evaporated milk, approximately
> Ice cream, coconut or other flavor of choice (optional)
> Maraschino cherries for garnish (optional)

Spoon the sweetened fruits, beans, corn, and flan into a tall glass. Add crushed ice to the top. Pour the evaporated milk over the mixture. Top with ice cream and maraschino cherries if desired. Serve with long-stemmed spoons.

YIELD: 1 serving.

Ginger Tea
Salabat

A sweet and spicy "tea" served during afternoon merienda.

During the Christmas season, there is often a pot of Salabat *brewing, as it is said to be good for the vocal chords. Since there is much caroling, this is a must!*

> ½ cup thinly sliced fresh ginger
> 6 cups water
> ½ cup packed light brown sugar

Gently boil the ginger in the water for about 30 minutes. Strain. Add the sugar and stir until dissolved. Serve hot.

YIELD: 4 to 6 servings.

TIP: If ginger flavor is too strong, add more boiling water.

Inspired by a recipe from Glenda Barretto, Via Mare Restaurant, Manila and Los Angeles.

VIETNAM

Moi qui vi cung den thu thuc an Viet Nam!
Welcome to Vietnamese cuisine!

Stretching a thousand miles long from China to the Gulf of Thailand, Vietnam is often described as a long bamboo pole with a rice basket hanging from each end. The fertile deltas of the Red River in the north and the Mekong River in the south are separated from each other by a long, narrow stretch of mountainous coastal land. These three areas have produced three regional cuisines, each identified with their major cities: Hanoi in the north, Hue in the center, and Saigon (Ho Chi Minh City) in the south.

The Vietnamese are of mixed Malay and Chinese origins. As in all of Southeast Asia, there was a strong Indian cultural influence in earlier ages, which remains in the form of widespread Buddhism. Ten centuries of Chinese rule have left an indelible stamp on Vietnamese culture and cuisine, and so to a lesser extent have the French, who colonized the country in the late sixteenth century. One result of this history is a distinct, highly complex, sophisticated cuisine that shares many ingredients with other Southeast Asian countries but shows strong Chinese and French influences.

Bach Ngo and Gloria Zimmerman, authors of *The Classic Cuisine of Vietnam,* first introduced me many years ago to the colorful, healthy, refreshing, and delightful cuisine of Vietnam. Ever since, it has been a favorite of my family. (I must make a disclaimer here: Although the rest of this book is based on my travels in Southeast Asia, Vietnam has not exactly welcomed American tourists in recent decades, and my experiences with Vietnamese food have been in this country. Fortunately, a number of Vietnamese immigrants, many of

375

them here in Illinois, have shared their knowledge, cooking skills, and memories of home with me.)

The northern region around Hanoi lies closest to China, and the food here shows the strongest Chinese influence. Stir-fried dishes, stews, soups, and the soupy rice porridge known as *chao* are popular. Northern food tends to be less hot and spicy than in central and southern Vietnam because there are fewer spices available. Black pepper and ginger are the predominant seasonings. Vegetables are usually cooked, as opposed to the south, where cooked foods are often combined with raw vegetables to give varied tastes and textures.

Tuan Nguyen, owner of Pasteur Restaurant in Chicago, introduced me to one of the favorite dishes of Hanoi, the beef and noodle soup *Pho Bo*. In Vietnam, and in Vietnamese neighborhoods in this country, this tasty soup is served all day long—for breakfast, midday snack, lunch, dinner, or after the movies. As people from the north have migrated south, it has become a favorite throughout Vietnam.

Although it is sometimes served in restaurants, *pho* is basically street or marketplace food. The aroma and taste will vary from one vendor to another, but the base is always a rich, aromatic beef stock. With a large wire strainer in one hand, the *pho* chef dips the noodles and bean sprouts in the boiling stock just long enough to heat the noodles and blanch the bean sprouts; with the other hand, he immerses a ladleful of beef into the stock to lightly cook the thinly sliced meat. He then puts the noodles and beef in a bowl, tops them with the boiling stock, and garnishes it with coriander. Southern-style *pho* restaurants also set out fish sauce, lime wedges, chiles, bean sprouts, and hot sauce for seasoning each bowl to taste.

In central Hue, the ancient imperial capital of Vietnam, the food is highly sophisticated, reflecting the pleasures of the royal palate. Spicing is more elaborate, with liberal use of chile peppers, and beautifully decorated presentations are *de rigueur*. Favorite dishes of this region include Sound Crepe, a combination crepe and omelet filled with shrimp, pork, mushrooms, bean sprouts, and coriander, named for the sound the batter makes when it hits the griddle, and Grilled Beef in Rice Papers, in which beef marinated in lemon grass, garlic, fish sauce, and seasonings is grilled, then wrapped in soft white rice papers along with cucumber, mint, and coriander, and dipped in the zesty hot sauce *nuoc cham*.

Ngoan Le, special assistant to the governor for Asian American affairs (Governor James R. Thompson, Illinois) is from Dalat, a former French resort in the central highlands south of Hue. This beautiful mountainous region, with its gorgeous waterfalls and pine forests, produces various kinds of lettuce, avocados, plums, strawberries, and cabbages, plus many other delectable vegetables. Because of the

mountains, the area is not suitable for rice growing. Large tea planta-
tions are located in the cool, dense forests.

Ngoan smiled frequently as she recalled fond memories of her
childhood there. She explained that mealtime is not as well-defined as
it is here in America and that often each meal is of the same degree of
heartiness. A typical breakfast at home in the city might be French
bread freshly purchased from the local bakery, dipped in sugar, devoured with condensed milk. Sometimes a child would eat a whole
loaf by himself.

Stopping on the way to school with her friends at her favorite
vendor, she would purchase *banh mi thit,* a mouth-watering sand-
wich on French bread. After toasting the bread over a charcoal fire
until it was just the perfect crunchiness and temperature, the vendor
sliced it and loaded it with wonderful delectables: a soft, spreadable
pork liver paté; next, a thin slice of another paté made from ground
pork, or some slices of barbecued pork, or head cheese; then *goi,*
shredded Chinese turnip, carrots, and cucumbers marinated in vinegar and a touch of sugar and chiles. This marvelous treat was topped
off with fresh mayonnaise, lettuce, coriander, and a hot spicy sauce.
All her friends would relish this treasure as they walked along together. In her words, this glorious creation "was heaven."

During school recesses, Ngoan and her classmates would run out
to the street vendors to snack on *qua,* freshly squeezed juice of
mangoes, guavas, or other succulent fruits in season. On the way
home from school, a favorite afternoon snack was *che,* warm or
chilled, pleasingly sweet soups. Her favorite was *che chuoi,* prepared
with slices of banana, sugar, tapioca pearls, and coconut milk, topped
with rich coconut cream.

Lee Tran, owner of Ba Le Restaurant in Chicago, serves many
varieties of *che,* all of them gratifying comfort foods. *Che bap,* made
from sticky rice and corn topped with coconut cream, and *che dau
trang,* black-eyed peas with sweet rice topped with rich coconut milk,
are reminiscent of snack foods I was served in Thailand. Because they
are very rich, they are rarely served as a dessert and are not included
in this chapter. Dessert in Vietnam is usually succulent fresh fruit or,
on special occasions, Coconut Flan.

In the hot, humid south, exotic fruits, sugarcane, vegetables, and
large coconut and rice crops grow in the fertile soils of the Mekong
River delta. Locally grown sugarcane and coconut are widely used;
one local favorite is *chao tom,* a delicious shrimp and pork paste that is
molded on sugarcane and grilled or baked.

Chinese, Indian, and French influences mingle in the food of
Saigon. In the delectable *banh cuon* (steamed rolled ravioli), an In-
dian-style thin ground-rice batter is poured onto a piece of muslin to

steam briefly. The soft crepe is gently scraped off and filled with a Chinese-influenced stuffing of minced pork and chopped Chinese black fungi. This tasty morsel is accompanied by a dipping sauce of fish sauce, vinegar, sugar, and chiles, with fresh mint and coriander for garnish.

Southern Vietnamese food is often spicier, sweeter, and heartier than in other parts of the country. Coconut milk is common, as are pineapples, tomatoes, and bean sprouts. A strong French influence shows in the fondness for long loaves of crusty white bread and the wide variety of ground pork products, all known by the French term *paté*. One of Ngoan's favorites is *paté chaud,* a seasoned pork ball wrapped in puff pastry, which is widely sold in bakeries.

Ngoan described three different kinds of soups common in Vietnamese cuisine. The first type is served early in a meal and is often Chinese in influence; Asparagus Crab Soup is an example. The second type, such as Hot and Sour Shrimp Soup, can be served over rice and is usually one of the main dishes of the meal. The third type is noodle soups, of which she says there must be at least twenty versions using different types of noodles, various toppings, and broths. These are a meal in themselves. A typical example is *hu tieu,* transparent bean threads in a chicken and pork stock with dried shrimp. This is topped with thinly sliced barbecued pork, shrimp, pork liver, coriander, a thin grasslike herb called *he,* and fried shallots.

Another southern favorite is *cha gio,* deep-fried spring rolls wrapped in lettuce and dipped in *nuoc cham.* Although we think of them as an appetizer, they are traditionally a full meal and are usually reserved for a special occasion such as a weekend get-together. Usually the mother and daughter are recruited to prepare these tasty delights, which take all day to make. The longest time is in cutting each ingredient to its proper size: mincing a large piece of pork, cutting carrots into very thin shreds, and onions and mushrooms into very thin slices. Today, Ngoan still cuts all the ingredients by hand, except for the pork, which she purchases already ground.

Rice is the staple of all areas. The Vietnamese prefer the long-grain type, which cooks up dry and flaky, and it appears in every meal. The long coastline, the Red River, and the Mekong have abundant supplies of seafood and fish, which is considered daily fare.

Fish sauce, *nuoc mam,* a salty, pungent sauce derived from fermented tiny anchovies, is another ingredient found throughout Vietnamese cooking. Playing the same role as soy sauce in Chinese cooking, it gives a subtle but essential flavor to most dishes. Mixed with lime juice, chiles, garlic, vinegar, and sugar, it becomes the zesty hot sauce called *nuoc cham* that appears practically at every meal. Every cook has a variation of this sauce, which is used as a salad dressing, a flavoring agent for cooked dishes, and a dipping sauce.

Meal patterns are basically similar to Chinese. In Ngoan's home, lunch or dinner would consist of a soup, a stir-fried dish such as broccoli with beef (seasoned with fish sauce, of course), and a main seafood or meat dish. Bowls and chopsticks are used to set the table.

Chopsticks may be the most visible sign of Chinese cultural influence; less obvious is a social and familial system based on the Confucian order. The Vietnamese revere their ancestors as sacred, and this extends to great respect for the elderly in everyday life. Rank in terms of age and relationship must be strictly observed. At Ngoan's dining-room table, she would show respect by asking her grandmother for permission to eat, then her father, and on down according to age until she had everyone's permission. In this way, she was properly trained in her position in her family order.

Tet, the lunar New Year, which may fall in January or February, is the most important of the Vietnamese holidays. The three-day holiday is filled with all sorts of religious and superstitious practices. The first person who comes and visits the family on New Year's Day is believed to bring them good or bad luck for the upcoming year, depending upon his moral conduct or luck. For this reason, he is usually a carefully chosen successful man with a good reputation. If, during the year, the family is stricken by misfortune, the visitor might have to take all the blame and won't be invited back the following year. Because of this belief, many people are hesitant to act as the first visitor of the year.

Many of the New Year customs followed by the Vietnamese are similar to those among the Chinese (see page 179). Many of the traditional foods for the New Year require days of preparation. Mrs. Lam Tam Hien of Van-Lang Restaurant in Wheaton, Illinois, fondly remembers the many candied sweets or *mut*—ginger, lotus seeds, persimmon, sweet potato, tamarind, winter melon—prepared by her mother for the New Year. She also made a succulent pork that took several days to marinate and preserve. First the pork was marinated in five-spice powder, sugar, salt, and fish sauce for a day, then it simmered on very low heat for three to four days to preserve it, as no cooking is allowed during *Tet*.

Symbolic rice cakes are an important part of *tet*. Dung Nguyen of Ba Le Restaurant in Chicago described two varieties: the northern *bang chung*, square sticky rice cakes filled with pork, mung beans, lots of black pepper, wrapped in banana leaves and steamed, which are said to represent the Earth; and *banh day*, round and sweeter rice cakes made from sticky rice, bananas, and coconut are popular in the central and south regions, and representative of Heaven.

The preparation of the rice cakes is a traditional family event. Dozens are made, to be devoured throughout the three-day *Tet* celebration. Everyone in the family helps, whether he can cook or not. A noncook might clean the banana leaves. Others will prepare the filling or wrap them. The cakes take hours to cook, giving all the relatives an occasion to stay up all night and catch up on everything that went on throughout the previous year.

In the home, the head of the family sets up a family altar with food and fruits. Peach blossoms are put around, representing luck and peace. At the end of the first day, which is spent paying respect to the ancestors, there is a family feast to welcome the ancestors to the home. Complicated and expensive foods must be served in attractive presentations to show respect for the ancestors: two or three kinds of soup, perhaps including an abalone soup or a special shark's fin soup, plus *cha gio,* lots of rice cakes, and an assortment of *mut.*

In celebrations and in everyday meals, the Vietnamese have used their natural foods with considerable awareness of color and textures to form new and unique flavors. Cooked foods are combined with crisp fresh vegetables and spiced with *nuoc cham* to elevate the food to a higher plateau. I am sure you will enjoy the outstanding flavors, delightful combinations of contrasting textures, and light, healthy foods of Vietnam as much as I do.

Chuc an ngon! Bon appetit!

TRADITIONAL VIETNAMESE MENUS

★☆★

FABULOUS VIETNAMESE FONDUE

6 people

Beef Fondue, *Bo Nhung Giam*

♦

Anchovy-Pineapple Dipping Sauce, *Mam Nem*

♦

Warm Beef Salad, *Bo Luc Lac*

♦

Beef Rice Soup, *Chao Thit Bo*

♦

Coconut Flan, *Banh Dua Ca Ra Men*

In Saigon, special occasions are often celebrated at Bo Bay Mon restaurants, which specialize in serving beef in many different ways. First a piping hot pot of broth is brought to the table in a charcoal-fired table brazier or fondue pot. Each person cooks individual portions of beef, while enjoying a leisurely time chatting with friends. The cooked beef is combined with marinated onions and vegetables, wrapped in soft white rice paper, and dipped in a tasty anchovy-based dipping sauce. Next a delicious Warm Beef Salad is served to refresh the palate. Traditionally, the meal is usually finished with Beef Rice Soup. The grand finale, a creamy comforting Coconut Flan, is a mouthwatering complement to the beef and the perfect end to a perfect evening!

The flan may be prepared the day before serving and chilled. In the morning, prepare the fondue dipping sauce, broth, rice sticks, and vegetable and beef platters; cover with plastic wrap and refrigerate. Prepare the vegetables and cut up and marinate the meat for the Warm Beef Salad. Prepare the beef and soup mixture for the Beef Rice Soup, but do not combine the two until serving time.

At serving time, reheat the fondue broth, and serve the fondue. Sauté the beef for the Warm Beef Salad and serve warm on watercress mixture. Reheat the Beef Rice Soup broth and combine with the seasoned beef. Unmold the Coconut Flan and serve.

A DELICIOUS VIETNAMESE DINNER

4 to 6 people

Fresh Beef Rolls, *Banh Hoi Thit Nuong*
◆
Asparagus Crab Soup, *Sup Mang Cua*
◆
Chicken Salad, *Goi Ga*
◆
*Steamed Fish, *Ca Hap*
◆
Stuffed Tomatoes, *Ca Chua Don Dau Hu*
◆
Rice
◆
Fresh Fruit
◆
Coffee

*If you prefer, serve Sweet and Sour Fish, *Ca Ran Chua Ngot*, in place of the Steamed Fish.

Here is a menu for a delicious Vietnamese meal that demonstrates the healthful, low-cholesterol, low-calorie nature of the cuisine without sacrificing a bit of flavor. Set your festive table with a red tablecloth, glowing red candles—both are good luck symbols—and Oriental fans or flowers for decoration. Arrange a pair of chopsticks, a plate, soup bowl, and spoon at each place setting.

Much of the preparation can be done ahead of time. The day before your dinner, grill the beef for the beef rolls.

The morning of the party, prepare the Asparagus Crab Soup, adding the cornstarch and egg when reheating before serving. Prepare the ingredients for the Chicken Salad, stuff the tomatoes, and prepare the fruit for dessert.

Several hours before serving, assemble the Fresh Beef Rolls, cover with plastic wrap, and refrigerate. Arrange the seasonings and toppings on the fish, cover with plastic wrap, and refrigerate. At serving time, steam the fish, cook the rice, toss the Chicken Salad, cook the tomatoes, and reheat the soup, adding the cornstarch mixture and egg.

STARTERS

Imperial Rolls, *Cha Gio Ga*
Fresh Beef Rolls, *Banh Hoi Thit Nuong*
Grilled Beef in Lettuce Packages, *Thit Nuong Cuon Xa Lach*
Triangle Spring Rolls, *Cha Gio Tom*
Shrimp Toast, *Banh Mi Chien Tom*
Fresh Shrimp Rolls, *Banh Trang Cuon Tom*
Shrimp in Lettuce Packages, *Xa Lach Cuon Tom*

SOUPS

Asparagus Crab Soup, *Sup Mang Cua*
Beef Rice Soup, *Chao Thit Bo*
Beef Noodle Soup, *Pho Bo*
Hot and Sour Shrimp Soup, *Canh Chua Tom*

MEAT

Basic Grilled Beef, *Thit Bo Nuong*
Stir-Fried Beef with Vegetables, *Bo Xao*
Stir-Fried Beef with Salad
Warm Beef Salad, *Bo Luc Lac*
Beef Fondue, *Bo Nhung Dam*

POULTRY

Lemon Grass Chicken, *Ga Xao Sa Ot*
Gingered Chicken, *Ga Xao Gung*
Grilled Lemon Grass Chicken, *Ga Nuong Sa*

FISH AND SEAFOOD

Steamed Fish, *Ca Hap*
Sweet and Sour Fish, *Ca Ran Chua Ngot*

SALADS AND VEGETABLES

Carrot Salad, *Goi Ca Rot*
Vegetable Platter, *Dia Rau Song*
Chicken Salad, *Goi Ga*
Chicken with Mint, *Ga Tron Rau Hung*
Barbecued Pork with Rice Noodle Salad, *Bun Thit Nuong*
Spicy Shrimp and Pork Salad, *Goi Tom*
Rice Noodles with Vegetables, Shrimp, and Peanuts, *Bun Tom Nuong*
Stuffed Tomatoes, *Ca Chua Don Dau Hu*
Cauliflower with Straw Mushrooms, *Bong Cai Xao Nam Rom*
Stir-Fried Mixed Vegetables with Peanuts, *Rau Cai Xao*

RICE, NOODLES, AND EGGS
Rice with Chicken, *Com Tay Cam*
Fried Rice with Tomato, *Com Rang Ca Chua*
Stir-Fried Beef with Noodles, *Bun Bo Xao*
Stir-Fried Shrimp and Bok Choy with Rice Noodles, *Hu Tieu Xao Tom*
Crab with Bean Threads, *Cua Xao Bun Tau*
Sound Crepe, *Banh Xeo*
Dried Rice Papers, *Banh Trang*

DIPS AND SAUCES
Spicy Fish Sauce, *Nuoc Cham*
Peanut Sauce, *Nuoc Leo*
Anchovy-Pineapple Dipping Sauce, *Mam Nem*

DESSERTS
Coconut Flan, *Banh Dua Ca Ra Men*

STARTERS

 ## Imperial Rolls
Cha Gio Ga

Delectable, thumb-size rolls containing minced pork or chicken, crab-meat, and cloud ears, wrapped in thin rice paper, and deep-fried until golden brown are served on special occasions.

This dish is the classic test of a Vietnamese bride's homemaking skill. Every bride is supposed to know how to produce Cha Gio Ga *of exactly the right crispness, color, and taste.*

When eating, wrap the Cha Gio Ga *in a lettuce leaf, add some coriander, mint, and other vegetables of your choice, and dip the whole bundle into chile hot* Nuoc Cham. *The refreshing mint combined with the smoothness of the minced chicken and crab, the flakiness of the rice paper, and the piquant* Nuoc Cham *dipping sauce make a delightful combination of tastes and textures.*

2 ounces fine bean threads, soaked in warm water for 20 minutes
   to soften, drained, chopped into 2-inch lengths
2 tablespoons cloud ears, soaked in warm water for 20 minutes to
   soften, drained, and finely shredded
12 ounces skinned, boned chicken breast, minced

6 ounces cooked crabmeat, flaked
3 cloves garlic, minced
3 tablespoons minced shallots
⅓ cup minced red onion
⅓ cup sugar
½ teaspoon freshly ground black pepper
28 sheets rice paper, 6½ inches in diameter *(banh trang)*
4 cups warm water (110° F)
⅓ cup sugar
1 egg white, lightly beaten
Oil for frying

Vietnamese Vegetable Platter (page 409)
Double recipe *Nuoc Cham* (page 425)

Prepare filling by combining bean threads, cloud ears, chicken, crab, garlic, shallots, red onion, sugar, and pepper in a bowl, and mix well. Set aside.

Put 1 quart warm water (110° F) into a bowl. Add the sugar and stir until dissolved. Dip 3 or 4 rice papers separately into the warm water for 2 to 3 seconds. Remove. Place the rice paper on a flat surface. Allow the rice paper to soften for 2 to 3 minutes. When the wrapper is soft and transparent, center about 1 to 2 teaspoons of the filling near the curved end of the paper, leaving space on both ends to seal ends of the roll. Fold and continue rolling to the top. Seal with egg white to keep packages together. Place the spring rolls, seam side down, on a tray. Cover with plastic wrap to prevent drying out before cooking. Continue until all wrappers are filled.

Heat oil in a wok or deep frying pan to 375° F. Add the spring rolls and fry a few at a time until golden brown and the filling is cooked. If it is not, lower the heat to 350° F and fry a little longer. Drain on paper towels and serve immediately or keep warm in a low oven until ready to serve.

Serve the rolls on a lettuce-lined plate with *Nuoc Cham* and Vietnamese Vegetable Platter.

To eat, roll each roll of *Cha Gio Ga* in a lettuce leaf along with a little coriander, mint, and vegetables of choice. Dip in *Nuoc Cham*.

YIELD: 28 rolls. (Allow 3 to 4 rolls per person.)

TIPS: If 6½-inch rice papers are unavailable, use seven 13½-inch-diameter rice papers, quartered. Prepare the rice papers as above. Fill each roll with 1 tablespoon filling, roll up, and seal with beaten egg white.

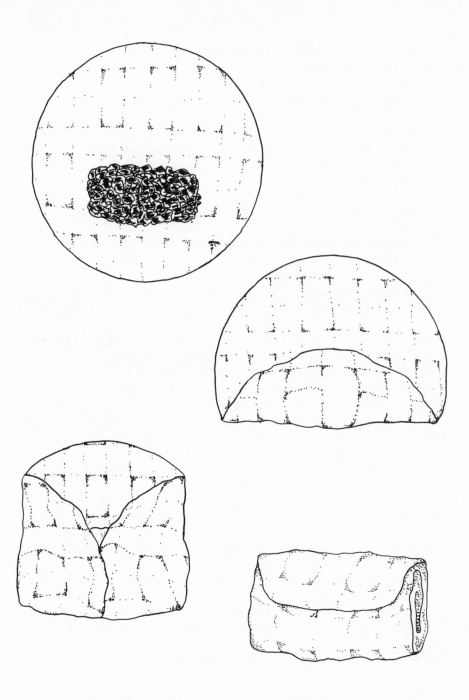

Substitute pork and shrimp for the chicken and crab or try your own combinations.

ADVANCE PREPARATION: The rolls can be assembled one day in advance, covered with plastic wrap, and refrigerated. Fry just before serving. The fried rolls may also be frozen. Reheat in a 350° F oven.

 ## Fresh Beef Rolls

Banh Hoi Thit Nuong

Savory grilled beef, combined with cucumber, mint, and coriander, then wrapped in soft white rice papers, is light and refreshing and a delightful party dish. You may prepare these morsels ahead or let your diners participate in the wrapping.

> 4 ounces thin rice sticks, soaked in warm water for 20 minutes, drained
> 6 sheets rice paper, 8½ inches in diameter (banh trang)
> ½ pound lean boneless top or bottom beef round, sliced wafer-thin into 1- by 2½-inch slices, cooked as in Basic Grilled Beef (page 388)
> ½ cucumber, peeled, seeds removed, cut lengthwise into thin 2-inch slices
> Fresh mint leaves
> Fresh coriander sprigs
> 20 Boston or other soft lettuce leaves (optional)
> Double recipe *Nuoc Cham* (page 425)

Heat 4 quarts water to boiling. Add the rice sticks and stir to separate. When the water returns to a boil, remove. Drain. Rinse with cold water. Drain. Dip each rice paper separately into warm water and place on a flat surface. Allow the paper to soften for 2 to 3 minutes or until soft and pliable. Alternate dipping the papers and filling the rolls so you will not have to wait for the rice papers to soften. (You may paint the rice papers with a pastry brush or spray with an atomizer filled with warm water instead of dipping them in water. Allow to soften before using.)

Place about 2 tablespoons beef, rice sticks, and 2 cucumber slices on a rice paper. Put 2 or 3 mint leaves and some coriander on top. Fold in the sides in envelope fashion and roll up tightly into a 3-inch cylinder. Repeat with remaining wrappers. Store seam side down. If desired, the beef packages may be wrapped with lettuce leaves. Serve with *Nuoc Cham.*

YIELD: 8 servings with other dishes.

ADVANCE PREPARATION: Rolls may be assembled several hours in advance, covered with plastic wrap, and refrigerated. If rolls become dry, spray with warm water, using an atomizer.

    Grilled Beef in Lettuce Packages
Thit Nuong Cuon Xa Lach

Crispy beef, fresh cucumber, mint, and lettuce dipped in piquant Nuoc Cham *provides a delightful and attractive appetizer or dinner accompaniment.*

> 8 to 10 green onions
> ½ pound grilled beef, prepared as in Basic Grilled Beef (page 00)
> ½ small cucumber, peeled, seeds removed, cut lengthwise into
>   thin 2-inch slices
> Fresh mint leaves
> Fresh coriander sprigs
> 8 to 10 Boston or other soft lettuce leaves
> Double recipe *Nuoc Cham* (page 425)

Blanch green onions in boiling water for 20 to 30 seconds to soften. Rinse with cold water. Drain.

Place 1 or 2 slices of barbecued beef on a lettuce leaf. Place cucumber slices, 2 or 3 mint leaves, and some coriander on top of beef. Fold in the sides of the lettuce leaf and roll tightly into a cylinder. Tie the bundle in the center with a green onion. Serve with *Nuoc Cham*.

YIELD: 8 servings.

ADVANCE PREPARATION: Prepare Basic Grilled Beef 1 day ahead. Assemble the rolls several hours ahead, cover with plastic wrap, and refrigerate. Serve at room temperature.

Triangle Spring Rolls
Cha Gio Tom

Many years ago Bach Ngo and Gloria Zimmerman, authors of The
Classic Cuisine of Vietnam, *showed me the preparation of these crispy
shrimp-filled appetizers. They have since become a favorite for entertaining.*

4 ounces crabmeat, flaked
½ pound finely ground pork
¼ cup chopped water chestnuts
½ small onion, minced
2 ounces bean threads, soaked in warm water for 20 minutes to
    soften, drained, cut into 1-inch pieces
2 shallots, minced
2 cloves garlic, minced
Freshly ground black pepper
12 sheets rice paper, 6 inches in diameter *(banh trang)*
2 eggs, lightly beaten
12 shrimp, shelled, with tails intact
3 to 4 cups oil for deep frying
12 lettuce leaves, Boston or romaine
1 small cucumber, thinly sliced
12 fresh coriander sprigs
36 mint leaves
Double recipe *Nuoc Cham* (page 425)

Combine the crabmeat, pork, water chestnuts, onion, bean threads,
shallots, garlic, and black pepper. Mix well.

Moisten the rice papers, one at time, covering the entire surface
with beaten egg. Allow to soften for a few seconds until they are
pliable. Alternate dipping the papers and filling the rolls so you will
not have to wait for the rice papers to soften. Fold one-third of the rice
paper over, making a semicircle with 1 flat edge.

Center 1 tablespoon of the filling on the rice paper. Place 1
shrimp on the filling, leaving the tail extended to serve as a handle.
Place 1 tablespoon of filling on top of the shrimp and mold the filling
completely around the shrimp. Fold the sides of the rice paper over
the filling to enclose it, forming a point where the shrimp tail extends.
Fold the curved part of the rice paper toward the shrimp tail. Tuck in
the corners. This should be triangular in shape with the shrimp tail
"handle" protruding about 1 inch.

Put oil into a large frying pan and place the rolls into the cold oil. Heat to moderate and fry, turning once, until golden, approximately 15 minutes. To serve, place the rolls in a lettuce leaf. Add cucumber slices, coriander sprigs, and 2 or 3 mint leaves, and wrap all into a package. Dip into *Nuoc Cham.*

YIELD: 12 rolls.

ADVANCE PREPARATION: The rolls may be cooked ahead and re-heated in a 350° F oven for about 20 minutes until crispy.

 ## Shrimp Toast
Banh Mi Chien Tom

The Vietnamese variation of Chinese Shrimp Toast!

½ pound shrimp, shelled, deveined, chopped
1 tablespoon chopped pork fat
1 shallot, minced
1 clove garlic, minced
1 green onion, minced
2 teaspoons fish sauce *(nuoc mam)*
1 egg white
1 teaspoon sugar
½ teaspoon salt
Dash freshly ground black pepper
2 tablespoons cornstarch
1 narrow loaf French bread, cut into thin slices
Oil for frying
Lettuce leaves
Nuoc Cham (page 425)

In a blender or food processor, combine shrimp, pork fat, shallot, garlic, and green onion, and process gently to a paste. Remove and put mixture into a bowl. Add the fish sauce, egg white, sugar, salt, pepper, and cornstarch, and stir until combined. Spread the shrimp paste on one side of the bread, making a mound in the center of each piece.

Heat oil in a frying pan to 375° F. Drop the toast, shrimp side down, into the oil. Fry until golden. Turn over gently and brown the other side. Remove and drain on paper towels. Keep warm in a 350° F oven while cooking remaining shrimp toast. Serve with lettuce leaves and *Nuoc Cham*.

YIELD: 6 servings.

ADVANCE PREPARATION: The bread slices may be spread with the shrimp paste, placed on a cookie sheet in a single layer, covered with plastic wrap, and refrigerated 2 hours before deep frying. Cooked Shrimp Toast can be frozen. Reheat in a 350° F oven on a rack over a baking pan.

 Fresh Shrimp Rolls
Banh Trang Cuon Tom

These delicately flavored rolls seasoned with mint, coriander, and peanuts are succulent as an appetizer or as part of a meal. Traditionally, the shrimp is "cooked" by marinating in lime juice for about 30 minutes. If you prefer, you may marinate the shrimp up to 12 hours for a more complete "cooking."

> 1 pound medium shrimp, shelled, deveined, cut in half
>   lengthwise
> ½ cup distilled white vinegar
> Dash of salt
> 2 tablespoons fresh lime juice
> 2 teaspoons fish sauce *(nuoc mam)*
> 2 shallots or 1 small onion, thinly sliced
> 1 garlic clove, minced
> ¼ teaspoon chili flakes
> ¼ teaspoon sugar
> 16 rice paper wrappers, 6½ inches in diameter *(banh trang)*
> 3 tablespoons chopped fresh coriander
> 3 tablespoons chopped fresh mint
> 2 tablespoons finely chopped unsalted dry-roasted peanuts
> Double recipe *Nuoc Cham* (page 425)

In a small bowl, combine shrimp, vinegar, and salt, and let soak for 30 minutes or until shrimp are firm and opaque. Remove shrimp and squeeze out any excess liquid. Return shrimp to the bowl. Add lime juice, fish sauce, shallots, garlic, chili flakes and sugar. Stir to mix. Cover. Refrigerate for 20 minutes, stirring occasionally.

Prepare the wrappers. Dip each rice paper into warm water and place on a flat surface. Allow the paper to soften for 2 to 3 minutes or until soft and pliable. Alternate dipping the papers and filling the rolls so you will not have to wait for the rice papers to soften. (You may paint the rice papers with a pastry brush or spray with an atomizer filled with warm water instead of dipping them in water. Allow to soften before using).

Center about 1½ tablespoons of the shrimp mixture along the lower edge of the rice paper wrapper. Sprinkle with coriander, mint, and chopped peanuts. Fold in the sides in an envelope pattern and roll them up tightly into a 3-inch cylinder. Repeat with remaining wrappers. Store with the seam side down. Serve with *Nuoc Cham*.

YIELD: 16 rolls.

ADVANCE PREPARATION: Rolls may be prepared several hours in advance, covered with plastic wrap, and refrigerated. If the rolls become dry, spray with warm water, using an atomizer.

 ## Shrimp in Lettuce Packages
Xa Lach Cuon Tom

A delightful combination of flavors and textures is found in this light "rolled salad."

> 4 ounces rice sticks, soaked in warm water for 20 minutes, drained
> 22 green onions
> 1 pound medium shrimp, cooked, sliced in half lengthwise
> 1 small cucumber, peeled, seeded, sliced lengthwise into thin 2-inch slices
> ¾ cup fresh coriander sprigs (tough stems removed)
> ¾ cup fresh mint leaves
> 22 Boston lettuce leaves
> Double recipe *Nuoc Cham* (page 425)

Heat 4 quarts water to boiling. Add the rice sticks and stir to separate. When the water returns to a boil, remove. Drain. Rinse with cold water. Drain. Cut into 2-inch pieces. Blanch green onions in hot water for 20 to 30 seconds, or until pliable. Rinse with cold water. Drain.

Place 4 pieces of shrimp, 1½ tablespoons rice sticks, 1 or 2 pieces of cucumber, 1 sprig of coriander, and 2 or 3 mint leaves on the narrow end of each lettuce leaf. Roll up lettuce into a package. Tie one green onion around the center of the lettuce. Trim the sides of the lettuce with a knife. Serve with *Nuoc Cham*.

YIELD: 22 packages.

ADVANCE PREPARATION: Assemble several hours before serving. Cover with plastic wrap and refrigerate.

SOUPS

 ## Beef Noodle Soup
Pho Bo

Your guests are sure to enjoy this low-calorie, light, easily assembled soup-plus-salad. Pho Bo *is nutritious, fragrantly spicy, and loved by all Vietnamese. It is a wonderful participation dish and is tasty for a luncheon or light supper.*

Savory piping-hot stock is poured over rice noodles and beef. Diners add bean sprouts, coriander, chiles, and lime to the fragrant soup. If you wish heartier fare, serve it as part of a meal. I prefer to make the deliciously flavored beef stock myself. If you desire, commercially prepared beef stock may be substituted, but your stock will lack the wonderful flavors of the long cooking of homemade stock.

3 large onions
1 tablespoon oil
5 pounds meaty beef bones (ribs, neck, or shank), trimmed of
    excess fat
8 to 10 ginger slices, smashed with the side of a cleaver
2 carrots, sliced
1 stick cinnamon
2 cardamom pods
3 star anise
4 whole cloves
1 teaspoon whole black peppercorns
2 cups (½ pound) fresh bean sprouts
½ pound beef sirloin, sliced very finely across the grain into bite-
    size pieces
1 green onion, finely sliced
¼ cup chopped coriander leaves
2 to 4 fresh red or green chiles, seeds removed, sliced, or 2
    tablespoons red pepper flakes

2 limes cut into 6 wedges
8 ounces rice sticks, soaked in hot water for 30 minutes, drained
2 to 3 tablespoons fish sauce (*nuoc mam*)
Freshly ground black pepper to taste

Slice 2 of the onions into ¼-inch slices. Heat 1 tablespoon oil in a frying pan. Add the sliced onion, and cook, stirring, until the outside layer has browned. Remove and drain. Slice the remaining onion into paper-thin slices and set aside.

Rinse bones and place in a stockpot. Cover with cold water. Bring slowly to a boil. Reduce heat and simmer, uncovered. As the stock heats, a residue will rise to the surface. For a clear stock, skim off the foam. When foaming stops after about 10 to 20 minutes, add the browned onions and the ginger, carrots, cinnamon, cardamom, star anise, cloves, and peppercorns. Bring to a boil. Simmer the stock, partially covered, from 6 to 12 hours, skimming regularly. If necessary, add more water during cooking to keep the bones covered. Strain the stock, and skim off and discard any fat from the surface. At serving time, season with fish sauce and salt to taste.

Blanch the bean sprouts in boiling water for 30 seconds. Drain Rinse with cold water. Drain.

Arrange the thinly sliced beef on a platter. Garnish with the reserved white onion slices and green onion. On another platter, arrange the bean sprouts, coriander, chiles, and limes. At serving time, plunge the rice sticks into boiling water to heat. Drain. Place in equal portions into soup bowls. Cover to keep warm. Meanwhile, heat the beef stock to boiling. Season to taste with fish sauce and black pepper. Pour into a soup tureen or chafing dish. At the table, place the soup on a portable burner to keep hot. Offer each guest a bowl of warm rice noodles. Each diner adds some beef and onion to a bowl. Ladle the hot stock over the meat, stirring to cook the meat. Add the bean sprouts, coriander, chiles, chile paste, and lime to taste. Enjoy hot, with chopsticks and a soup spoon.

YIELD: 6 to 8 servings.

TIP: Substitute prepared beef broth for homemade. Simmer ginger, carrots, cinnamon, star anise, cloves, and black peppercorns in the prepared stock for 30 minutes. Strain. Season with fish sauce and black pepper.

ADVANCE PREPARATION: The stock may be prepared up to three days in advance and refrigerated. Arrange the beef and bean sprout dishes several hours before serving. Cover with plastic wrap and refrigerate. Bring to room temperature before serving. Heat the rice noodles and stock just before serving.

 ## Asparagus Crab Soup
Sup Mang Cua

A delicate, easily prepared light soup.

1 can white asparagus
1 teaspoon oil
1 clove garlic, minced
2 shallots, minced
½ pound crabmeat, flaked
6 cups chicken stock
1 tablespoon fish sauce (*nuoc mam*)
1 tablespoon cornstarch dissolved in 2 tablespoons water
1 large egg, lightly beaten
Dash white pepper
¼ cup chopped fresh coriander leaves
¼ cup green onions, green part only

Drain asparagus, reserving liquid. Cut asparagus into 1½-inch lengths. Heat a medium soup pot over high heat. Add oil. Add garlic, shallots, and crab, and stir-fry over high heat for 2 to 3 minutes. Add chicken stock, reserved asparagus liquid, and asparagus. Stir until soup comes to a boil. Add fish sauce. Reduce heat to low, and simmer 1 minute. Add dissolved cornstarch, stirring in a circular motion as the soup thickens. Drop the egg into the soup while stirring. Remove from heat. Add white pepper. Stir. Garnish with coriander and green onions.

YIELD: 6 servings.

ADVANCE PREPARATION: Prepare soup several hours before serving. Add cornstarch and egg prior to serving.

Beef Rice Soup
 ### *Chao Thit Bo*

In Saigon, this soup is traditionally served after Beef Fondue.

6 ounces lean ground beef
1 small onion, minced
2 tablespoons fish sauce (*nuoc mam*)
Freshly ground black pepper to taste
2 tablespoons oil
1 teaspoon finely minced fresh ginger
⅓ cup rice
2 tablespoons fish sauce (*nuoc mam*)
2 teaspoons sugar
1 teaspoon salt
2 garlic cloves, minced
1 tablespoon lemon grass, minced, bottom 6 inches only
    (optional)
½ ounce bean threads, soaked in warm water for 20 minutes,
    drained, cut into 2-inch lengths
1 tablespoon chopped fresh coriander
1 green onion, green part only, chopped
2 tablespoons chopped roasted peanuts
Freshly ground black pepper
Nuoc Cham (page 425), (optional)

In a soup tureen, combine beef, onion, 1 tablespoon fish sauce, and black pepper to taste. Set aside.

Heat 1 tablespoon oil in a 4-quart pan. Add the ginger and rice. Stir until the rice becomes milky white and puffs, about 1 minute. Add 7 cups water. Bring to a boil. Reduce to simmer and cook, partially covered, for about 20 minutes, or until the rice is tender. Add the remaining fish sauce, sugar, and salt. Stir gently to mix.

Heat remaining 1 tablespoon oil in a skillet. Add the garlic and lemon grass. Sauté over low heat until fragrant, about 1 minute. Add to the soup and stir. Add the bean threads. Bring the soup to a boil. Pour the hot soup over the beef mixture. Using chopsticks or a fork, break up the meat into small pieces. The meat will be cooked instantly by the boiling broth. Sprinkle with coriander, green onion, peanuts, and freshly ground black pepper. Serve with *Nuoc Cham*.

YIELD: 4 to 6 servings.

ADVANCE PREPARATION: Prepare the beef and soup mixtures several hours ahead. Reheat the soup and add to the seasoned beef just before serving. Serve hot.

 ## Hot and Sour Shrimp Soup
Canh Chua Tom

Tender shrimp and mushrooms are combined with tangy lemon grass, lime, and the fire of chile. This soup, which resembles the Thai Tom Yum Koong, *is a favorite among my students. In Vietnam, the soup is often served over rice during a meal, or it can be a meal in itself.*

1 pound medium shrimp with shells
3 stalks fresh lemon grass
1 tablespoon oil
5 cups chicken stock
1 can (15 ounces) straw mushrooms, drained
½ teaspoon minced lime zest
1 small tomato, cut into thin wedges
2 green onions, thinly sliced
1½ cups bean sprouts
3 tablespoons lime juice
¼ cup fish sauce (*nuoc mam*)
¼ to ½ teaspoon chili powder
¼ teaspoon freshly ground black pepper
2 tablespoons coarsely chopped fresh coriander leaves
1 fresh red chile, seeds removed, thinly sliced

Peel, wash, and devein shrimp, reserving shells. Cut shrimp in half lengthwise. Cut off top of lemon grass stalk and pound with side of a cleaver. Pound the bottom 6 inches to release flavors. Cut into 1-inch lengths. Add oil to a saucepan and heat. Add shrimp shells and stir-fry until golden and bright pink. Add chicken stock and lemon grass tops. Bring to a boil over high heat. Reduce heat and simmer for 20 minutes. Strain the stock and return to saucepan. Add the straw mushrooms, lime zest, remaining lemon grass, and tomato wedges. Bring to a boil. Reduce heat and simmer 4 minutes. Add shrimp and cook until pink and opaque, about 2 minutes. Remove from heat. Stir in green onions, bean sprouts, lime juice, fish sauce, chili powder, and pepper. Taste. Add more fish sauce and lime juice if desired. Garnish with coriander and chile slices. Serve at once.

YIELD: 4 to 6 servings.

TIPS: If straw mushrooms are large, cut into halves or quarters.

ADVANCE PREPARATION: The shrimp shells may be stir-fried and the stock cooked 1 day ahead and refrigerated. For optimum flavor, reheat stock, add remaining ingredients, and finish cooking at serving time.

POULTRY

 Lemon Grass Chicken
★ *Ga Xao Sa Ot* ★

Aromatic lemon grass, chiles, and mint are combined to make this spicy Vietnamese favorite.

6 chicken legs or thighs, boned, skinned (about 1¼ pounds
 trimmed chicken)
2 stalks lemon grass, bottom 6 inches only, minced
3 tablespoons fish sauce *(nuoc mam)*
¼ teaspoon freshly ground black pepper
2 cloves garlic, minced
1 tablespoon oil
2 fresh red chiles, seeded, shredded into 1½-inch lengths
3 green onions, shredded into 1½-inch lengths
1½ teaspoons sugar
3 tablespoons fresh mint or basil leaves, or a combination
 (optional)
⅓ cup unsalted roasted peanuts
Vietnamese Vegetable Platter (page 409)

Cut up chicken into 1-inch cubes. Combine the lemon grass, 2 tablespoons fish sauce, pepper, and garlic. Add to the chicken and mix thoroughly. Set aside and let marinate for ½ to 1 hour.

In a wok or skillet, heat oil over medium-high heat. Add chicken and stir-fry until chicken is no longer pink, approximately 3 to 4 minutes. Add a little water to the mixture, if necessary, to prevent scorching. When chicken is done, add remaining fish sauce, chiles, green onions, and sugar. Stir for 30 seconds. Toss with mint or basil. Garnish with peanuts. Serve with rice and Vietnamese vegetable platter.

YIELD: 4 servings.

TIP: To obtain best results, fresh lemon grass should be used.

VARIATIONS: Chicken breasts may be substituted for the legs and thighs. The dark meat is juicier and is preferred for this dish.

Substitute ¾ teaspoon red pepper powder for fresh red chiles.

 ## Gingered Chicken
Ga Xao Gung

Flavorful ginger, lemon grass, sweet brown sugar, and spicy black pepper commingle to make this an enticing dish. The Vietnamese use a generous amount of black pepper and cook it in a clay pot. They prefer to use moist, flavorful chicken thighs.

4 chicken thighs, boned, cut into 2-inch pieces
2 tablespoons shredded fresh ginger
2 tablespoons chopped onion
2 stalks lemon grass, bottom 6 inches only, minced
½ cup plus 2 tablespoons fish sauce (*nuoc mam*)
2 tablespoons oil
2 garlic cloves, chopped
3 tablespoons brown sugar
4 green onions, cut into 2-inch lengths
2 to 3 teaspoons black pepper or to taste

In a bowl, combine chicken, ginger, onion, lemon grass, and fish sauce. Let marinate 30 minutes.

Heat oil in a pan over high heat. Add garlic and fry 10 seconds. Add the chicken mixture and stir-fry until golden. Add brown sugar. Stir to carmelize. Add 1 cup water. Bring to a boil. Reduce heat and simmer, covered, 10 minutes. Add green onions and black pepper. Continue to cook another 5 to 10 minutes. Serve with rice.

YIELD: 3 servings.

TIP: Chicken breasts may be used, but they will not be as flavorful.

ADVANCE PREPARATION: The flavors of the dish improve if it is cooked one day ahead and reheated. Reheat just before serving, adding green onions and black pepper at this time.

Grilled Lemon Grass Chicken
★ *Ga Nuong Sa* ★

 2 stalks minced lemon grass, bottom 6 inches only
 ⅛ teaspoon ground cinnamon
 ½ teaspoon ground coriander
 ⅓ teaspoon white pepper
 2 tablespoons soy sauce
 1 tablespoon fish sauce *(nuoc mam)*
 1 teaspoon brown sugar
 1½ tablespoons oil
 8 whole chicken legs or breasts
 Double recipe *Nuoc Cham* (page 425)
 Vegetable Platter (page 409)

Pound or process lemon grass to a coarse mixture. Add cinnamon,
coriander, white pepper, soy sauce, fish sauce, brown sugar, and oil.
Mix well. Place chicken in a shallow dish. Add marinade and mix
well. Let chicken marinate in the refrigerator for 3 to 4 hours, turning
occasionally.

Remove the chicken from the refrigerator 15 minutes before
cooking. Grill over a medium hot fire, turning, until cooked
throughout. Baste occasionally with marinade during cooking. Serve
with *Nuoc Cham* and a Vegetable Platter.

YIELD: 8 servings with other dishes.

MEAT

 Basic Grilled Beef
★ *Thit Bo Nuong* ★

*Grilled beef is a basic ingredient of many Vietnamese recipes. Usually it
is served with other accompaniments.*

 1 pound lean boneless top or bottom beef round

MARINADE:

 2 stalks lemon grass, bottom 6 inches only, thinly sliced
 2 teaspoons minced garlic

3 tablespoons minced shallots
1 small fresh green or red chile, seeds removed, minced
2 teaspoons sugar
1 tablespoon fish sauce (nuoc mam)
1 teaspooon Chinese sesame oil
1 tablespoon white sesame seeds

Chill beef until firm. Slice into thin ⅛- by 1- by 2-inch slices.

Prepare marinade. In a mortar, processor, or blender, combine the lemon grass, garlic, shallots, and chile. Pound or process to a paste. Add the sugar, fish sauce, and sesame oil, and continue processing until well blended. Mix in the sesame seeds. Add the mixture to the sliced meat and combine. Marinate for 30 minutes to 1 hour.

Grill the meat briefly over a hot charcoal fire until just firm to touch, or cook in the oven. Preheat oven to 450°F. Line the bottom and sides of a baking pan with aluminum foil, and place the meat on the foil. Let the slices touch each other to prevent the meat from drying. Bake about 5 to 10 minutes or until just firm to touch. Cool the beef to room temperature.

TIP: Beef will be easier to slice if partially frozen.

ADVANCE PREPARATION: Cook one day in advance. Refrigerate, covered.

 ## Stir-Fried Beef with Vegetables
Bo Xao

Colorful vegetables and hearty beef unite in this flavorful stir-fry.

½ pound boneless beef sirloin or flank steak
¼ teaspoon freshly ground black pepper
1 tablespoon fish sauce (nuoc mam)
1 garlic clove, minced
6 ounces broccoli flowerets
½ teaspoon thin soy sauce
2 teaspoons oyster sauce
½ cup chicken stock or water
1 tablespoon cornstarch dissolved in 2 tablespoons water
4 tablespoons oil
½ medium onion, halved lengthwise, cut into ⅓-inch wedges
1 medium green or red bell pepper, cut into 1- by ⅓-inch strips
2 celery stalks, leaves removed, cut on the diagonal into ¼-inch
   slices

1 large tomato, cut into ⅓-inch wedges
3 green onions, shredded into 1½-inch lengths

Chill beef until firm. Slice across the grain into paper-thin ¹⁄₁₆- to ⅛-inch slices. Then cut meat into slices ¾- inch wide by 2 inches long. Sprinkle meat with black pepper, ½ teaspoon fish sauce, and half the chopped garlic. Stir. Allow to marinate for 1 to 2 hours, refrigerated.

Cut broccoli flowerets lengthwise into thin slices. Combine remaining fish sauce, soy sauce, oyster sauce, chicken stock, and cornstarch. Set aside.

Heat a wok over high heat. Add 2 tablespoons oil and heat. Add broccoli, onion, peppers, and celery. Stir-fry for 2 minutes. Add tomatoes and green onions. Stir-fry for an additional 1 to 2 minutes. Remove from wok and set aside. Add remaining 2 tablespoons oil to wok. Heat. Add the beef. Stir-fry for 2 minutes, or until browned. Return the vegetables to the wok. Recombine sauce mixture and add to wok. Cook, stirring, for approximately 30 seconds, or until sauce is opaque and has thickened slightly. Serve with rice and *Nuoc Cham*.

YIELD: 2 to 3 servings.

 ## Stir-Fried Beef with Salad

This dish is often served on individual metal sizzling platters, garnished with vegetables.

1 pound flank steak, cut into ⅛- by 2- by 2-inch strips
2 cloves garlic, minced
1 tablespoon fish sauce (*nuoc mam*)
3 tablespoons soy sauce
1 teaspoon sugar
5 tablespoons oil
1 medium onion, sliced into ¼-inch strips
2 to 4 small dried red chiles, soaked in warm water for 5 minutes
     or until softened, drained, seeds removed, minced
2 tablespoons beef stock or water
12 leaves Boston or red leaf lettuce
2 medium tomatoes, each cut into 6 slices
12 coriander sprigs

Marinate meat in garlic, fish sauce, 1 tablespoon soy sauce, ½ teaspoon sugar, and 1 tablespoon oil for 2 hours in refrigerator, covered.

Combine ½ teaspoon sugar, chiles, 2 tablespoons soy sauce, and beef stock in a small bowl. Heat wok over high heat. Add 2 tablespoons oil and heat. Add onion. Stir-fry 1 to 2 minutes. Remove and put in a bowl. Add steak and stir-fry 2 to 3 minutes, or until done. Add chile mixture to wok, and stir. Add cooked onion. Stir 30 seconds. Remove from heat. Place several lettuce leaves on 4 individual plates. Place a quarter of beef in the center of each serving. Garnish each plate with tomato slices and coriander sprigs.

YIELD: 4 servings.

 ## Warm Beef Salad
Bo Luc Lac

This is delicious as an appetizer or late night snack.

1 pound beef sirloin, eye of round, or filet of beef cut into ⅛- by
    1- by 2-inch strips
8 cloves garlic, minced
1 tablespoon fish sauce (*nuoc mam*)
1 tablespoon soy sauce
1½ teaspoons sugar
1 medium red onion, sliced into paper-thin slices
2 tablespoons distilled white vinegar
1 tablespoon olive oil
¼ teaspoon salt
2 tablespoons oil
2 cups watercress, washed, drained
1 green onion, thinly sliced
Freshly ground black pepper

Marinate steak in half the garlic, fish sauce, soy sauce, and ½ teaspoon sugar for 1 hour in refrigerator. Place the onion in a small bowl. Add the vinegar, olive oil, 1 teaspoon sugar, and salt. Toss well. Set aside to marinate for 10 minutes. Remove only the tough, heavy stems of the watercress. Combine the watercress with the onion mixture and place on a serving plate.

Heat 2 tablespoons oil in wok or skillet. Add the remaining garlic, and stir until fragrant and golden brown. Add the beef and saute quickly over high heat, shaking the pan to sear the beef. (The beef should be medium rare.) Pour the cooked meat over the onion and watercress. Garnish with green onion. Sprinkle with freshly ground black pepper. Serve with French bread.

YIELD: 4 servings.

ADVANCE PREPARATION: Marinate the beef and onions several hours before serving. Combine the watercress and onion mixture, and saute the beef just before serving.

 ## Beef Fondue
Bo Nhung Dam

In Saigon, special occasions are often celebrated by going to a Bo Bay Mon restaurant, which specialize in serving Beef Fondue.

6 ounces thin rice sticks *(bun)* soaked in warm water for 20
  minutes, drained
Vegetable Platter (page 409)

BEEF PLATTER:

1 pound sirloin of beef or eye of round, partially frozen until firm,
  trimmed of fat, sliced paper thin across the grain
2 medium onions, peeled, thinly sliced, separated into rings
2 green onions, chopped
2 tablespoons oil
Freshly ground black pepper

FONDUE BROTH:

2 tablespoons oil
3 garlic cloves, minced
2 tablespoons chopped fresh lemon grass (bottom 6 inches only)
6 thin slices fresh ginger
1 cup distilled white vinegar
3 tablespoons sugar
1 tablespoon salt

8 ounces rice paper rounds *(banh trang)*, 6½ inches in diameter
1 cup coarsely ground roasted peanuts
2 green onions chopped
Anchovy-Pineapple Dipping Sauce (page 426)

Heat 4 quarts water to boiling. Add the rice sticks and stir to separate. When the water returns to a boil, remove. Drain. Rinse with cold water. Drain. Cut into 2 inch pieces. Place in a bowl for serving.

Arrange the Vegetable Platter on 1 or 2 serving dishes. Cover with plastic wrap. Set aside.

Arrange the beef slices in overlapping layers on 1 or 2 round platters. Garnish with onion rings and green onions. Sprinkle the oil and black pepper over all. Cover with plastic wrap. To prepare the broth, heat oil. Add the garlic, lemon grass, and ginger. Stir-fry until fragrant, about 20 seconds. Add vinegar, sugar, salt, and 1¾ cup water. Bring to a boil. Set aside.

To serve, place the rice papers on a serving plate. Give each diner a shallow soup bowl of warm water and an individual dipping sauce bowl. Place the beef and vegetable platters, rice stick bowl, and peanuts on the table. Heat the fondue broth. Transfer to a tabletop fondue pot. Garnish with chopped green onions.

Take a rice paper and dip it briefly into the water bowl to soften the wrapper and make it pliable. Place the rice paper on a dinner plate. Place a lettuce leaf and a selection of salad vegetables and herbs, some rice sticks, and a teaspoon of ground peanuts on the paper near the center.

Using chopsticks, dip a few slices of beef and onion rings into the simmering fondue broth. Cook until the beef looses its pinkness on the outside. (The beef should cook quickly, about 1 minute.) Remove the cooked beef and onions, and place on top of the salad ingredients and rice paper. Roll the rice paper into a neat package (folding the ends in). Dip it into the anchovy sauce and eat out of the hand. Before or after a roll is consumed, cook the beef and onion in the simmering broth for the next wrap and roll session.

YIELD: 4 to 6 servings.

TIP: *Nuoc Cham* may be substituted for the Anchovy-Pineapple Dipping Sauce if desired.

ADVANCE PREPARATION: Prepare the dipping sauce, broth, rice sticks, vegetable and beef platters the morning of serving. Refrigerate, covered with plastic wrap. Before serving, bring the dipping sauce, vegetables, and rice sticks to room temperature. Reheat the broth when ready to serve.

FISH AND SEAFOOD

 Steamed Fish
Ca Hap

Colorful vegetables are attractively placed on flavorful fish in this healthy, low-calorie, and elegant steamed entree. This dish demonstrates the aesthetic appeal of Vietnamese cuisine as well as the Chinese influence.

    1 whole pike, sea bass, striped bass, or whitefish (about 2
        pounds), cleaned and scaled, with head and tail intact
    ½ teaspoon salt
    1 teaspoon sugar
    Freshly ground black pepper
    4 teaspoons fish sauce (*nuoc mam*)
    2 teaspoons peeled shredded fresh ginger
    2 cloves garlic, chopped
    1 piece celery, sliced on diagonal into thin slices
    1 small onion, thinly sliced
    ¼ cup shredded bamboo shoots
    10 lily buds, soaked in hot water for 20 minutes, drained, tough
        tips removed
    4 Chinese black mushrooms, soaked in hot water for 20 minutes
        or until spongy, drained, stems removed, shredded
    ½ ounce bean threads, soaked in hot water for 20 minutes or
        until softened, drained, cut into 2-inch lengths
    1 firm ripe tomato, cut into small wedges
    2 green onions, shredded into 1½-inch lengths
    3 tablespoons peanut oil (optional)

Wash fish and pat dry with paper towels. Make 3 diagonal slashes 1 inch apart on each side of fish. Place the fish on a heatproof platter. Combine the salt, sugar, pepper, and fish sauce, and rub the outside and inside of the fish with the mixture. Marinate the fish for 30 minutes.

Arrange the ginger, garlic, celery, onion, bamboo shoots, lily buds, and black mushrooms on the fish. Place the bean threads on top of the vegetables. Arrange the tomato wedges on top of the fish and around the edges. Garnish with green onions.

Place the fish upright on a heatproof plate on a rack in a steamer or large roasting pan. Fill the steamer with boiling water to within 1 inch of the top of rack. Cover, turn heat to medium high, and steam the fish about 10 minutes per pound until fish is no longer translucent, adding more boiling water to the pan if necessary. Remove platter from the steamer. Carefully slip the fish on top of a large serving platter. Heat oil in a small pan until very hot but not smoking. Stand away from fish and pour the hot oil over the entire surface of the fish to give it a nice glaze. Serve.

YIELD: 2 to 3 servings.

ADVANCE PREPARATION: Arrange ingredients on top of fish. Cover with plastic wrap. Refrigerate.

 ## Sweet and Sour Fish
Ca Ran Chua Ngot

Many Asian countries have their version of this classic dish. One of my favorites is from Vietnam. This exciting version provides both distinctive flavors and a beautiful presentation. It is deep-fried and glazed with a rich vegetable sauce and will be the sensation of your dinner.

Oil for deep frying
1 tablespoon ginger, minced
1 tablespoon garlic, minced
4 large Chinese dried black mushrooms, soaked in hot water for
     20 minutes or until softened, drained, tough stems removed,
     shredded
20 dried lily buds, soaked in hot water for 20 minutes or until
     softened, drained
1 small onion, peeled, cut into ¼-inch slices
1 medium carrot, peeled, cut into ¼-inch by 1½-inch shreds
1 medium celery stalk, cut into ¼-inch by 1½-inch shreds
3 green onions, shredded into 1½-inch lengths
1 small firm ripe tomato, cut in half, sliced into ¼-inch wedges

SAUCE MIXTURE. Combine and set aside

1 tablespoon oyster sauce
1 tablespoon soy sauce
⅓ cup plus 2 tablespoons sugar
½ cup distilled white vinegar
1 tablespoon Chinese sesame oil
1 fresh red or green chile, seeded, cut into thin shreds
2 teaspoons cornstarch dissolved in 1 tablespoon water

1 whole red snapper (about 2½ pounds), cleaned, scaled, with
     head and tail intact

½ teaspoon salt
⅓ cup cornstarch
Coriander sprigs for garnish (optional)

In a wok or heavy pan, heat 3 tablespoons oil on moderate heat. Add ginger and garlic, and stir-fry for 10 seconds. Add mushrooms, lily buds, onion, carrot, celery, and green onions, and stir-fry for 2 to 3 minutes. Add the tomato, and stir for 1 minute longer. Recombine sauce mixture and add to pan. Stir until the sauce is translucent and slightly thickened. Cover pan and set aside.

Wash fish and pat dry. Make 3 diagonal slashes 1 inch apart on each side of fish. Rub inside and out with salt, and set aside for 30 minutes. Dry fish again with paper towels. Just before frying, coat the fish completely with the cornstarch.

In the meantime, heat a wok or shallow roasting pan large enough to hold fish. Add the oil and heat to 375° F. Gently lower the fish into the oil head first and immerse it in the oil. Ladle the hot oil over the fish and shift the fish occasionally while frying. Deep-fry about 3 to 6 minutes on each side, or just long enough for the fish to be firm and delicately browned, turning it carefully with a spatula. Remove gently with 2 spatulas, tilting it over the wok to drain. Drain on paper towels. Place on a large, heated serving platter. Reheat the sauce and pour over the fish, spreading vegetables attractively on the top. Garnish with coriander. Serve immediately.

YIELD: 2 to 3 servings.

ADVANCE PREPARATION: The fish may be deep-fried 1 to 2 hours before serving. Refry to heat and crisp fish just before serving. Reheat sauce and pour over fish.

SALADS AND VEGETABLES

 ## Carrot Salad
Goi Ca Rot

A popular accompaniment to Vietnamese meals.

½ cup water
3 tablespoons lemon juice
3 tablespoons sugar
⅛ to ¼ teaspoon red pepper powder
¼ teaspoon salt
2 medium carrots, shredded into 2-inch lengths

Combine water, lemon juice, sugar, red pepper powder, and salt in a bowl. Stir until sugar dissolves. Add shredded carrots. Cover and refrigerate 2 hours or longer to allow flavors to blend.

YIELD: 1 cup, approximately.

TIP: Shredded Chinese turnip (daikon, lo bok), celery, onion, bell pepper, or a mixture of these vegetables may also be prepared in this manner.

 ## Vegetable Platter
Dia Rau Song

A salad or vegetable platter is served as an accompaniment to almost all Vietnamese meals. In Vietnam, many aromatic leaves are included as well as several varieties of mint, which are not found in the United States.

A vegetable platter should include:

Soft leaf lettuce, such as Boston, separated into leaves (allow approximately 3 leaves per person)
6 green onions, cut into 2-inch lengths
1 cup fresh mint leaves
1 cup fresh Asian or regular basil leaves
1 cup fresh coriander leaves
1 cucumber, peeled, cut in half lengthwise, sliced thinly crosswise

4 ounces fresh bean sprouts
1 carrot, thinly sliced
Lime slices (optional)

Place the lettuce in a mound in the center of the serving dish. Put the green onions, mint, basil, and coriander around the lettuce in separate mounds. Arrange the cucumber, bean sprouts, and carrot in separate mounds on the platter. Garnish with lime slices.

TIP: Additions to the vegetable platter might include sliced red onion, shredded Chinese turnip (daikon lobok), fresh sweet basil, lemon basil, or dill.

 ## Chicken Salad
Goi Ga

A seductively appealing juxtaposition of fragrances and tastes, Goi Ga *is superb as a first course with cocktails or as part of a meal.*

3 cups shredded Chinese cabbage
2 carrots, shredded into 1½-inch lengths
½ cucumber, peeled, seeds removed, shredded into 1 ½-inch lengths
1 tablespoon salt
2 fresh red chiles, seeds removed, finely sliced
1 small onion, cut into very fine slices
1 clove garlic, crushed
2 tablespoons cider or white vinegar
2 tablespoons sugar
1 tablespoon fish sauce (*nuoc mam*)
2 tablespoons fresh lime juice
1⅓ cups shredded cooked chicken
3 tablespoons crushed unsalted dry-roasted peanuts
¼ cup fresh coriander leaves

Put cabbage, carrots, and cucumber in separate bowls. Sprinkle ⅓ of the salt in each bowl and let stand for 20 minutes. Rinse each vegetable and squeeze dry.

Combine chiles, onion, garlic, vinegar, sugar, fish sauce, and lime juice. Stir to dissolve sugar. Add to vegetables and toss well. Place vegetables on a plate. Top with cooked chicken. Garnish with crushed peanuts and coriander.

YIELD: 3 to 4 servings.

ADVANCE PREPARATION: Prepare chicken and vegetables several hours before serving. Assemble 1 hour prior to meal. Cover with plastic wrap.

 ## Chicken with Mint
★ *Ga Tron Rau Hung*

Serve this easily prepared piquant salad as an appetizer or as part of a meal.

    1 chicken breast
    ½ onion, sliced into paper-thin slices and separated
    ½ cup distilled white vinegar
    ¼ teaspoon salt
    ⅛ teaspoon freshly ground black pepper
    ¼ cup minced mint leaves

Bring 1½ quarts water to a boil. Add chicken breast and return to boil. Reduce heat and simmer for 20 minutes. Remove breast and rinse with cold water. Remove skin and meat from bone. Using your fingers, shred the chicken meat.

Cover onion slices with white vinegar and let marinate for 15 minutes. Drain and rinse with cold water. Combine chicken, onion, salt, pepper, and mint leaves. Mix well. Serve.

YIELD: 3 to 4 servings with other dishes.

TIP: Cook chicken 1 day ahead. Shred chicken and combine ingredients on day of serving. The flavor will improve if allowed to stand 1 to 2 hours before serving.

 ## Barbecued Pork with Rice Noodle Salad
★ *Bun Thit Nuong*

Inviting in appearance and irresistible in taste, this salad is superb and can easily be doubled or tripled for entertaining. I have varied from the traditional Vietnamese service to make it easier for an American buffet.

    1 fresh red or green chile pepper, seeds removed, minced
    3 shallots, minced
    2 cloves garlic, minced
    2 teaspoons sugar

1½ tablespoons fish sauce (*nuoc mam*)

⅛ teaspoon black pepper

2 teaspoons lime juice

1 pound pork butt or loin, partially frozen, sliced paper thin against the grain

8 ounces thin rice vermicelli, soaked in warm water for 30 minutes, drained

1 teaspoon vegetable oil

3 carrots, shredded into fine 2-inch matchsticks

2 cups bean sprouts

2 to 3 heads Boston lettuce, cored, leaves detached, washed, dried

Double recipe *Nuoc Cham* (page 425)

⅓ cup fresh coriander leaves

½ cup fresh mint leaves

¾ cucumber, cut in half, seeded, thinly sliced

3 green onions, thinly sliced

¼ cup chopped unsalted roasted peanuts

Pound or process the chile, shallots, garlic, and sugar to a paste. Add the fish sauce, black pepper and lime juice. Mix. Combine the paste mixture and the meat. Marinate for 30 minutes.

Grill the meat over charcoal or cook in the oven using the following method. Preheat the oven to 450° F. Line a baking pan with aluminum foil. Arrange the pork on the foil in overlapping slices. (If pieces are separated, they may become too dry when cooking.) Bake for 5 to 10 minutes, or until just firm to touch. Remove from oven. Cool. Slice into ½- by 2-inch pieces. Bring 4 quarts water to a boil. Add the rice sticks to the water and stir until separated. As soon as the water returns to a boil, remove. Drain. Rinse with cold water. Drain. Toss with the oil.

Bring 2 cups of water to a boil. Add the shredded carrots and bean sprouts. Blanch in the boiling water for 15 seconds. Remove. Drain. Rinse with cold water. Drain. Add to the noodles and toss.

Line a large round platter with the lettuce leaves. Combine one quarter of the *Nuoc Cham* with the noodle mixture. Add the meat and 2 tablespoons each of chopped coriander and chopped mint leaves. Add more *Nuoc Cham* if necessary. The salad should be completely coated with the *Nuoc Cham*. Place the salad in the center of the lettuce. Arrange the cucumber slices around the salad mixture. Sprinkle the salad with green onions and chopped peanuts. Garnish with sprigs of mint and coriander. Serve cold or at room temperature with additional *Nuoc Cham* on the side. To serve in lettuce packages, let each guest place a spoonful or two of noodle mixture on the lettuce, folding it before eating.

YIELD: 4 servings as a main course or 8 with other dishes.

ADVANCE PREPARATION: Prepare ingredients in advance. Store separately in plastic bags. Assemble the salad 1 to 2 hours in advance. Cover with plastic wrap. Refrigerate.

SERVING METHOD, VIETNAMESE STYLE: Place the cooked pork in a bowl and sprinkle with *Nuoc Cham* to cover the pork almost completely. Add 2 to 3 tablespoons chopped peanuts and sprinkle with green onions. Arrange the vegetables on a separate dish. Each person is given a bowl containing a small amount of the rice noodles. The diner takes a little of each vegetable and the pork and puts them on the noodles and eats from the noodle bowl, adding more *Nuoc Cham* if desired.

Spicy Shrimp and Pork Salad
Goi Tom

Tasty and colorful, this typical Vietnamese salad has a superb blending of tastes and textures.

    ½ pound medium shrimp, shelled and deveined
    ½ pound boneless pork loin
    2 carrots, shredded into 1½-inch lengths
    1 medium cucumber, peeled, seeds removed, shredded into very
        thin 1½-inch lengths
    3 stalks celery, shredded into thin 1½-inch lengths
    1 tablespoon salt
    1 small red onion, very thinly sliced
    ⅓ cup chopped fresh coriander leaves
    3 tablespoons chopped fresh mint leaves
    3 tablespoons distilled white vinegar
    3 tablespoons sugar
    1½ tablespoons fish sauce (*nuoc mam*)
    1 clove garlic, crushed
    2 tablespoons fresh lime juice
    Romaine lettuce leaves
    1 to 2 fresh red chiles, seeded, shredded
    3 tablespoons unsalted roasted peanuts, chopped

Cook shrimp in boiling water until they are opaque, about 2 to 3 minutes. Drain. Cool. Cut each shrimp in half lengthwise. Put pork in a small saucepan. Cover with cold water. Bring to a simmer over moderate heat, and cook until tender, about 25 minutes. Drain. Let cool. Cut into thin 2-inch shreds.

Place carrots, cucumber, and celery in separate bowls. Add ⅓ of the salt to each bowl. Allow to stand for 20 minutes. Rinse salt off and squeeze to remove water. Combine carrots, cucumber, celery, and onion with pork, shrimp, ¼ cup of the coriander, and 2 tablespoons of the mint leaves. In a small dish, combine vinegar, sugar, fish sauce, garlic, and lime juice. Stir until sugar dissolves. Add to salad ingredients and mix to combine. To serve, place salad on lettuce leaves. Sprinkle the salad with remaining coriander, mint, chiles, and chopped peanuts. Serve.

YIELD: 4 to 6 servings.

TIP: Pork belly (uncured bacon) is quite often used for this dish. If you prefer to use pork belly in place of the pork loin, cook for approximately 20 minutes. Cool and shred.

ADVANCE PREPARATION: Prepare all ingredients ahead of time. Combine salad 1 hour before serving.

Rice Noodles with Vegetables, Shrimp, and Peanuts
Bun Tom Nuong

Colorful and refreshing, this "salad" is inviting in appearance and irresistible in taste!

8 ounces rice sticks, soaked in warm water for 20 minutes, or
    until soft and pliable, drained
1 teaspoon oil
¾ cup fresh bean sprouts
1 carrot, shredded into 2-inch lengths
½ cucumber, seeded, shredded into 2-inch lengths
2 cups shredded romaine lettuce
¼ cup chopped fresh coriander
¼ cup chopped fresh mint (optional)
3 tablespoons chopped unsalted roasted peanuts
8 ounces shelled, deveined, cooked shrimp
Double recipe *Nuoc Cham* (page 425)

Heat 4 quarts water to boiling. Add the rice sticks and stir to separate. When the water returns to a boil, remove. Drain. Rinse with cold water. Drain the noodles. Toss with oil. Blanch the bean sprouts in boiling water for 30 seconds. Rinse with cold water. Drain.

To serve, use 6 separate serving bowls. Place some bean sprouts, carrot, cucumber, and lettuce in the bottom of each bowl. Sprinkle on some of the coriander, mint, and peanuts in each bowl. Distribute the noodles among the bowls. Place the cooked shrimp on the noodles. Garnish with remaining coriander, mint, and peanuts. Serve with *Nuoc Cham*.

YIELD: 6 servings with other dishes.

TIP: A single large bowl may be used for serving if desired. Place the ingredients in the bowl as in single servings.

ADVANCE PREPARATION: Prepare ingredients ahead and store in plastic wrap in refrigerator. Assemble a half hour before serving.

 ## Stuffed Tomatoes
Ca Chua Don Dau Hu

A beautiful, delicately flavored presentation.

> 4 medium firm ripe tomatoes
> ½ teaspoon salt
> 1 garlic clove, crushed
> White part of ½ leek
> ¼ cup drained straw mushrooms
> 8 ounces bean curd (*tofu*)
> 2 tablespoons crumbled bean threads, soaked in warm water for
>   20 minutes, drained, finely chopped
> ¼ teaspoon sugar
> Salt and white pepper to taste
> 2 tablespoons oil
> 6 teaspoons chopped roasted peanuts
> Coriander leaves for garnish (optional)
> *Nuoc Cham* (page 425)

Wash and dry the tomatoes. Cut off a thin slice from the stem end of each tomato and scoop out the pulp. Season the tomato shells lightly with salt and rub the inside of each tomato with the garlic clove.

Invert on a rack to drain for about 15 minutes. Dry the inside of the tomatoes with a paper towel. To clean the leek, cut in half and wash carefully to free the leaves of grit. Chop leek. Reserve 4 straw mushrooms for garnish, and chop the remaining mushrooms. Mash the bean curd to a paste. Add the chopped straw mushrooms, bean threads, leek, and sugar. Season to taste with salt and pepper. Mix. Fill the tomatoes with the mixture. Garnish with whole straw mushrooms.

Heat a frying pan. Add the oil. Put the tomatoes into the pan, stuffed side down. Cook on medium heat, covered, for 2 to 3 minutes, or until lightly browned. Turn tomatoes and fry for 2 to 3 minutes longer. Remove from heat. Sprinkle with peanuts. Garnish with coriander leaves. Serve with *Nuoc Cham*.

YIELD: 4 servings.

TIP: To crumble bean threads, place noodles in a food processor and process a few seconds, or put the noodles in a paper bag and hit with the side of a cleaver until broken into small pieces. This will prevent the bean threads from scattering.

ADVANCE PREPARATION: Tomatoes may be stuffed hours ahead and refrigerated. If liquid accumulates after stuffing, drain before cooking. They may also be cooked ahead and reheated.

 Cauliflower with Straw Mushrooms
Bong Cai Xao Nam Rom

An easily prepared, delicate vegetable combination that is equally delicious served hot or at room temperature.

> 2 leeks
> 2 tablespoons fish sauce *(nuoc mam)*
> 2 cups cauliflowerets, cut lengthwise into thin slices
> ½ teaspoon sugar
> 1 cup drained straw mushrooms
> 1 tablespoon oil

Clean leeks by cutting in half and washing carefully to free the leaves of grit. Slice white part only into thin slices. Combine fish sauce, 2 tablespoons water, and sugar in a bowl. Heat frying pan over high heat. Add oil. Add leeks and cauliflower and stir for 1 minute. Reduce heat to medium. Add 2 tablespoons water. Cover and cook for 2 minutes. Add straw mushrooms and fish sauce mixture. Stir to combine. Cover and cook an additional 2 minutes. Remove from heat and serve.

YIELD: 4 servings.

TIP: If the straw mushrooms are large, cut in half before cooking.

 ## Stir-Fried Mixed Vegetables with Peanuts *Rau Cai Xao*

Crisp vegetables in a tangy sauce are garnished with peanuts in this easily prepared dish.

1 to 2 tablespoons oil
3 green onions, shredded into 2-inch lengths
1 carrot, shredded into 2-inch lengths
2 ounces snow peas, strings removed, cut on the diagonal into thin shreds
½ green or red bell pepper, cut into 2- by ¼-inch strips
2 cups shredded Chinese cabbage
2 tablespoons chicken stock or water
1 tablespoon fish sauce *(nuoc mam)*
1 teaspoon oyster sauce
Salt to taste
Freshly ground pepper to taste
¼ cup coarsely chopped unsalted roasted peanuts

In a wok or skillet, heat oil over medium-high heat. Add green onions, carrot, snow peas, and pepper. Stir-fry for 30 seconds. Add cabbage shreds and stir-fry until cabbage has just softened. Add stock, fish sauce, oyster sauce, salt and pepper. Stir-fry for 30 seconds or until liquid has been absorbed. If desired, add more fish sauce, and salt and pepper to taste. Transfer to a serving platter. Garnish with peanuts.

YIELD: 3 to 4 servings.

TIP: In a Vietnamese stir-fry, very little oil is used. If necessary to keep the foods from sticking, add chicken stock or water to final cooking stage.

RICE, NOODLES, AND EGGS

 ## Rice with Chicken
Com Tay Cam

This very popular Vietnamese rice dish is traditionally prepared in a Chinese-style clay pot. In this version, I have chosen to use a flameproof casserole. The preparation method is similar to an Indian pilaf. It is easily prepared and can be a one-dish meal combining tasty chicken with mushrooms.

1 chicken breast, boned, skinned, cut into ½-inch cubes
1 tablespoon fish sauce (*nuoc mam*)
1 tablespoon soy sauce
1 tablespoon oyster sauce
1 teaspoon Chinese sesame oil
3 cloves garlic, minced
¼ teaspoon salt or to taste
Freshly ground black pepper
1 teaspoon oil
2 shallots, minced
1 tablespoon minced fresh ginger
1 cup canned straw mushrooms, drained
Chinese dried black mushrooms, soaked in water until softened,
    about 20 minutes, drained, stems removed, shredded
1 tablespoon cornstarch dissolved in 4 tablespoons water

RICE:

2 cups long-grain rice, rinsed, and drained for 10 minutes until
    dry
2 tablespoons oil
3 shallots, minced
2 cloves garlic, minced
2½ cups chicken broth

Nuoc Cham (page 425)
Vegetable Platter (page 409)

Combine chicken with fish sauce, soy sauce, oyster sauce, sesame oil, 1 clove garlic, salt, and pepper. Let marinate 20 to 30 minutes. Heat oil in wok or skillet. Add shallots, ginger, and remaining garlic. Add marinated chicken and stir-fry over medium heat about 3 to 4 minutes, or until done. Add straw and Chinese mushrooms and stir-fry for 1 minute. Add cornstarch mixture and cook until opaque and slightly thickened. Remove and set aside.

Heat 2 tablespoons oil over medium heat in a flameproof casserole or heavy-bottomed pan. Add shallots and garlic, and fry until lightly browned. Add drained rice and fry until the rice is thoroughly coated with the oil and begins to brown (about 3 minutes), stirring to prevent burning. Add 2½ cups chicken broth. Stir well to keep rice from settling. Bring to a boil. Reduce heat and simmer, partially covered, for approximately 10 to 15 minutes, or until most of the water is absorbed and the surface of the rice has steamy holes. Quickly place the reserved chicken and mushrooms on top of the rice. Try not to allow too much steam to escape. Cover the pan with a tight-fitting lid, and continue cooking over very low heat for 10 minutes longer. Remove from the heat and let rice rest, covered, for 5 minutes to allow the fragile grains to firm up. Do not stir the rice during the final 15 minutes of steaming and resting. Uncover and fluff the rice with a fork. Serve hot with *Nuoc Cham* and a Vegetable Platter.

YIELD: 4 to 6 servings.

TIPS: The rice will remain warm for approximately 20 minutes after resting.

Fresh mushrooms cut into ½-inch slices may be substituted for the straw and Chinese dried black mushrooms.

 ## Fried Rice with Tomato
Com Rang Ca Chua

An attractive, simply prepared rice dish.

> 2 tablespoons oil
> 1 small onion, minced
> 2 cloves garlic, minced
> 2 tablespoons tomato paste
> ½ cup water
> ⅓ teaspoon sugar
> 4 cups cold cooked rice
> 1½ cups cooked peas
> Salt and pepper to taste
> 2 tablespoons butter (optional)

Heat oil in a pan over high heat. Add onion and garlic, and stir-fry until onion is transparent. Add tomato paste, water, and sugar, and cook, stirring, for 1 minute. Add cooked rice, peas, salt, and pepper. Stir-fry 2 to 3 minutes, or until well combined and heated through. If using butter, add and stir until melted. Mix well.

YIELD: 2 to 3 servings.

 ## Stir-Fried Beef with Noodles
Bun Bo Xao

An interesting juxtaposition of tastes and textures makes this light, refreshing Vietnamese dish a winner. Savory beef, thin rice sticks, peanuts, and vegetables are wrapped in a lettuce package and dipped in fragrant Nuoc Cham. *Serve* Bun Bo *as an appetizer or as part of a meal. It makes wonderful picnic fare.*

> 5 ounces rice sticks, soaked in warm water 20 minutes to soften,
>   drained
> 3 tablespoons oil
> 3 cups chopped onion
> 1 pound sirloin or rump steak, chilled until firm, cut into very
>   thin ½- by 1½- by ⅛-inch strips
> 1½ tablespoons fish sauce *(nuoc mam)*
> ¼ teaspoon freshly ground black pepper
> ⅓ cup chopped unsalted roasted peanuts
>
> Lettuce leaves
> Vegetable Platter (page 409)
> *Nuoc Cham* (page 425)

Bring 4 quarts water to a boil. Add the rice sticks to the water, and stir until separated. As soon as the water returns to a boil, remove. Drain the noodles. Cover with foil to keep warm.

Heat 2 tablespoons oil in a large skillet or wok. Add onion, and stir-fry until soft and golden brown. Remove and set aside. Add 1 tablespoon oil to pan. Add the meat, and stir-fry until well browned. Add the cooked onion. Stir. Add the fish sauce and pepper. Cook, stirring, for about 30 seconds. Place on a platter. Garnish with peanuts.

To eat, let your guests wrap some rice noodles, meat, and vegetables in a lettuce leaf. Dip parcels into *Nuoc Cham.*

YIELD: 4 servings.

VARIATION: Divide warm rice sticks among 4 to 6 deep bowls. Add beef, onion, and cucumber slices to each bowl. Sprinkle generously with peanuts. Pour some of the *Nuoc Cham* over the rice sticks and serve the remaining *Nuoc Cham* in a small bowl.

This dish is equally good when served at room temperature.

Stir-Fried Shrimp and Bok Choy with Rice Noodles
Hu Tieu Xao Tom

The Chinese influence is shown in this colorful meal-in-one, combining fragrant shrimp and crispy bok choy.

SAUCE:

    4 teaspoons fish sauce (*nuoc mam*)
    1 tablespoon oyster sauce
    ½ cup water
    1 teaspoon sugar
    ¼ teaspoon freshly ground black pepper
    1 teaspoon cornstarch
    8 ounces fresh rice noodles, cut into ½-inch-thick slices, or
        6 ounces flat, dried rice vermicelli
    4 tablespoons oil
    3 cloves garlic, chopped
    1 medium onion, sliced
    8 ounces bok choy, tough stems removed, cut into 2-inch
        sections
    8 ounces shelled, deveined shrimp
    2 green onions, cut into 2-inch lengths

In a small bowl, combine the fish sauce, oyster sauce, water, sugar, pepper, and cornstarch. Set aside. Blanch the fresh rice noodles in boiling water for 15 to 20 seconds. Rinse. Drain. Set aside. (If using dried rice noodles, soak in hot water for 20 minutes. Cook in 4 quarts boiling water for 1 to 2 minutes or until *al dente*. Drain and rinse well. Do not overcook as they will become mushy when stir-fried. Drain.)

Heat a wok or skillet over high heat. Add 2 tablespoons oil. Heat. Add the garlic, and stir until fragrant. Add the onion, and stir-fry until soft. Add bok choy, and stir-fry for 1 minute. Remove and set aside. Add 2 tablespoons oil. Add the shrimp and stir-fry until shrimp is cooked. Add the cooked vegetables and green onions. Stir. Recombine the sauce mixture, and add to the wok. Stir-fry until the sauce thickens slightly. Add the noodles, and stir until heated through. Serve hot.

YIELD: 4 servings.

TIP: Beef, chicken, pork, or a combination of these ingredients may be used in place of shrimp.

 ## Crab with Bean Threads
Cua Xao Bun Tau

Delicate, refreshing, and easily prepared, this delicious dish can be served as a part of brunch as well as dinner.

    2 tablespoons oil
    1 clove garlic, minced
    2 shallots, minced
    6 ounces crabmeat, flaked
    4 ounces bean threads, soaked in warm water for 20 minutes,
        drained, cut into 4-inch lengths
    ⅓ cup frozen peas, defrosted
    2 green onions, shredded into 1½-inch lengths
    2 teaspoons fish sauce *(nuoc mam)*
    ½ teaspoon white pepper

Heat oil in a wok or frying pan over high heat. Add garlic and shallots, and stir-fry for 10 seconds. Add the crab, and stir-fry until very lightly browned. Add the bean threads, peas, green onions, and ¼ cup of water. Stir-fry for 1 to 2 minutes to allow noodles to absorb the water. Add the fish sauce and pepper, and stir to combine. Serve.

YIELD: 4 servings.

Sound Crepe
Banh Xeo

Tempting, crisp crepes combine a happy union of ingredients and are a favorite in Saigon. The name comes from the sound the crepe batter makes when it sizzles on the griddle. They make a wonderful light luncheon or brunch and are equally delightful as part of a meal.

1⅛ cups rice flour
⅛ teaspoon turmeric
¼ teaspoon salt (optional)
2 green onions green part only, thinly sliced
¾ cup oil
½ pound boneless pork loin, cut into 1½-inch shreds
1 ¾ teaspoons fish sauce *(nuoc mam)*
2 cloves garlic, minced
3 shallots, chopped
½ teaspoon freshly ground black pepper
½ pound medium shrimp, shelled, deveined, cut in half
12 medium mushrooms, thinly sliced
10 eggs, beaten
7 ounces fresh bean sprouts
11 or 12 Boston or other soft lettuce leaves
½ cucumber, peeled, seeds removed, thinly sliced lengthwise
     into 2-inch strips
Mint or coriander leaves
Double recipe *Nuoc Cham* (page 425)

In a bowl, combine rice flour with 1¼ cups cold water and whisk together until smooth. Add turmeric, salt, and green onions, and mix well. Let rest for 15 minutes.

Combine pork, 1 teaspoon fish sauce, half the garlic, shallots, and black pepper. Mix well. Add remaining fish sauce, garlic, shallots, and black pepper to the shrimp. Mix well.

Heat 2 tablespoons oil in a 10-inch nonstick skillet. Add pork mixture. Stir-fry until half done. Add shrimp mixture and mushrooms. Stir-fry until cooked through. Remove and set aside. Add 1 tablespoon oil. Heat. Stir the rice flour batter and ladle 3 tablespoons into the pan. Tilt the pan to allow the batter to evenly disperse. Turn the heat down to medium and cover. Cook 1 minute. Pour 3 tablespoons of the egg mixture over all, tilting it to run out beyond the edges of the crepe. Cover and cook until the eggs are set and nearly dry, about 2 to 3 minutes. Uncover. Add 2 tablespoons of the cooked mixture and scatter 1 to 2 tablespoons bean sprouts over the crepe. Fold in half, adding ½ tablespoon oil if necessary to prevent sticking. Cover and cook 30 seconds on each side or until the crepe is very crisp. Transfer to a warm platter. Keep warm in a low oven while preparing remaining crepes. Repeat, using the remaining filling, rice flour batter, and egg mixture. Serve garnished with lettuce, cucumber, mint or coriander, and *Nuoc Cham*.

YIELD: 10 crepes.

TIP: The Vietnamese prefer pork belly (uncured bacon) for this dish. You may substitute this for the pork loin, or use all pork or all shrimp. For a vegetarian version, use shredded fried tofu instead of the pork and combine the fresh mushrooms with sliced button, straw, or Chinese dried black mushrooms.

 ## Dried Rice Papers
Banh Trang

Thin, translucent rice papers are prepared from rice flour, water, and salt. The mixture is steamed, then dried on woven bamboo mats, which give them their crosshatch pattern. They come in two shapes, triangular or round (6½, 8½, and 13½ inches in diameter), and are sold in Asian markets.

To store, wrap the rice papers carefully and place in an airtight container. If they are exposed to moisture, it will be absorbed and the edges will curl, making them unusable.

Most rice papers now come from Thailand in packages labeled in Vietnamese (*Banh Trang*). When fried, they are much crisper than Chinese wrappers. They are also used uncooked as a fresh wrapper for cooked foods.

To use the rice papers as wrappers, dip 2 or 3 papers separately in a large bowl of warm water (about 110° F) for 2 to 3 seconds, or brush with a moistened pastry brush or spray them lightly with water from an atomizer. After dampening, let the wrappers rest until just pliable. Use the wrappers as they become pliable and alternate between moistening and wrapping. If allowed to sit in water, the rice papers will disintegrate.

Serving moistened uncooked rice papers can be very touchy. If the papers are too moist, they will stick together. Spraying the papers with an atomizer works best. They will become pliable and almost soggy. Let the papers stand for 15 to 20 minutes, allowing them to dry slightly, but still be pliable. Stack the damp papers on a plate and cover with plastic wrap. Put a very lightly dampened kitchen towel on top until ready to serve. These must be consumed within 5 to 10 minutes after wrapping. If allowed to stand too long once served, they will become dry and hard to handle.

When frying or cooking rice papers, I prefer to soak the rice paper sheets in sugared water to give them a crisper texture and a more attractive golden color. Dissolve ⅓ cup sugar in 1 quart of warm water (110° F) and proceed as for the uncooked rice papers.

DIPS AND SAUCES

 Spicy Fish Sauce
Nuoc Cham

An exciting, tangy hot sauce, which might be considered Vietnam's version of the sambal *of Indonesia and Malaysia. Each cook has his own formula for* Nuoc Cham. *It is used to add spice to almost any cooked dish, as a dressing for salads, and as a dipping sauce. It is served during almost every Vietnamese meal.*

2 tablespoons rice vinegar
3 tablespoons fresh lime juice
¼ cup fish sauce (*nuoc mam*)
¼ cup water
2 tablespoons sugar
1 clove garlic, minced
1 fresh hot red chile, seeds removed, minced, or ½ teaspoon red
    pepper flakes, or ¼ teaspoon red (cayenne) pepper powder
1 tablespoon long fine, carrot shreds

Combine rice vinegar, lime juice, fish sauce, water, and sugar in a small bowl. Stir until the sugar dissolves. Add garlic, chile, and carrots. Stir. Cover and let stand for at least 1 hour to blend flavors.

YIELD: 1 cup.

ADVANCE PREPARATION: Nuoc Cham can be refrigerated in a glass container for several days.

Peanut Sauce
Nuoc Leo

1 tablespoon fish sauce (*nuoc mam*)
¼ cup hoisin sauce
¼ cup chicken stock or water
1 clove garlic, minced
1 fresh red chile, seeded, minced
2 tablespoons ground dry-roasted unsalted peanuts

Combine the fish sauce, hoisin sauce, and chicken stock in a small bowl. Stir to blend. Garnish with garlic, chile, and peanuts. Serve.

Anchovy-Pineapple Dipping Sauce
Mam Nem

2 cloves garlic, minced
1 fresh red chile, seeded, chopped
2 tablespoons sugar
1 can (2 ounces) flat anchovies, including oil
2 tablespoons fish sauce (*nuoc mam*)
¼ cup fresh lime or lemon juice
2 tablespoons pineapple juice or water

Pound or process half the garlic, chile, and sugar to a smooth paste. Add the anchovies and mash to a smooth paste. Stir in the fish sauce, lemon juice, and pineapple juice. Mix well. Sprinkle remaining garlic over the top. Set aside.

TIP: Two tablespoons chopped fresh pineapple may be added to the sauce.

ADVANCE PREPARATION: Prepare the dipping sauce the morning of serving. Refrigerate. Before serving, bring the dipping sauce to room temperature.

DESSERTS

 Coconut Flan
Banh Du Ca Ra Men

Here is a dessert combining French techniques with Vietnamese flavors.

CARAMEL:

⅔ cup sugar
¼ cup water

CUSTARD:

1 cup fresh or canned coconut milk
1 cup milk
¼ cup sugar
4 eggs
1 teaspoon vanilla extract

Prepare the caramel. In a small pan, combine sugar and water, and swirl (shake pan with a circular motion) over moderately high heat until the sugar has dissolved completely. Then let the sugar boil, swirling the pan occasionally, until the syrup turns a molasses brown. This will take approximately 10 minutes. Remove saucepan from the heat as soon as the desired color is reached. If you let it darken too much, it will have a bitter taste. Pour the carmelized syrup into a flan mold or individual heatproof small bowls or cups, tilting and swirling the molds to evenly coat the entire bottom. Be very careful not to burn yourself, as the syrup will be very hot.

Prepare the custard. Combine the coconut milk, milk, and sugar in a medium saucepan over low heat. Scald until the sugar dissolves completely. Remove from the heat. In a large bowl, whisk the eggs and vanilla. Gradually whisk the hot coconut milk into the eggs, blending thoroughly. Strain the custard into the caramel-coated flan mold. Place the filled mold into a large baking pan and place on the middle shelf of the oven. Pour boiling water around the mold to come halfway up the mold. Bake for 40 minutes to 1 hour if using a single mold, 30 to 40 minutes if using individual ramekins, or until a knife inserted in the center of the custard comes out clean. Remove from the oven and cool to room temperature out of the water bath. When cool, cover with plastic wrap or aluminum foil, and refrigerate until thoroughly chilled, preferably for 8 hours.

To serve, run a knife around the edge of the mold. Holding the mold and a plate firmly together, turn them over. Tap the plate on a flat surface to allow the custard to slide out on to the serving plate. Serve chilled.

YIELD: 5 to 6 servings.

ADVANCE PREPARATION: Prepare 1 to 2 days ahead. Refrigerate covered. Unmold when serving.

GLOSSARY

Annatto seeds (Achuete, Atsuete): The hard, reddish seeds of the annatto tree used to give food a reddish color in Filipino cooking. When soaked in hot water, the seeds produce a reddish-orange liquid. It is also available as a bottled liquid. To obtain the reddish color, a mixture of paprika and turmeric, stirred into a little water, may be substituted.

Bagoong: A salty fermented sauce or paste made from small shrimps or fish, used as an accompaniment to main dishes in Philippine cuisine.

Bamboo shoots: Bamboo shoots add sweetness, delicacy, and crunch to dishes. Sometimes they can be found fresh in Asian markets, but they are readily available in cans. Drain the bamboo shoots; if they have a tinny taste, blanch them in water. They may be kept in a glass container in the refrigerator for a few days. Change the water daily.

Banana leaves: These large, flat green leaves are the "aluminum foil" of Southeast Asia. They are used as placemats, to line and decorate elaborate dishes, to line steamers, and to wrap food. When used as a wrapper for steamed foods, they impart a delicate flavor (page 26). The leaves may be purchased frozen in Asian and Latin American markets. If unavailable, substitute aluminum foil.

Basil: Many different varieties of fresh basil exist. Sweet basil, holy basil, a purple-stemmed variety, and lemon basil are sometimes available in Thai grocery stores. It is used as an ingredient as well as a garnish, and adds a slightly peppery yet cooling flavor. You may use any sweet basil. If it is unavailable, substitute mint, even though their flavors differ. Dried basil is a very poor substitute.

Bean Curd (Tofu): Bean curd is made from soybean powder and is high in protein, low in calories, and very inexpensive. It comes in water in square cakes measuring about 2½ to 3 inches. Firm tofu is best in stir-fried dishes and soups. If fresh when purchased, it will keep about a week in the refrigerator. Change the water daily.

Bean curd, pressed (Bean cakes, Tofu, pressed): Firm and compact cakes about 3 inches square by 1 inch thick usually found in the refrigerated section. Water is extracted from fresh bean curd to make them solid. The cake is then simmered in

429

water, soy sauce, star anise, and sugar, giving the bean curd a subtle taste that absorbs and complements many food flavors.

Bean curd sheets: Frozen or dried bean curd (tofu) sheets are used as wrappers for stuffed foods or as a meat substitute.

Bean sprouts: Sprouted from the mung beans, these give a wonderful texture to many dishes. Purchase crisp white sprouts with a fresh smell. If possible, use the sprouts the same day they are purchased. If not, blanch them in boiling water for 30 seconds, drain, and refresh with cold water. Store in cold water in the refrigerator for a day or two, changing the water daily. Never use canned bean sprouts. Bean sprouts can easily be grown at home and will sprout in 2 to 3 days.

Bean threads (Cellophane noodles, Transparent noodles, Glass noodles, Chinese vermicelli): These hard, thin, opaque noodles are made from ground mung beans and are often sold in bundles of small individual packages. They are usually soaked briefly in warm water before cooking and add texture to soups and stir-fried dishes. Bean threads can also be fried in hot oil for a few seconds, turning them into crisp, white strands that are wonderful for garnishes or as a base for salads.

Belacan: *See* Shrimp paste.

Blachan: *See* Shrimp paste. This Dutch-Indonesian spelling of "belacan" is still used on commercial packaging.

Black beans, fermented: Also known as salted black beans, these small black fermented soy beans have a wonderful flavor when combined with garlic. Soak briefly in water and rinse to remove the salt. Available in cans, plastic bags, and bottles. Will keep indefinitely in a tightly covered glass jar.

Bean paste, yellow: A salty, pungent soybean paste used in Chinese cooking.

Bok choy (Chinese cabbage): A white-stalked, green-leafed vegetable that has a taste resembling Swiss chard. The center section, known as the heart, is topped with yellow flowers and is extremely delicate and tender.

Cabbage: Both the Western and Chinese varieties of cabbage are used. If a recipe calls for celery cabbage, use the long, compact, green type.

Candlenut (Kemiri): A hard, oily nut used for flavoring and thickening curries. Macadamia nuts may be substituted.

Cardamom: This queen of spices has aromatic pods that contain a number of small seeds. The pods and seeds are used in sweet and savory dishes, particularly in curries. For optimum results, grind the seeds just before using. Cardamom also comes in a powdered form, but it is better to grind your own.

Cellophane noodles: *See* Bean threads.

Chiles (chilies) fresh red and green: Fresh chiles are a rich source of Vitamin A and C, and are used extensively in Southeast Asian cooking. As there are many varieties of chiles, it might take a little experimenting to ascertain their "heat."

Usually, the smaller the chiles, the hotter they taste. The tiny "bird" chile peppers from Thailand are fiery hot and have a wonderful flavor. Use one-quarter of the amount called for in the recipe.

In Southeast Asia, the seeds, which produce the predominant hotness, are usually not removed. For most of the recipes in this book, the seeds are removed, leaving the rich flavor of the chiles.

Choose fresh red Jalapeno, Serranos, or other hot chiles such as the Fresno or Anaheim chiles. Red chiles are generally milder than green ones because they sweeten as they ripen. Purchase chiles that are bright, with no brownish spots. If red chiles are unavailable, fresh green chiles may be substituted.

One note of caution—when handling fresh chiles, you may need to wear rubber gloves if you have very sensitive hands. Handle the chiles carefully. When cutting them, be sure not to touch your eyes or lips, and to wash your hands thoroughly with soap and water. Before preparing other foods, wash your knife and chopping board.

Chiles may be stored loosely wrapped in a paper towel inside a plastic bag in the refrigerator. They may also be washed, dried, and frozen whole in a plastic container. The texture will suffer, but they can be used for paste mixtures or for recipes calling for minced chiles. *Sambal Ulek* can be substituted in a pinch if fresh chiles are unavailable. I have also substituted dried red chiles soaked in warm water until softened, chili flakes, or a mixture of chili powder and a small amount of minced red bell pepper.

I have toned down the recipes in the book by using fewer chiles. If you desire to dine as the Southeast Asians, increase the amount of chiles or simply add some *sambal* to your dishes at the table.

Chiles, dried red: Dried red chiles are available in most markets. In Southeast Asian cooking, they are often soaked in water to soften before being ground with other spices. If they are unavailable, dried chile flakes may be substituted.

Chile (chili) sauce: There are many bottled varieties. The best known Thai chile paste is *Sriracha* sauce. It comes in mild, medium, and hot versions. *Sambal Ulek* is the Indonesian version. A homemade version of *Sambal Ulek* appears on page 321.

Chile (chili) powder (Red pepper powder): A pungent, aromatic powder made from dried red chiles.

Chinese beans (Yard-long green beans): These grow up to a yard long and are slightly crunchier than regular green beans. They are sold in Asian markets and are often part of ceremonial dishes as they symbolize long life. Look for slender, smooth pods. Substitute string beans.

Chinese dried black mushrooms: Brownish-black dried mushrooms with caps about 1 to 2 inches in diameter. The large, thick mushrooms with curled edges, light skins, and highly cracked surfaces are best. The mushrooms impart a distinctive flavor and must be soaked in warm water until spongy, about 20 to 30 minutes. Stems are seldom used, as they are quite tough. Store in a tightly covered glass container.

Chinese sausages (Lop cheong): Rich, rather sweet, small, slender pork sausages, which freeze well. Substitute chopped spiced ham.

Chinese sesame oil: An aromatic amber-colored oil made from toasted sesame seeds and used as a seasoning. It has a totally different flavor from that sold in health-food stores.

Chinese turnip (Daikon, Lo bok, Icicle radish): A long or large white Oriental or Japanese radish, which can grow up to 2 feet in length.

Cilantro: *See* Coriander.

Chicharon: Fried pork rind used in Filipino dishes.

Chorizo de Bilbao: Highly spiced sausage of Spanish origin.

Cloud ears (Tree ears, Wood ears): This Chinese fungus grows on trees. It is almost always sold dried and provides an unusual texture and contrast to a dish.

Coconut milk: One of the most important ingredients in Southeast Asian cooking. The milk is the white liquid that is squeezed from grated coconut meat and not the juice inside the coconut. *See* Fundamentals (page 22).

Coriander, fresh (Cilantro, Chinese parsley): Widely used in Southeast Asia, it looks like flat-leafed parsley. It has a pungent, earthy, citrus-like flavor, and is used in cooking as well as in garnishing. Wash, dry, and wrap in paper toweling. Store in a plastic bag in the refrigerator for 1 week. You can substitute parsley for garnish, but there is no substitute for the flavor.

Coriander roots: The roots of the coriander plant are used extensively in Thai cooking and can be found in Thai grocery stores. If they are unavailable, use the bottom 1 inch of the stems. The roots can be chopped and frozen.

Coriander seed: One of the flavoring ingredients in curries. Sold whole or ground. It has an entirely different flavor than coriander leaves and cannot be used as a substitute.

Cumin: The ground seed is an important part of curry powders and spice mixtures. Caraway may be substituted, but use a third of the given amount of cumin.

Curry leaves: Curry leaves have a mild sweet-spicy aroma. Bay leaves may be substituted.

Daikon: *See* Chinese turnip.

Daun Pandan: *See* Pandanus.

Daun Salam: An aromatic leaf used in Indonesian cooking. Bay leaf may be substituted, although the taste will not be exact.

Dried shrimp paste *(Kapee, Belacan, Terasi):* A pungent paste prepared from fermented shrimp. It is an acquired taste, but is very important in the preparation of curries. Shrimp paste is sold either fresh or in cakes, often labeled "blachan" (the old Dutch-Indonesian spelling). The recipes in this book are written for the dried form except where noted in the individual recipe. Tightly sealed in a jar, it will keep indefinitely, unrefrigerated.

Shrimp paste is rarely used in the raw form. When added to an uncooked mixture, it is usually toasted in foil in a dry skillet before adding it to the finished product.

Durian: A large, globular, odorus fruit with a hard, spiny shell. The taste of the creamy flesh has been described as akin to that of cheese or custard, but its aroma is considered repugnant.

Eggplant (Chinese eggplant, Japanese eggplant): The long, thin lavender Chinese eggplant or smaller nearly black Japanese eggplant is sweet and tender.

Eggplant, Thai (Pea eggplant): Small green pea-shaped eggplant. Used raw for chile sauces or in curry dishes.

Fermented black beans: *See* Black beans, fermented.

Fish sauce: Known as *nam pla* in Thailand, *patis* in the Philippines, and *nuoc mam* in Vietnam, this thin, translucent, salty brown liquid is made from salted shrimp or fish. Milder in flavor than soy sauce, it is an important seasoning in Thailand, the Philippines, and Vietnam.

Five-spice powder: This powdered Chinese spice powder is a combination of ground star anise, fennel, cinnamon, cloves, and Szechuan pepper.

Galangal: Known as *ka* in Thailand, *laos* in Indonesia, and *lengkaus* in Malaysia, this member of the ginger family gives a special aromatic flavor to curries and soups. It can be purchased frozen or dried. If dried, soak in warm water until soft before grinding with other spices to make a paste. Use ¼ less dried galangal than fresh called for in recipe. Ground dried galangal, sometimes labeled *"laos powder"* is also available. A ⅛-inch-thick stick of dried galangal is equal to ½ teaspoon powdered. Ginger may not be substituted.

Garam masala: An aromatic combination of Indian spices. See page 27 for recipe.

Ghee (Clarified butter): Sold in tins in Indian grocery stores, ghee is pure butter fat without any of the milk solids. It may be prepared at home.

White radish: *See* Chinese turnip.

Ginger: This aromatic rhizome of the ginger plant provides a sharp, pungent flavor and pleasing aroma. Often ginger available in the United States is "old" ginger and should be peeled before using.

Green onions: Known as scallions in some parts of the country.

Hoisin sauce: A dark, brownish-red sauce with a slightly sweet hot flavor, used in Chinese cooking. It is made from soybeans, flour, sugar, salt, garlic, chiles, and spices. Store in a jar in the refrigerator for 1 to 2 months.

Ka (Kha): *See* Galangal.

Kaffir lime leaves (Makrut): The leaves from the Kaffir lime tree add a lemon-lime flavor and are added whole or shredded to curries and soups. They are available fresh or frozen in Asian grocery stores. Whole dried leaves and powdered leaves, *bai makrut,* are also available in Asian markets. One whole leaf is equal to ¼ teaspoon powder. Substitute citrus leaves where available.

Kapee: *See* Shrimp paste.

Kecap manis: A thick, sweet soy sauce from Java with a molasses base. It is the basis for sauces and marinades for many Indonesian dishes. *Kecap manis* comes bottled in many Asian grocery stores with the old spelling "ketjap." It can also be made at home (page 321).

Kemiri nuts: *See* Candlenuts.

Krupuk udang: *See* Shrimp crackers.

Laos: *See* Galangal.

Lemon grass: Known as *takrai* in Thai and *sereh* in Indonesia, this is one of the most common herbs in Southeast Asian cooking. Lemon grass has long, hard, grayish-green, lemony smelling grasslike leaves, and gives dishes a wonderful citrus flavor. It can be found in many Western markets.

To use fresh lemon grass, peel off the outer leaves. Only the bottom 6 inches of the lemon grass is used. Because it is fairly hard, it is best to slice crosswise into very thin slices before grinding to a paste or it will not grind properly.

It is best stored with the root end in a little water, which prevents it from drying out. Stalks of fresh lemon grass can also be frozen. If unavailable, the best substitute is very thinly peeled lemon rind, although it's taste is not anything like the real thing! The zest of half a lemon is equal to 1 stalk of lemon grass.

Lemon grass also comes in a dried form, which has to be soaked in hot water for 1 hour before using. I prefer to use lemon zest to the dried form.

Lily buds (Lily flowers, Golden needles, Tiger lily buds): Long, narrow, dried lily buds, about 2 to 3 inches long. They have a mild, flowery fragrance, and add an interesting texture to dishes. Soak in hot water for 15 minutes or until soft, and trim away the tough stems.

Macapuno: An abnormal coconut prized for its soft, creamy flesh, it has a different texture than normal coconuts. It is preserved as balls or strips in thick syrup.

Mushrooms, dried Chinese black: *See* Chinese dried black mushrooms.

Mushrooms, straw: Small yellowish mushrooms, which are available in cans. They are crisp in texture, fragrant, and very tasty.

Nam pla: *See* Fish sauce.

Noodles, bean thread: *See* Bean threads.

Noodles, fresh rice: *See* Rice noodles, fresh.

Noodles, rice sticks: *See* Rice sticks.

Nuoc mam: *See* Fish sauce.

Oils: For most of the recipes, I would suggest using peanut or unsaturated vegetable oil. Olive oil is used only in Spanish or Filipino cooking. Most recipes do not specify a certain oil, leaving the choice up to you.

Oyster-flavored sauce: A thick brown sauce prepared from oysters cooked in soy sauce and brine. Its rich flavor makes foods smooth, subtle, and velvety. It can be stored for several months without refrigeration.

Palm sugar: A coarse brown sugar refined from palm sap. It is used throughout Southeast Asia and has a rich, smooth flavor. It is sold in hard blocks or in a smooth paste in Asian markets. Substitute dark brown sugar.

Pandan (screwpine): Used as a flavoring in rice and curries as well as a green coloring agent in sweets. It is also available in a powdered form. You can substitute vanilla, but the flavor will not be the same.

Patis: *See* Fish sauce.

Plum sauce: A sweet and spicy Chinese sauce made from plums, chiles, ginger, spices, vinegar, and sugar. Sold in jars or cans.

Red ginger: Preserved ginger slices, used as a garnish and flavoring.

Rice flour (Rice powder): Flour ground from rice.

Rice papers, dried (Banh trang): There is no substitute for Vietnamese rice paper. It is a round, tissue-thin, brittle crepe, made of rice, salt, and water. They are available in 6½, 8½, and 13½-inch sizes in Asian markets. Most of them are imported from Thailand. (*See* page 424).

Rice Noodles, fresh: These are available in Asian markets and will keep refrigerated for about 2 days. Both the cut and sheet noodles come with a light coating of oil, which should be removed by pouring boiling water over them.

Rice sticks (Rice vermicelli, Rice flour noodles): Thin, brittle dried noodles made from ground rice. Since they are already cooked, they need only to be rehydrated. For best texture, soak before heating to remove the starch. They are used in soups, stir-fried dishes, and should be cooked *al dente*. When deep-fried briefly, they become puffy and crisp and can be used as a garnish. To prevent them from splattering all over your kitchen, separate the rice sticks in a large paper bag.

Rice vermicelli: *See* Rice sticks.

Rice wine, Chinese (Shaoxing wine): Brewed from glutinous rice. Pale dry sherry can be substituted.

Saffron: The world's most expensive spice. It is the dried stigma of the saffron crocus. The threadlike strands are dark orange in color and have a strong perfume. Saffron is used in Indian dishes. Soak the threads in warm water and add both the threads and the water to the dish. Beware of inexpensive saffron, as it is probably an inferior substitute.

Salted black beans: *See* Black beans, fermented.

Sambal oelek: The old Dutch-Indonesian spelling of *Sambal Ulek* sometimes seen on commercially purchased *Sambal Ulek*.

Sambal ulek: A combination of chiles and salt preserved in vinegar. It is used in seasoning pastes and sauces, and can be used as a substitute for fresh chiles. A recipe for the homemade version appears on page 321.

Sesame oil: *See* Chinese sesame oil.

Shallots: Small, purplish onions with red-brown skin, which resemble garlic cloves in shape. They are much less expensive in Asian markets than in Western stores. If unavailable, substitute yellow onions or the white bottoms of green onions.

Shrimp crackers (Krupuk udang): Thin, flat dried chips, which when fried in hot oil puff up to two to three times their original size. If stored in a tightly covered container prior to cooking, they will keep indefinitely. Used as a side dish or as a garnish for dishes.

Shrimp, dried: Tiny dried shrimp used in many forms for both texture and flavor. Store in a tightly sealed jar.

Shrimp paste: Known as *kapee* in Thailand, *belacan* in Malaysia, and *terasi* in Indonesia, this dark-colored, dry paste is made of fermented shrimp and has a pungent odor. It is an essential ingredient in Southeast Asian cooking and comes in two forms—a soft pinkish mixture sold in jars and a firm brownish brick. The recipes in this book are written for the dried brick form, sometimes labeled with the old Dutch-Indonesian spelling *"blachan."* Tightly sealed in a jar, it will keep indefinitely at room temperature.

Shrimp paste is never used uncooked. If it is not cooked in a spice paste mixture, wrap it in foil and toast it in a dry skillet before using.

Shrimp paste, dried: *See* Shrimp paste.

Sriracha sauce: *See* Chile sauce.

Star anise: A small dried star-shaped, licorice-flavored spice with many pods. When a recipe calls for one whole star anise, it means eight individual pods.

Straw mushrooms:*See* Mushrooms, straw.

Sweet soy sauce: *See* kecap manis.

Tamarind: The beanlike fruit of this tropical tree. It adds an interesting tartness to curries, other dishes, and beverages. The prepared pulp is sold in packages in Asian markets. (See recipe for Tamarind Water on page 25.) Some Thai and Indian stores sell a concentrate that can be diluted with 6 parts water before use. Frozen orange-juice concentrate can be substituted for a similar taste but not color.

Tausi: Black soy beans, salted and fermented, used in Philippine cooking.

Terasi: *See* Shrimp paste.

Tofu: *See* Bean curd.

Tofu cakes: *See* Bean curd cakes.

Tofu, pressed: *See* Bean curd, pressed.

Trasi: *See* Shrimp paste.

Tree ears: *See* Cloud ears.

Turmeric: In Southeast Asia, this bright orange relative of the ginger family is sold fresh and is pounded with other aromatics to make spice paste mixtures. The turmeric sold in Asian markets is powdered. The recipes in this book are written for powdered turmeric.

Ubod: The heart of a palm, usually a coconut tree, eaten either raw or cooked as a vegetable. It is available in jars in Asian or Filipino markets.

Wood ears: *See* Cloud ears.

U.S. AND METRIC CONVERSION TABLE

VOLUME

Symbol	When you know:	Multiply by:	To find:
tsp	teaspoons	5.0	milliliters
tbsp	tablespoons	15.0	milliliters
fl oz	fluid ounces	29.57	milliliters
c	cups	0.24	liters
pt	pints	0.47	liters
qt	quarts	0.95	liters
gal	gallons	3.8	liters
ml	milliliters	0.034	fluid ounces

MASS
(Weight)

oz	ounces	28.35	grams
lb	pounds	0.45	kilograms
g	grams	0.035	ounces
kg	kilograms	2.2	pounds

TEMPERATURE

°F	Fahrenheit	5/9 (after subtracting 32)	Celcius

LENGTH

in	inches	2.5	centimeters

QUICK ROUNDED MEASUREMENTS FOR EASY REFERENCE

VOLUME

1/4 tsp	= 1/24 oz	=	1 ml
1/2 tsp	= 1/12 oz	=	2 ml
1 tsp	= 1/6 oz	=	5 ml
1 tbsp	= 1/2 oz	=	15 ml
1 c	= 8 oz	=	250 ml
4 c (1 qt)	= 32 oz	=	1 liter

MASS
(WEIGHT)

1 oz		=	30 g
4 oz		=	115 g
8 oz		=	225 g
16 oz	= 1 lb	=	450 g
32 oz	= 2 lb	=	900 g
36 oz	= 2¼ lb	=	1,000 g (1 kg)

INDEX